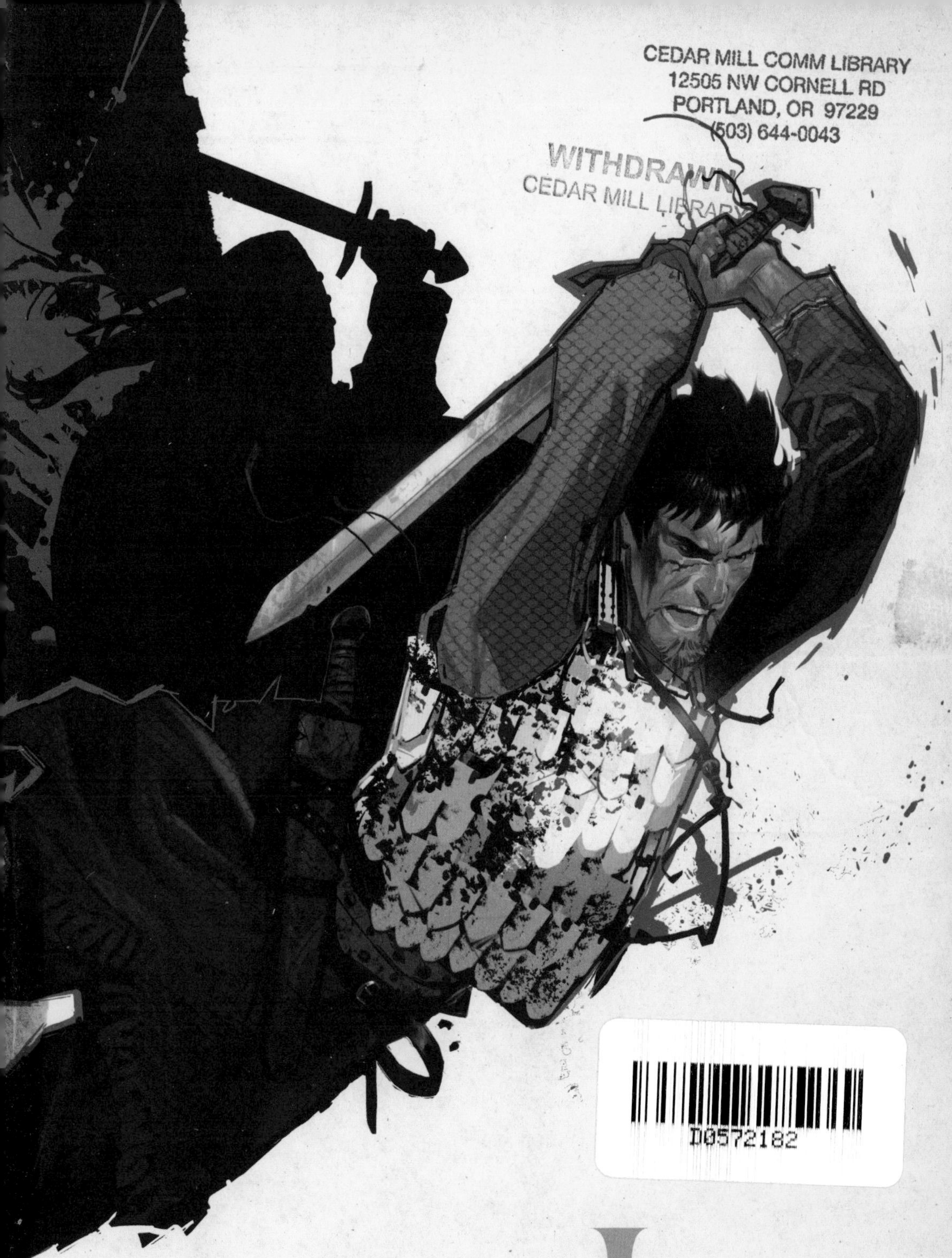

NORTHLANDERS

BOOK ONE: SVEN THE RETURNED

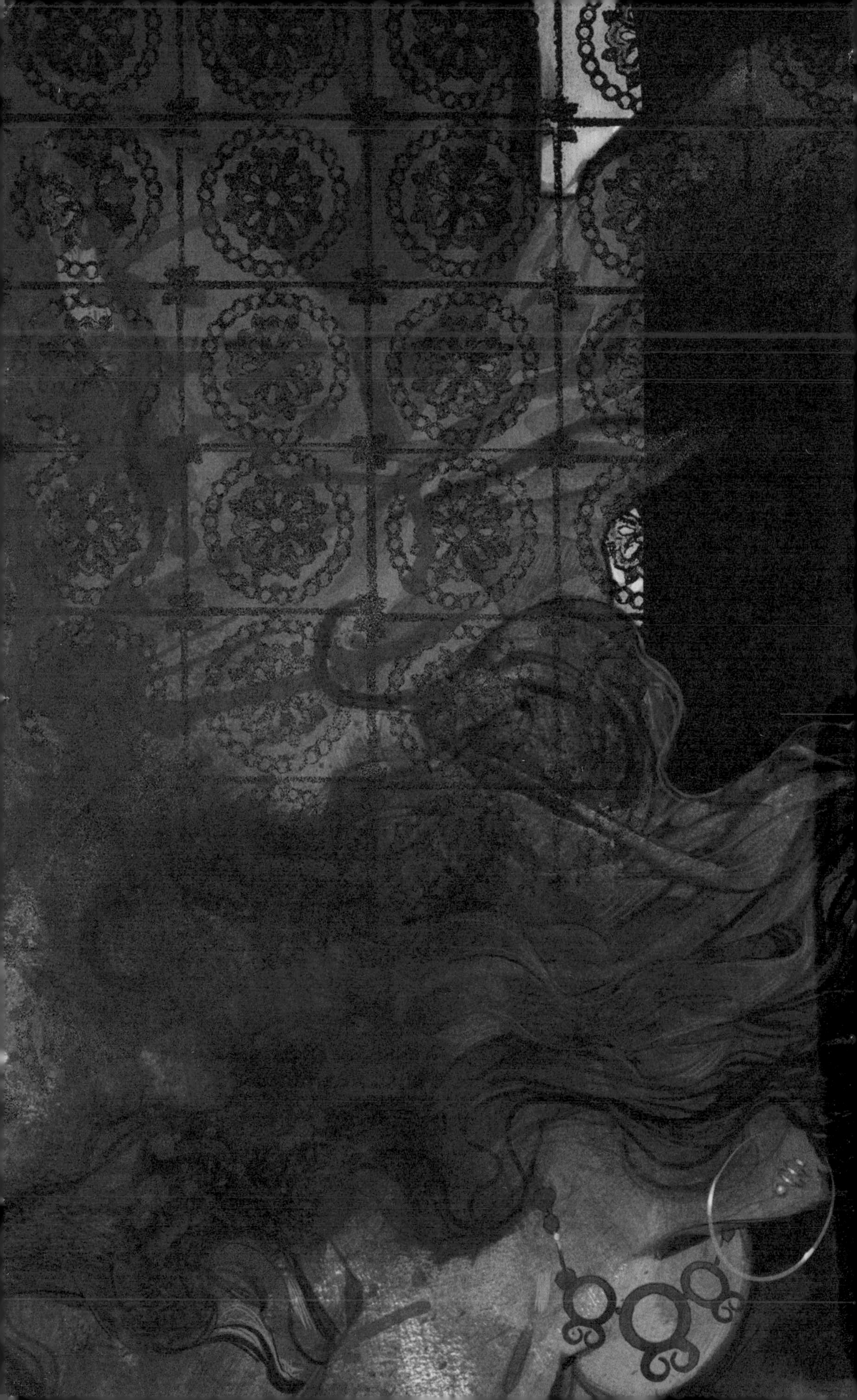

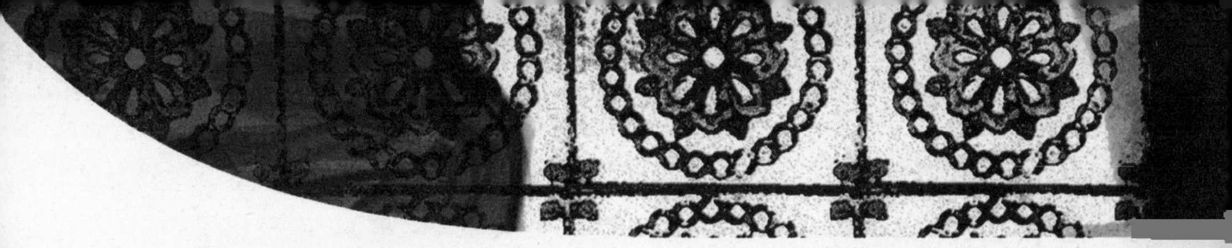

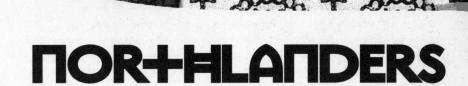

NORTHLANDERS

BOOK ONE: SVEN THE RETURNED

Brian Wood Writer **Davide Gianfelice** Artist

Dave McCaig Colorist **Travis Lanham** Letterer

Original series covers by **Massimo Carnevale**

NORTHLANDERS created by **Brian Wood**

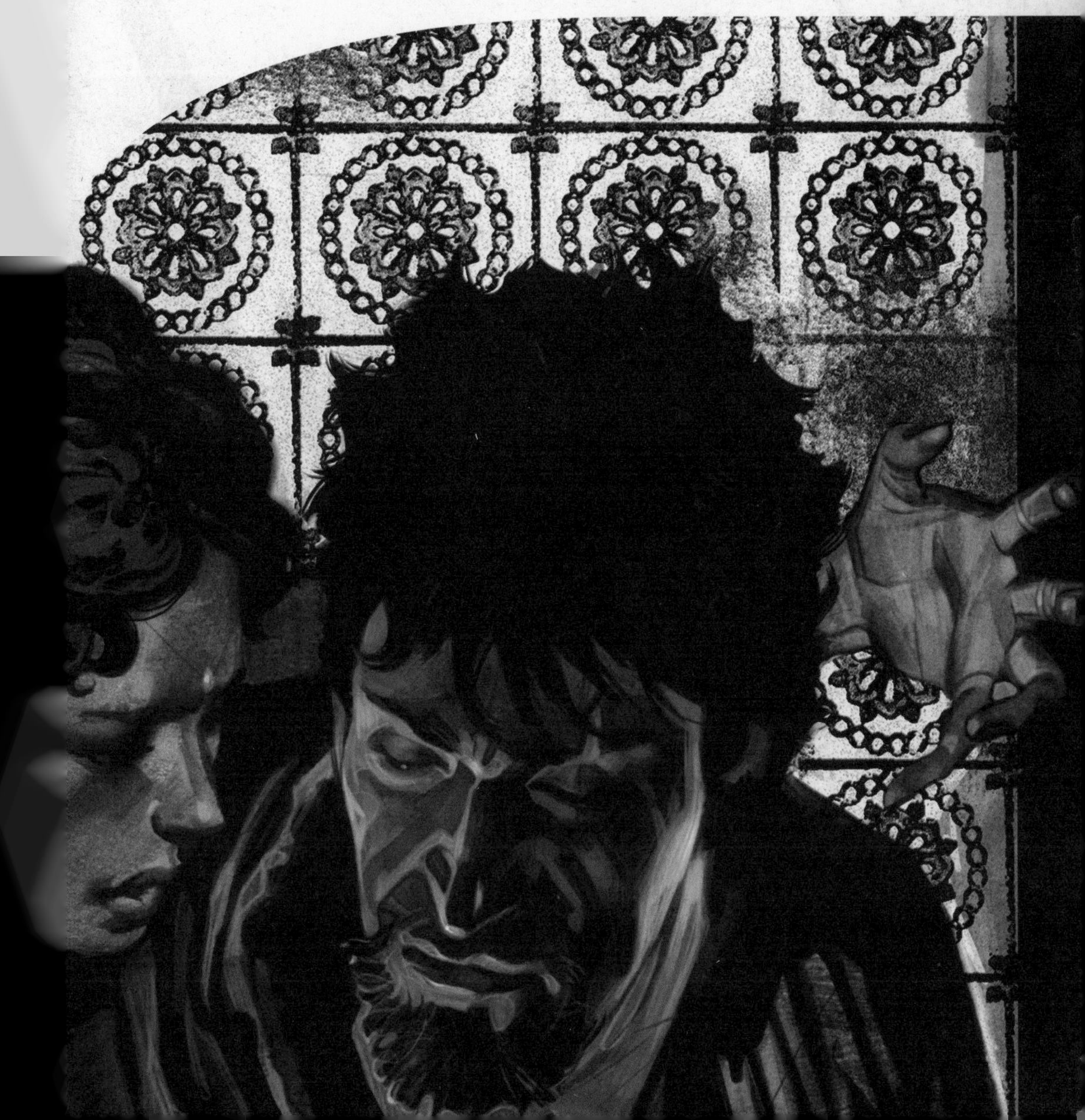

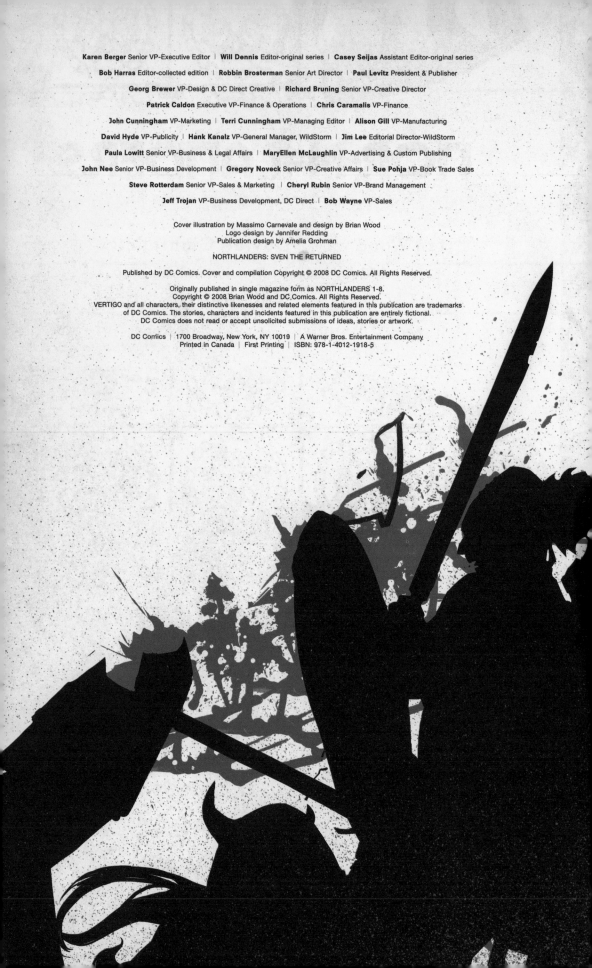

Cover illustration by Massimo Carnevale and design by Brian Wood
Logo design by Jennifer Redding
Publication design by Amelia Grohman

NORTHLANDERS: SVEN THE RETURNED

DC Comics | 1700 Broadway, New York, NY 10019 | A Warner Bros. Entertainment Company
Printed in Canada | First Printing | ISBN: 978-1-4012-1918-5

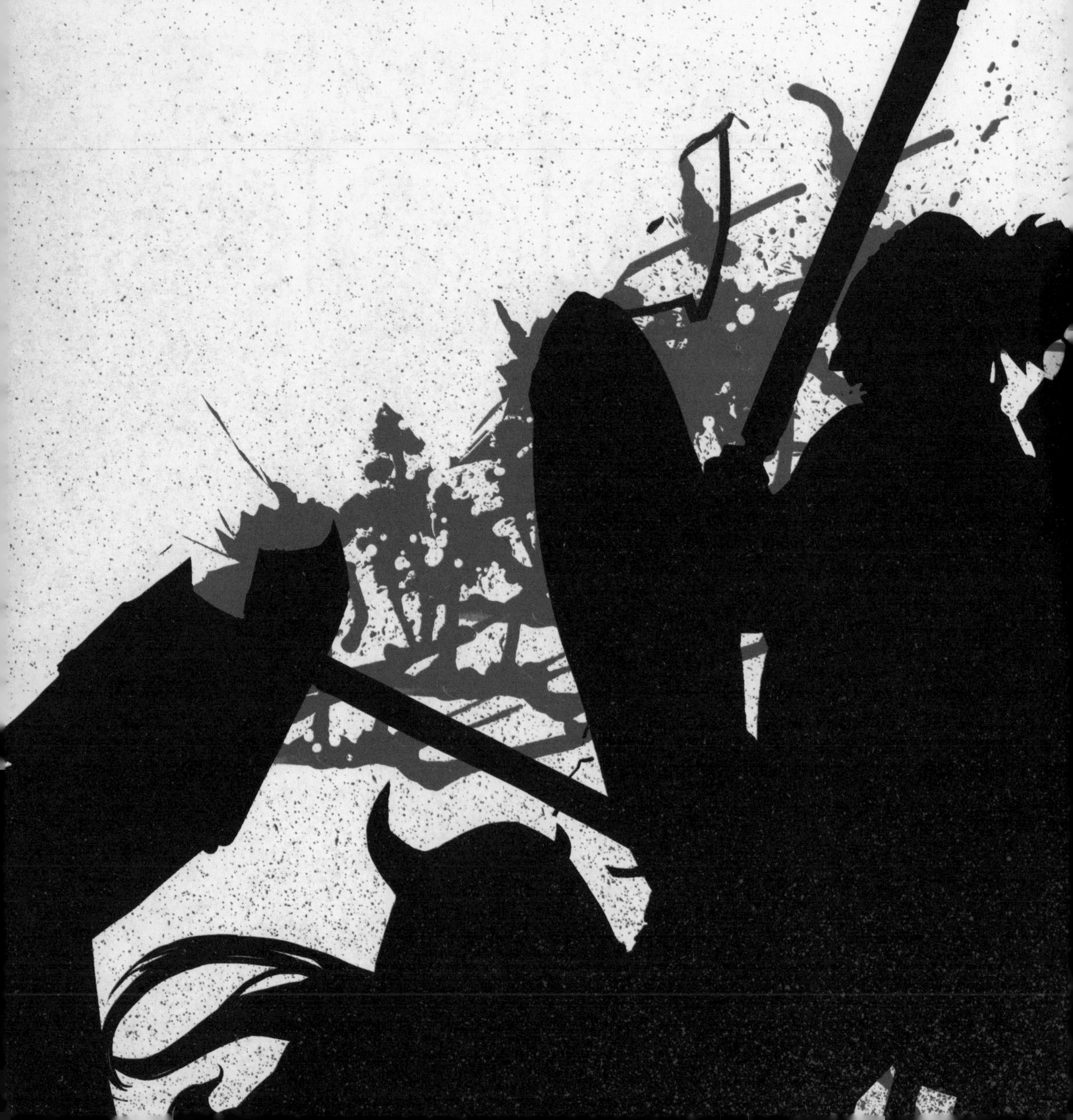

1 As High Summer Passes

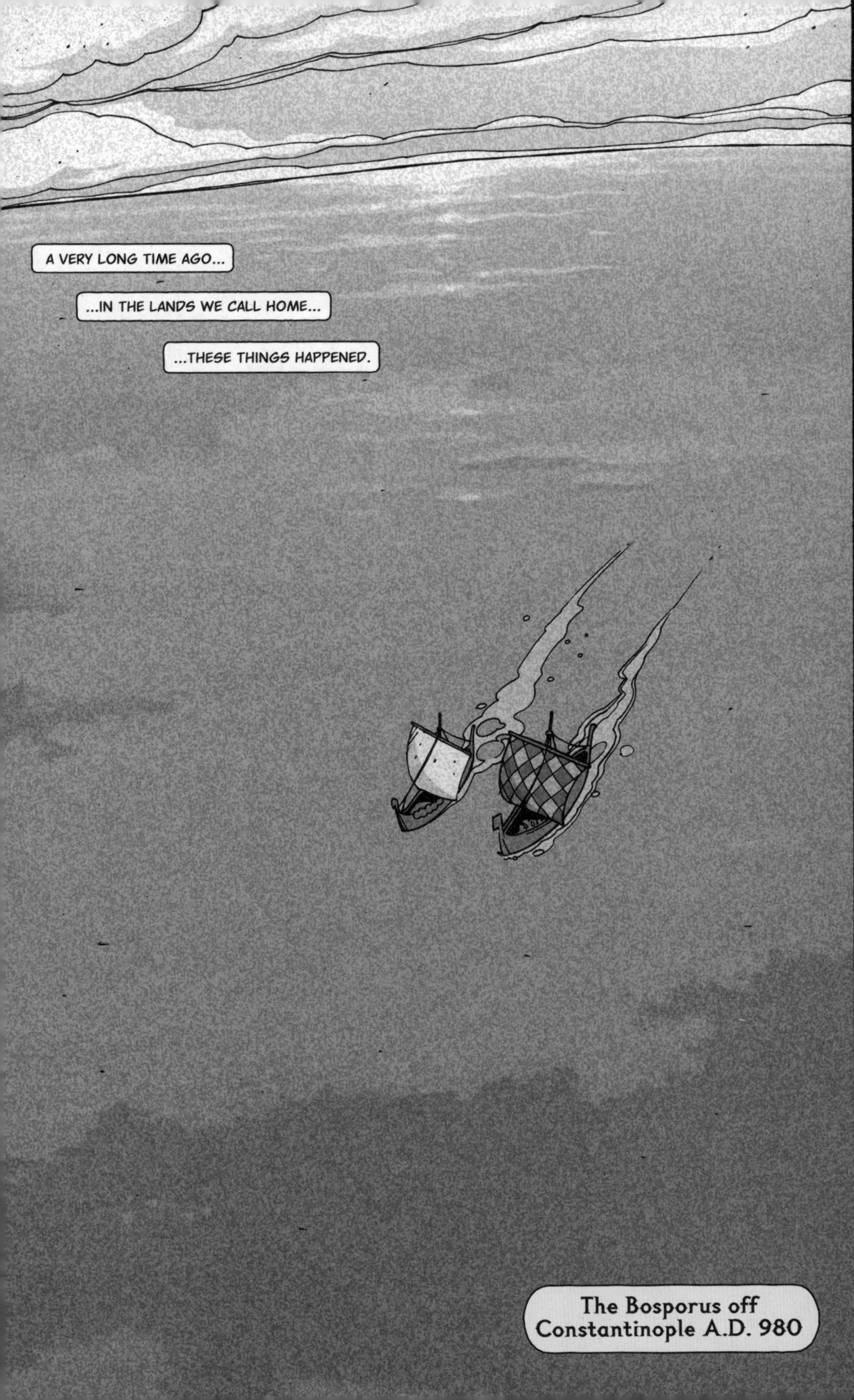
A VERY LONG TIME AGO...
...IN THE LANDS WE CALL HOME...
...THESE THINGS HAPPENED.
The Bosporus off Constantinople A.D. 980

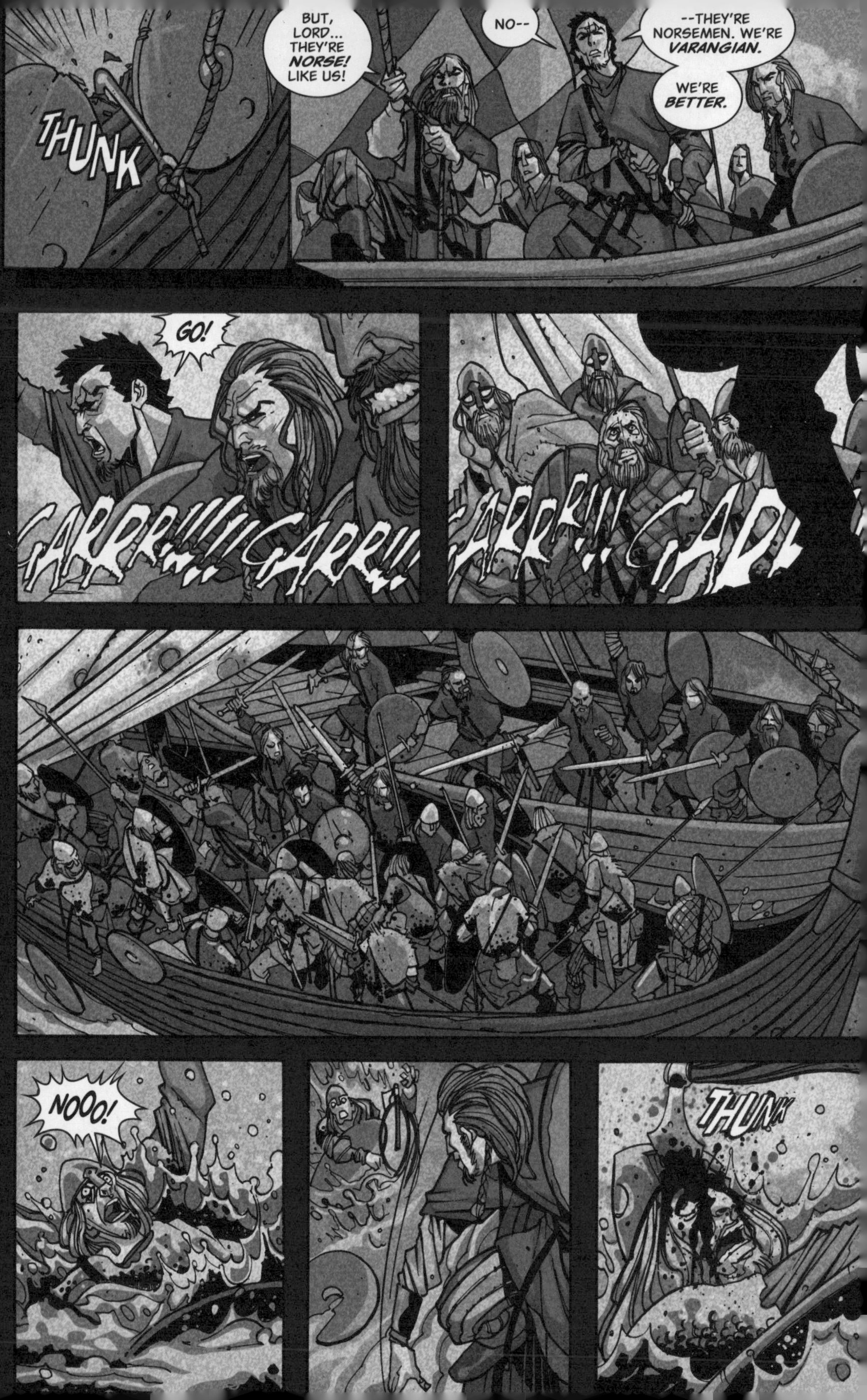
THUNK
BUT, LORD... THEY'RE NORSE! LIKE US!
NO--
--THEY'RE NORSEMEN. WE'RE VARANGIAN.
WE'RE BETTER.
GO!
GARRR!!!
GARRR!!!
GARRR!!!
GARR
NOOO!
THUNK

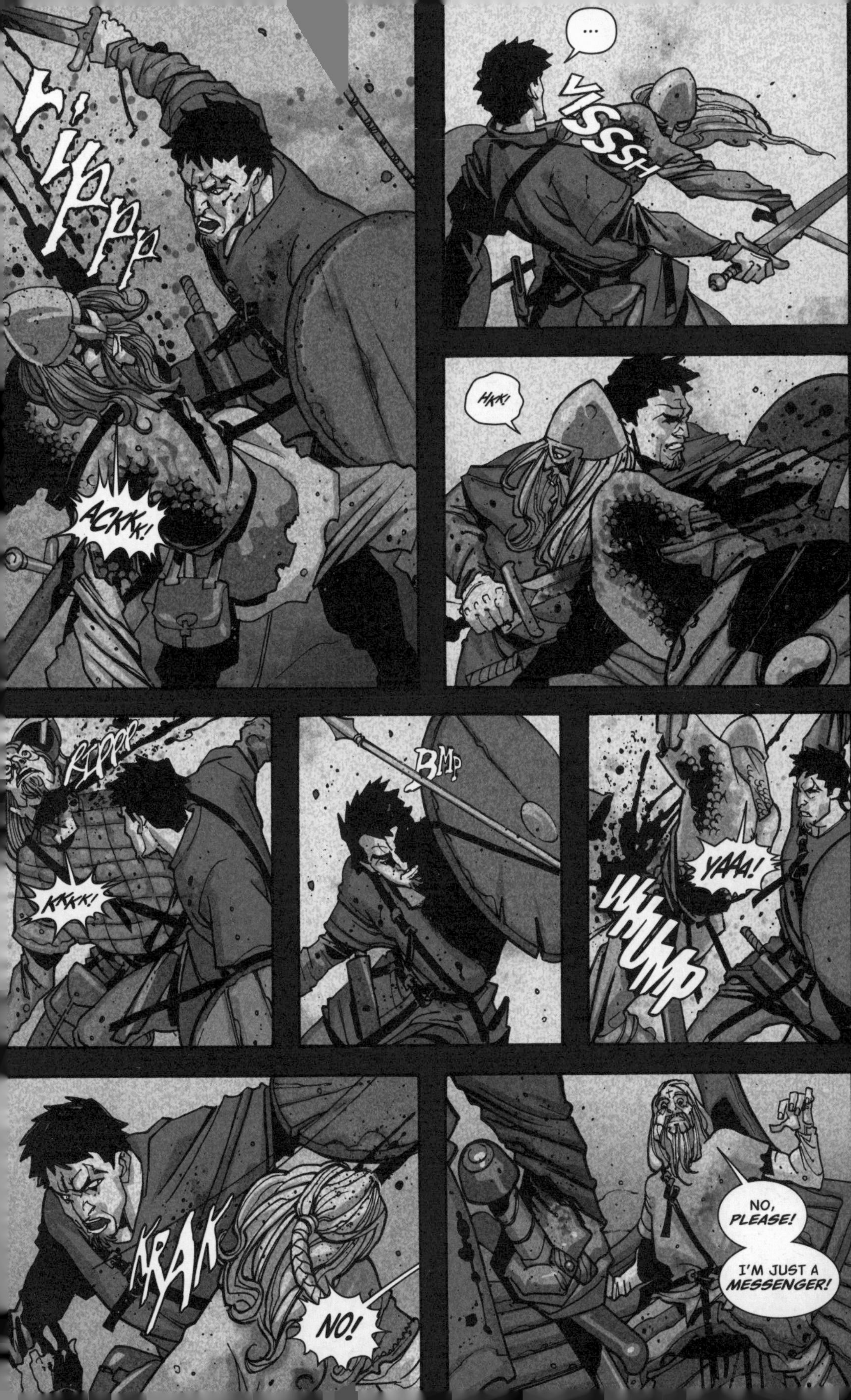
RIPPP
ACKKK!
...
VISSSH
HKK!
RIPPP
KKKK!
BMP
YAAA!
WHUMP
KRAK
NO!
NO, PLEASE!
I'M JUST A MESSENGER!

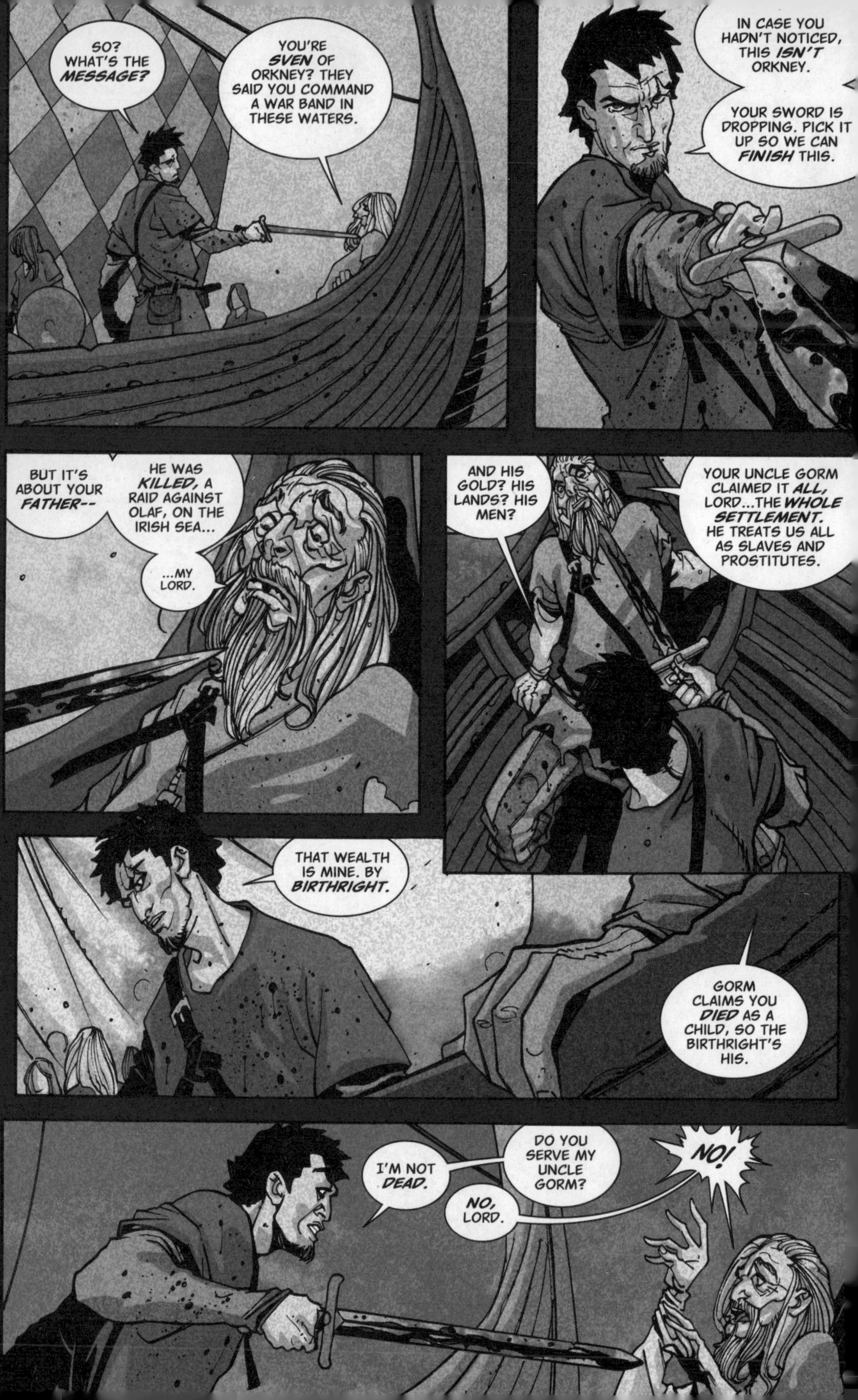
SO? WHAT'S THE MESSAGE?
YOU'RE SVEN OF ORKNEY? THEY SAID YOU COMMAND A WAR BAND IN THESE WATERS.
IN CASE YOU HADN'T NOTICED, THIS ISN'T ORKNEY.
YOUR SWORD IS DROPPING. PICK IT UP SO WE CAN FINISH THIS.
BUT IT'S ABOUT YOUR FATHER--
HE WAS KILLED, A RAID AGAINST OLAF, ON THE IRISH SEA...
...MY LORD.
AND HIS GOLD? HIS LANDS? HIS MEN?
YOUR UNCLE GORM CLAIMED IT ALL, LORD...THE WHOLE SETTLEMENT. HE TREATS US ALL AS SLAVES AND PROSTITUTES.
THAT WEALTH IS MINE. BY BIRTHRIGHT.
GORM CLAIMS YOU DIED AS A CHILD, SO THE BIRTHRIGHT'S HIS.
I'M NOT DEAD.
DO YOU SERVE MY UNCLE GORM?
NO, LORD.
NO!

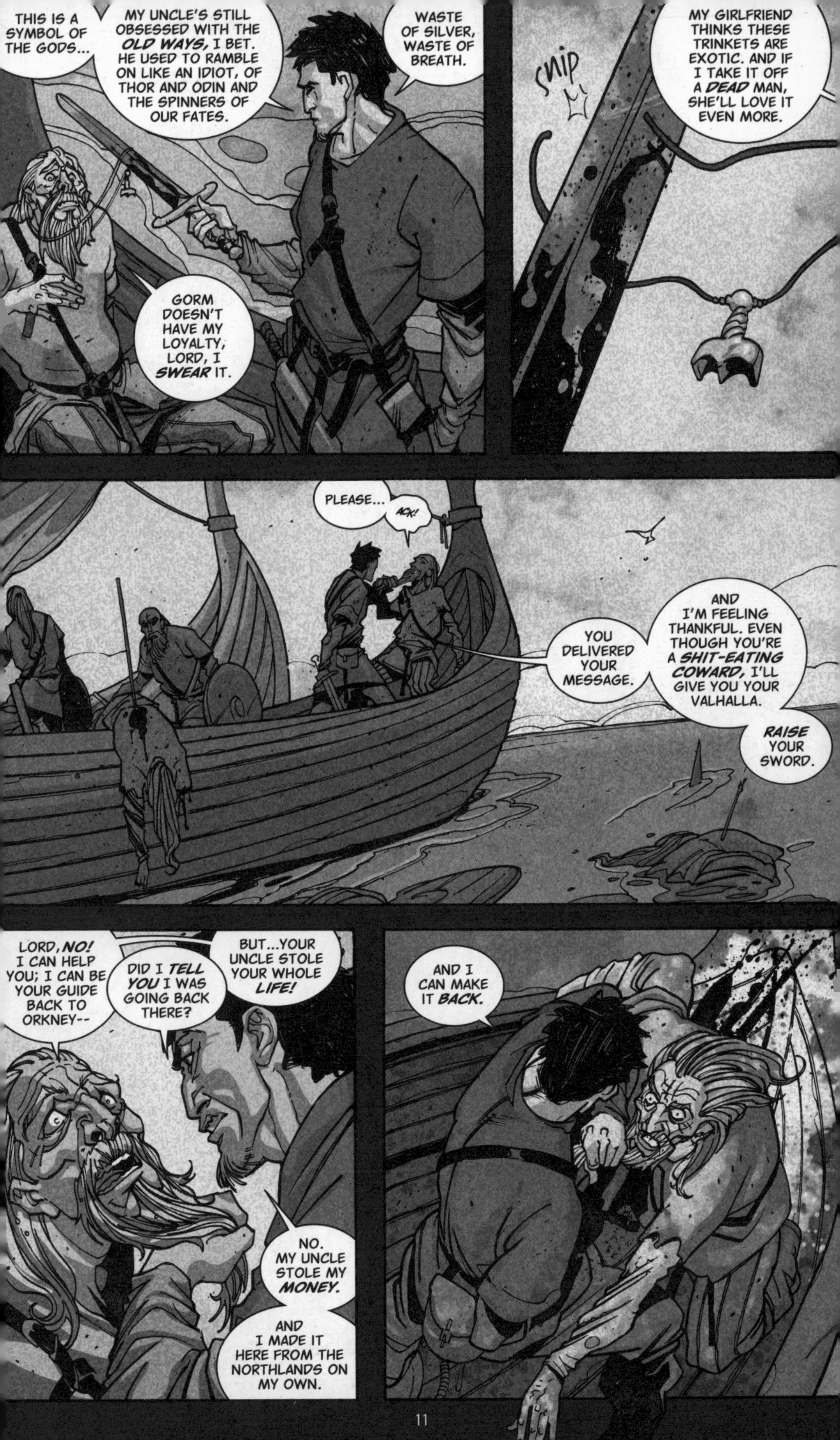
THIS IS A SYMBOL OF THE GODS...
MY UNCLE'S STILL OBSESSED WITH THE OLD WAYS, I BET. HE USED TO RAMBLE ON LIKE AN IDIOT, OF THOR AND ODIN AND THE SPINNERS OF OUR FATES.
WASTE OF SILVER, WASTE OF BREATH.
GORM DOESN'T HAVE MY LOYALTY, LORD, I SWEAR IT.
SNIP
MY GIRLFRIEND THINKS THESE TRINKETS ARE EXOTIC. AND IF I TAKE IT OFF A DEAD MAN, SHE'LL LOVE IT EVEN MORE.
PLEASE...
ACK!
YOU DELIVERED YOUR MESSAGE.
AND I'M FEELING THANKFUL. EVEN THOUGH YOU'RE A SHIT-EATING COWARD, I'LL GIVE YOU YOUR VALHALLA.
RAISE YOUR SWORD.
LORD, NO! I CAN HELP YOU; I CAN BE YOUR GUIDE BACK TO ORKNEY--
DID I TELL YOU I WAS GOING BACK THERE?
BUT...YOUR UNCLE STOLE YOUR WHOLE LIFE!
NO. MY UNCLE STOLE MY MONEY.
AND I MADE IT HERE FROM THE NORTHLANDS ON MY OWN.
AND I CAN MAKE IT BACK.

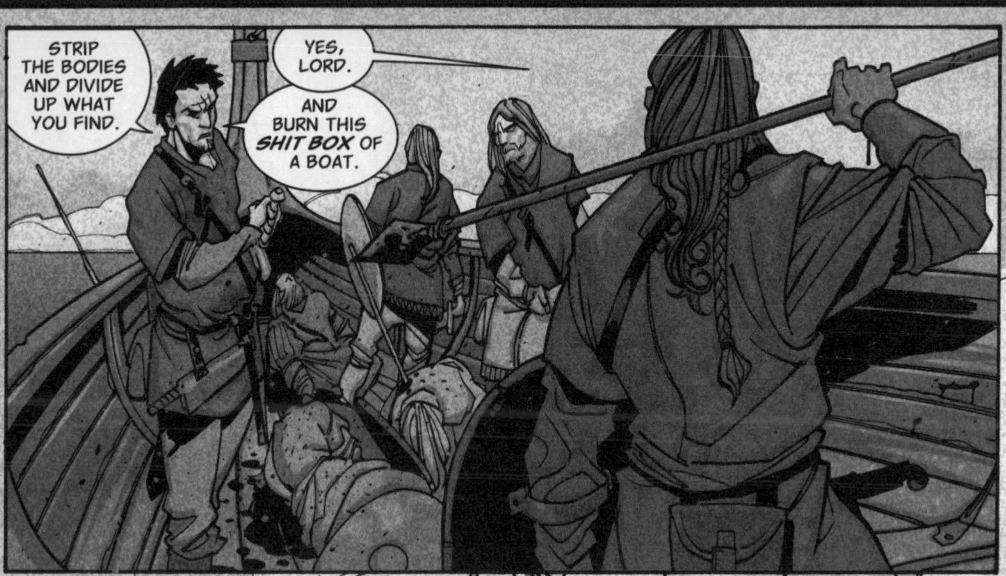
STRIP THE BODIES AND DIVIDE UP WHAT YOU FIND.
YES, LORD.
AND BURN THIS SHIT BOX OF A BOAT.

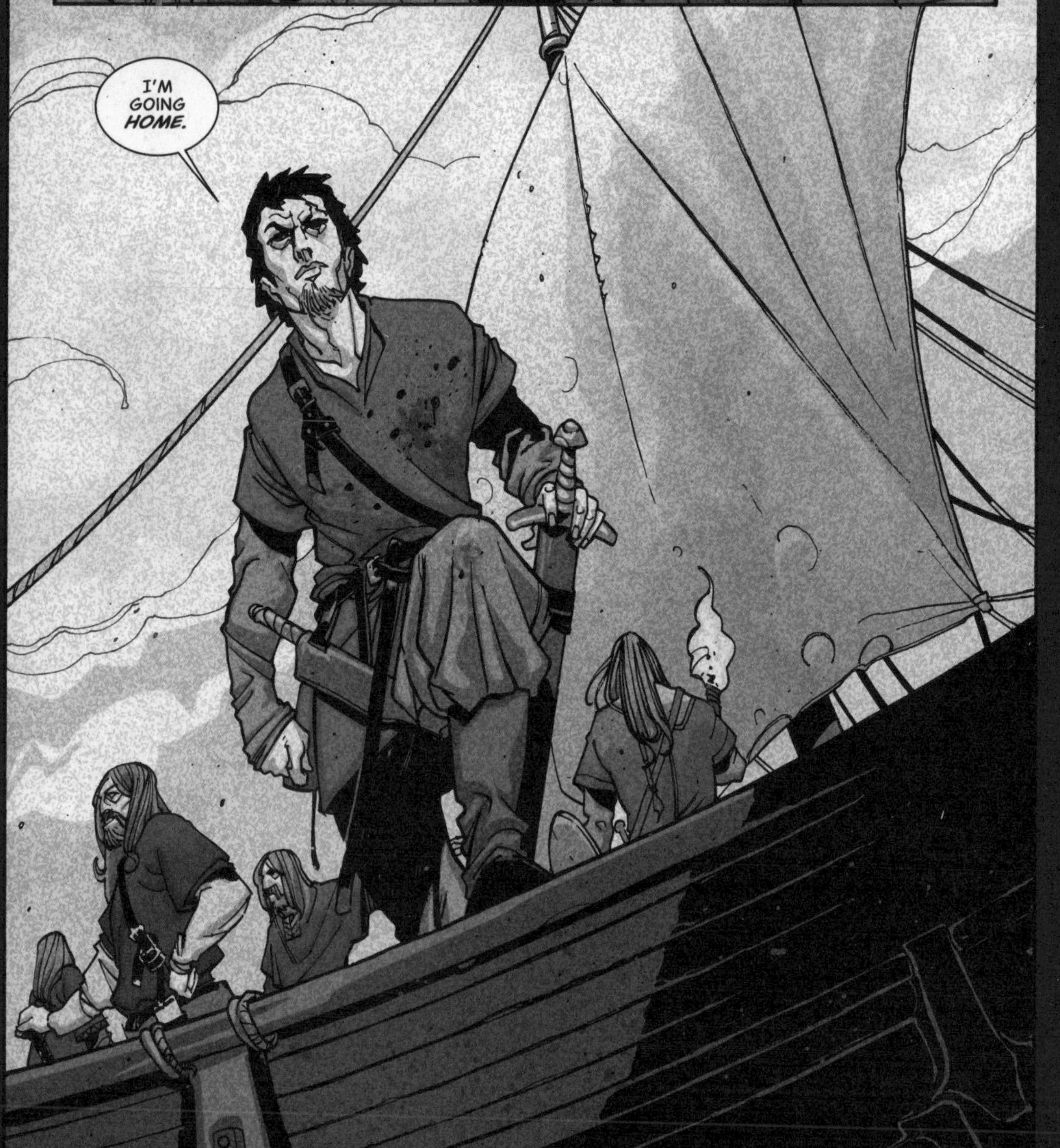
I'M GOING HOME.

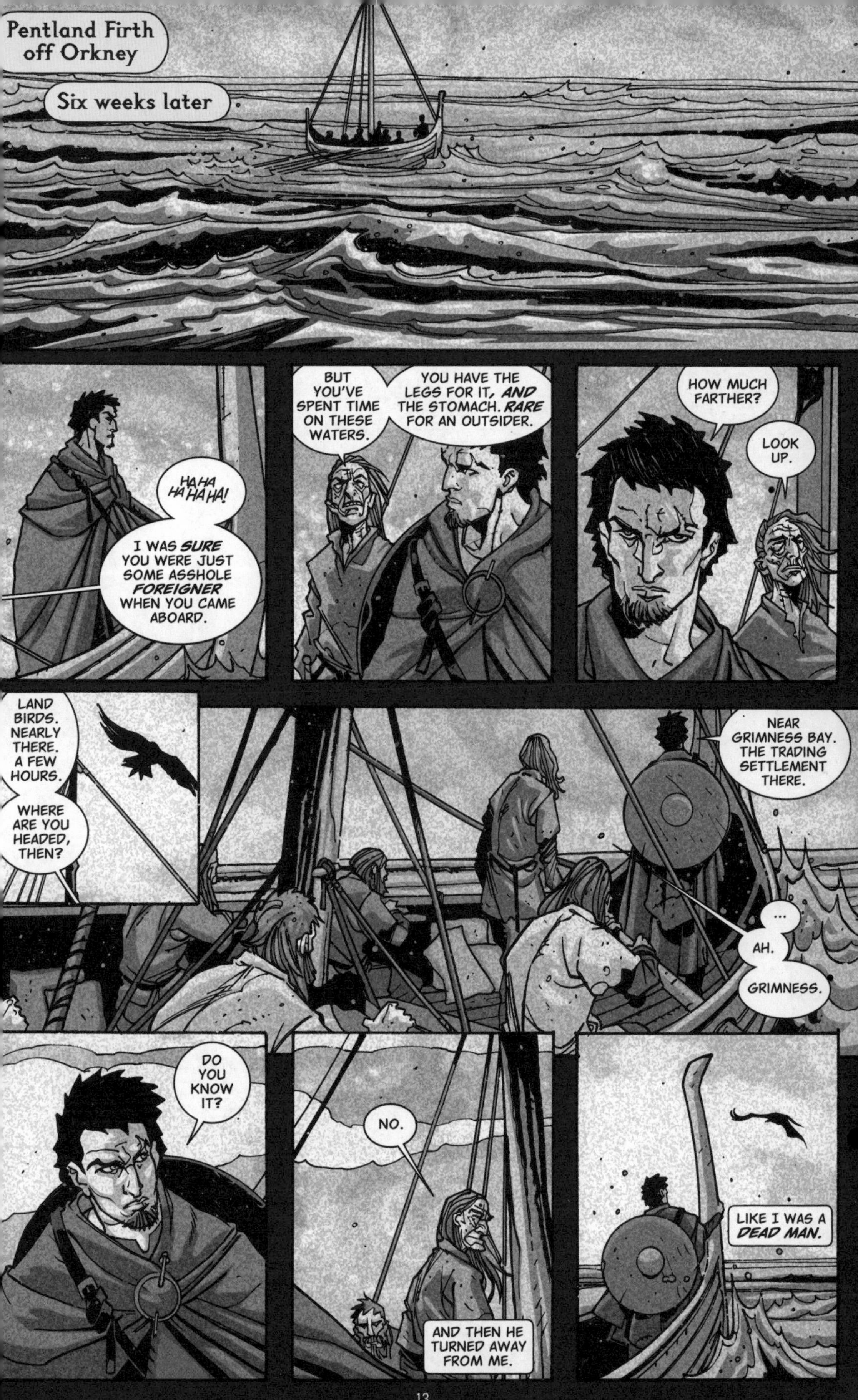
Pentland Firth off Orkney
Six weeks later
HA HA HA HA HA!
I WAS SURE YOU WERE JUST SOME ASSHOLE FOREIGNER WHEN YOU CAME ABOARD.
BUT YOU'VE SPENT TIME ON THESE WATERS.
YOU HAVE THE LEGS FOR IT, AND THE STOMACH. RARE FOR AN OUTSIDER.
HOW MUCH FARTHER?
LOOK UP.
LAND BIRDS. NEARLY THERE. A FEW HOURS.
WHERE ARE YOU HEADED, THEN?
NEAR GRIMNESS BAY. THE TRADING SETTLEMENT THERE.
...
AH.
GRIMNESS.
DO YOU KNOW IT?
NO.
AND THEN HE TURNED AWAY FROM ME.
LIKE I WAS A DEAD MAN.

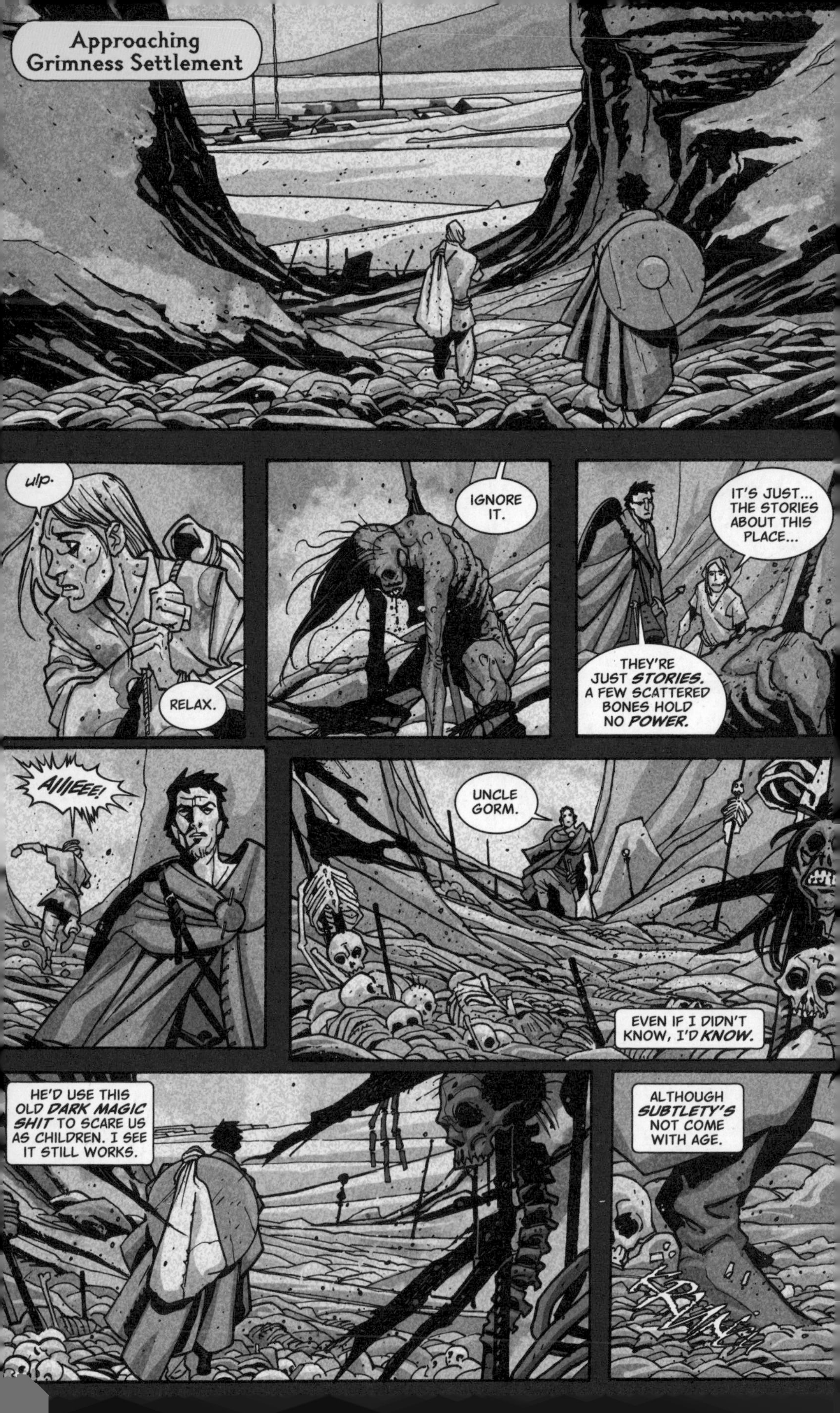
Approaching Grimness Settlement
ulp.
RELAX.
IGNORE IT.
IT'S JUST... THE STORIES ABOUT THIS PLACE...
THEY'RE JUST STORIES. A FEW SCATTERED BONES HOLD NO POWER.
AIIIEEE!
UNCLE GORM.
EVEN IF I DIDN'T KNOW, I'D KNOW.
HE'D USE THIS OLD DARK MAGIC SHIT TO SCARE US AS CHILDREN. I SEE IT STILL WORKS.
ALTHOUGH SUBTLETY'S NOT COME WITH AGE.

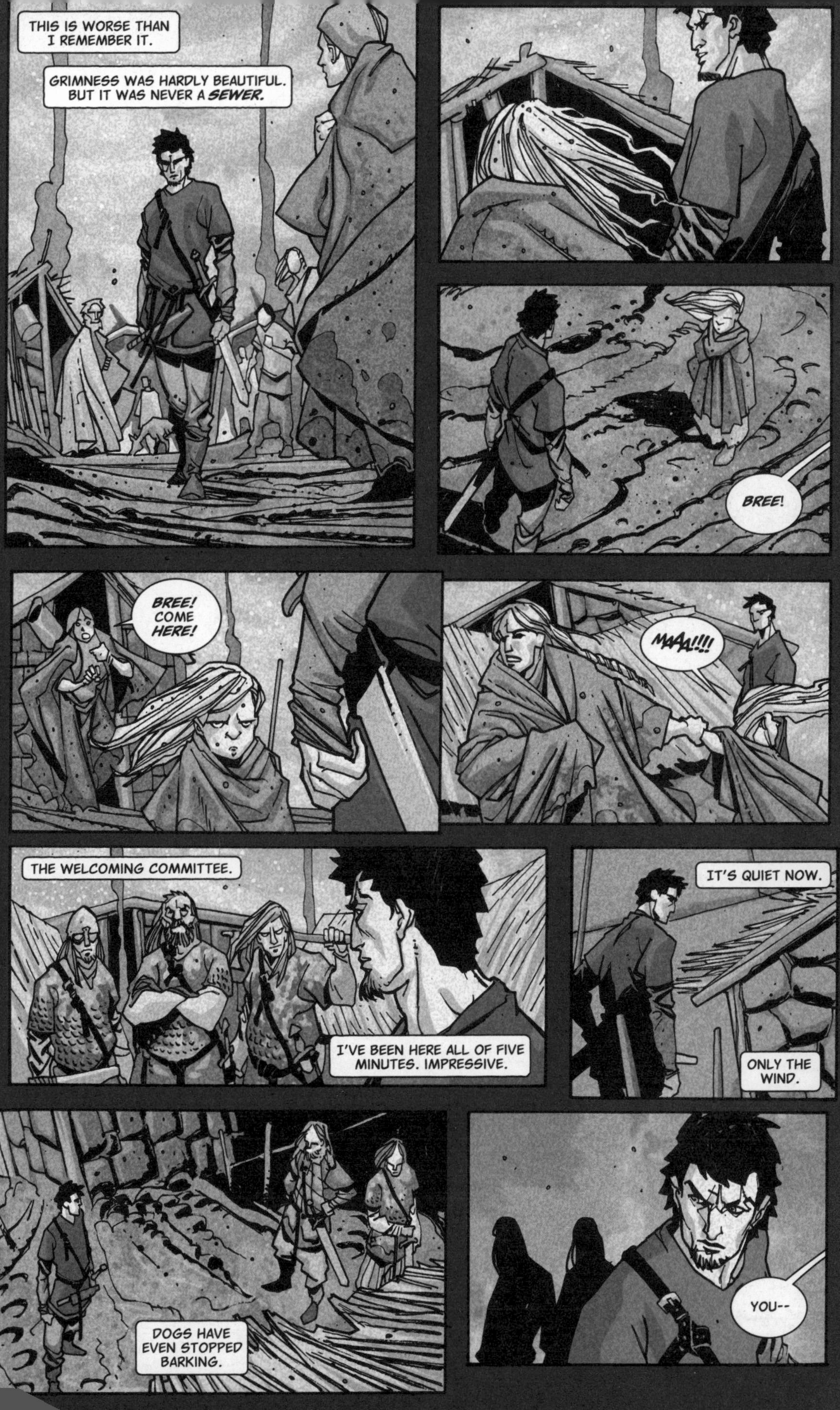
THIS IS WORSE THAN I REMEMBER IT.
GRIMNESS WAS HARDLY BEAUTIFUL. BUT IT WAS NEVER A *SEWER.*
BREE!
BREE! COME HERE!
MAAA!!!!
THE WELCOMING COMMITTEE.
I'VE BEEN HERE ALL OF FIVE MINUTES. IMPRESSIVE.
IT'S QUIET NOW.
ONLY THE WIND.
DOGS HAVE EVEN STOPPED BARKING.
YOU--

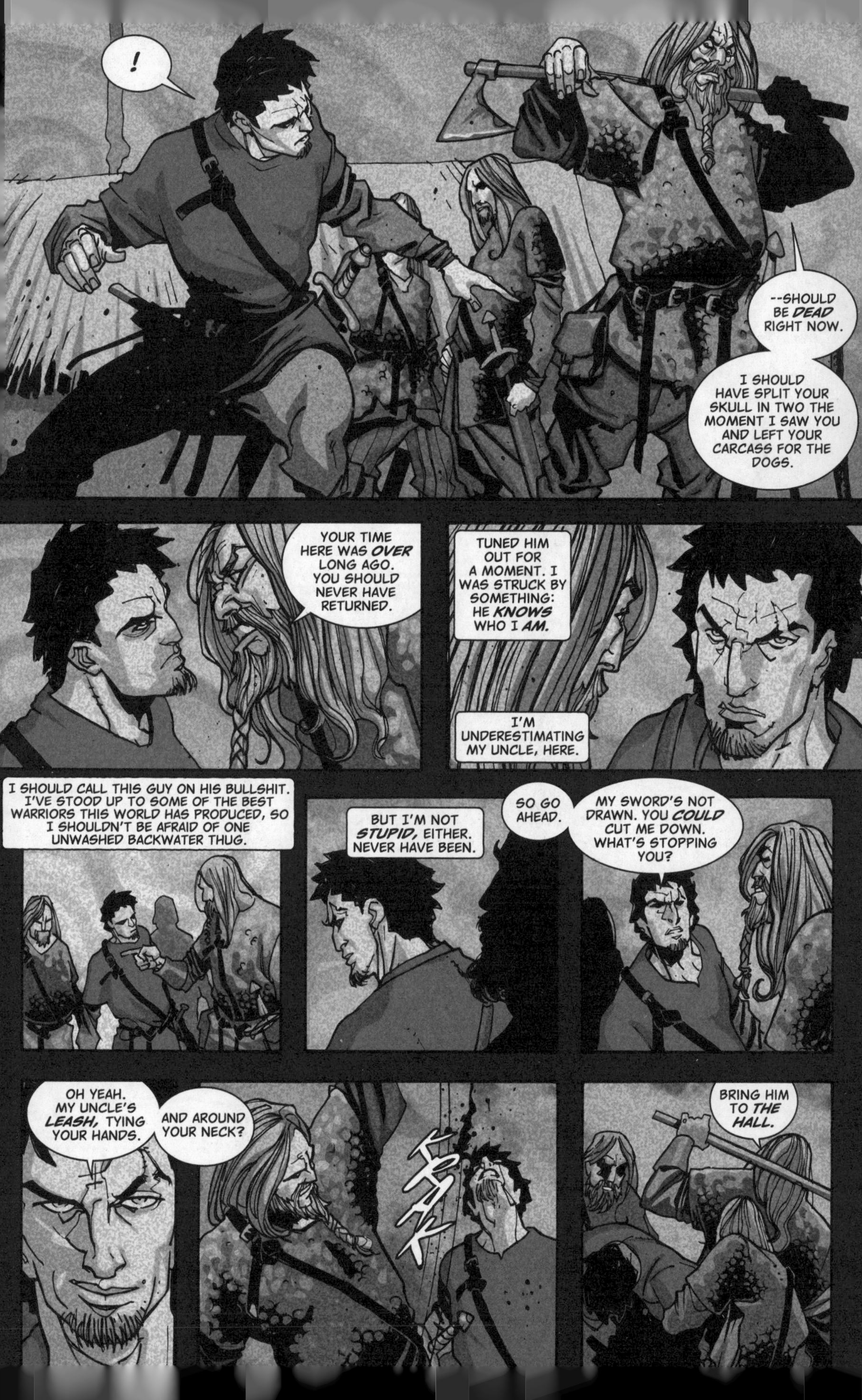
!
--SHOULD BE DEAD RIGHT NOW.
I SHOULD HAVE SPLIT YOUR SKULL IN TWO THE MOMENT I SAW YOU AND LEFT YOUR CARCASS FOR THE DOGS.
YOUR TIME HERE WAS OVER LONG AGO. YOU SHOULD NEVER HAVE RETURNED.
TUNED HIM OUT FOR A MOMENT. I WAS STRUCK BY SOMETHING: HE KNOWS WHO I AM.
I'M UNDERESTIMATING MY UNCLE, HERE.
I SHOULD CALL THIS GUY ON HIS BULLSHIT. I'VE STOOD UP TO SOME OF THE BEST WARRIORS THIS WORLD HAS PRODUCED, SO I SHOULDN'T BE AFRAID OF ONE UNWASHED BACKWATER THUG.
BUT I'M NOT STUPID, EITHER. NEVER HAVE BEEN.
SO GO AHEAD.
MY SWORD'S NOT DRAWN. YOU COULD CUT ME DOWN. WHAT'S STOPPING YOU?
OH YEAH. MY UNCLE'S LEASH, TYING YOUR HANDS.
AND AROUND YOUR NECK?
KRAK
BRING HIM TO THE HALL.

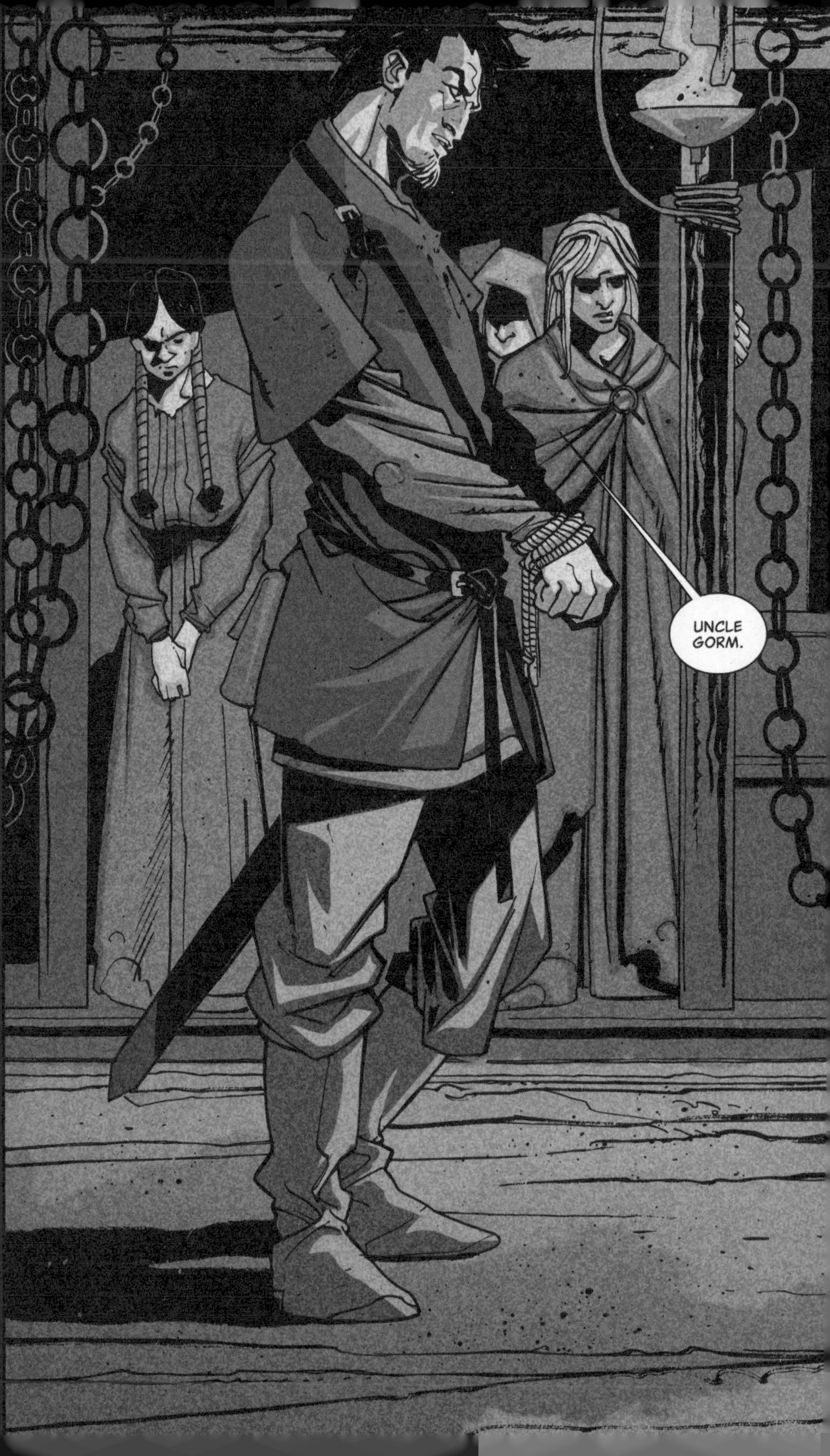
UNCLE GORM.

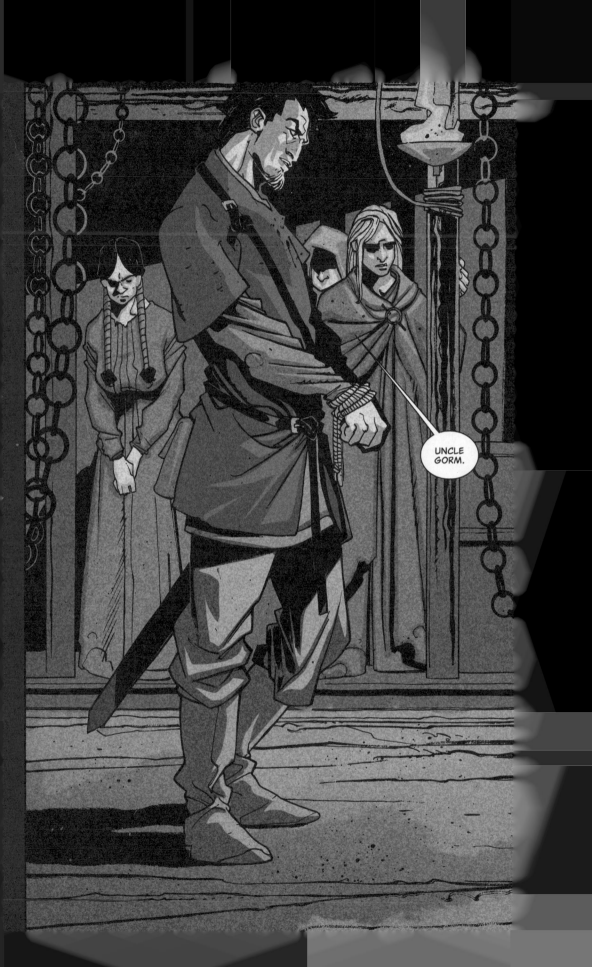

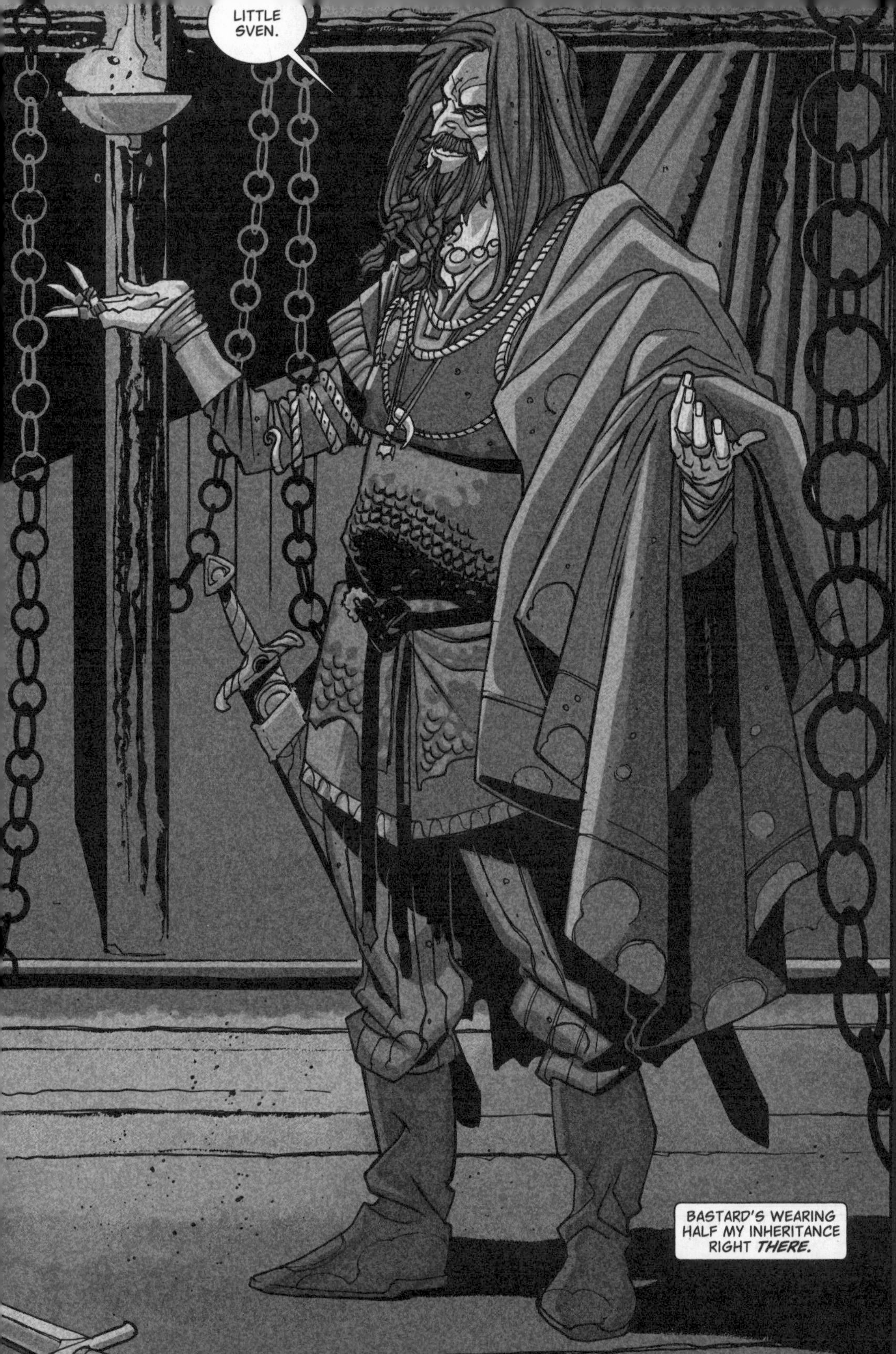
LITTLE SVEN.
BASTARD'S WEARING HALF MY INHERITANCE RIGHT *THERE.*

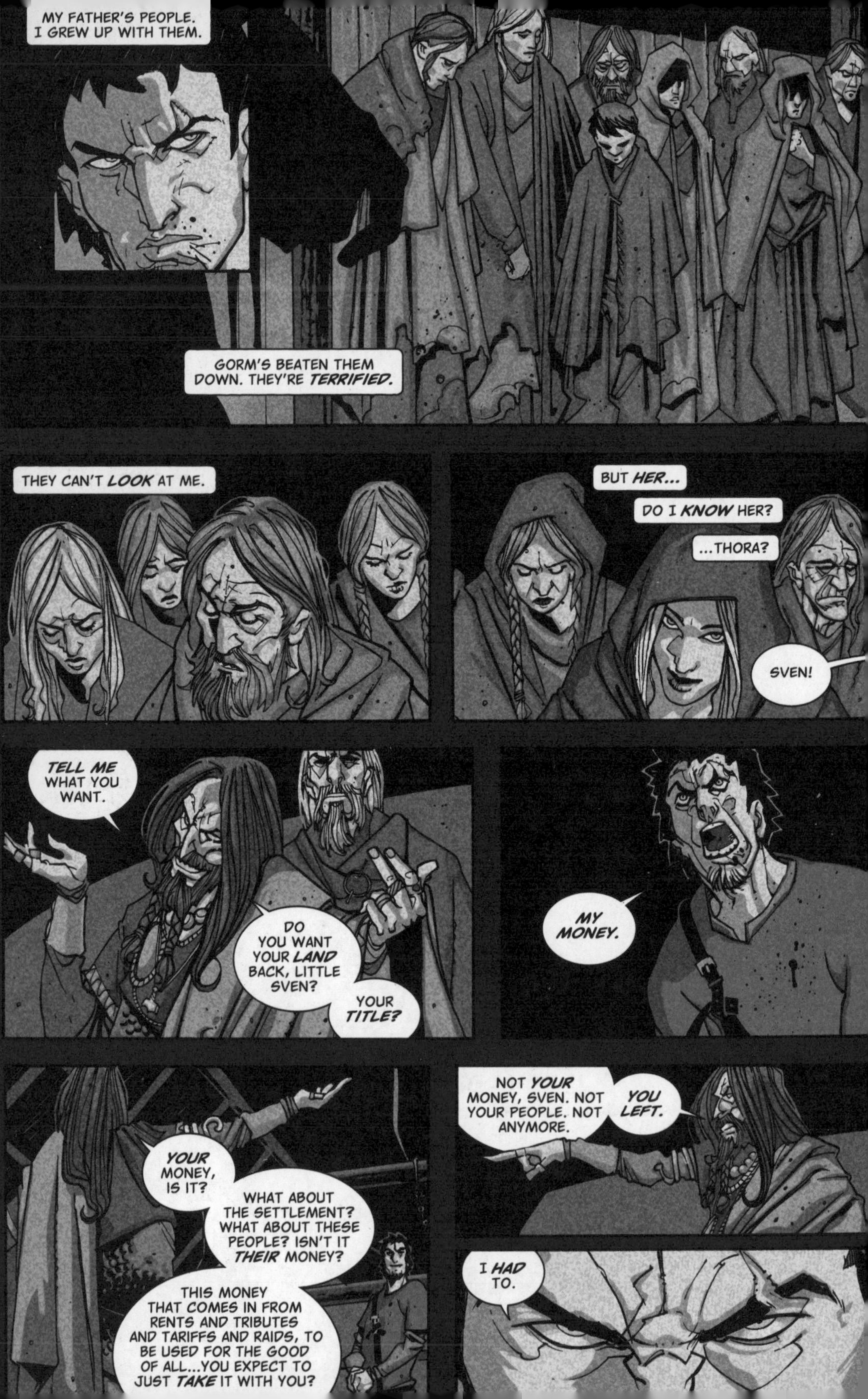
MY FATHER'S PEOPLE. I GREW UP WITH THEM.
GORM'S BEATEN THEM DOWN. THEY'RE *TERRIFIED.*
THEY CAN'T *LOOK* AT ME.
BUT *HER...*
DO I *KNOW* HER?
...THORA?
SVEN!
TELL ME WHAT YOU WANT.
DO YOU WANT YOUR *LAND* BACK, LITTLE SVEN?
YOUR *TITLE?*
MY MONEY.
YOUR MONEY, IS IT?
WHAT ABOUT THE SETTLEMENT? WHAT ABOUT THESE PEOPLE? ISN'T IT *THEIR* MONEY?
THIS MONEY THAT COMES IN FROM RENTS AND TRIBUTES AND TARIFFS AND RAIDS, TO BE USED FOR THE GOOD OF ALL...YOU EXPECT TO JUST *TAKE* IT WITH YOU?
NOT *YOUR* MONEY, SVEN. NOT YOUR PEOPLE. NOT ANYMORE.
YOU LEFT.
I *HAD* TO.

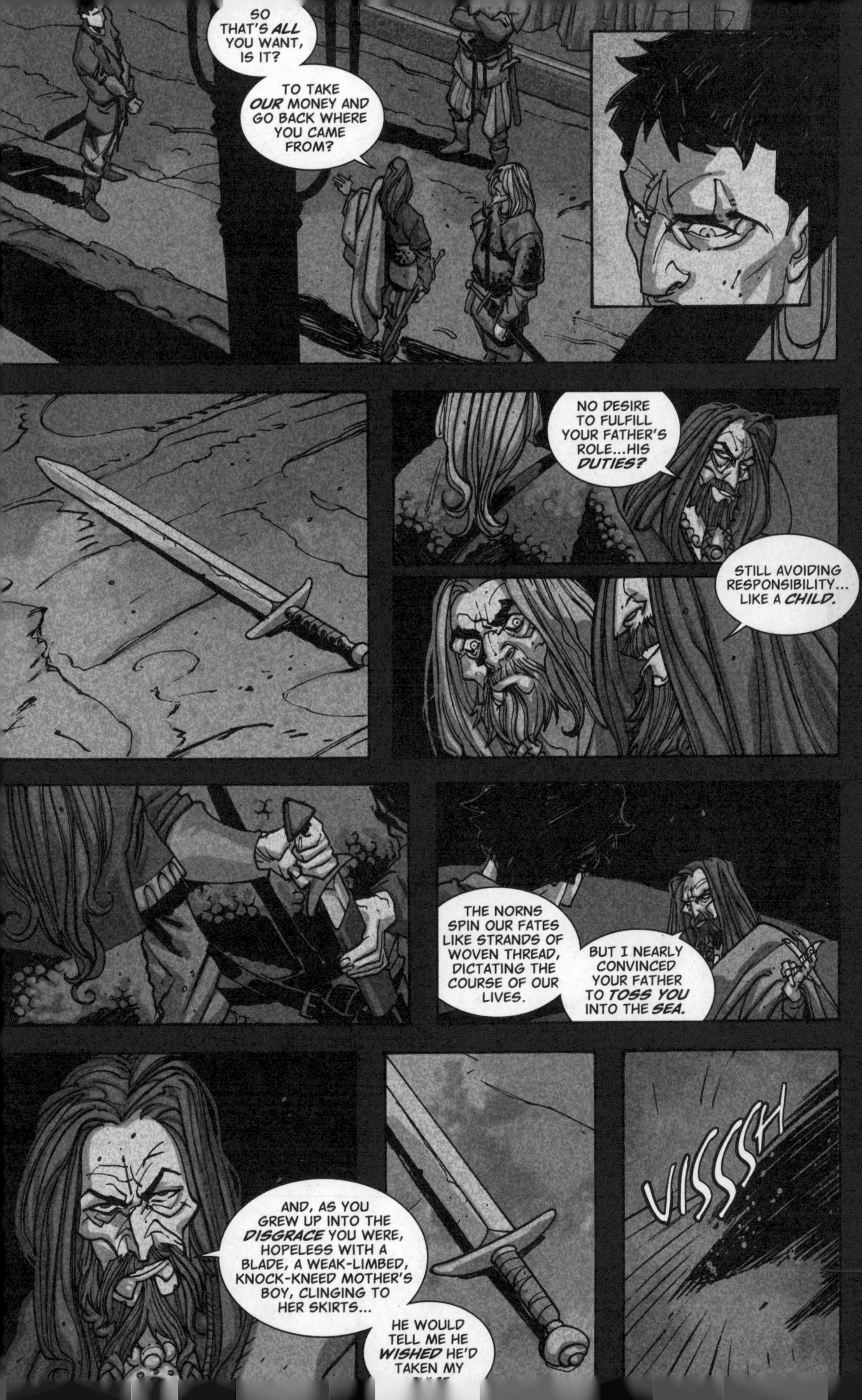
SO THAT'S ALL YOU WANT, IS IT?
TO TAKE OUR MONEY AND GO BACK WHERE YOU CAME FROM?
NO DESIRE TO FULFILL YOUR FATHER'S ROLE...HIS DUTIES?
STILL AVOIDING RESPONSIBILITY... LIKE A CHILD.
THE NORNS SPIN OUR FATES LIKE STRANDS OF WOVEN THREAD, DICTATING THE COURSE OF OUR LIVES.
BUT I NEARLY CONVINCED YOUR FATHER TO TOSS YOU INTO THE SEA.
AND, AS YOU GREW UP INTO THE DISGRACE YOU WERE, HOPELESS WITH A BLADE, A WEAK-LIMBED, KNOCK-KNEED MOTHER'S BOY, CLINGING TO HER SKIRTS...
HE WOULD TELL ME HE WISHED HE'D TAKEN MY
VISSSH

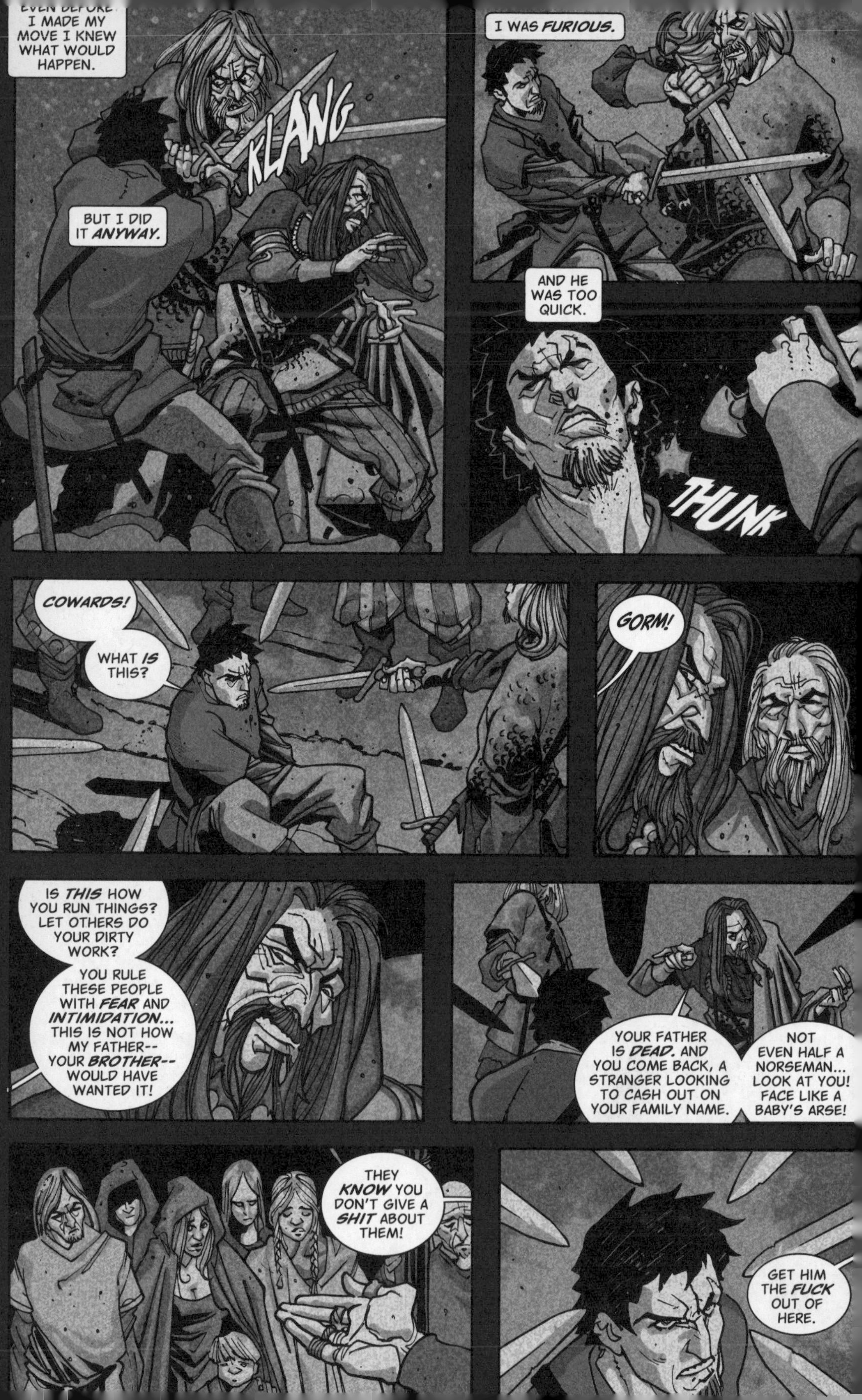
I MADE MY MOVE I KNEW WHAT WOULD HAPPEN.
KLANG
BUT I DID IT ANYWAY.
I WAS FURIOUS.
AND HE WAS TOO QUICK.
THUNK
COWARDS!
WHAT IS THIS?
GORM!
IS THIS HOW YOU RUN THINGS? LET OTHERS DO YOUR DIRTY WORK?
YOU RULE THESE PEOPLE WITH FEAR AND INTIMIDATION... THIS IS NOT HOW MY FATHER-- YOUR BROTHER-- WOULD HAVE WANTED IT!
NOT EVEN HALF A NORSEMAN... LOOK AT YOU! FACE LIKE A BABY'S ARSE!
YOUR FATHER IS DEAD. AND YOU COME BACK, A STRANGER LOOKING TO CASH OUT ON YOUR FAMILY NAME.
THEY KNOW YOU DON'T GIVE A SHIT ABOUT THEM!
GET HIM THE FUCK OUT OF HERE.

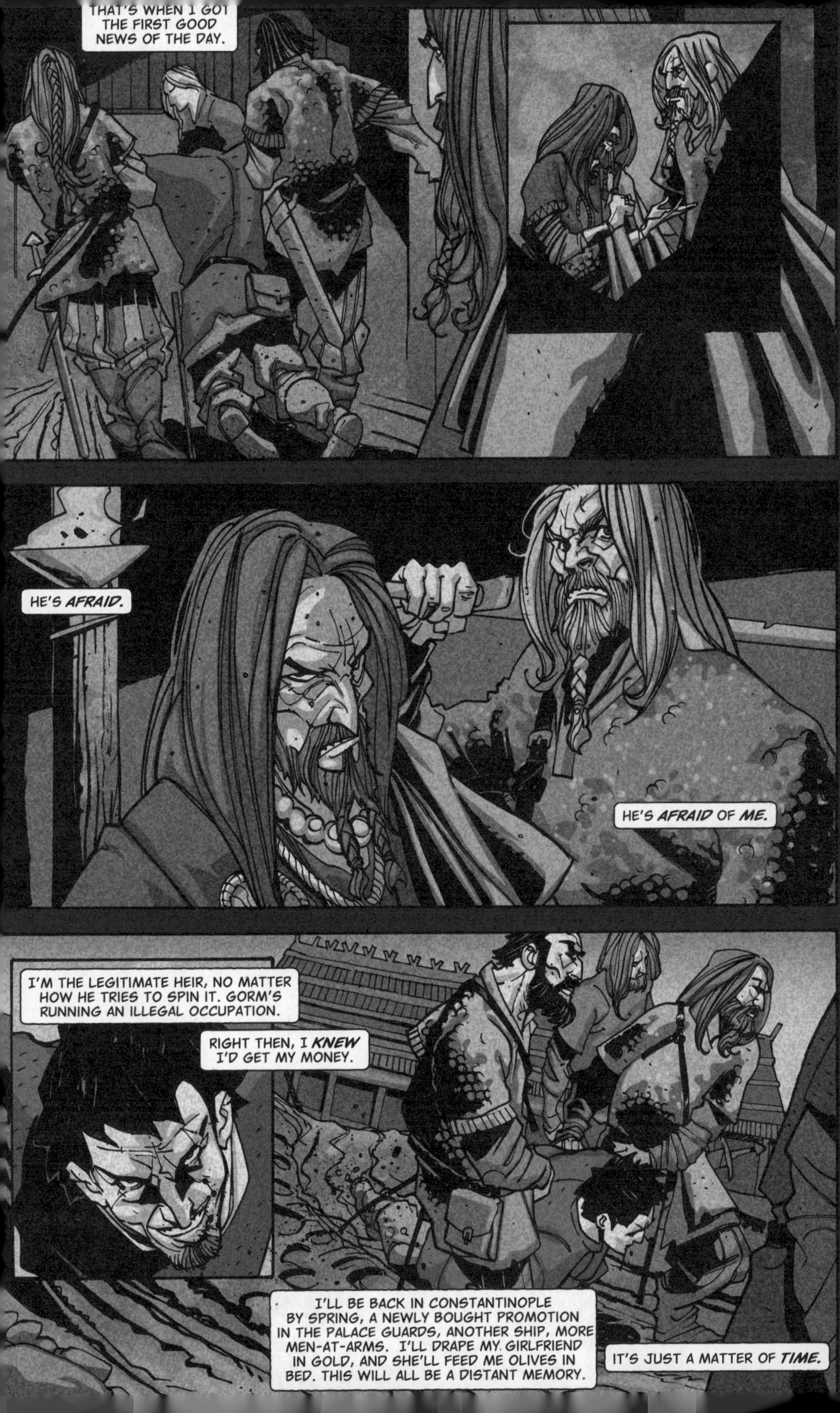
THAT'S WHEN I GOT THE FIRST GOOD NEWS OF THE DAY.
HE'S *AFRAID.*
HE'S *AFRAID* OF *ME.*
I'M THE LEGITIMATE HEIR, NO MATTER HOW HE TRIES TO SPIN IT. GORM'S RUNNING AN ILLEGAL OCCUPATION.
RIGHT THEN, I *KNEW* I'D GET MY MONEY.
I'LL BE BACK IN CONSTANTINOPLE BY SPRING, A NEWLY BOUGHT PROMOTION IN THE PALACE GUARDS, ANOTHER SHIP, MORE MEN-AT-ARMS. I'LL DRAPE MY GIRLFRIEND IN GOLD, AND SHE'LL FEED ME OLIVES IN BED. THIS WILL ALL BE A DISTANT MEMORY.
IT'S JUST A MATTER OF *TIME.*

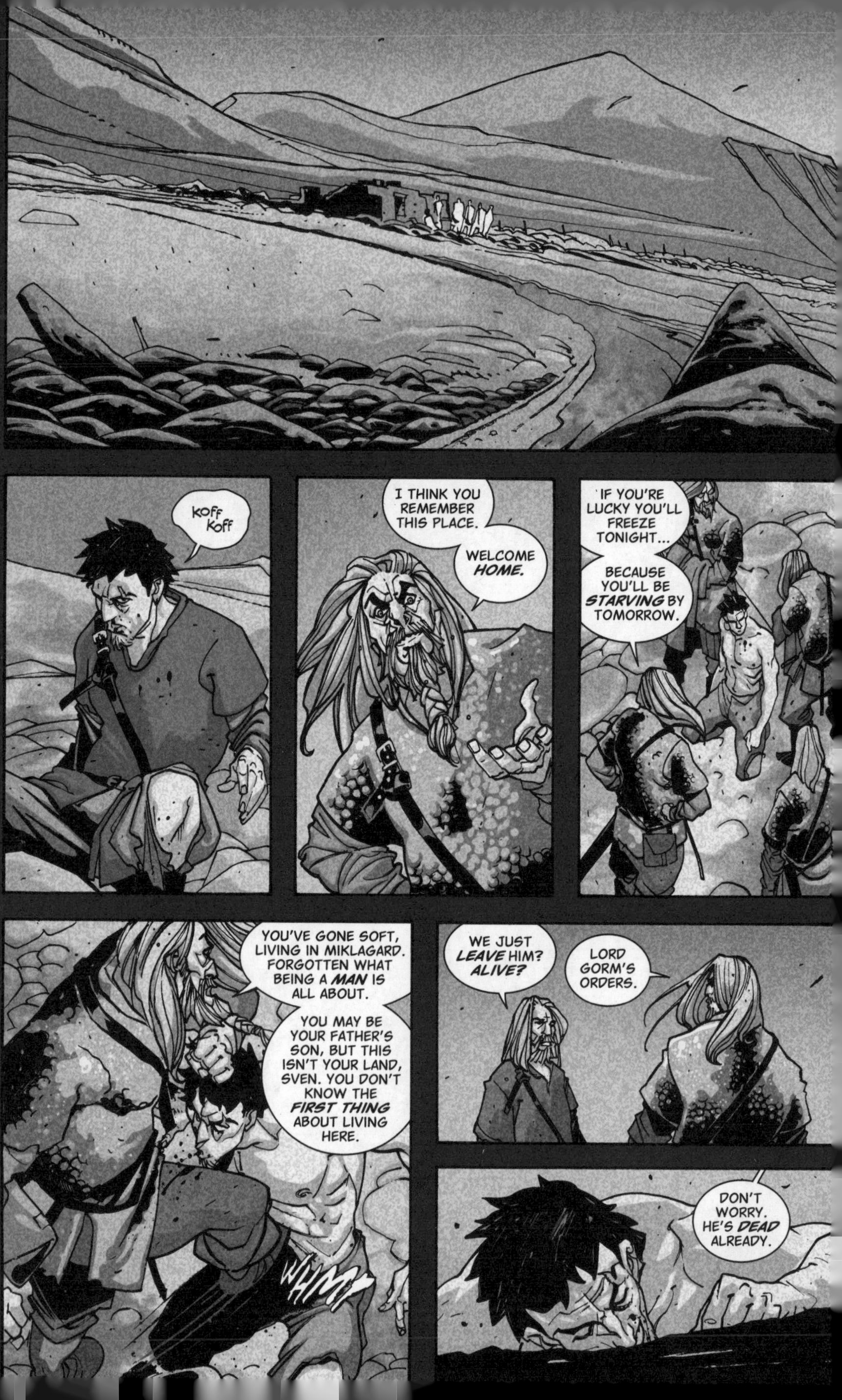
KOFF KOFF
I THINK YOU REMEMBER THIS PLACE.
WELCOME HOME.
IF YOU'RE LUCKY YOU'LL FREEZE TONIGHT...
BECAUSE YOU'LL BE STARVING BY TOMORROW.
YOU'VE GONE SOFT, LIVING IN MIKLAGARD. FORGOTTEN WHAT BEING A MAN IS ALL ABOUT.
YOU MAY BE YOUR FATHER'S SON, BUT THIS ISN'T YOUR LAND, SVEN. YOU DON'T KNOW THE FIRST THING ABOUT LIVING HERE.
WHUMP
WE JUST LEAVE HIM? ALIVE?
LORD GORM'S ORDERS.
DON'T WORRY. HE'S DEAD ALREADY.

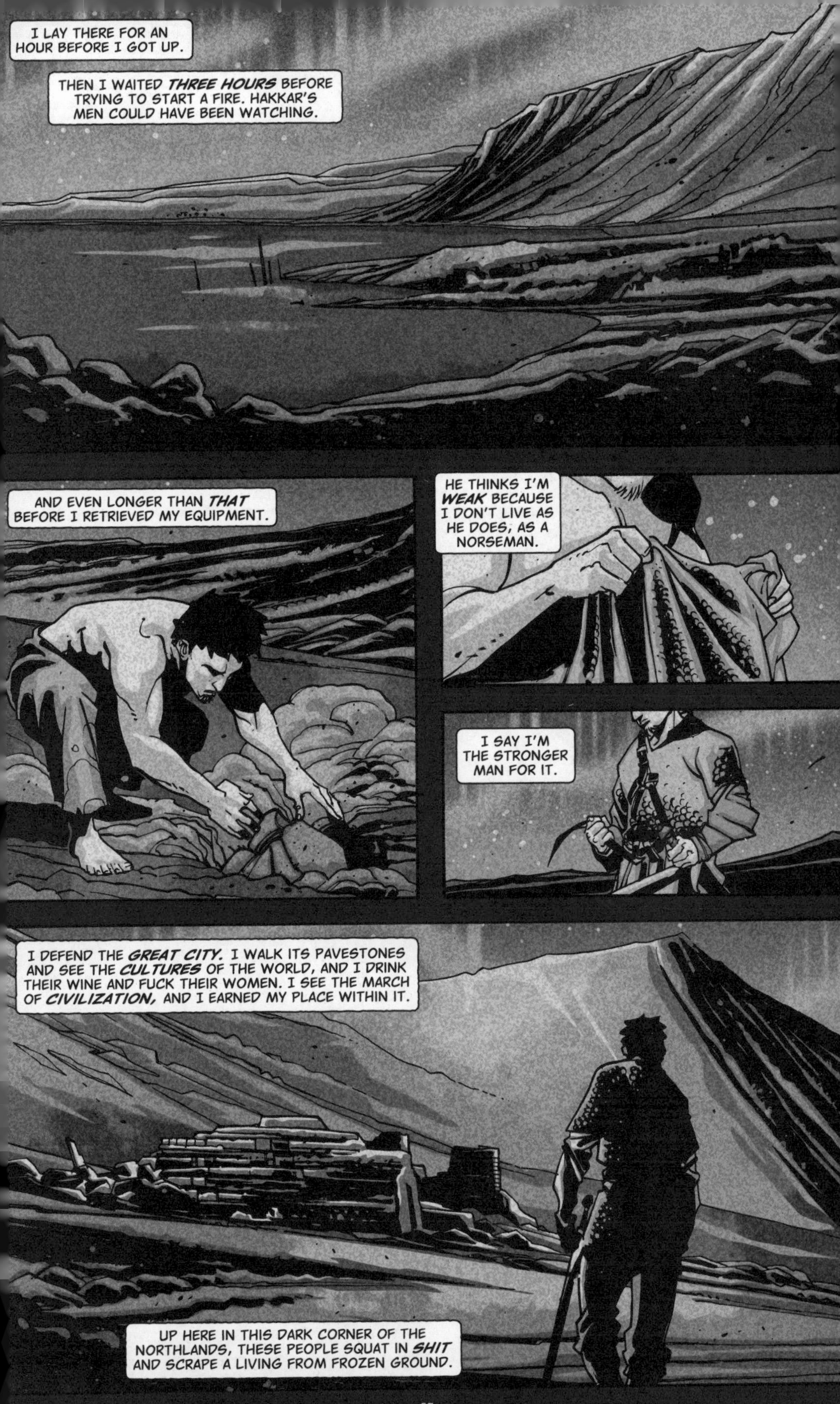
I LAY THERE FOR AN HOUR BEFORE I GOT UP.
THEN I WAITED *THREE HOURS* BEFORE TRYING TO START A FIRE. HAKKAR'S MEN COULD HAVE BEEN WATCHING.
AND EVEN LONGER THAN *THAT* BEFORE I RETRIEVED MY EQUIPMENT.
HE THINKS I'M *WEAK* BECAUSE I DON'T LIVE AS HE DOES, AS A NORSEMAN.
I SAY I'M THE STRONGER MAN FOR IT.
I DEFEND THE *GREAT CITY.* I WALK ITS PAVESTONES AND SEE THE *CULTURES* OF THE WORLD, AND I DRINK THEIR WINE AND FUCK THEIR WOMEN. I SEE THE MARCH OF *CIVILIZATION,* AND I EARNED MY PLACE WITHIN IT.
UP HERE IN THIS DARK CORNER OF THE NORTHLANDS, THESE PEOPLE SQUAT IN *SHIT* AND SCRAPE A LIVING FROM FROZEN GROUND.

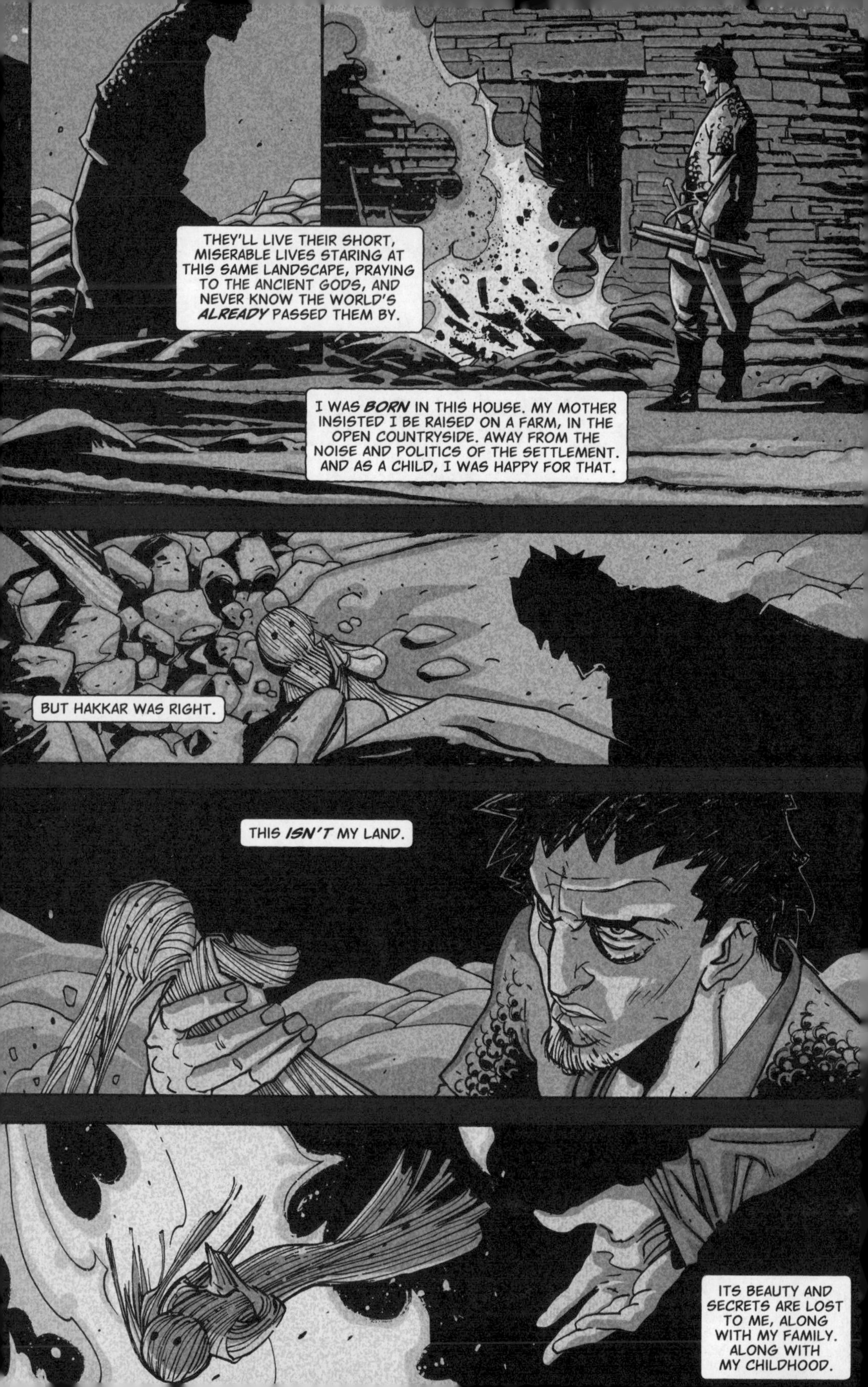
THEY'LL LIVE THEIR SHORT, MISERABLE LIVES STARING AT THIS SAME LANDSCAPE, PRAYING TO THE ANCIENT GODS, AND NEVER KNOW THE WORLD'S ALREADY PASSED THEM BY.
I WAS BORN IN THIS HOUSE. MY MOTHER INSISTED I BE RAISED ON A FARM, IN THE OPEN COUNTRYSIDE. AWAY FROM THE NOISE AND POLITICS OF THE SETTLEMENT. AND AS A CHILD, I WAS HAPPY FOR THAT.
BUT HAKKAR WAS RIGHT.
THIS ISN'T MY LAND.
ITS BEAUTY AND SECRETS ARE LOST TO ME, ALONG WITH MY FAMILY. ALONG WITH MY CHILDHOOD.

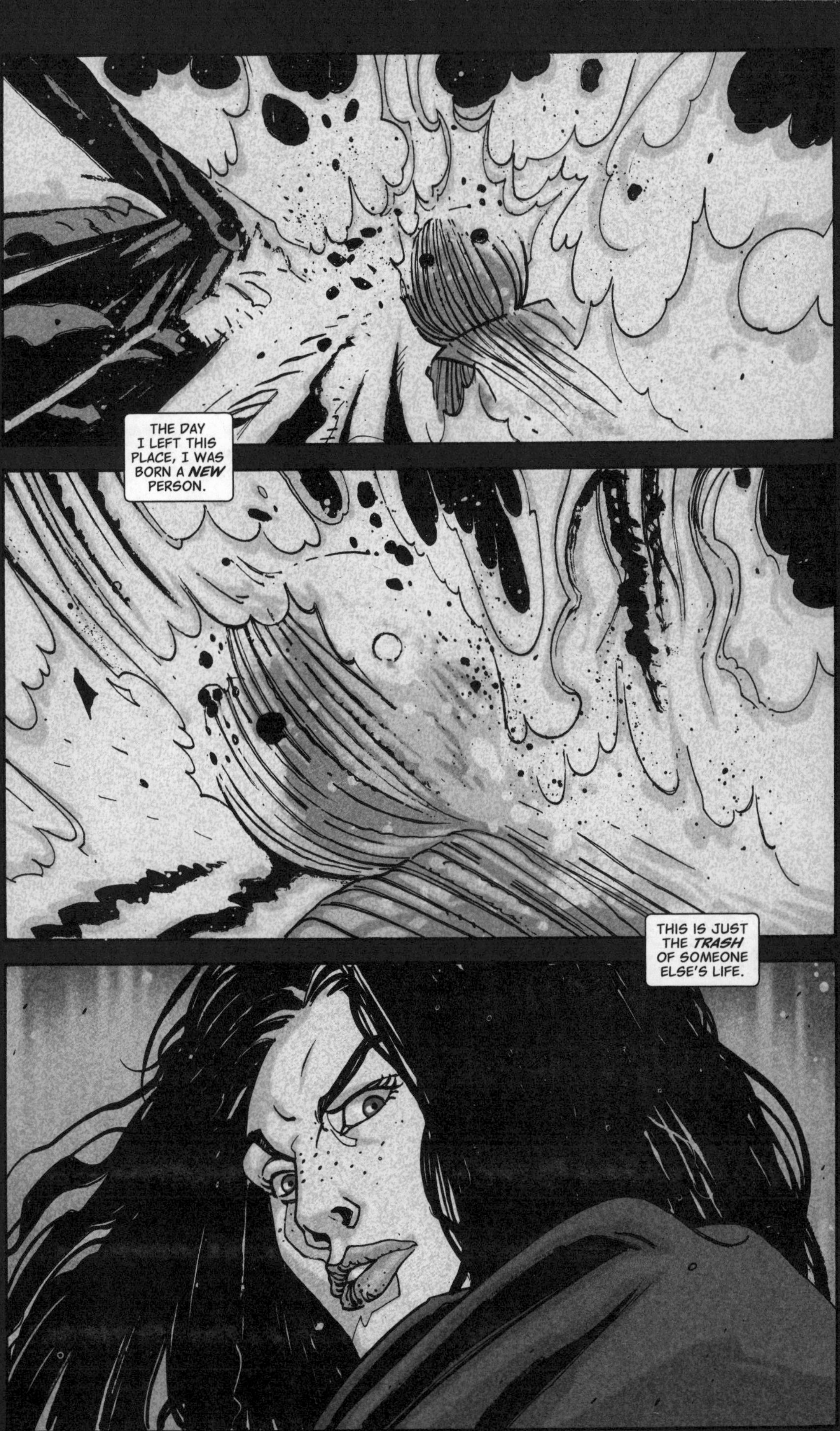
THE DAY I LEFT THIS PLACE, I WAS BORN A NEW PERSON.
THIS IS JUST THE TRASH OF SOMEONE ELSE'S LIFE.

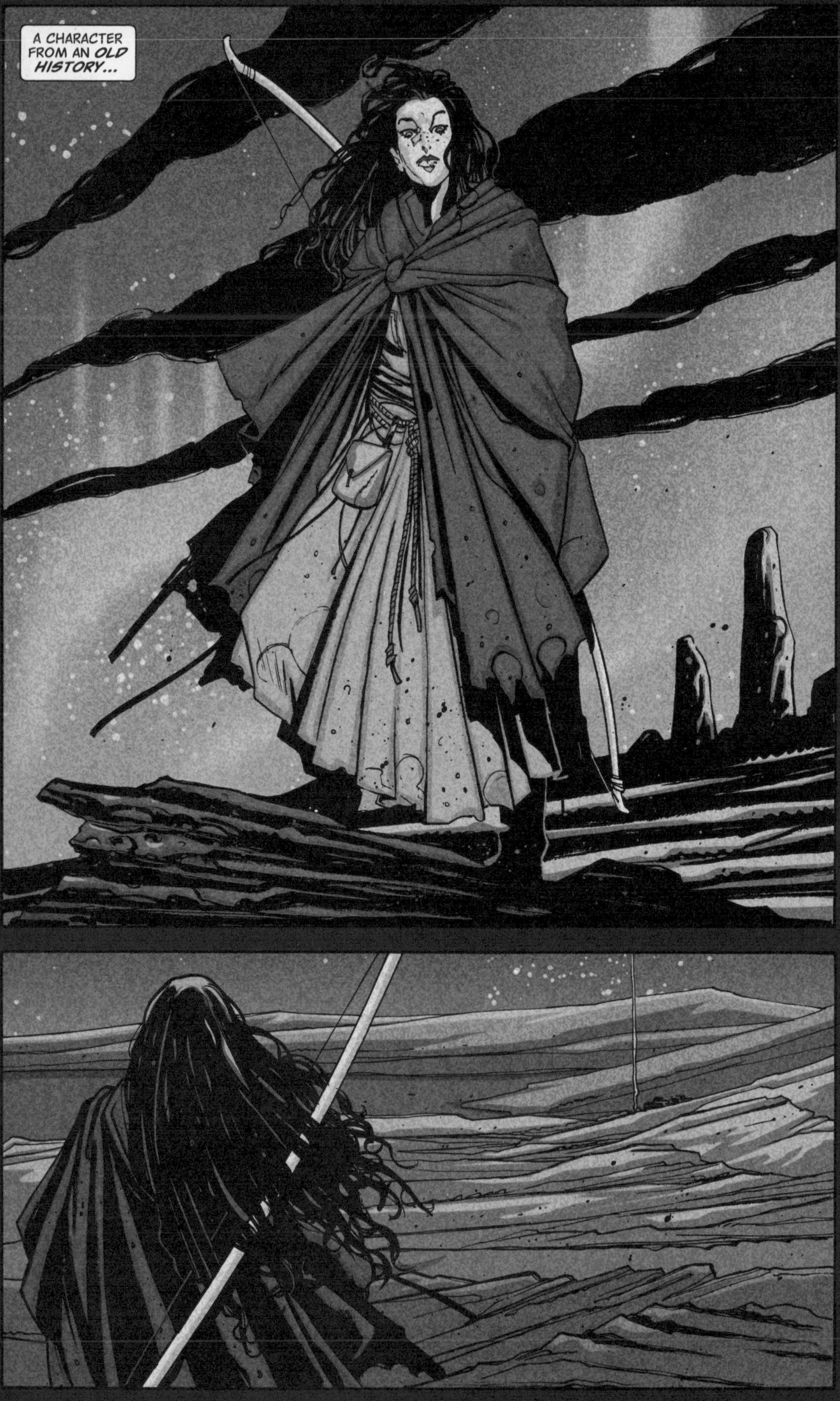
A CHARACTER FROM AN OLD HISTORY...

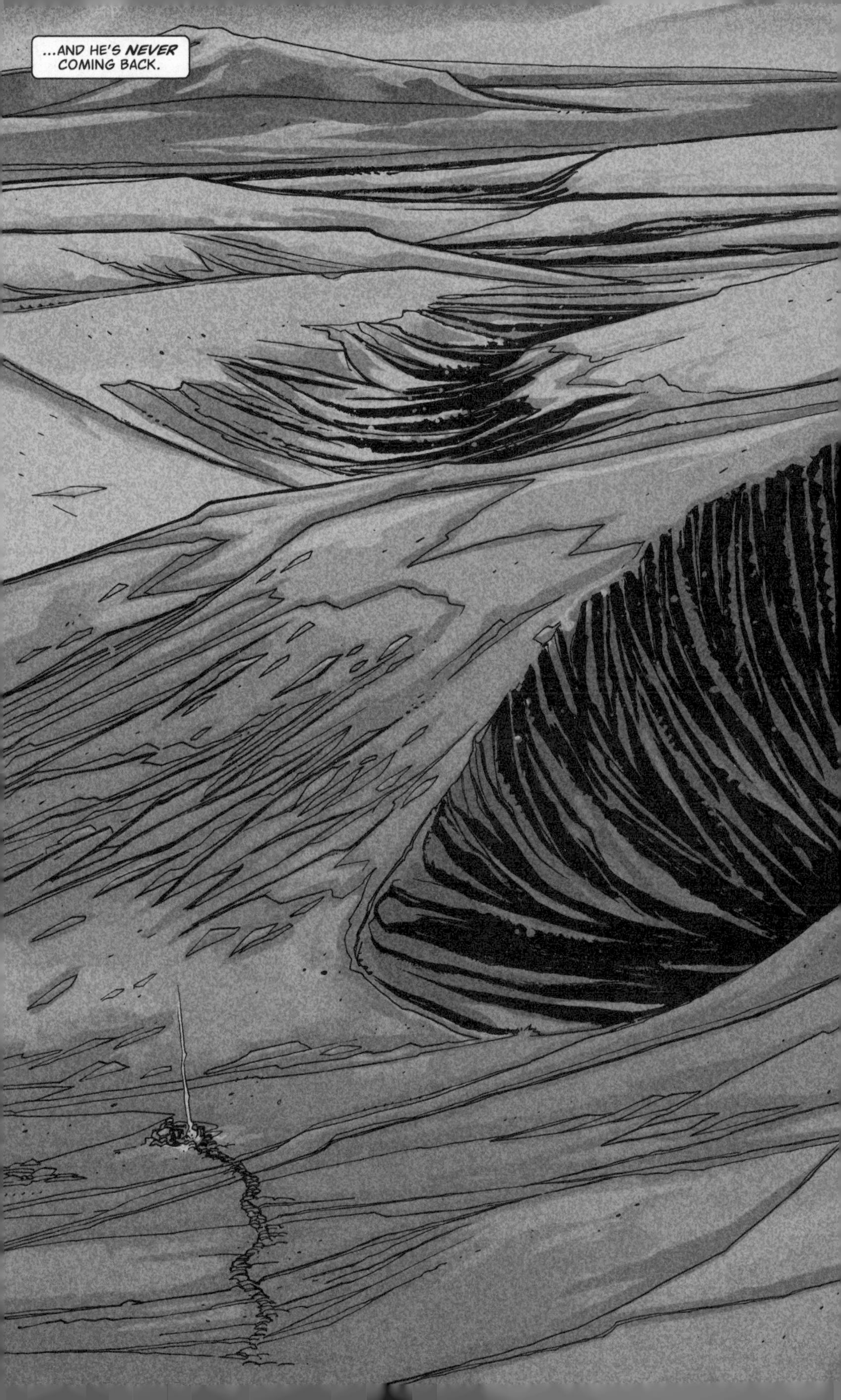
...AND HE'S NEVER COMING BACK.

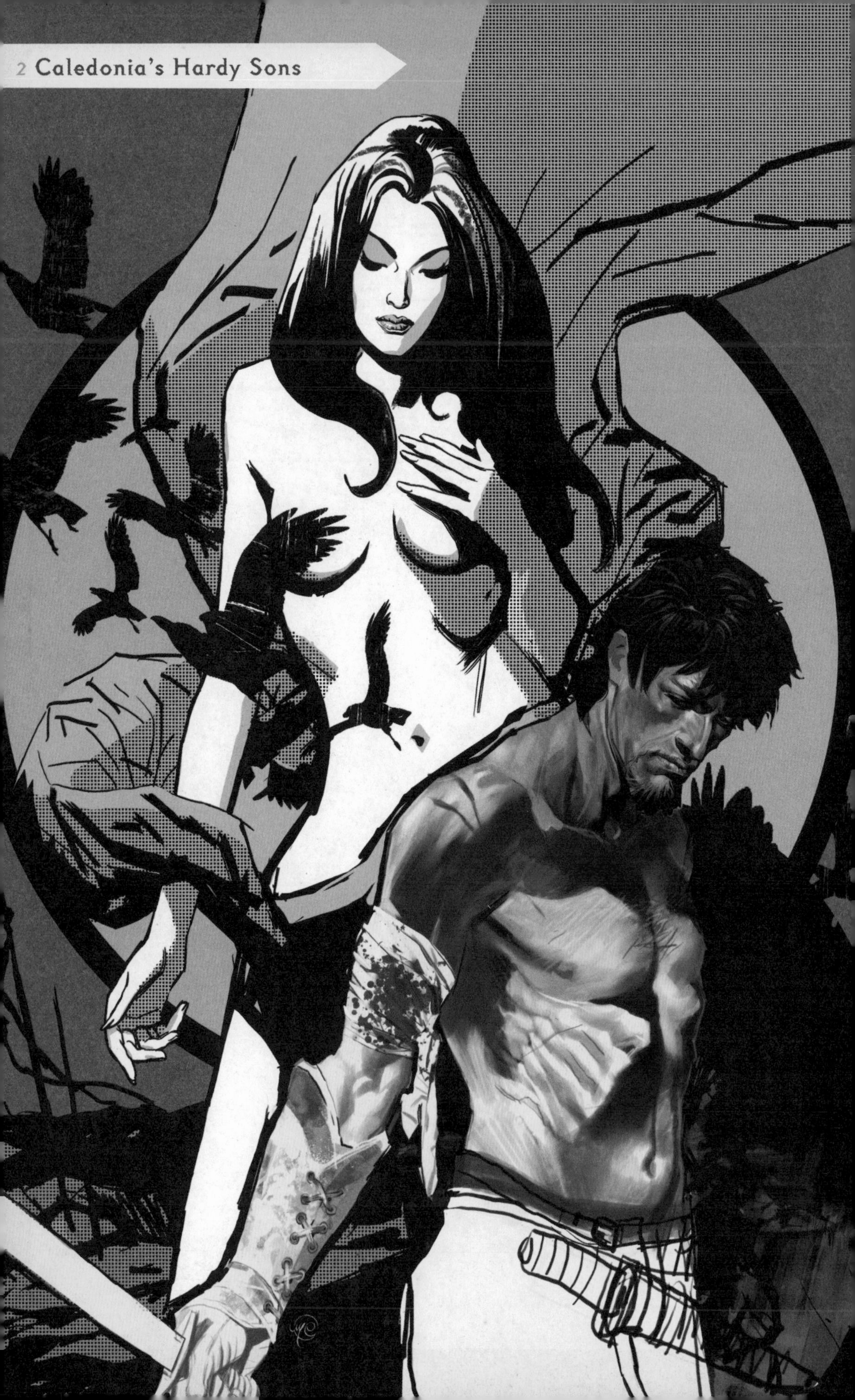

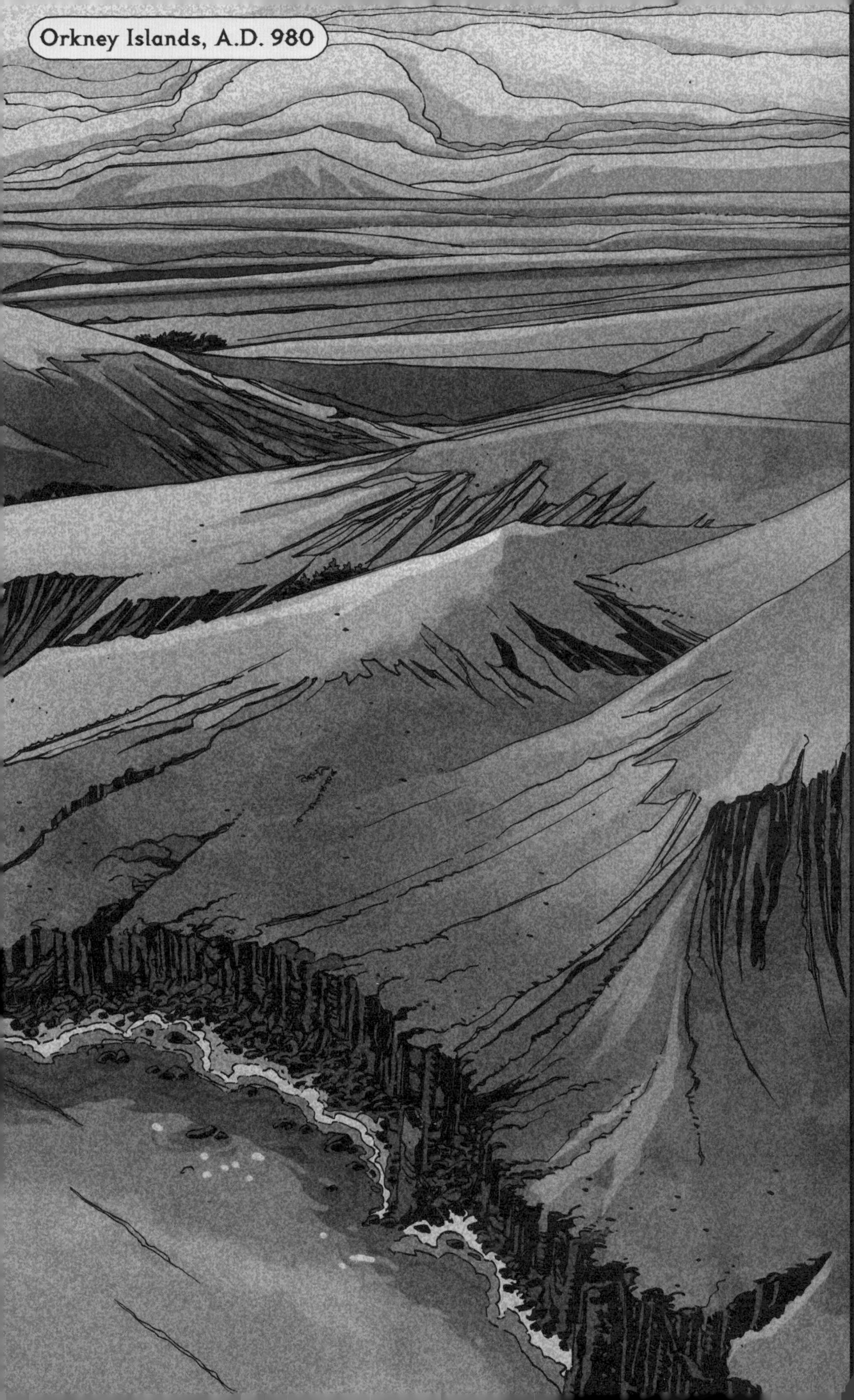
Orkney Islands, A.D. 980

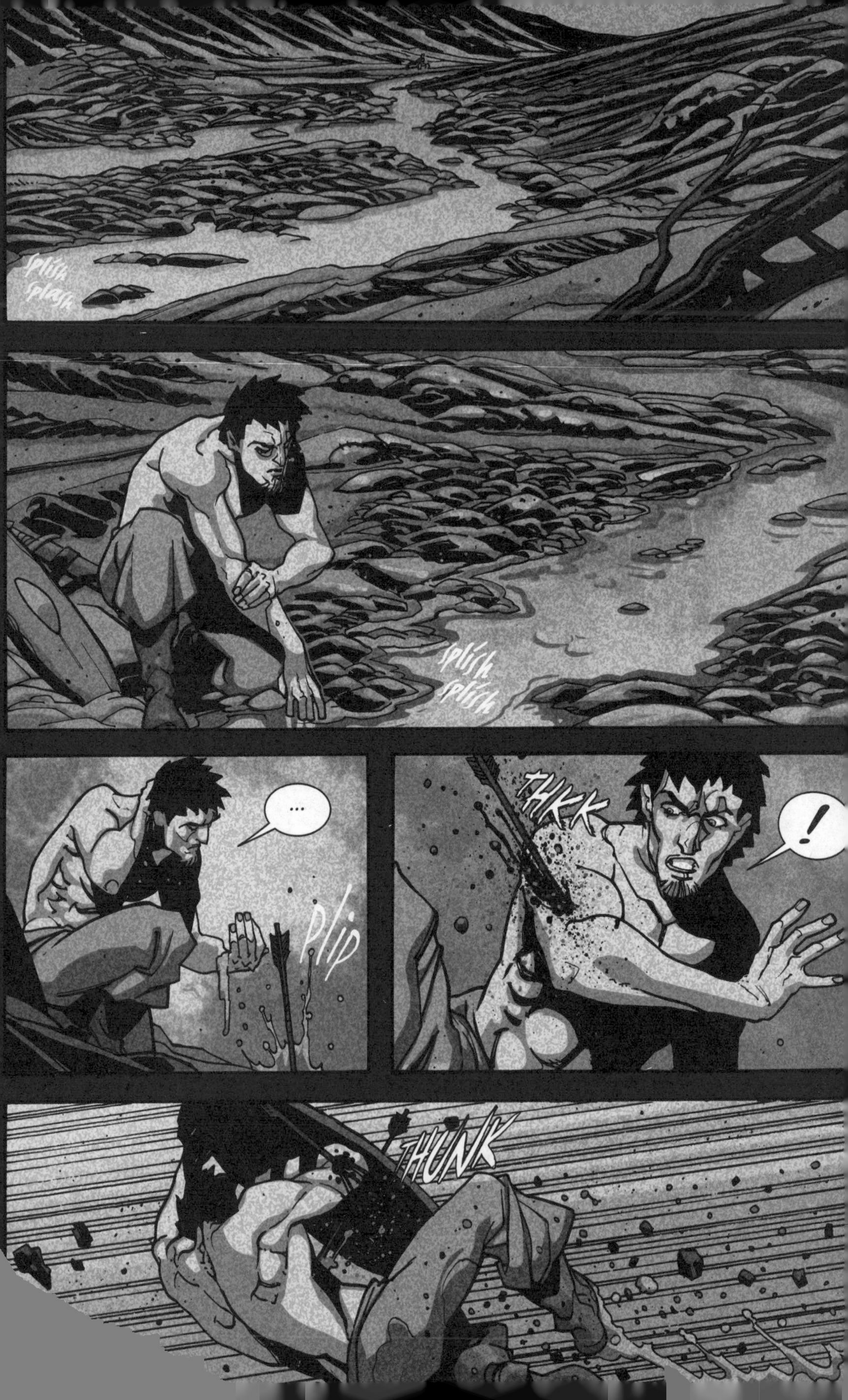
splish
splash
splish
splish
...
plip
THKK
!
THUNK

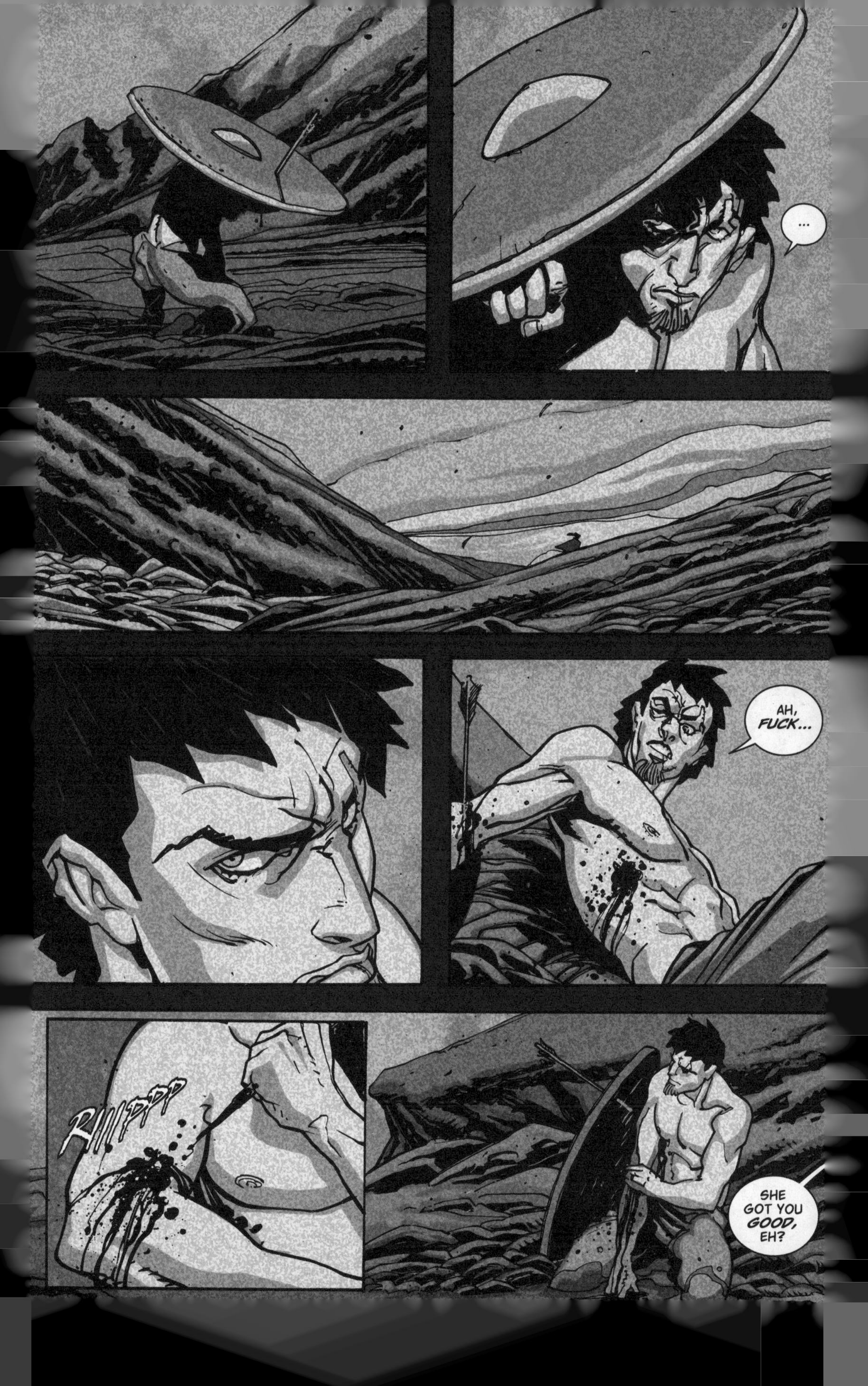
...
AH, FUCK...
RIIIIPPP
SHE GOT YOU GOOD, EH?

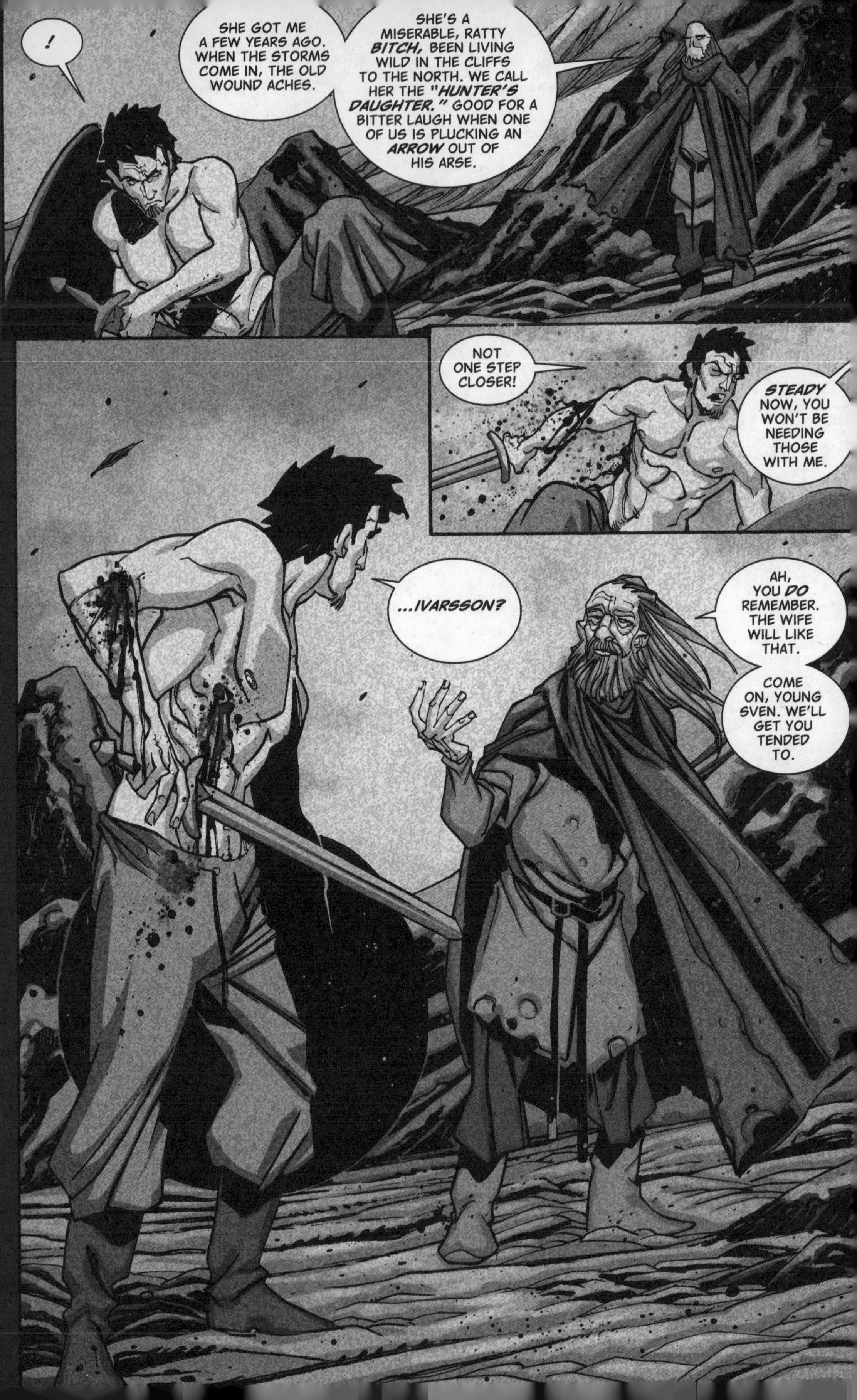
!
SHE GOT ME A FEW YEARS AGO. WHEN THE STORMS COME IN, THE OLD WOUND ACHES.
SHE'S A MISERABLE, RATTY *BITCH,* BEEN LIVING WILD IN THE CLIFFS TO THE NORTH. WE CALL HER THE *"HUNTER'S DAUGHTER."* GOOD FOR A BITTER LAUGH WHEN ONE OF US IS PLUCKING AN *ARROW* OUT OF HIS ARSE.
NOT ONE STEP CLOSER!
STEADY NOW, YOU WON'T BE NEEDING THOSE WITH ME.
...IVARSSON?
AH, YOU *DO* REMEMBER. THE WIFE WILL LIKE THAT.
COME ON, YOUNG SVEN. WE'LL GET YOU TENDED TO.

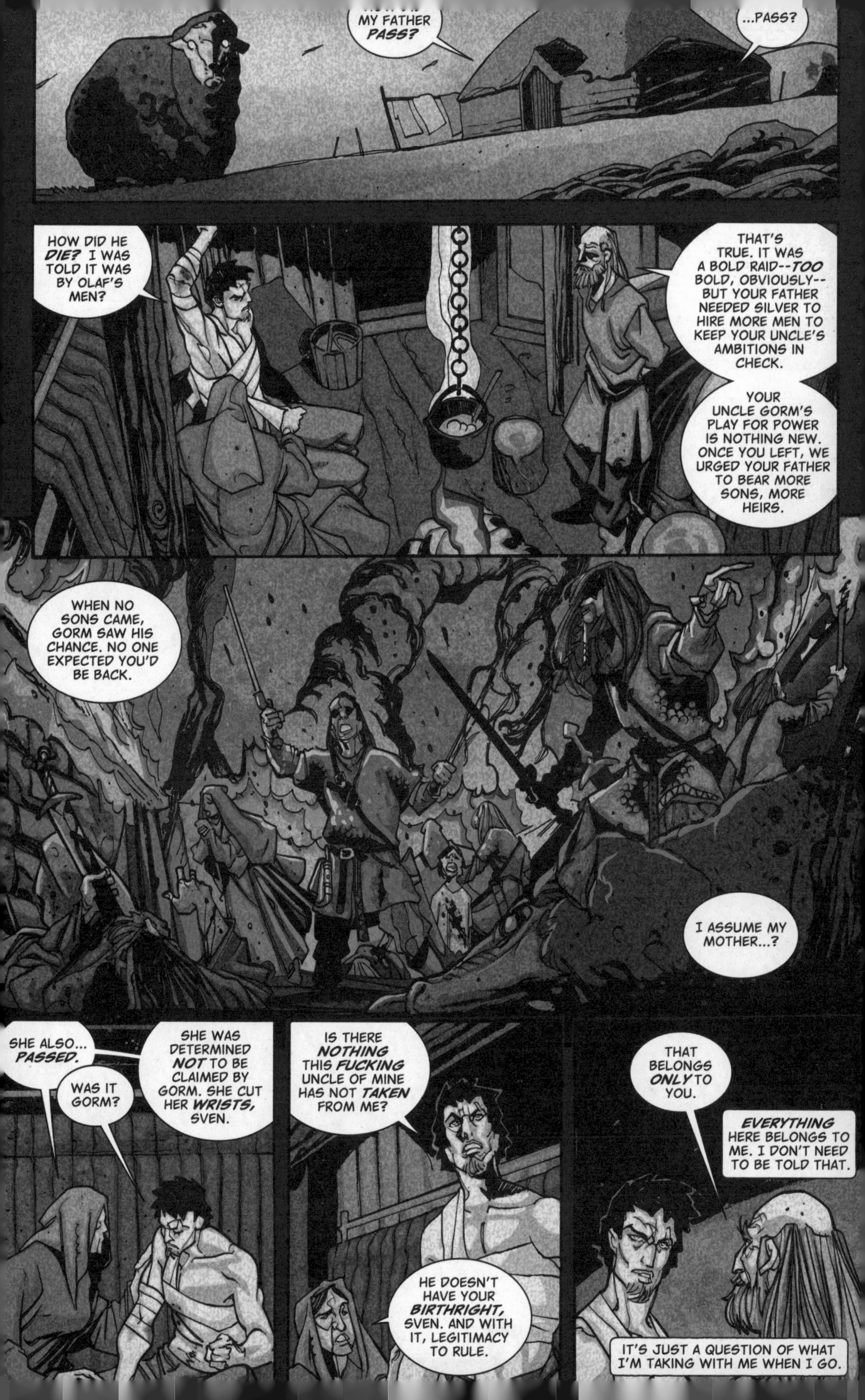
MY FATHER PASS?
...PASS?
HOW DID HE DIE? I WAS TOLD IT WAS BY OLAF'S MEN?
THAT'S TRUE. IT WAS A BOLD RAID--TOO BOLD, OBVIOUSLY--BUT YOUR FATHER NEEDED SILVER TO HIRE MORE MEN TO KEEP YOUR UNCLE'S AMBITIONS IN CHECK.
YOUR UNCLE GORM'S PLAY FOR POWER IS NOTHING NEW. ONCE YOU LEFT, WE URGED YOUR FATHER TO BEAR MORE SONS, MORE HEIRS.
WHEN NO SONS CAME, GORM SAW HIS CHANCE. NO ONE EXPECTED YOU'D BE BACK.
I ASSUME MY MOTHER...?
SHE ALSO... PASSED.
WAS IT GORM?
SHE WAS DETERMINED NOT TO BE CLAIMED BY GORM. SHE CUT HER WRISTS, SVEN.
IS THERE NOTHING THIS FUCKING UNCLE OF MINE HAS NOT TAKEN FROM ME?
HE DOESN'T HAVE YOUR BIRTHRIGHT, SVEN. AND WITH IT, LEGITIMACY TO RULE.
THAT BELONGS ONLY TO YOU.
EVERYTHING HERE BELONGS TO ME. I DON'T NEED TO BE TOLD THAT.
IT'S JUST A QUESTION OF WHAT I'M TAKING WITH ME WHEN I GO.

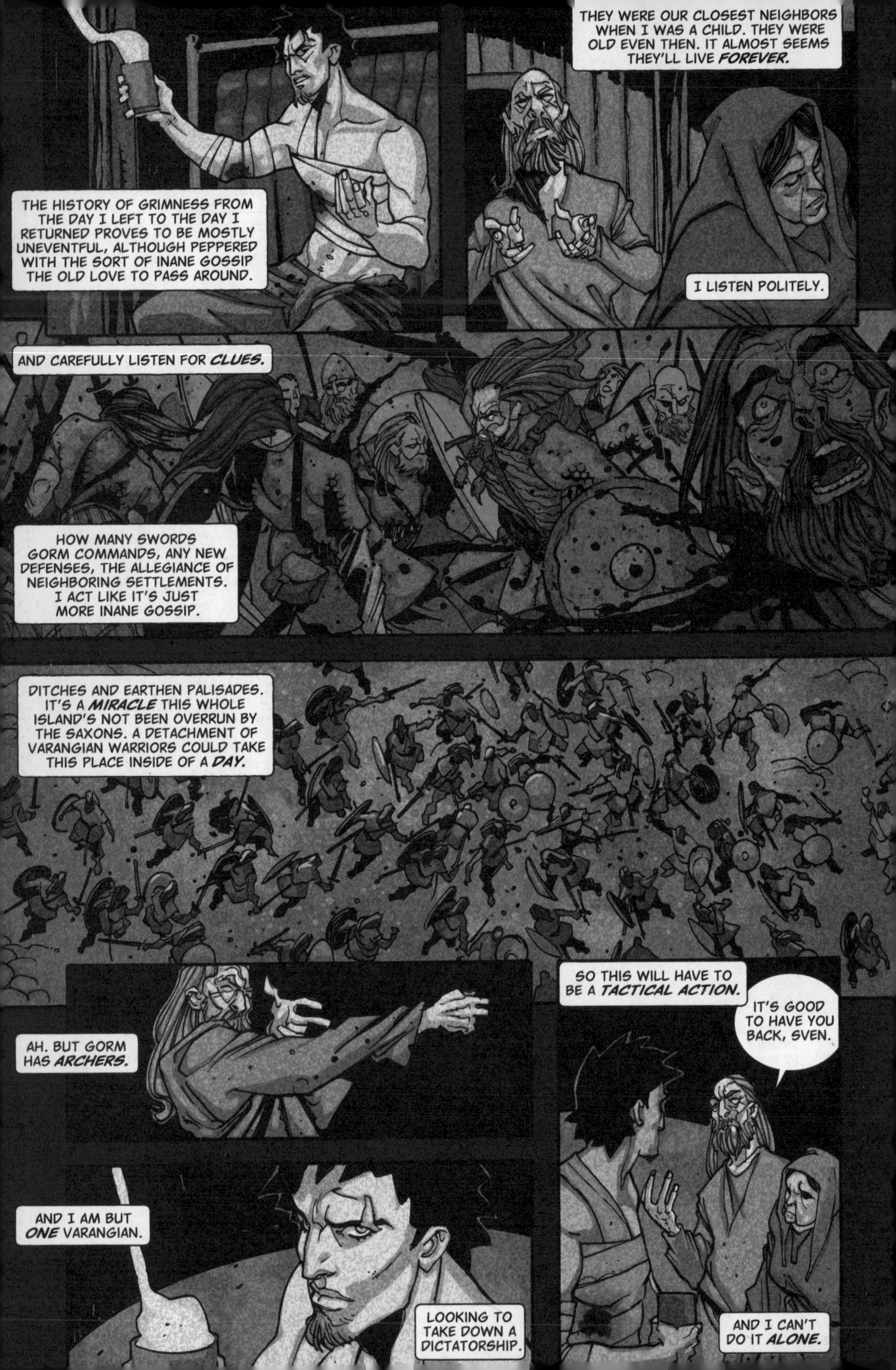
THE HISTORY OF GRIMNESS FROM THE DAY I LEFT TO THE DAY I RETURNED PROVES TO BE MOSTLY UNEVENTFUL, ALTHOUGH PEPPERED WITH THE SORT OF INANE GOSSIP THE OLD LOVE TO PASS AROUND.
THEY WERE OUR CLOSEST NEIGHBORS WHEN I WAS A CHILD. THEY WERE OLD EVEN THEN. IT ALMOST SEEMS THEY'LL LIVE *FOREVER.*
I LISTEN POLITELY.
AND CAREFULLY LISTEN FOR *CLUES.*
HOW MANY SWORDS GORM COMMANDS, ANY NEW DEFENSES, THE ALLEGIANCE OF NEIGHBORING SETTLEMENTS. I ACT LIKE IT'S JUST MORE INANE GOSSIP.
DITCHES AND EARTHEN PALISADES. IT'S A *MIRACLE* THIS WHOLE ISLAND'S NOT BEEN OVERRUN BY THE SAXONS. A DETACHMENT OF VARANGIAN WARRIORS COULD TAKE THIS PLACE INSIDE OF A *DAY.*
AH. BUT GORM HAS *ARCHERS.*
AND I AM BUT *ONE* VARANGIAN.
LOOKING TO TAKE DOWN A DICTATORSHIP.
SO THIS WILL HAVE TO BE A *TACTICAL ACTION.*
IT'S GOOD TO HAVE YOU BACK, SVEN.
AND I CAN'T DO IT *ALONE.*

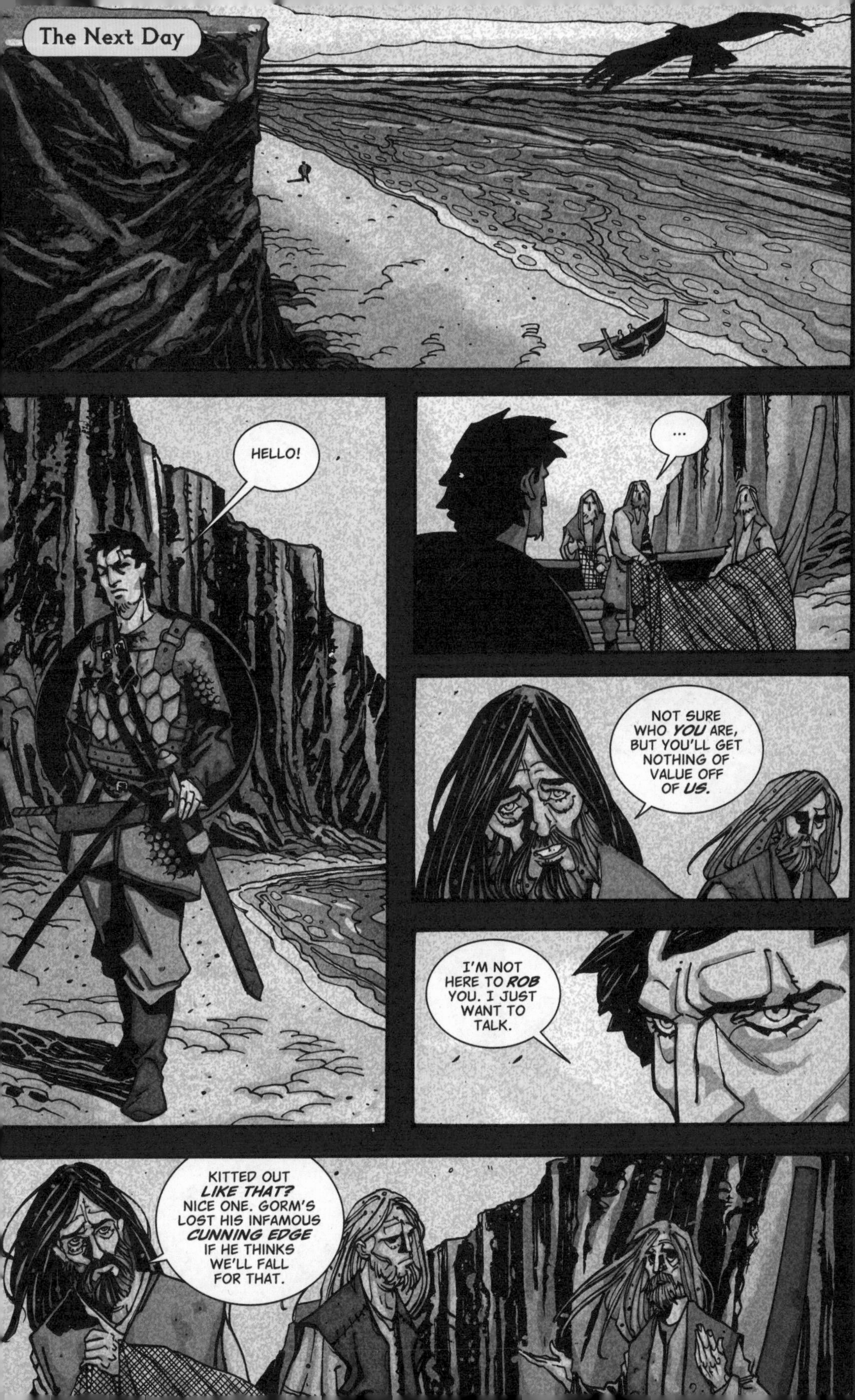
The Next Day
HELLO!
...
NOT SURE WHO YOU ARE, BUT YOU'LL GET NOTHING OF VALUE OFF OF US.
I'M NOT HERE TO ROB YOU. I JUST WANT TO TALK.
KITTED OUT LIKE THAT? NICE ONE. GORM'S LOST HIS INFAMOUS CUNNING EDGE IF HE THINKS WE'LL FALL FOR THAT.

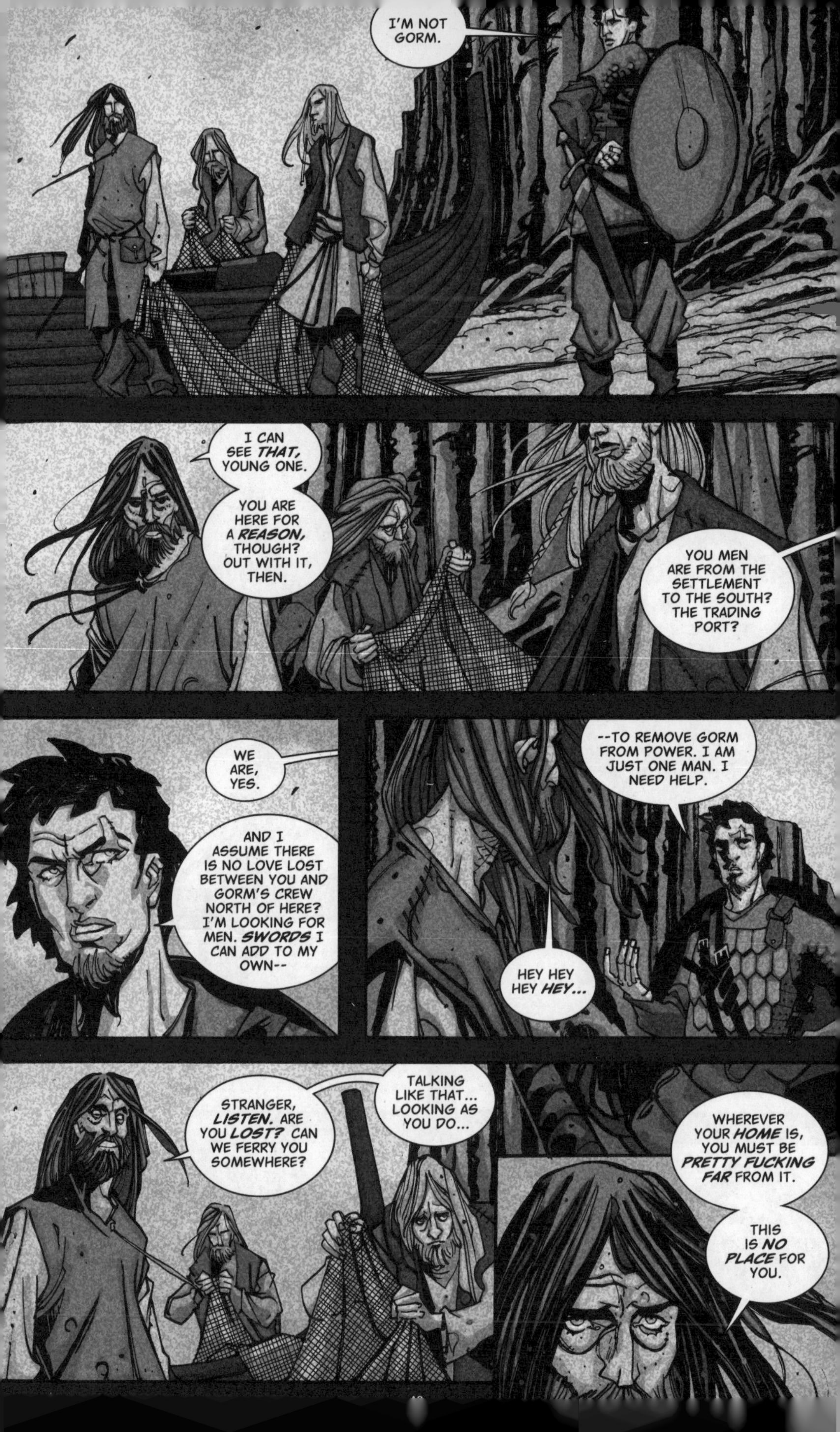
I'M NOT GORM.
I CAN SEE THAT, YOUNG ONE.
YOU ARE HERE FOR A REASON, THOUGH? OUT WITH IT, THEN.
YOU MEN ARE FROM THE SETTLEMENT TO THE SOUTH? THE TRADING PORT?
WE ARE, YES.
AND I ASSUME THERE IS NO LOVE LOST BETWEEN YOU AND GORM'S CREW NORTH OF HERE? I'M LOOKING FOR MEN. SWORDS I CAN ADD TO MY OWN--
--TO REMOVE GORM FROM POWER. I AM JUST ONE MAN. I NEED HELP.
HEY HEY HEY HEY...
STRANGER, LISTEN. ARE YOU LOST? CAN WE FERRY YOU SOMEWHERE?
TALKING LIKE THAT... LOOKING AS YOU DO...
WHEREVER YOUR HOME IS, YOU MUST BE PRETTY FUCKING FAR FROM IT.
THIS IS NO PLACE FOR YOU.

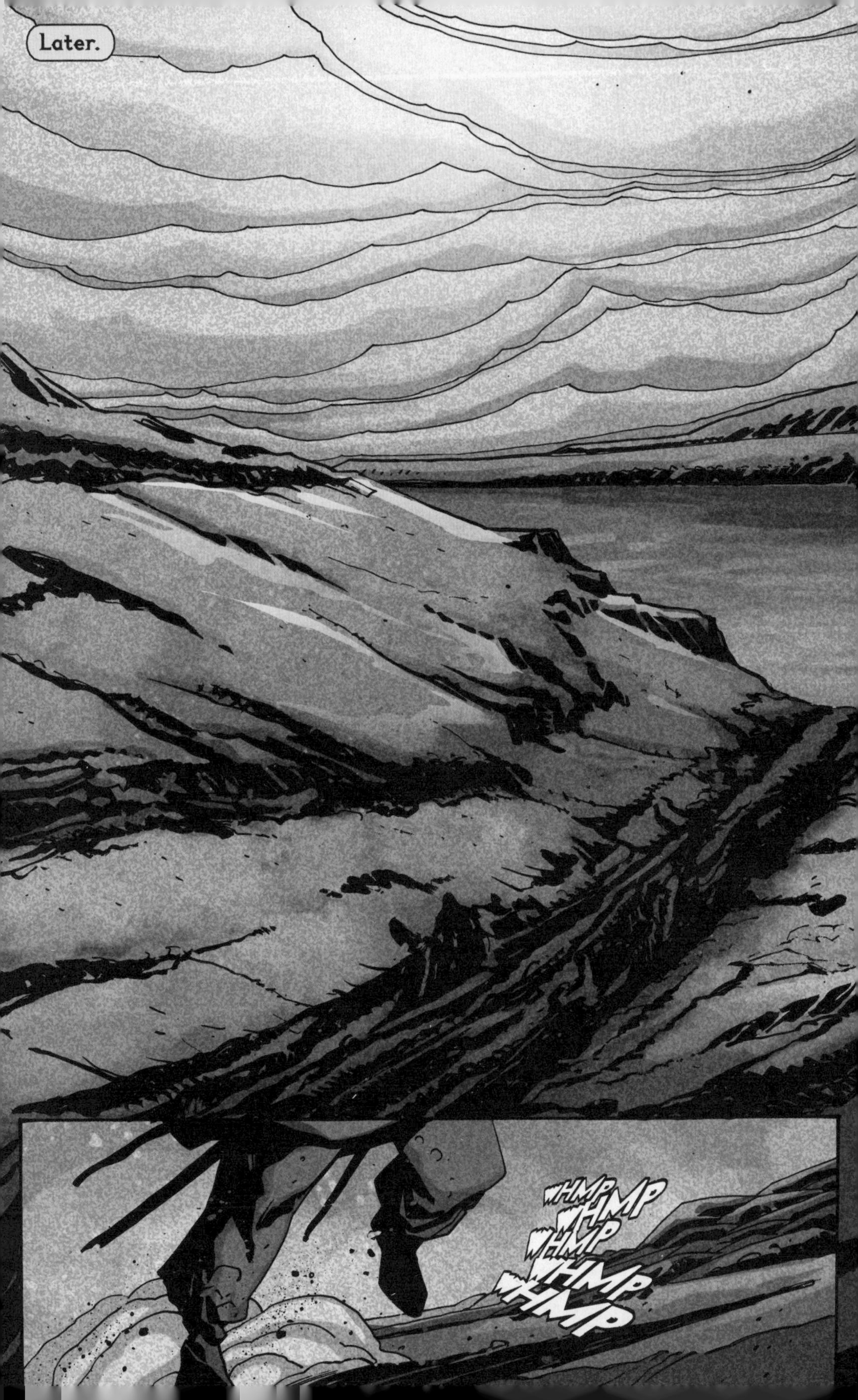
Later.
WHMP WHMP WHMP WHMP WHMP WHMP

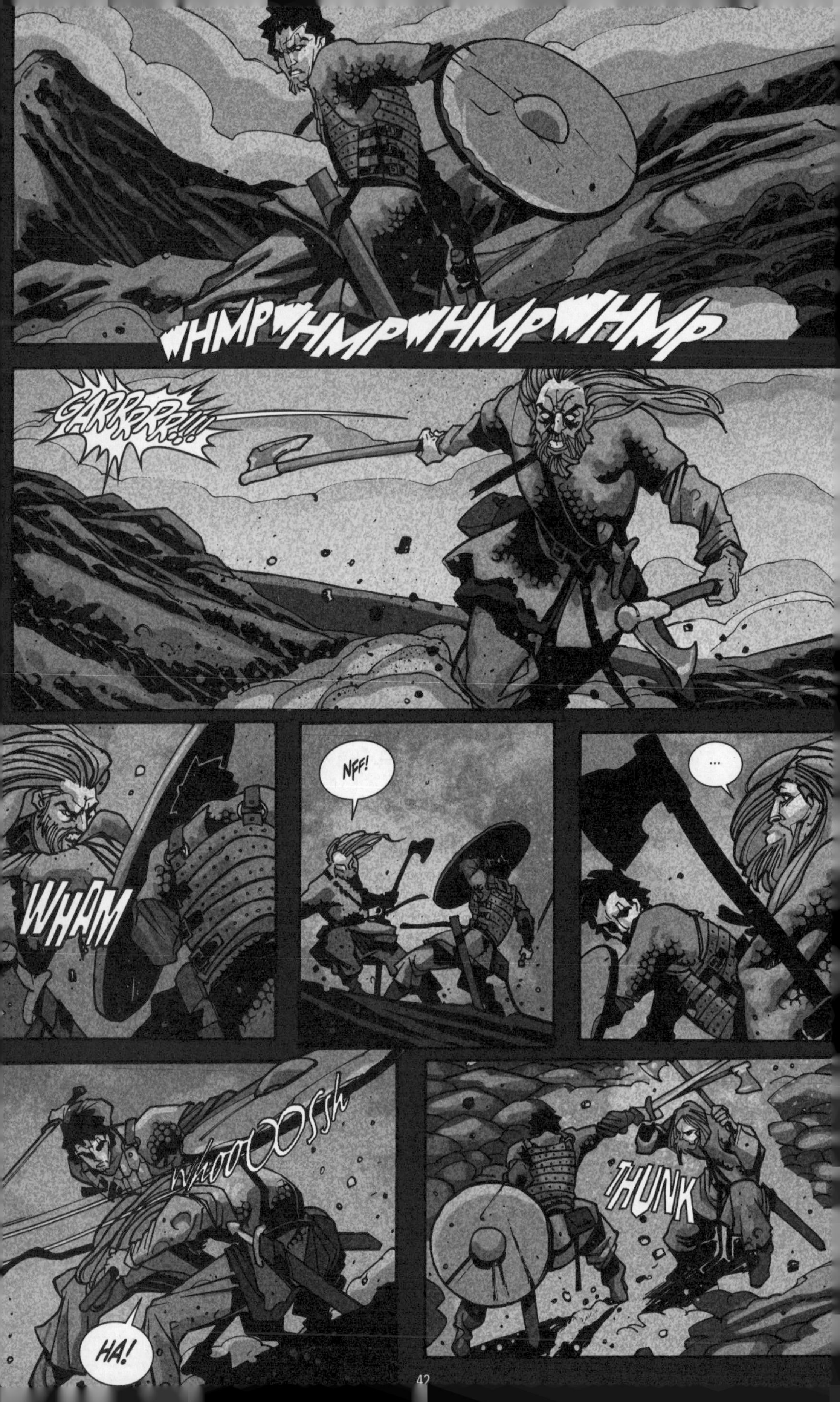
WHMP WHMP WHMP WHMP
GARRRRR!!!
WHAM
NFF!
...
WHOOOOSSH
HA!
THUNK

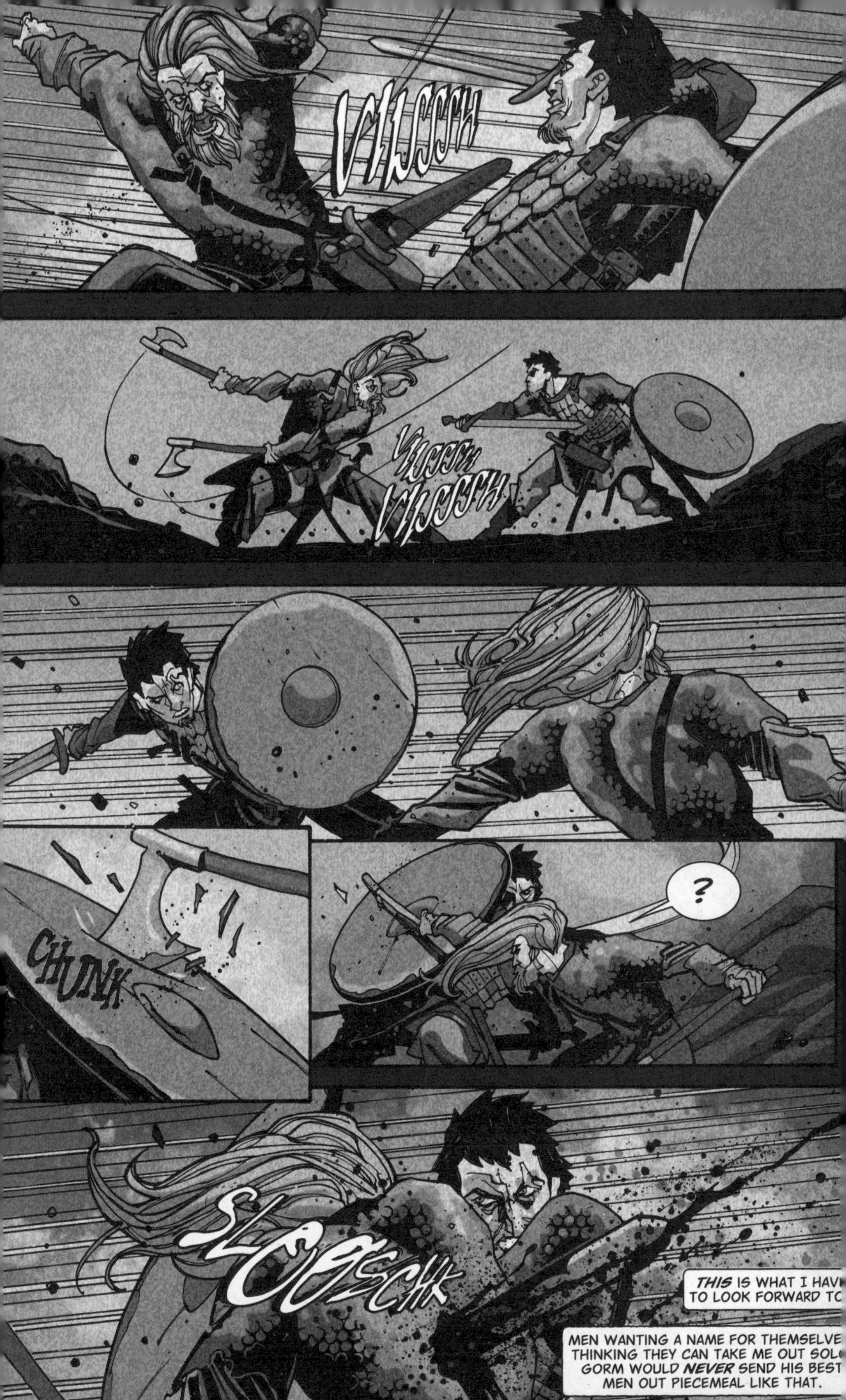
CHUNK
?
SLOOSCHK
THIS IS WHAT I HAV
TO LOOK FORWARD TO
MEN WANTING A NAME FOR THEMSELVE
THINKING THEY CAN TAKE ME OUT SOL
GORM WOULD NEVER SEND HIS BEST
MEN OUT PIECEMEAL LIKE THAT.

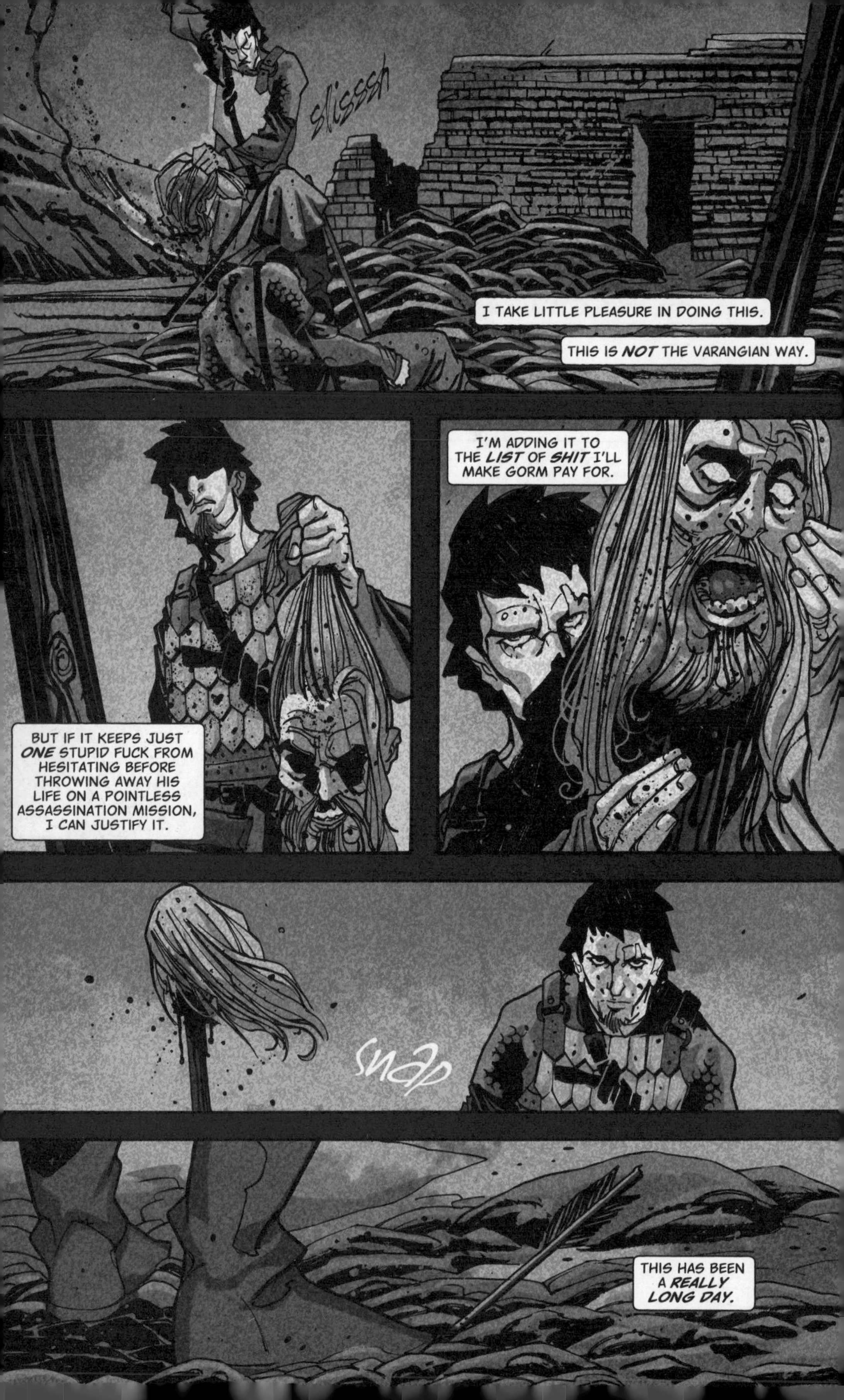
SLISSSH
I TAKE LITTLE PLEASURE IN DOING THIS.
THIS IS NOT THE VARANGIAN WAY.
BUT IF IT KEEPS JUST ONE STUPID FUCK FROM HESITATING BEFORE THROWING AWAY HIS LIFE ON A POINTLESS ASSASSINATION MISSION, I CAN JUSTIFY IT.
I'M ADDING IT TO THE LIST OF SHIT I'LL MAKE GORM PAY FOR.
SNAP
THIS HAS BEEN A REALLY LONG DAY.

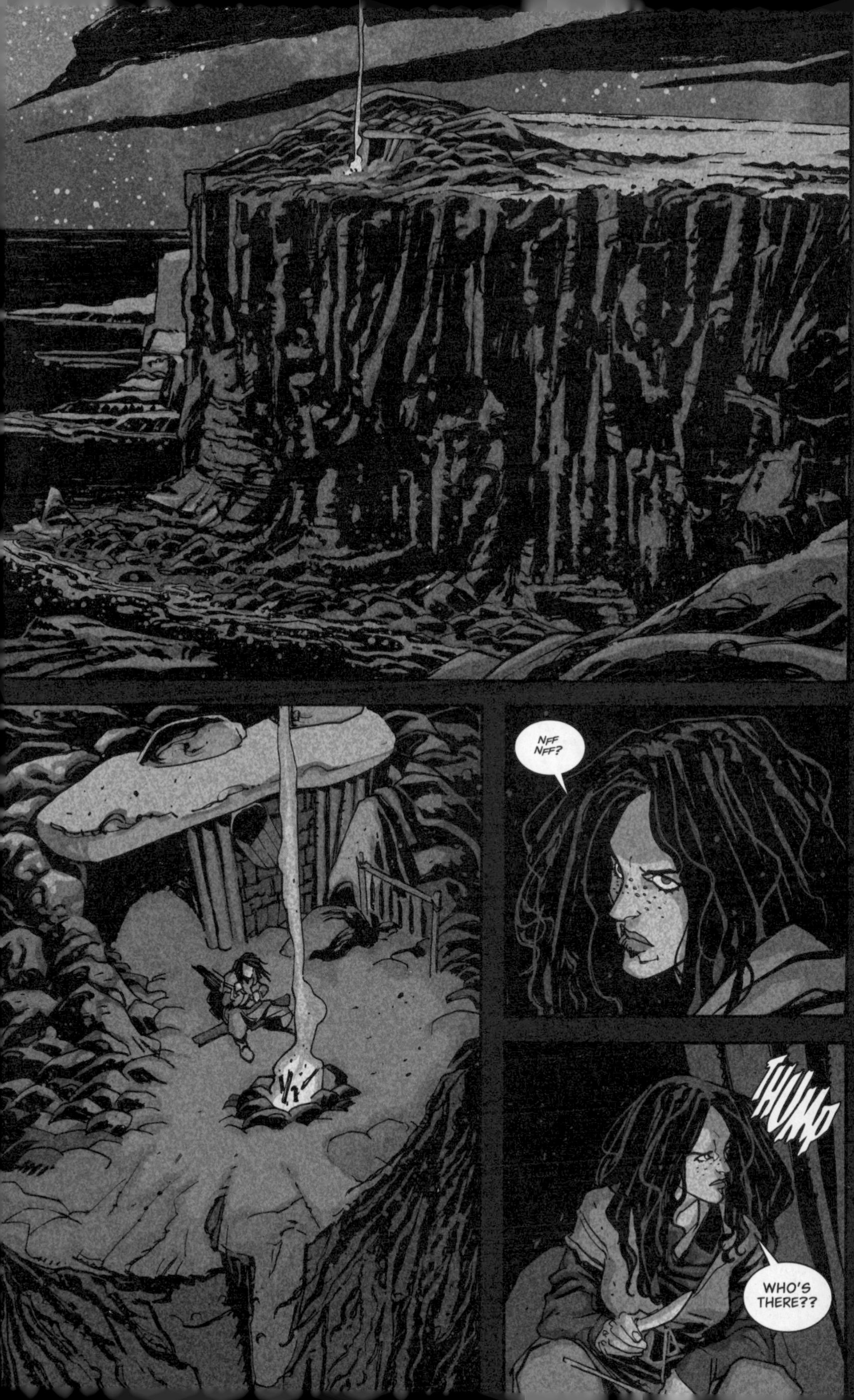
NFF NFF?
THUMP
WHO'S THERE??

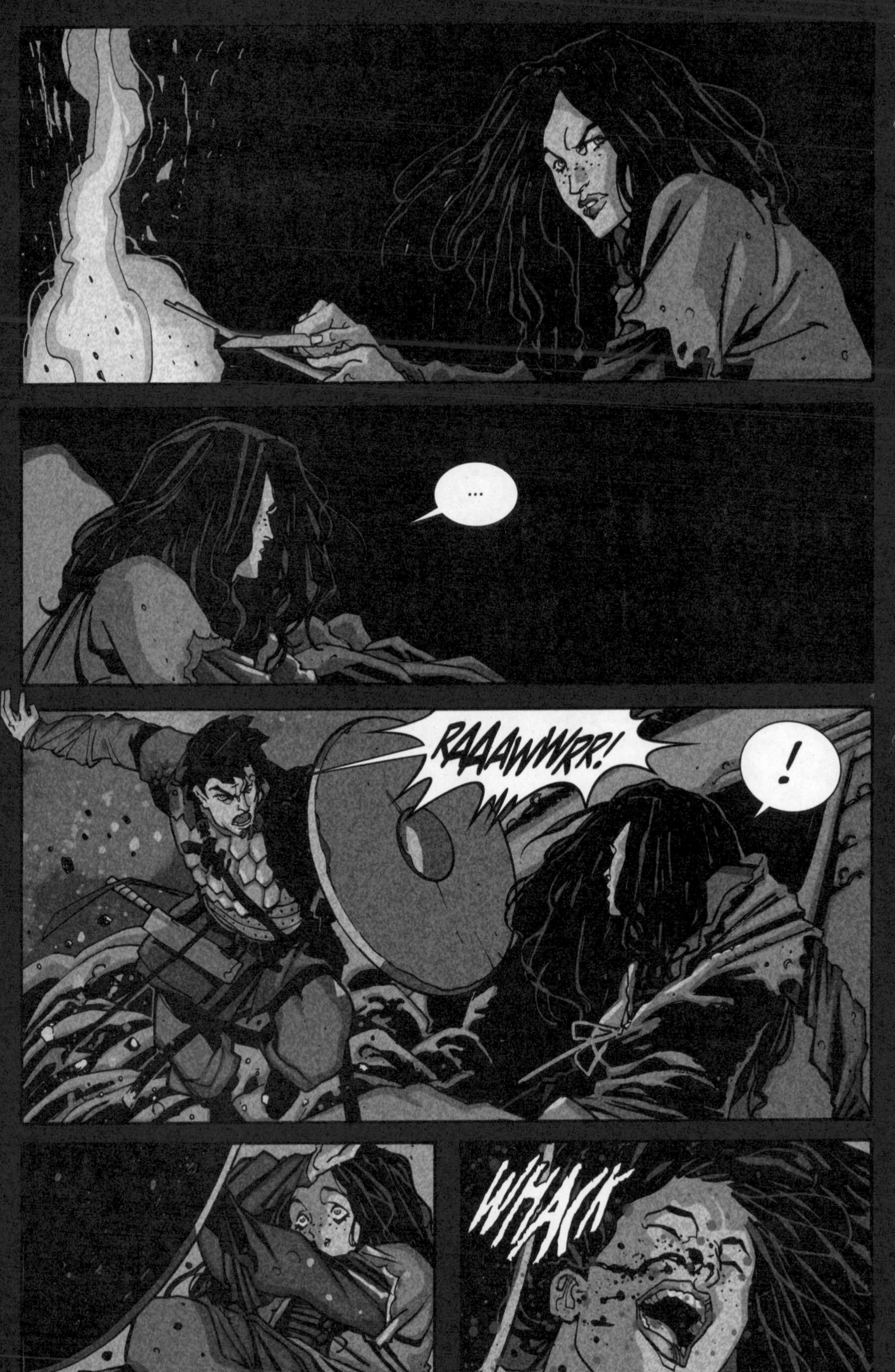
...
RAAAWWRR!
!
WHACK

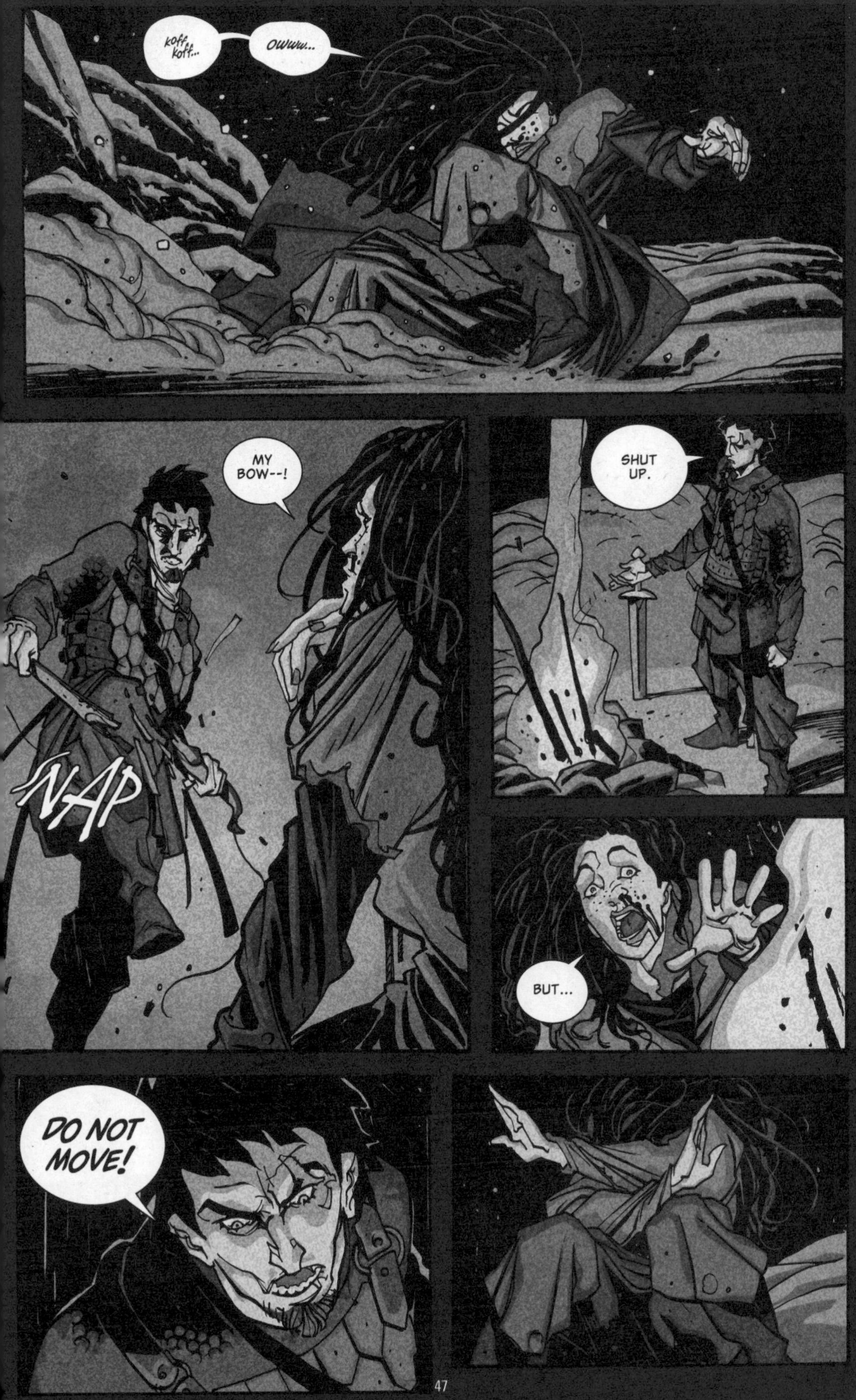
koff koff...
owww...
MY BOW--!
SNAP
SHUT UP.
BUT...
DO NOT MOVE!

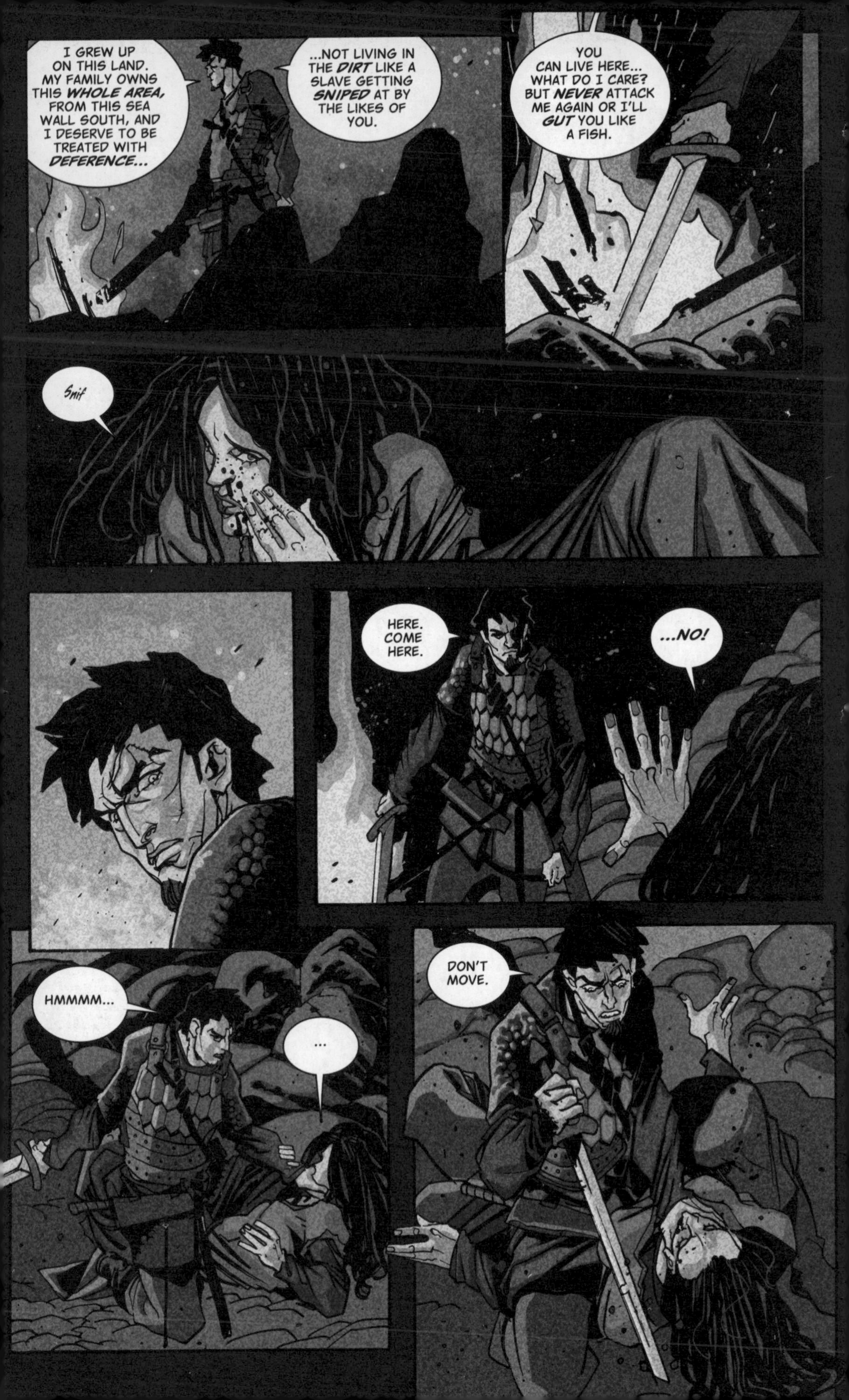
I GREW UP ON THIS LAND. MY FAMILY OWNS THIS WHOLE AREA, FROM THIS SEA WALL SOUTH, AND I DESERVE TO BE TREATED WITH DEFERENCE...
...NOT LIVING IN THE DIRT LIKE A SLAVE GETTING SNIPED AT BY THE LIKES OF YOU.
YOU CAN LIVE HERE... WHAT DO I CARE? BUT NEVER ATTACK ME AGAIN OR I'LL GUT YOU LIKE A FISH.
Snif
HERE. COME HERE.
...NO!
HMMMM...
...
DON'T MOVE.

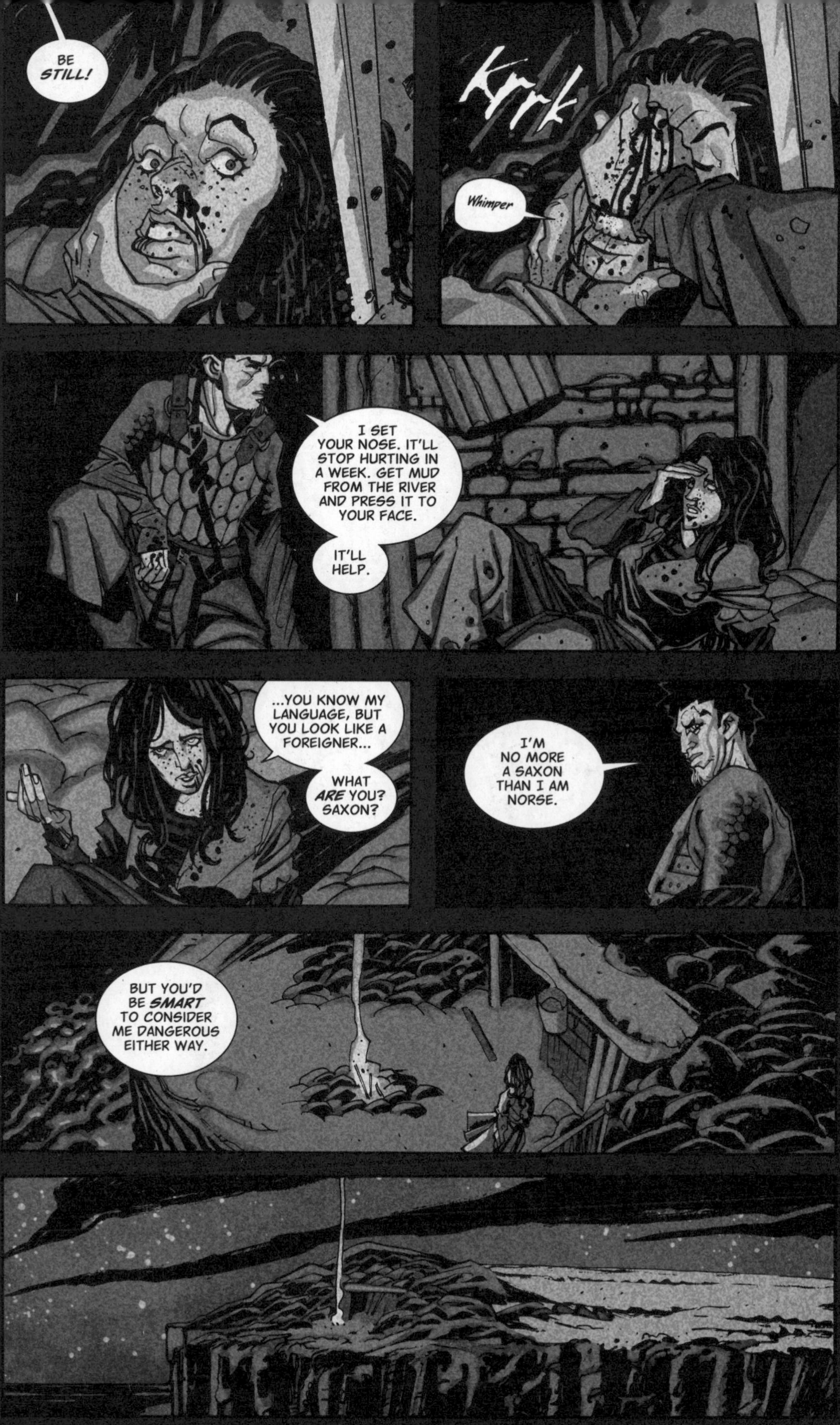
BE STILL!
Krrk
Whimper
I SET YOUR NOSE. IT'LL STOP HURTING IN A WEEK. GET MUD FROM THE RIVER AND PRESS IT TO YOUR FACE.
IT'LL HELP.
...YOU KNOW MY LANGUAGE, BUT YOU LOOK LIKE A FOREIGNER...
WHAT ARE YOU? SAXON?
I'M NO MORE A SAXON THAN I AM NORSE.
BUT YOU'D BE SMART TO CONSIDER ME DANGEROUS EITHER WAY.

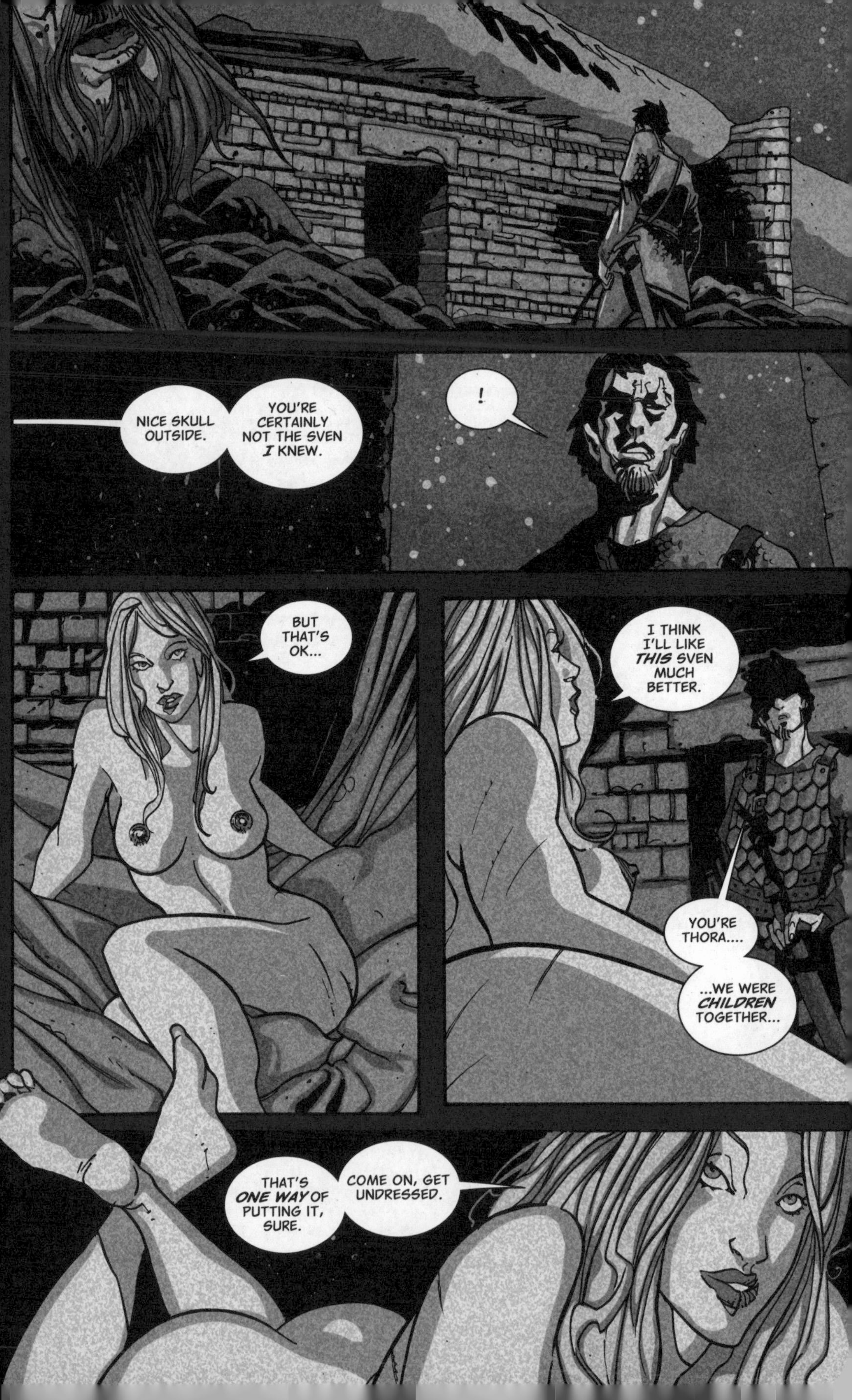
NICE SKULL OUTSIDE.
YOU'RE CERTAINLY NOT THE SVEN I KNEW.
!
BUT THAT'S OK...
I THINK I'LL LIKE THIS SVEN MUCH BETTER.
YOU'RE THORA....
...WE WERE CHILDREN TOGETHER...
COME ON, GET UNDRESSED.
THAT'S ONE WAY OF PUTTING IT, SURE.

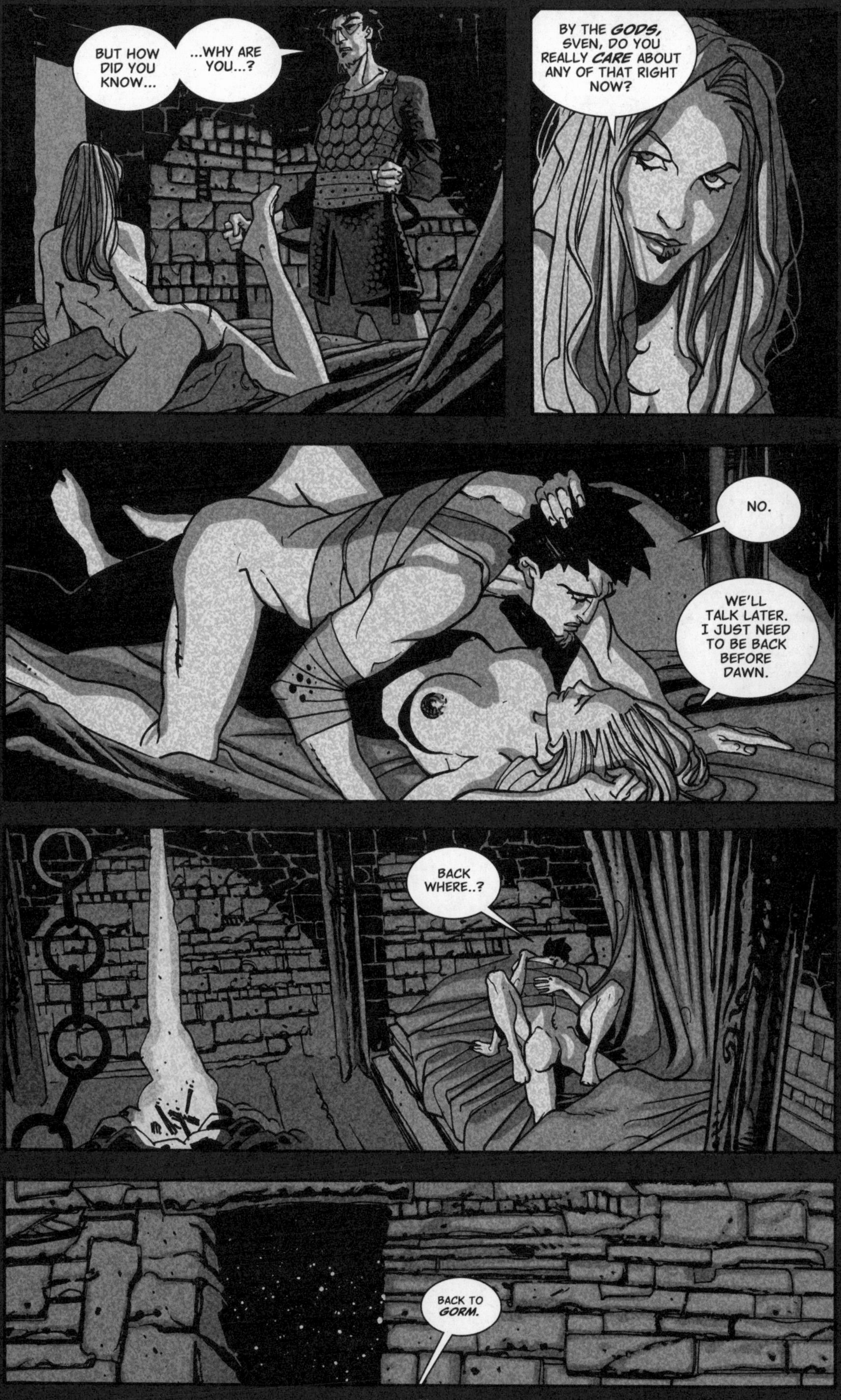
BUT HOW DID YOU KNOW...
...WHY ARE YOU...?
BY THE GODS, SVEN, DO YOU REALLY CARE ABOUT ANY OF THAT RIGHT NOW?
NO.
WE'LL TALK LATER. I JUST NEED TO BE BACK BEFORE DAWN.
BACK WHERE..?
BACK TO GORM.

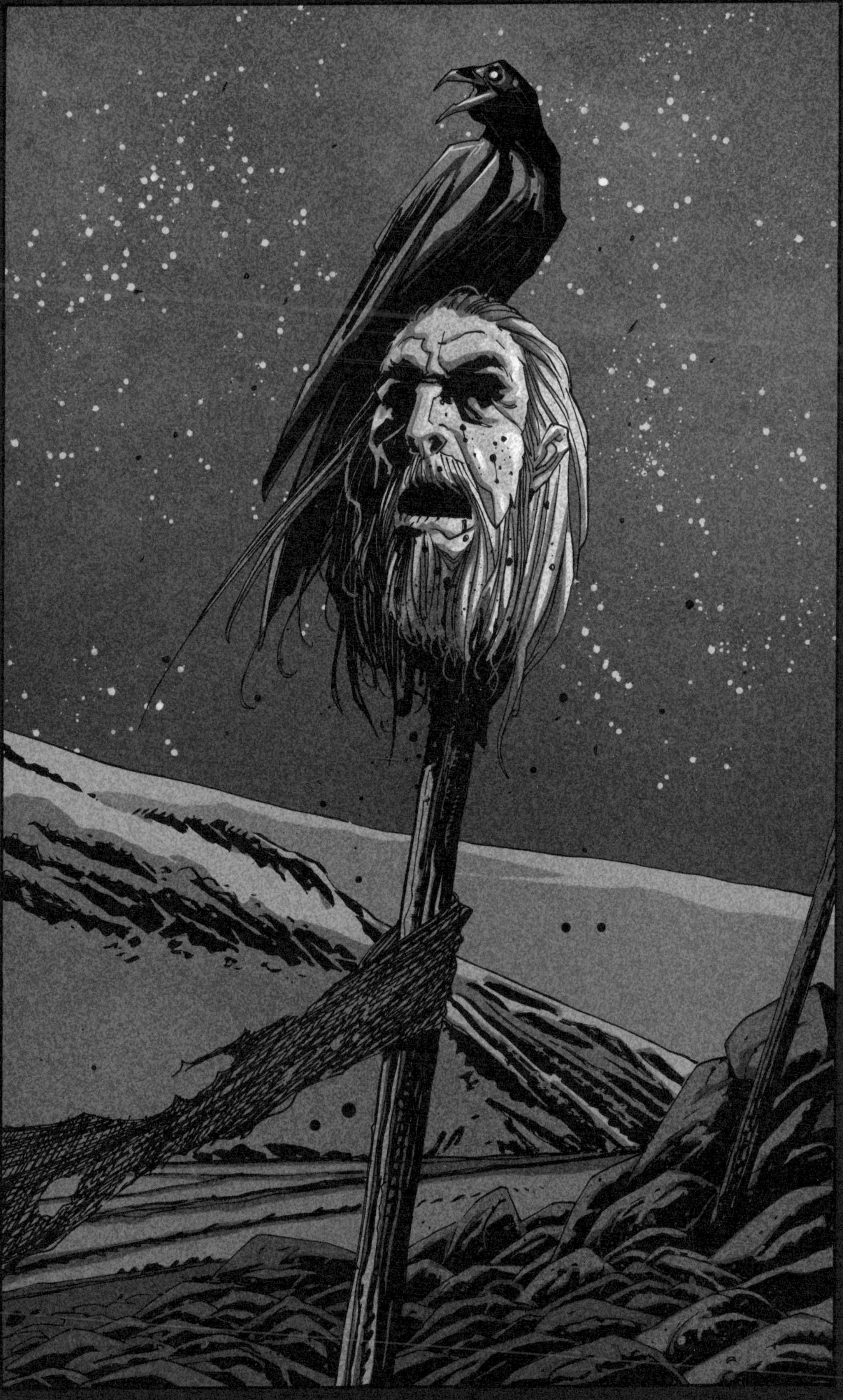

3 The Drovers Lads

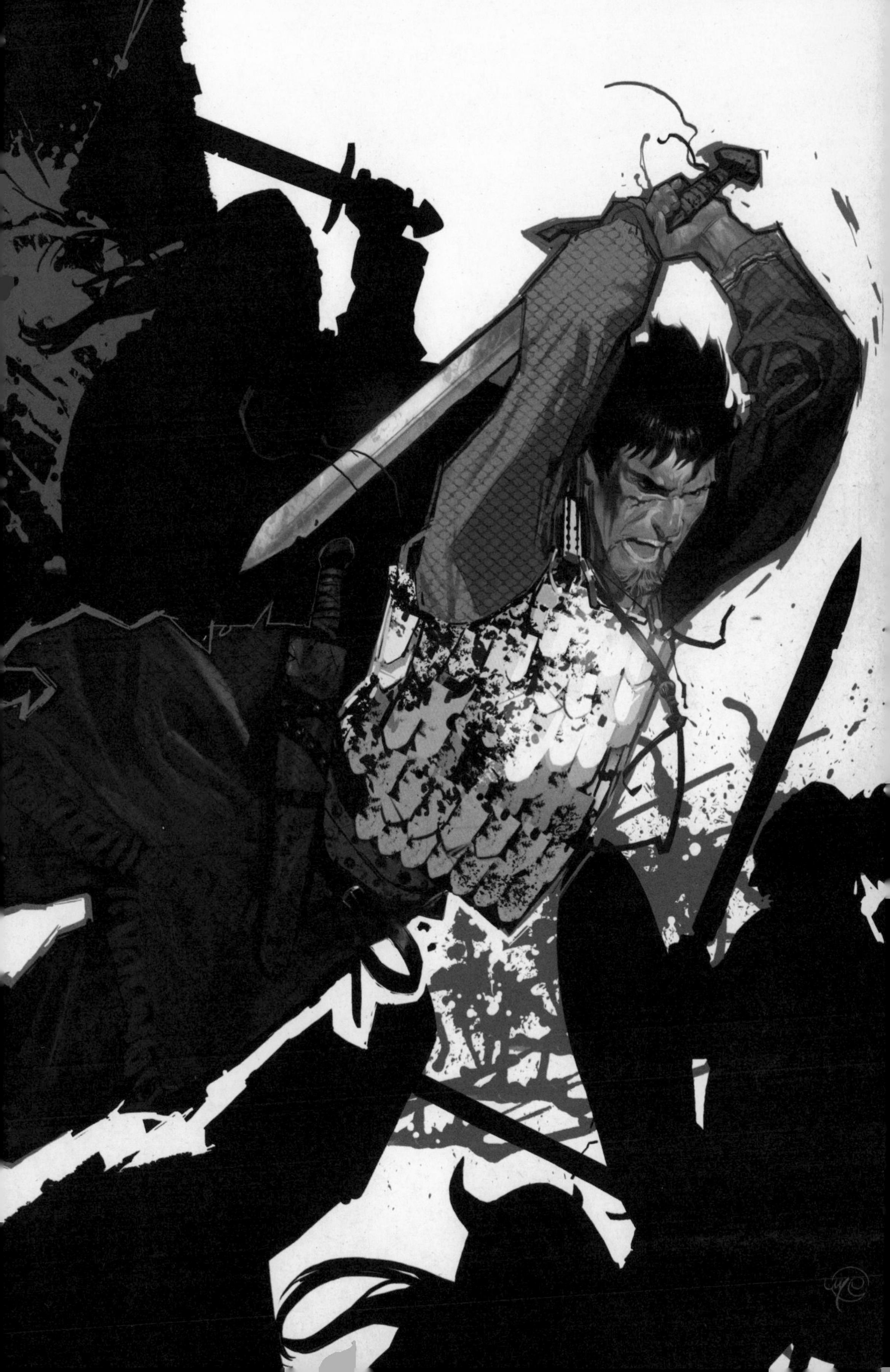

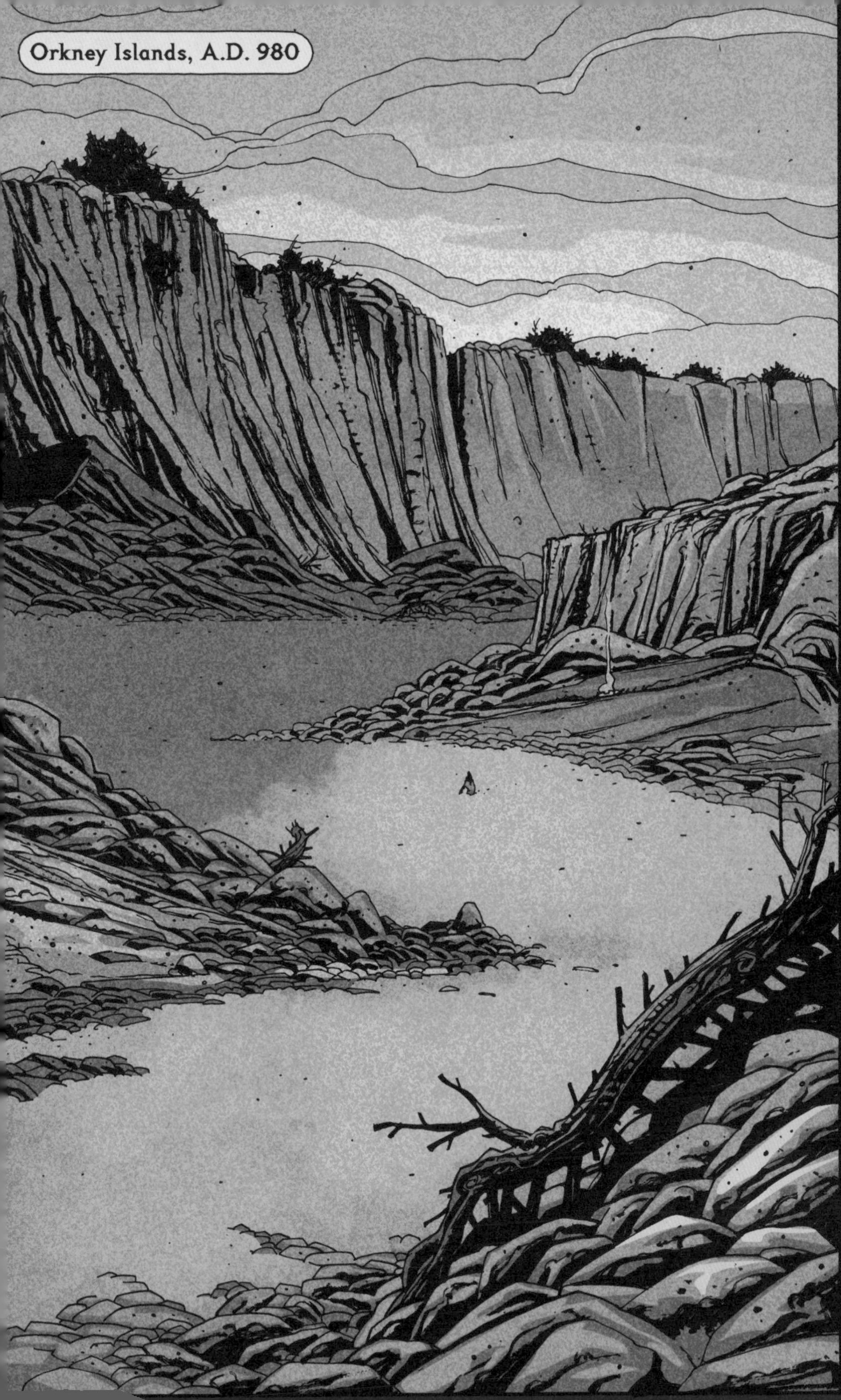
Orkney Islands, A.D. 980

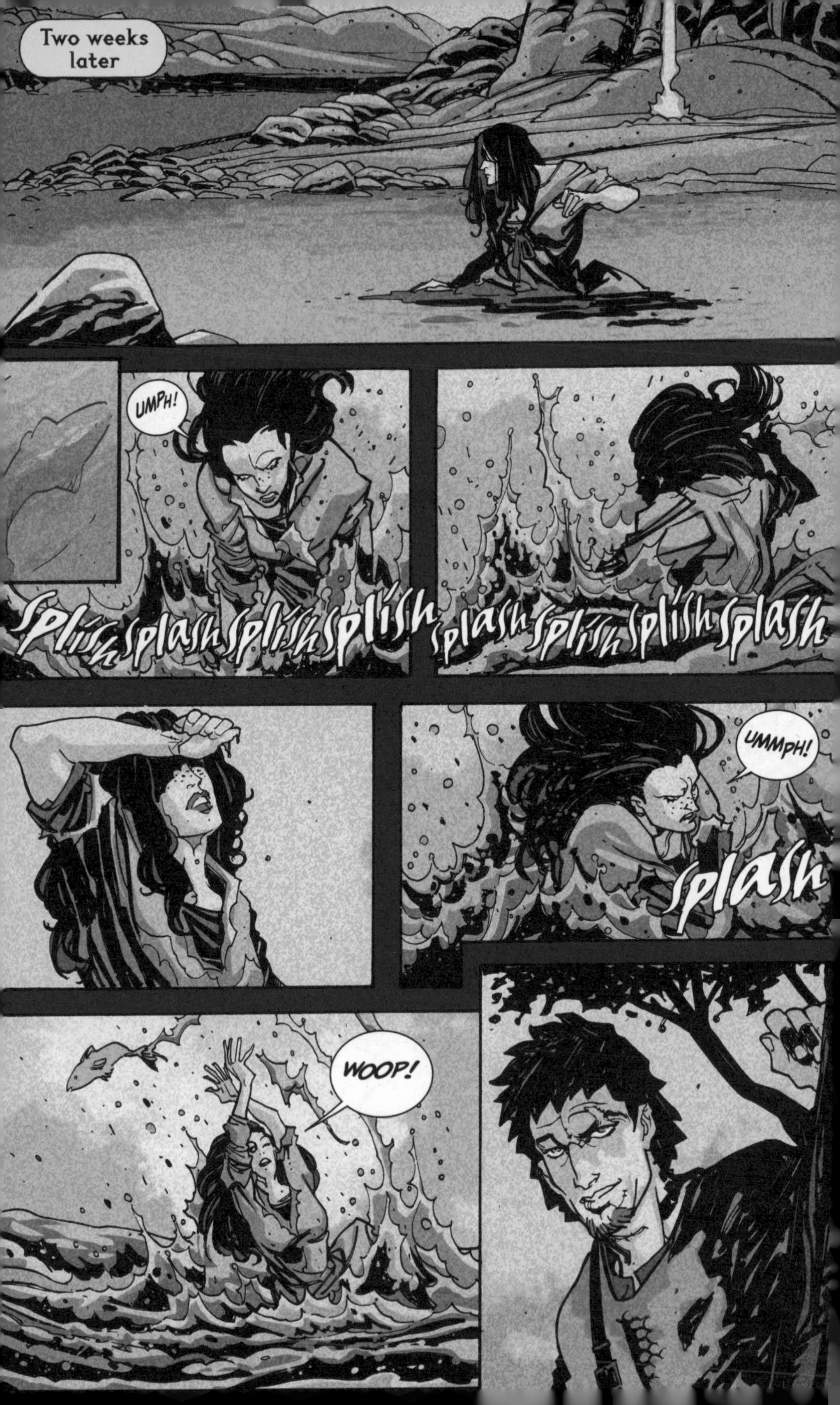
Two weeks later
UMPH!
Splish Splash Splish Splish
Splash Splish Splish Splash
UMMPH!
Splash
WOOP!

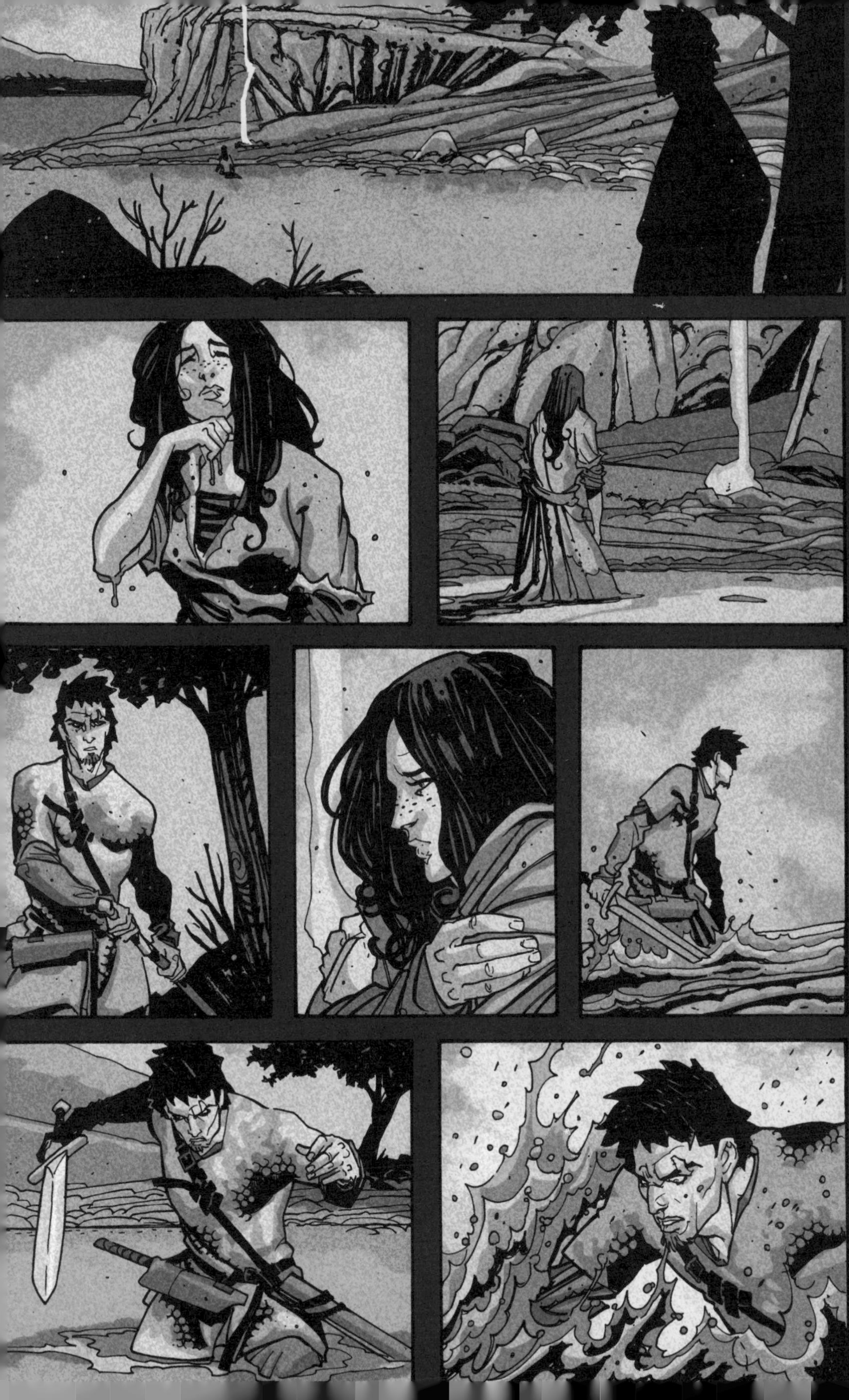

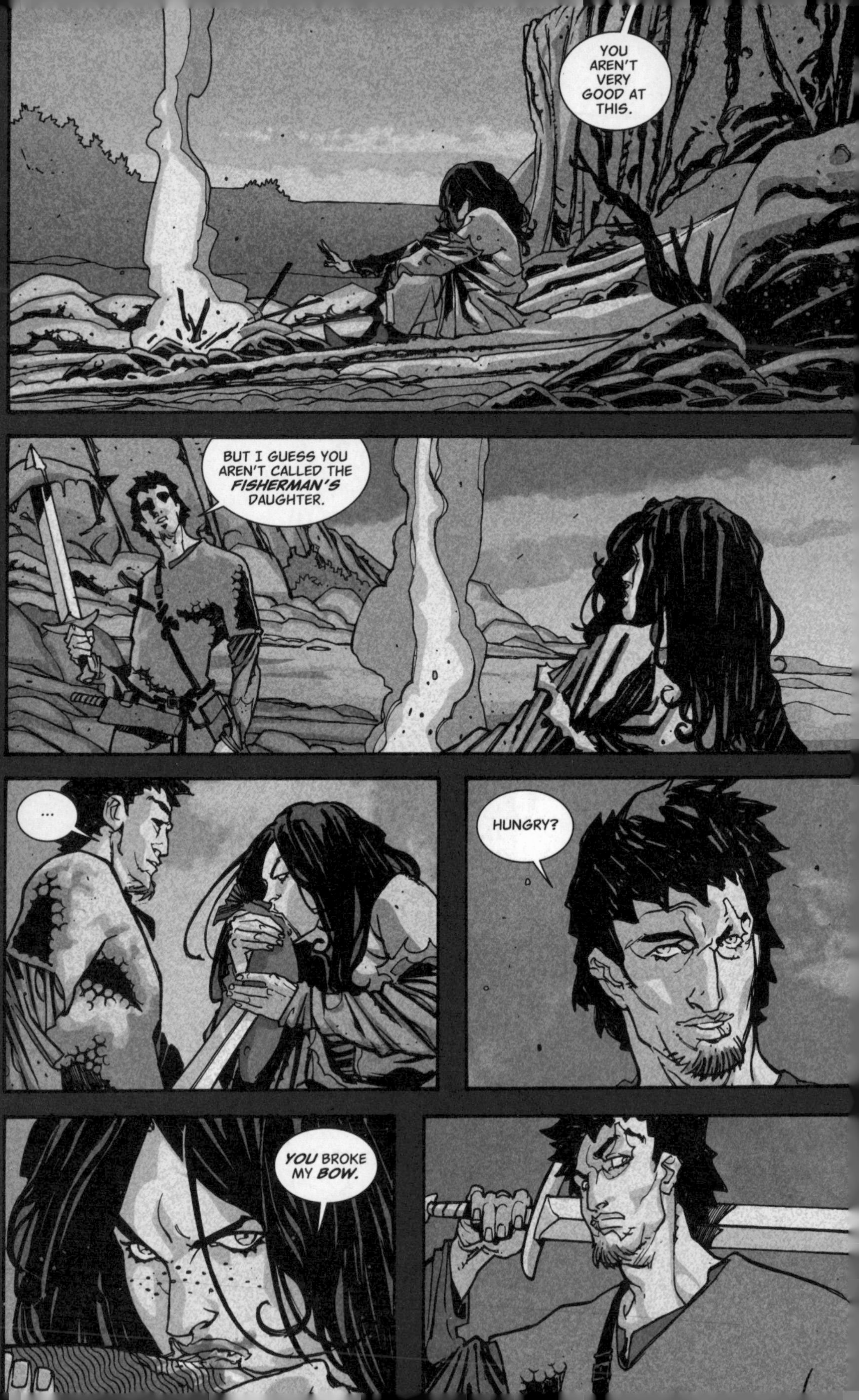
YOU AREN'T VERY GOOD AT THIS.
BUT I GUESS YOU AREN'T CALLED THE *FISHERMAN'S* DAUGHTER.
...
HUNGRY?
YOU BROKE MY *BOW.*

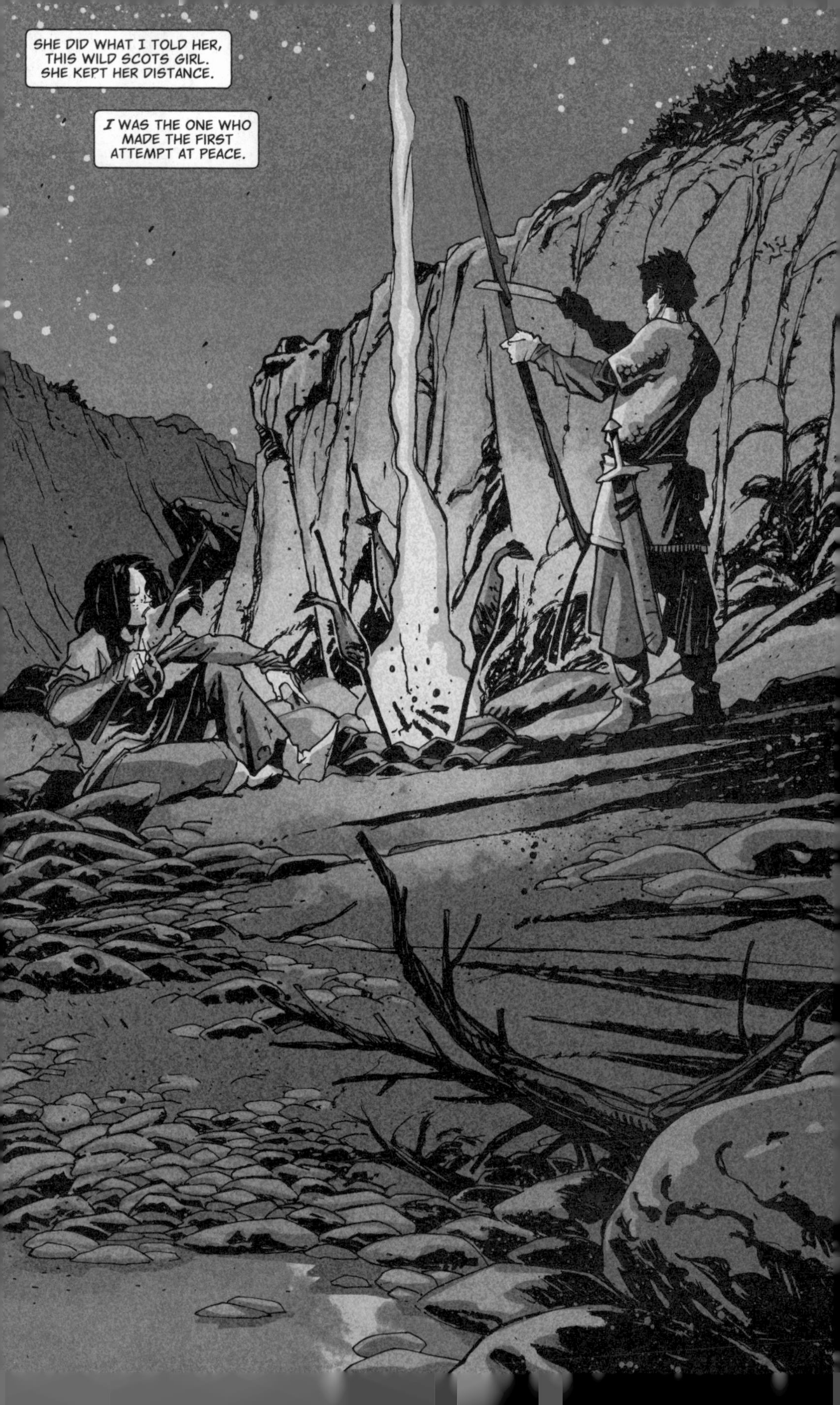
SHE DID WHAT I TOLD HER, THIS WILD SCOTS GIRL. SHE KEPT HER DISTANCE.
I WAS THE ONE WHO MADE THE FIRST ATTEMPT AT PEACE.

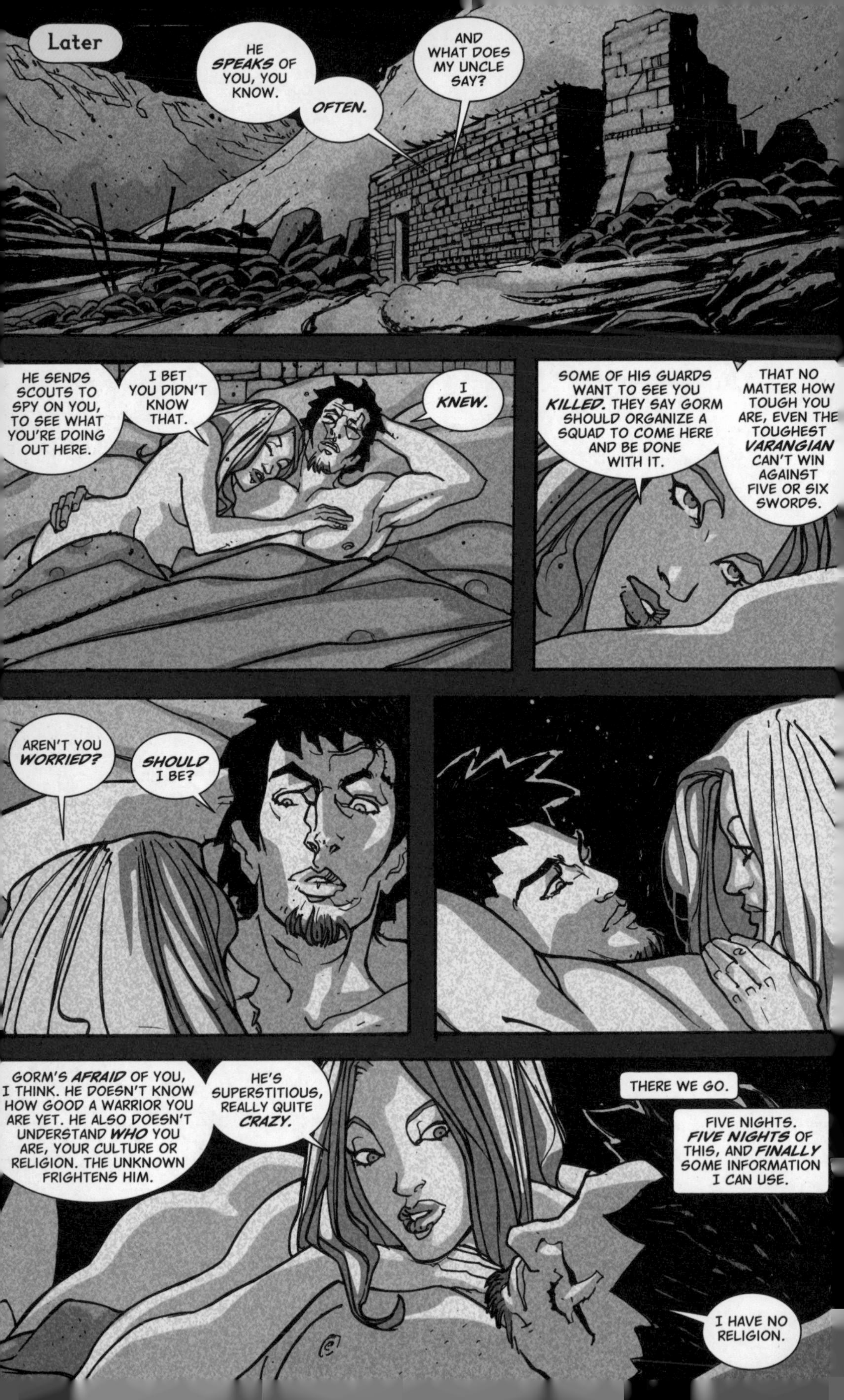
Later
HE SPEAKS OF YOU, YOU KNOW.
OFTEN.
AND WHAT DOES MY UNCLE SAY?
HE SENDS SCOUTS TO SPY ON YOU, TO SEE WHAT YOU'RE DOING OUT HERE.
I BET YOU DIDN'T KNOW THAT.
I KNEW.
SOME OF HIS GUARDS WANT TO SEE YOU KILLED. THEY SAY GORM SHOULD ORGANIZE A SQUAD TO COME HERE AND BE DONE WITH IT.
THAT NO MATTER HOW TOUGH YOU ARE, EVEN THE TOUGHEST VARANGIAN CAN'T WIN AGAINST FIVE OR SIX SWORDS.
AREN'T YOU WORRIED?
SHOULD I BE?
GORM'S AFRAID OF YOU, I THINK. HE DOESN'T KNOW HOW GOOD A WARRIOR YOU ARE YET. HE ALSO DOESN'T UNDERSTAND WHO YOU ARE, YOUR CULTURE OR RELIGION. THE UNKNOWN FRIGHTENS HIM.
HE'S SUPERSTITIOUS, REALLY QUITE CRAZY.
THERE WE GO.
FIVE NIGHTS. FIVE NIGHTS OF THIS, AND FINALLY SOME INFORMATION I CAN USE.
I HAVE NO RELIGION.

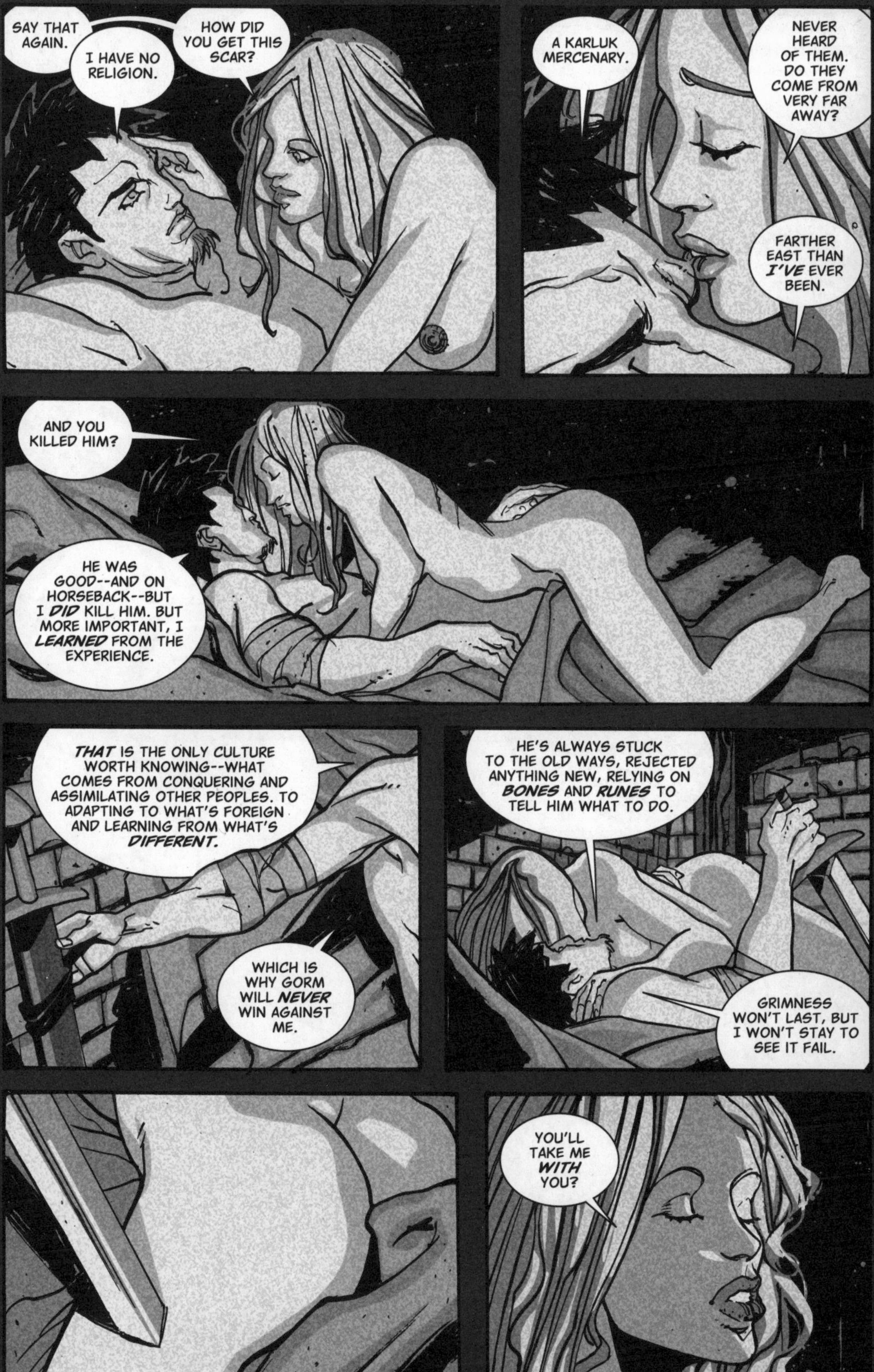
SAY THAT AGAIN.
I HAVE NO RELIGION.
HOW DID YOU GET THIS SCAR?
A KARLUK MERCENARY.
NEVER HEARD OF THEM. DO THEY COME FROM VERY FAR AWAY?
FARTHER EAST THAN I'VE EVER BEEN.
AND YOU KILLED HIM?
HE WAS GOOD--AND ON HORSEBACK--BUT I DID KILL HIM. BUT MORE IMPORTANT, I LEARNED FROM THE EXPERIENCE.
THAT IS THE ONLY CULTURE WORTH KNOWING--WHAT COMES FROM CONQUERING AND ASSIMILATING OTHER PEOPLES. TO ADAPTING TO WHAT'S FOREIGN AND LEARNING FROM WHAT'S DIFFERENT.
WHICH IS WHY GORM WILL NEVER WIN AGAINST ME.
HE'S ALWAYS STUCK TO THE OLD WAYS, REJECTED ANYTHING NEW, RELYING ON BONES AND RUNES TO TELL HIM WHAT TO DO.
GRIMNESS WON'T LAST, BUT I WON'T STAY TO SEE IT FAIL.
YOU'LL TAKE ME WITH YOU?
EVERY NIGHT THORA ASKS ME.

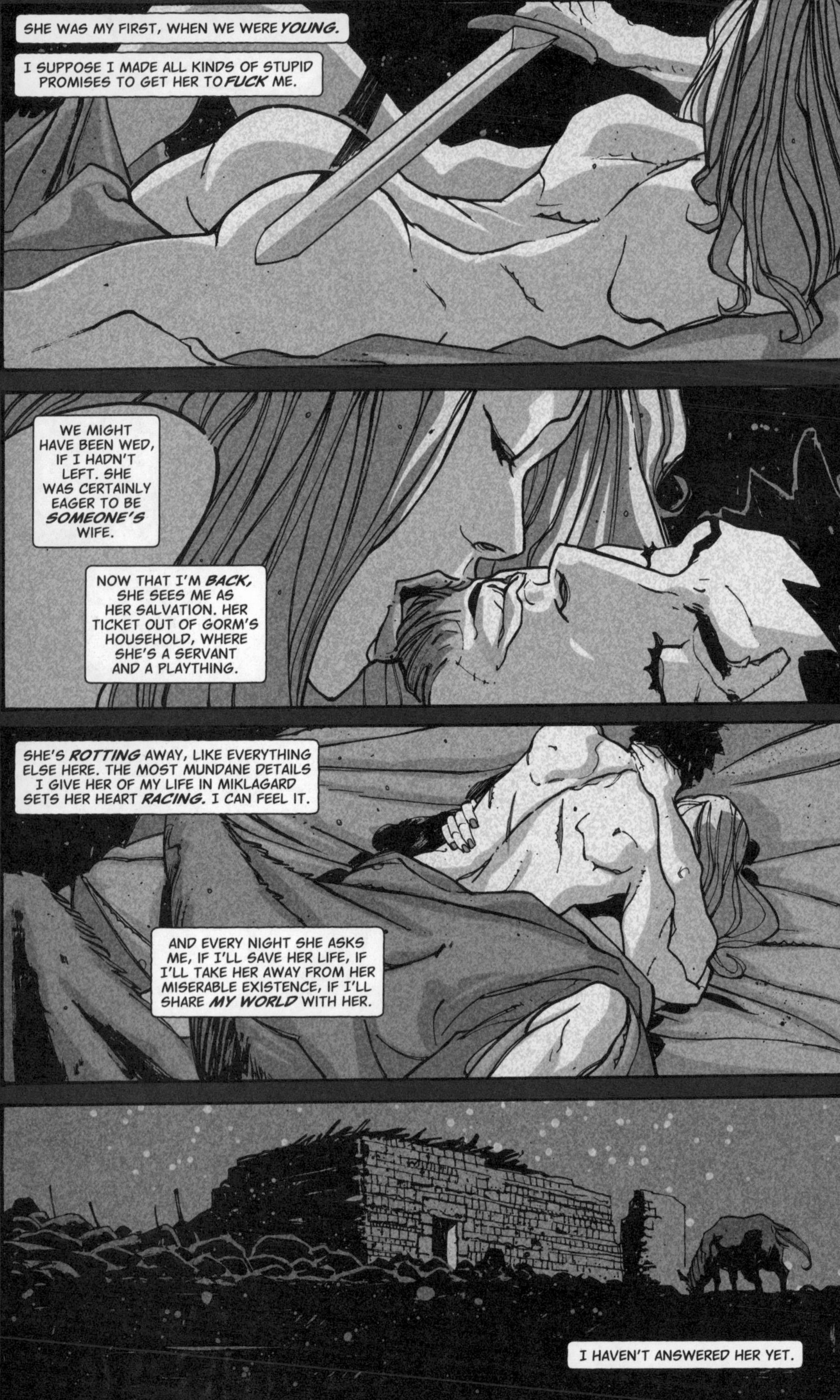
SHE WAS MY FIRST, WHEN WE WERE YOUNG.
I SUPPOSE I MADE ALL KINDS OF STUPID PROMISES TO GET HER TO FUCK ME.
WE MIGHT HAVE BEEN WED, IF I HADN'T LEFT. SHE WAS CERTAINLY EAGER TO BE SOMEONE'S WIFE.
NOW THAT I'M BACK, SHE SEES ME AS HER SALVATION. HER TICKET OUT OF GORM'S HOUSEHOLD, WHERE SHE'S A SERVANT AND A PLAYTHING.
SHE'S ROTTING AWAY, LIKE EVERYTHING ELSE HERE. THE MOST MUNDANE DETAILS I GIVE HER OF MY LIFE IN MIKLAGARD SETS HER HEART RACING. I CAN FEEL IT.
AND EVERY NIGHT SHE ASKS ME, IF I'LL SAVE HER LIFE, IF I'LL TAKE HER AWAY FROM HER MISERABLE EXISTENCE, IF I'LL SHARE MY WORLD WITH HER.
I HAVEN'T ANSWERED HER YET.

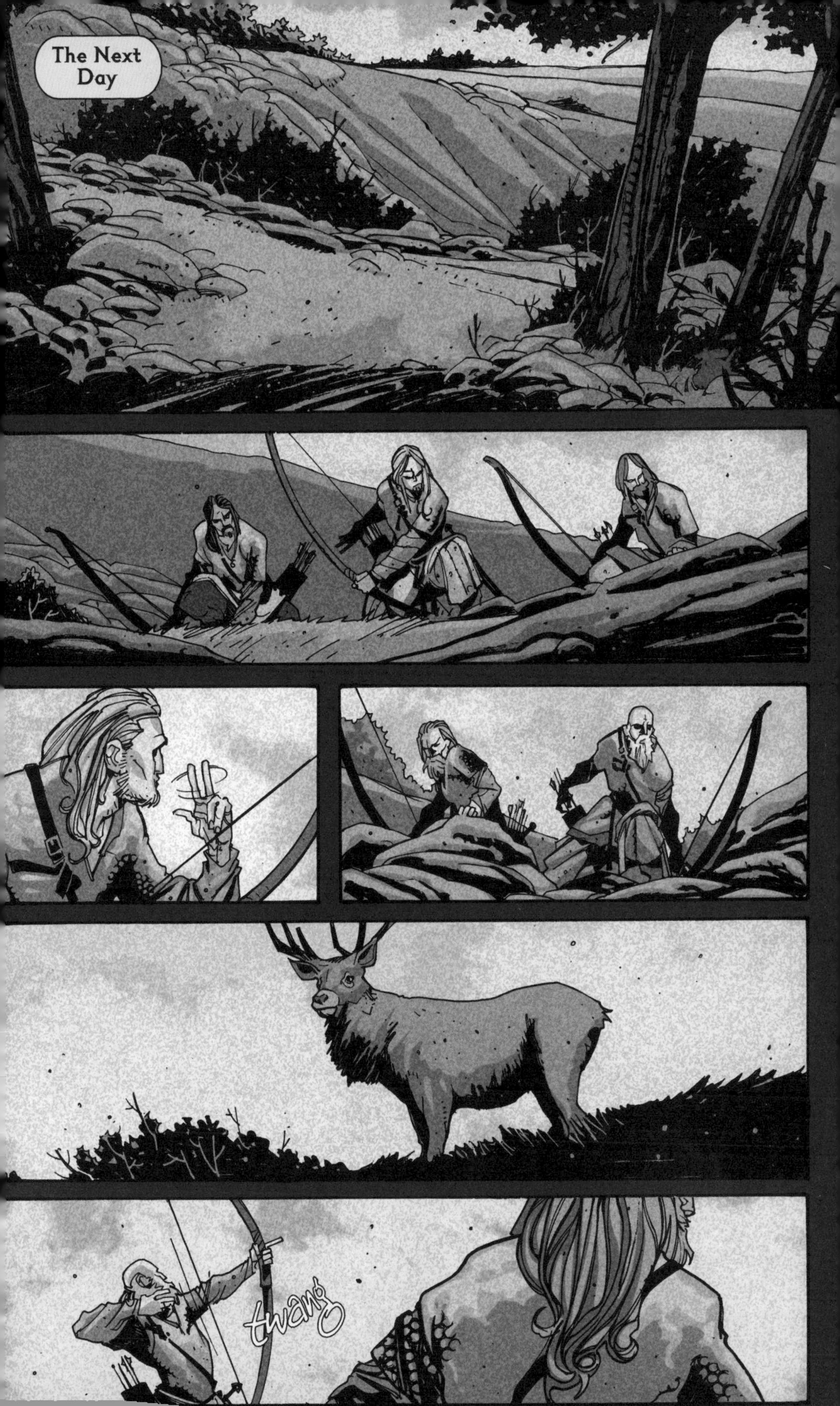
The Next Day
twang

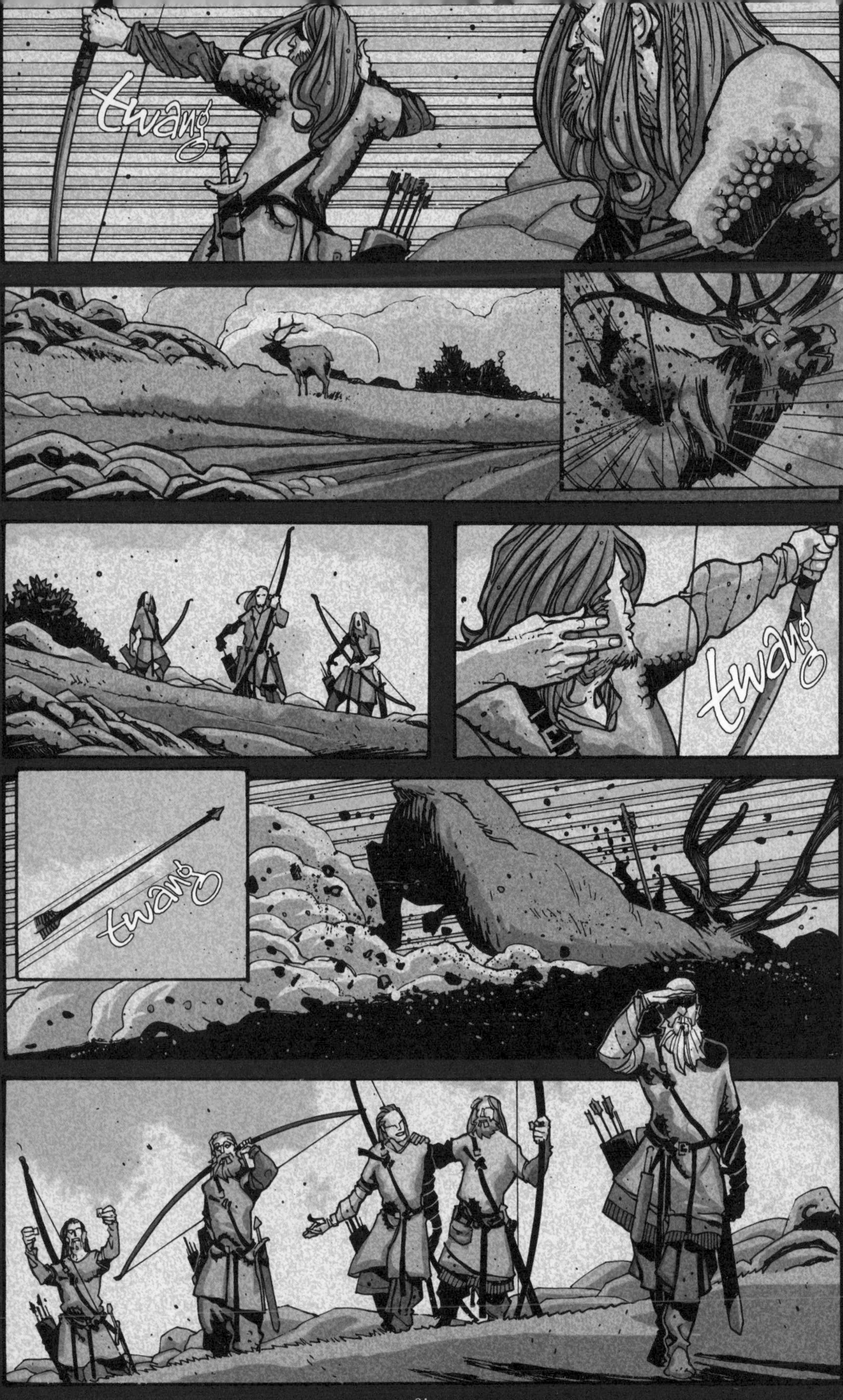
twang
twang
twang

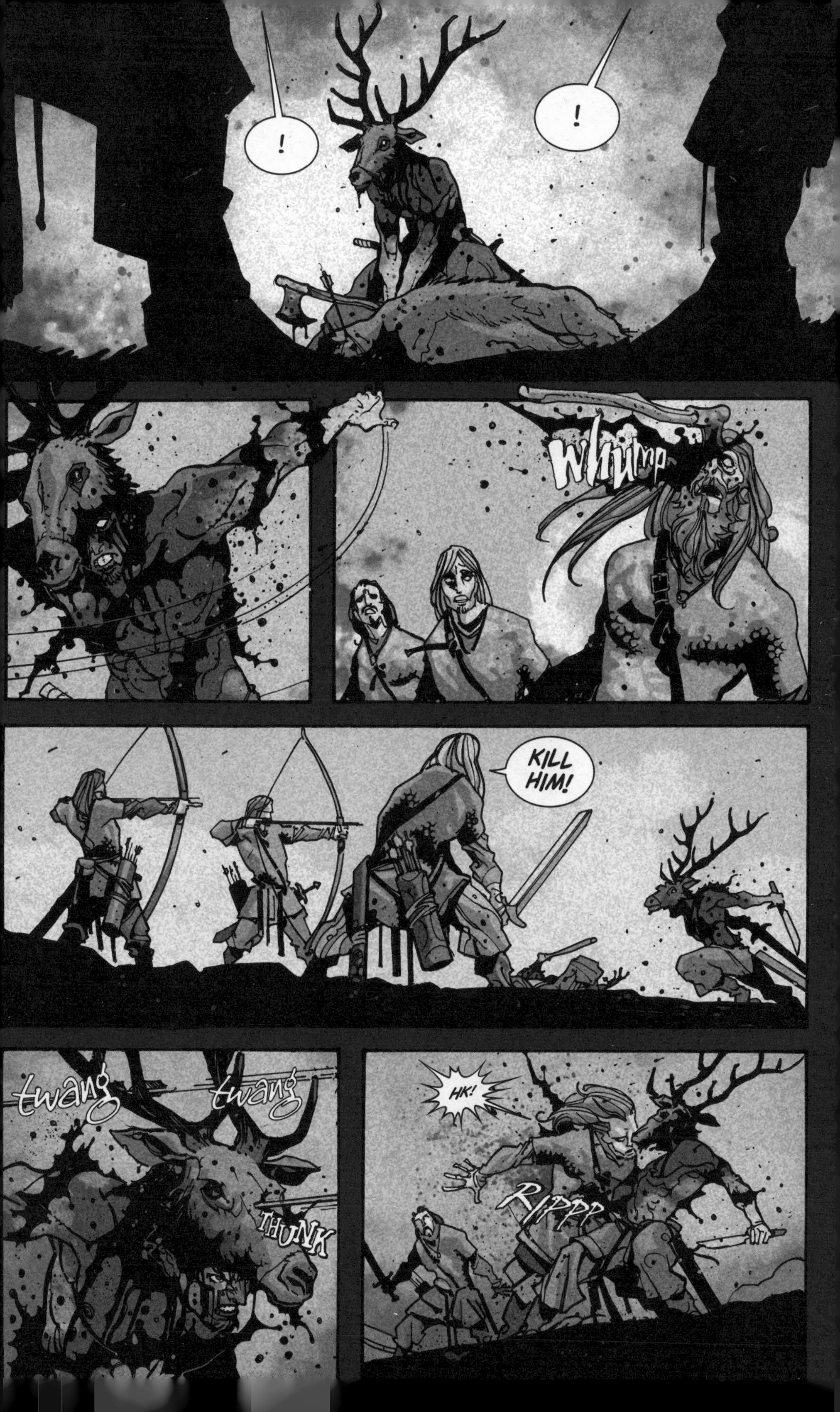
!
!
WHUMP
KILL HIM!
twang
twang
THUNK
HK!
RIPPP

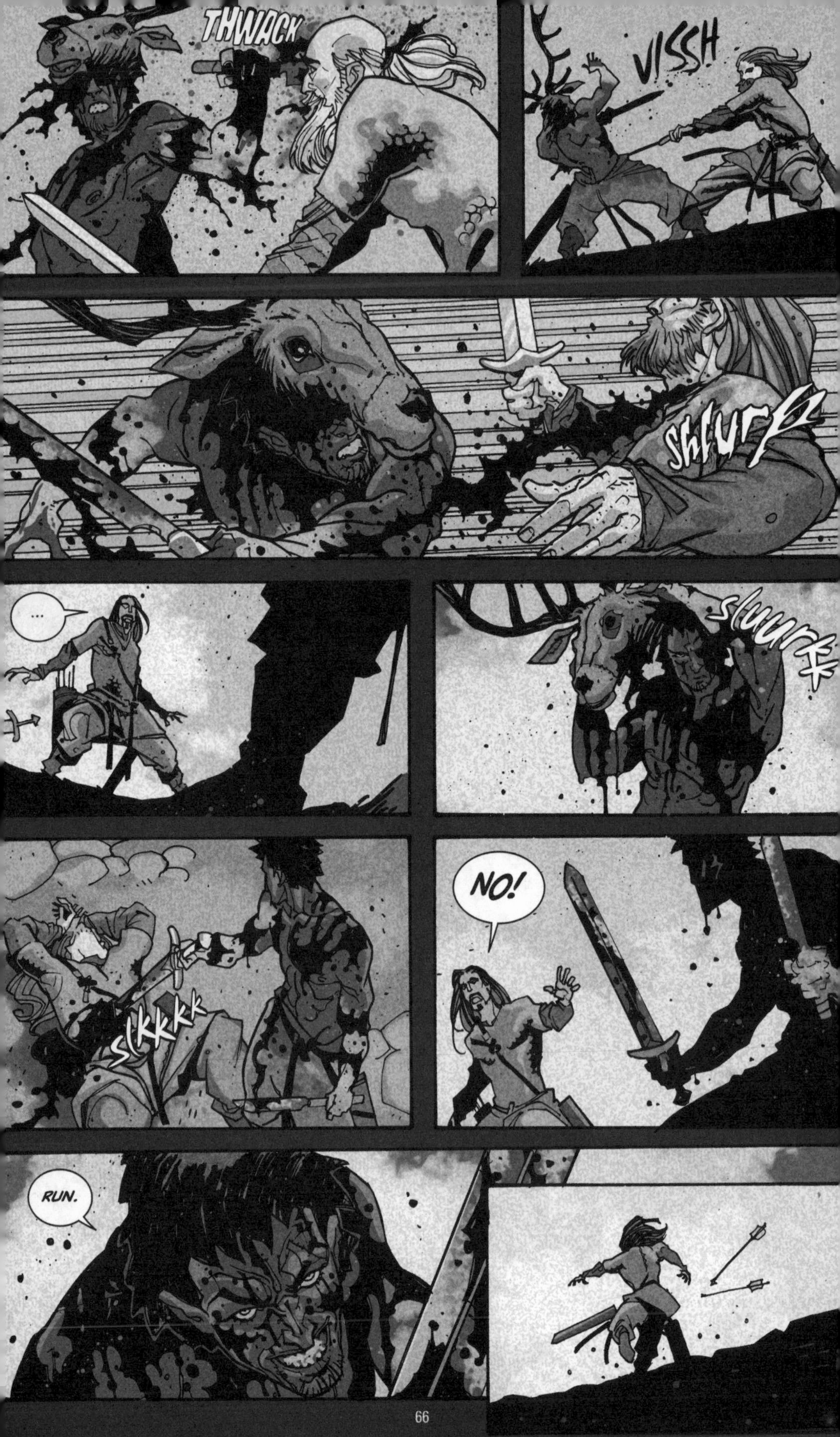
THWACK
VISSH
SHLURP
...
SLUURKK
SLKKKK
NO!
RUN.

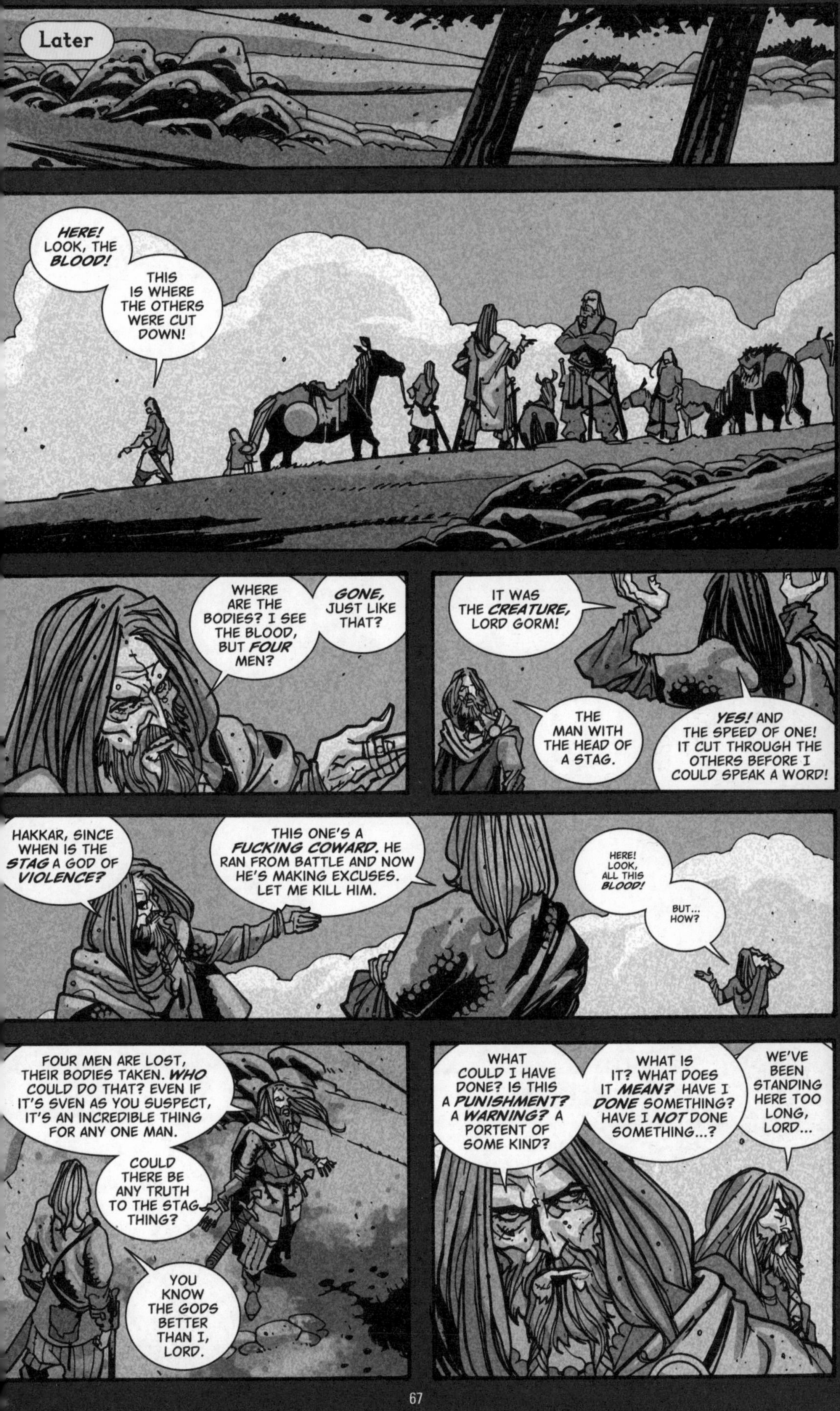

Later
HERE! LOOK, THE BLOOD!
THIS IS WHERE THE OTHERS WERE CUT DOWN!
WHERE ARE THE BODIES? I SEE THE BLOOD, BUT FOUR MEN?
GONE, JUST LIKE THAT?
IT WAS THE CREATURE, LORD GORM!
THE MAN WITH THE HEAD OF A STAG.
YES! AND THE SPEED OF ONE! IT CUT THROUGH THE OTHERS BEFORE I COULD SPEAK A WORD!
HAKKAR, SINCE WHEN IS THE STAG A GOD OF VIOLENCE?
THIS ONE'S A FUCKING COWARD. HE RAN FROM BATTLE AND NOW HE'S MAKING EXCUSES. LET ME KILL HIM.
HERE! LOOK, ALL THIS BLOOD!
BUT... HOW?
FOUR MEN ARE LOST, THEIR BODIES TAKEN. WHO COULD DO THAT? EVEN IF IT'S SVEN AS YOU SUSPECT, IT'S AN INCREDIBLE THING FOR ANY ONE MAN.
COULD THERE BE ANY TRUTH TO THE STAG THING?
YOU KNOW THE GODS BETTER THAN I, LORD.
WHAT COULD I HAVE DONE? IS THIS A PUNISHMENT? A WARNING? A PORTENT OF SOME KIND?
WHAT IS IT? WHAT DOES IT MEAN? HAVE I DONE SOMETHING? HAVE I NOT DONE SOMETHING...?
WE'VE BEEN STANDING HERE TOO LONG, LORD...

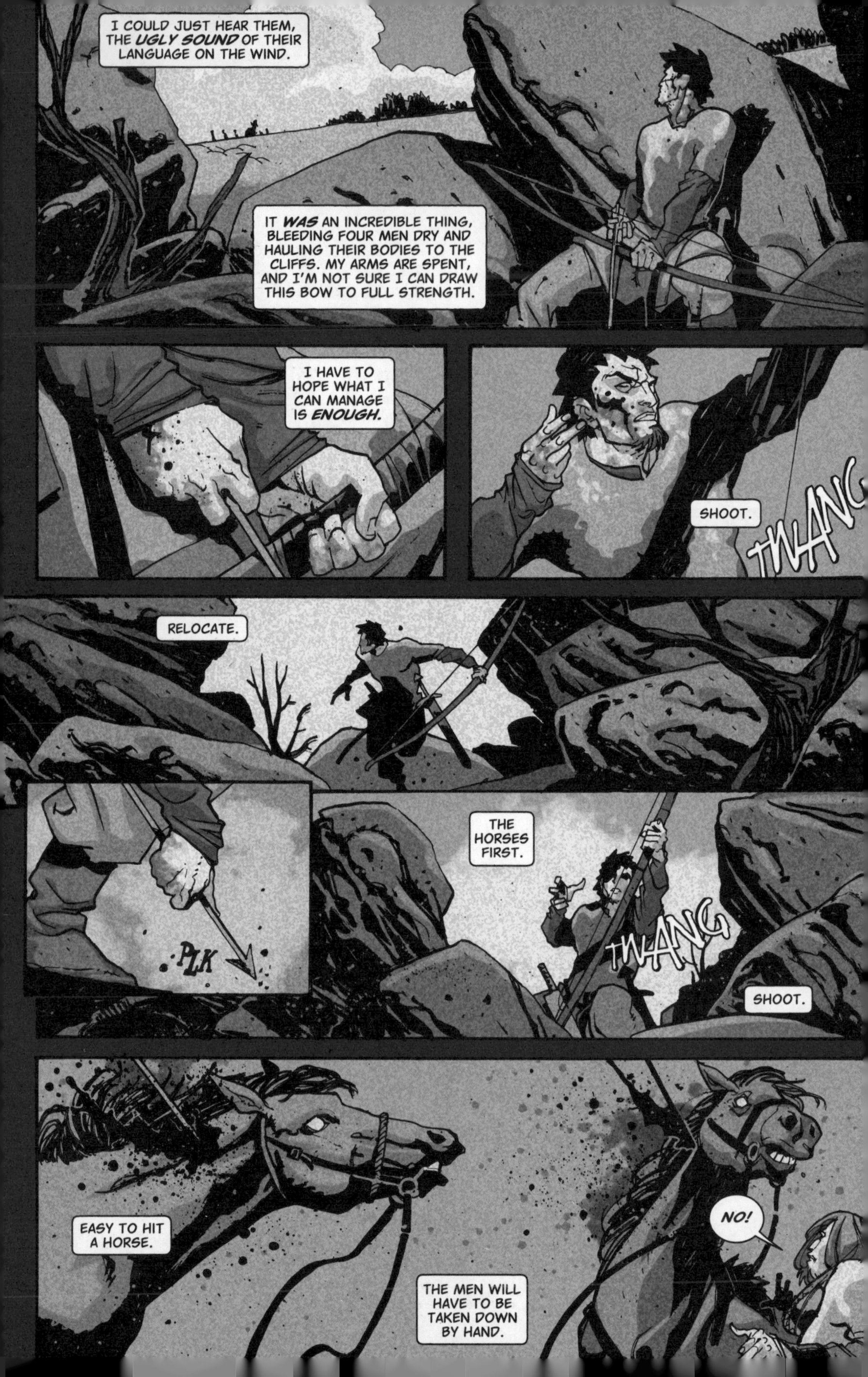

I COULD JUST HEAR THEM, THE UGLY SOUND OF THEIR LANGUAGE ON THE WIND.
IT WAS AN INCREDIBLE THING, BLEEDING FOUR MEN DRY AND HAULING THEIR BODIES TO THE CLIFFS. MY ARMS ARE SPENT, AND I'M NOT SURE I CAN DRAW THIS BOW TO FULL STRENGTH.
I HAVE TO HOPE WHAT I CAN MANAGE IS ENOUGH.
SHOOT.
TWANG
RELOCATE.
PLK
THE HORSES FIRST.
TWANG
SHOOT.
EASY TO HIT A HORSE.
THE MEN WILL HAVE TO BE TAKEN DOWN BY HAND.
NO!

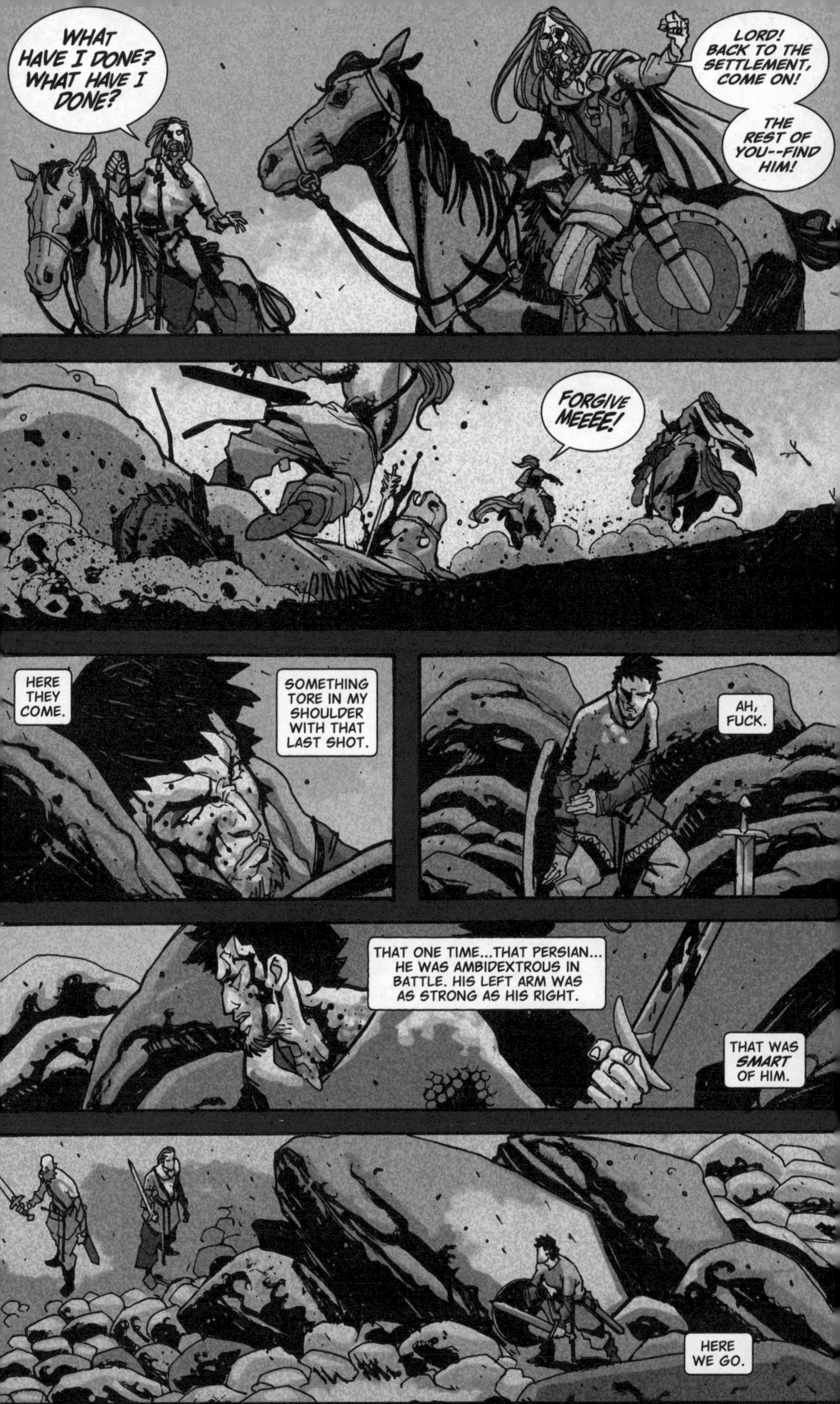
WHAT HAVE I DONE? WHAT HAVE I DONE?
LORD! BACK TO THE SETTLEMENT, COME ON!
THE REST OF YOU--FIND HIM!
FORGIVE MEEEE!
HERE THEY COME.
SOMETHING TORE IN MY SHOULDER WITH THAT LAST SHOT.
AH, FUCK.
THAT ONE TIME...THAT PERSIAN... HE WAS AMBIDEXTROUS IN BATTLE. HIS LEFT ARM WAS AS STRONG AS HIS RIGHT.
THAT WAS SMART OF HIM.
HERE WE GO.

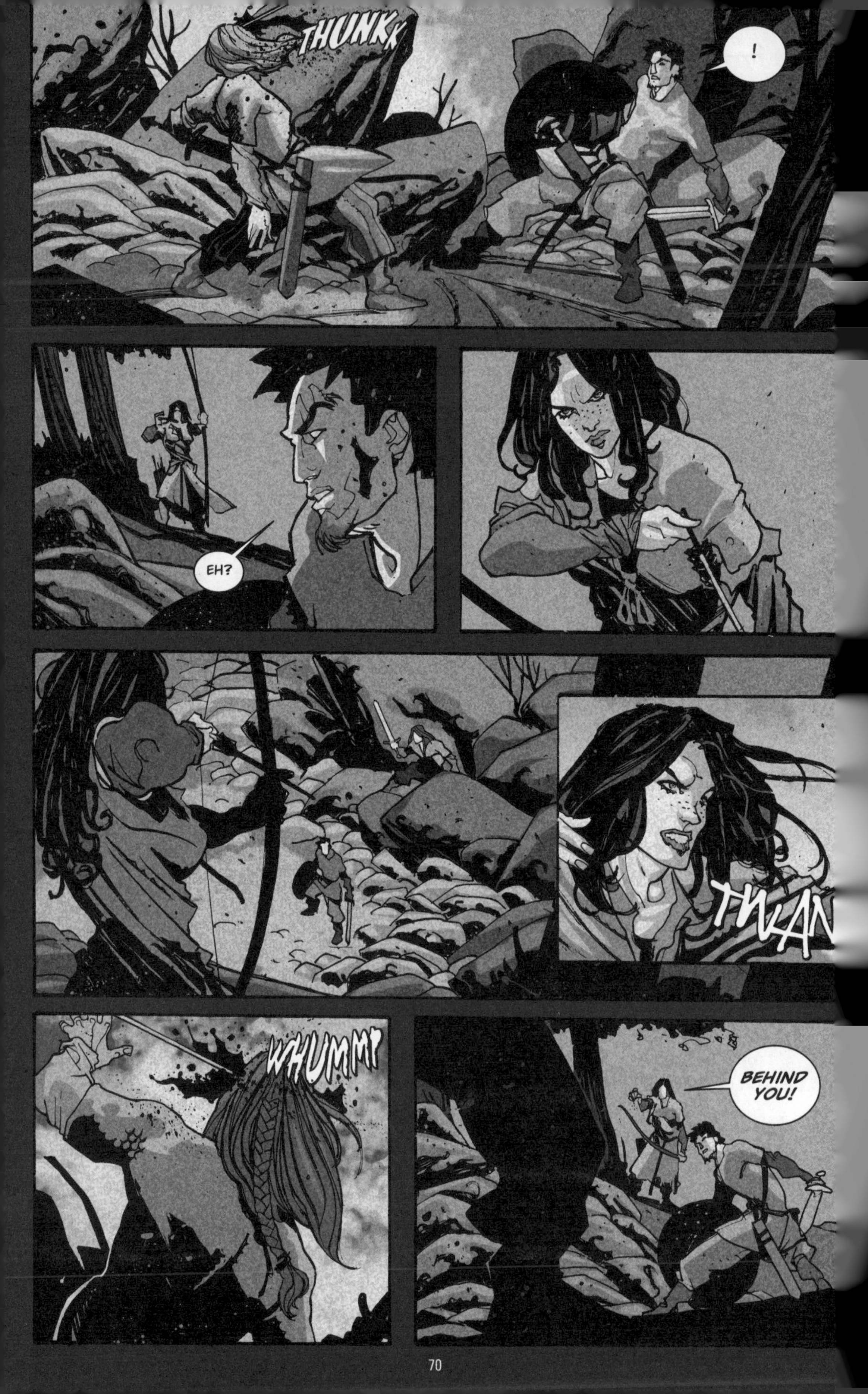
THUNKK
!
EH?
TWAN
WHUMM
BEHIND YOU!

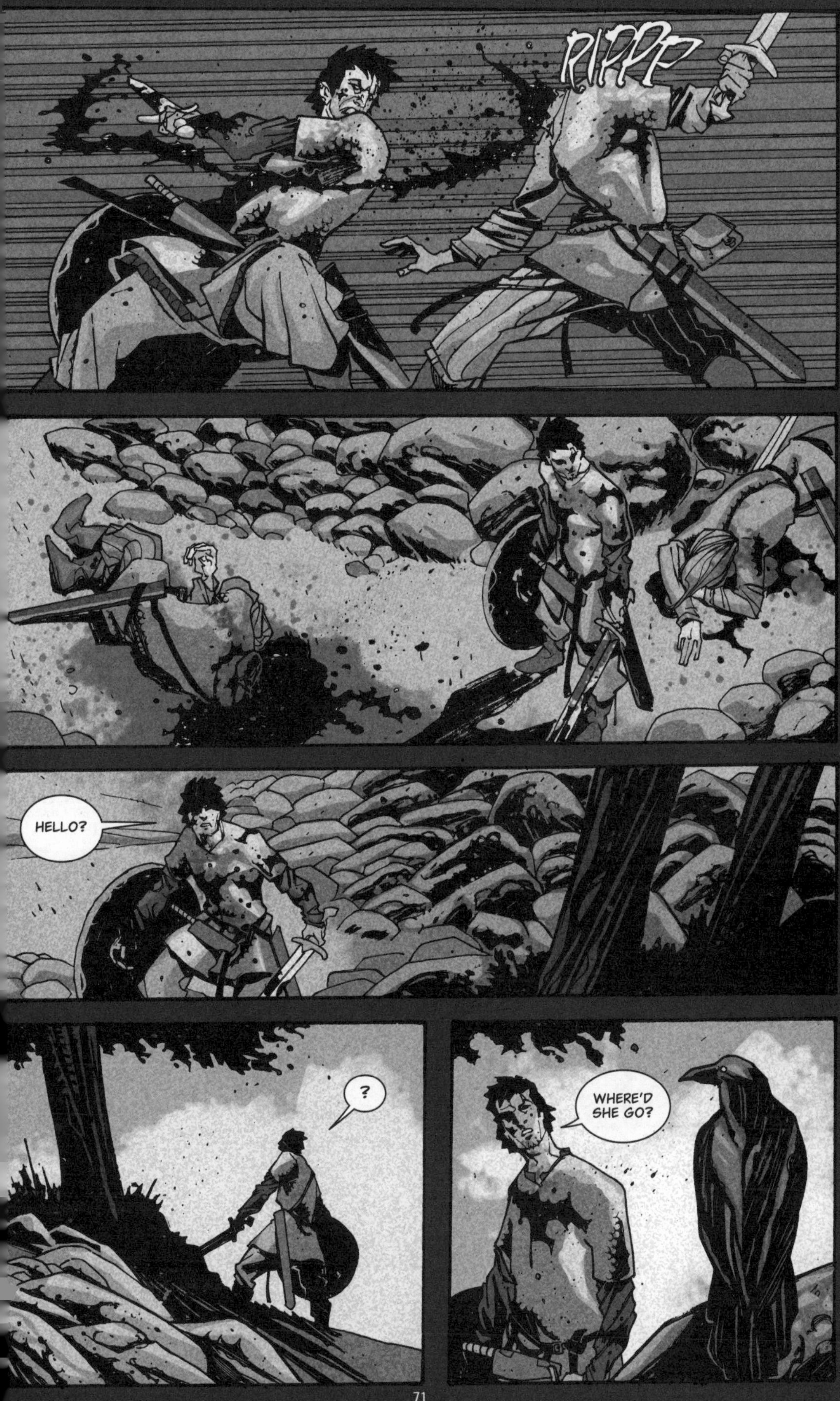
RIPPP
HELLO?
?
WHERE'D SHE GO?

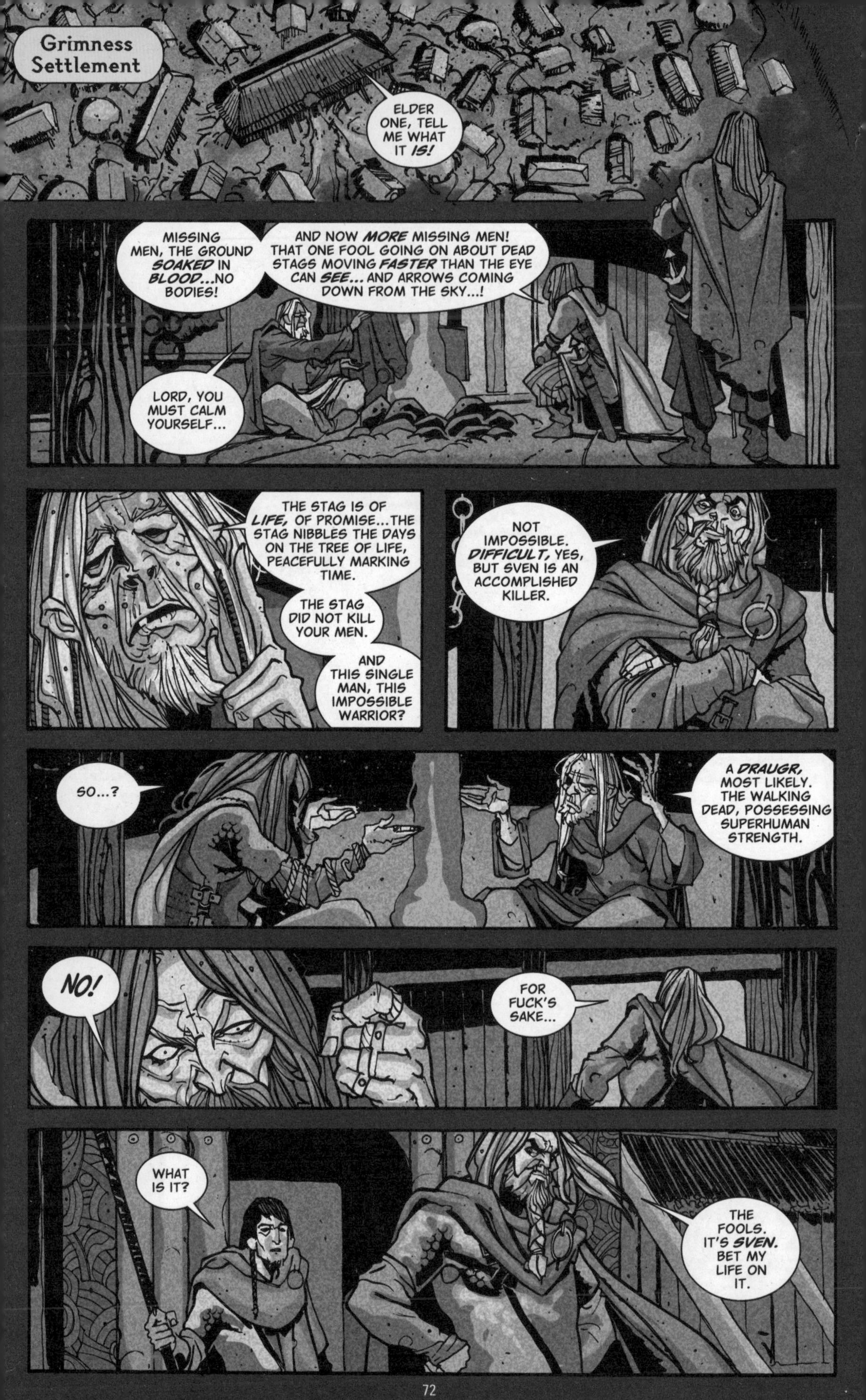

Grimness Settlement
ELDER ONE, TELL ME WHAT IT IS!
MISSING MEN, THE GROUND SOAKED IN BLOOD...NO BODIES!
AND NOW MORE MISSING MEN! THAT ONE FOOL GOING ON ABOUT DEAD STAGS MOVING FASTER THAN THE EYE CAN SEE... AND ARROWS COMING DOWN FROM THE SKY...!
LORD, YOU MUST CALM YOURSELF...
THE STAG IS OF LIFE, OF PROMISE...THE STAG NIBBLES THE DAYS ON THE TREE OF LIFE, PEACEFULLY MARKING TIME.
THE STAG DID NOT KILL YOUR MEN.
AND THIS SINGLE MAN, THIS IMPOSSIBLE WARRIOR?
NOT IMPOSSIBLE. DIFFICULT, YES, BUT SVEN IS AN ACCOMPLISHED KILLER.
SO...?
A DRAUGR, MOST LIKELY. THE WALKING DEAD, POSSESSING SUPERHUMAN STRENGTH.
NO!
FOR FUCK'S SAKE...
WHAT IS IT?
THE FOOLS. IT'S SVEN. BET MY LIFE ON IT.

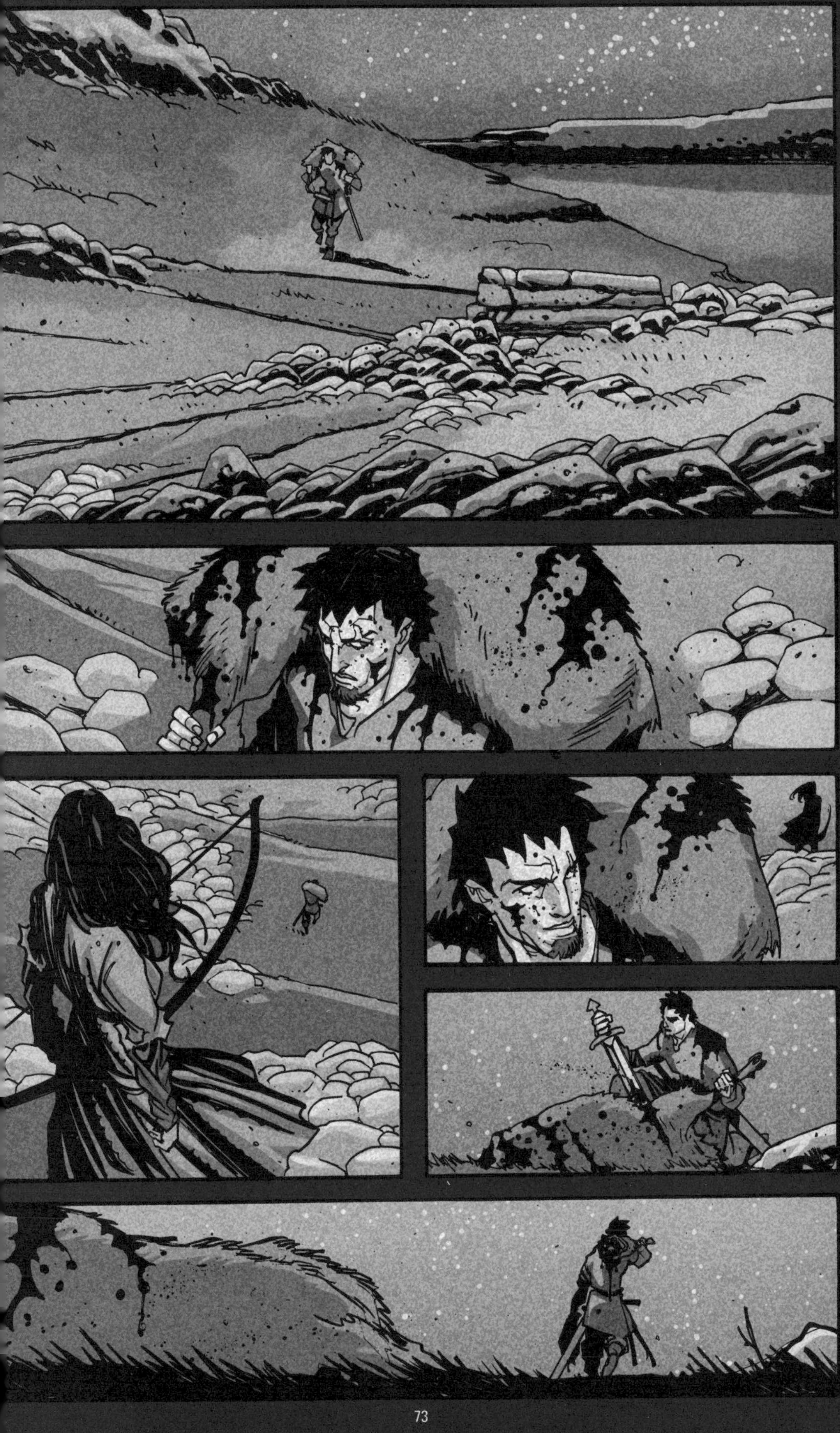

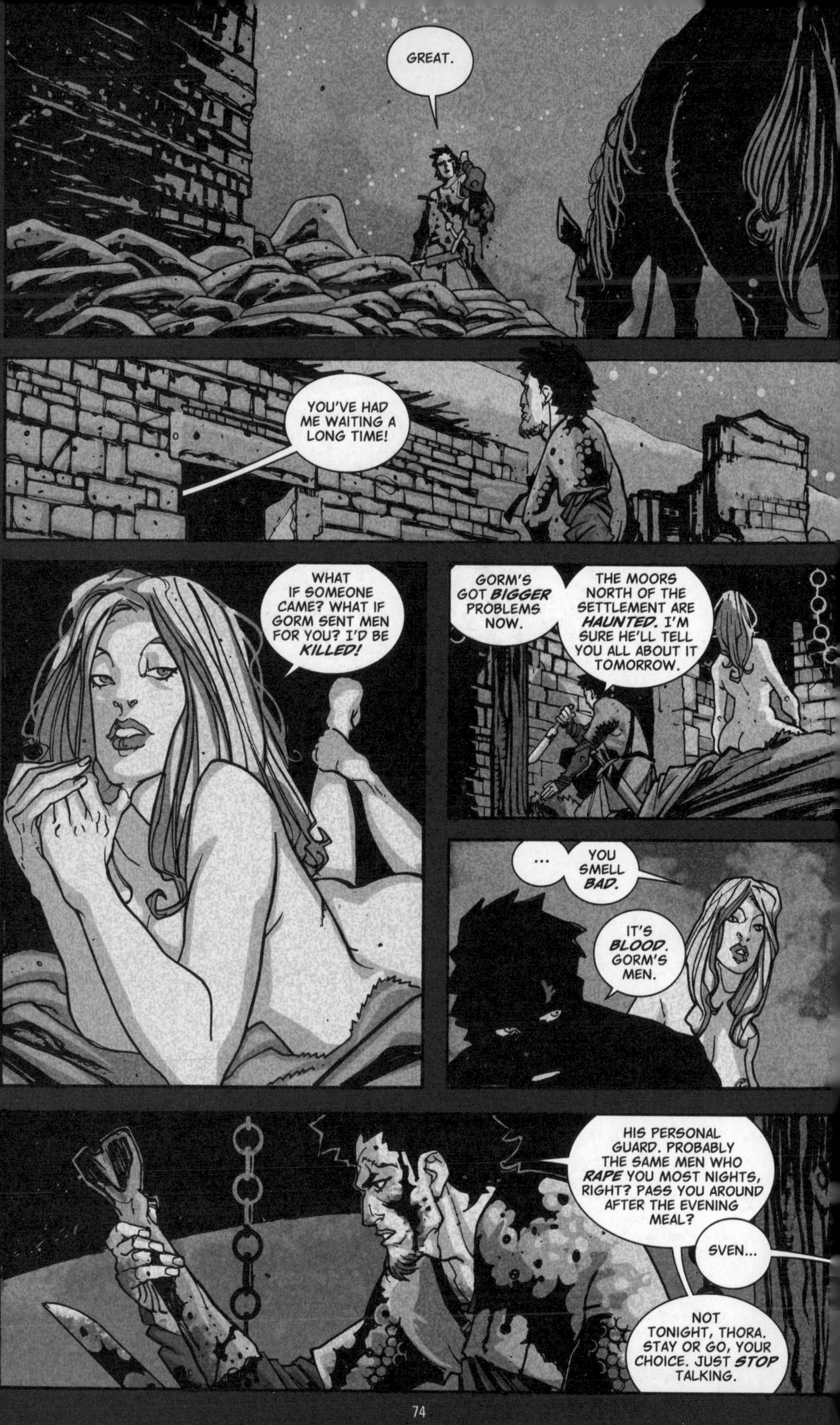

GREAT.
YOU'VE HAD ME WAITING A LONG TIME!
WHAT IF SOMEONE CAME? WHAT IF GORM SENT MEN FOR YOU? I'D BE KILLED!
GORM'S GOT BIGGER PROBLEMS NOW.
THE MOORS NORTH OF THE SETTLEMENT ARE HAUNTED. I'M SURE HE'LL TELL YOU ALL ABOUT IT TOMORROW.
...
YOU SMELL BAD.
IT'S BLOOD. GORM'S MEN.
HIS PERSONAL GUARD. PROBABLY THE SAME MEN WHO RAPE YOU MOST NIGHTS, RIGHT? PASS YOU AROUND AFTER THE EVENING MEAL?
SVEN...
NOT TONIGHT, THORA. STAY OR GO, YOUR CHOICE. JUST STOP TALKING.

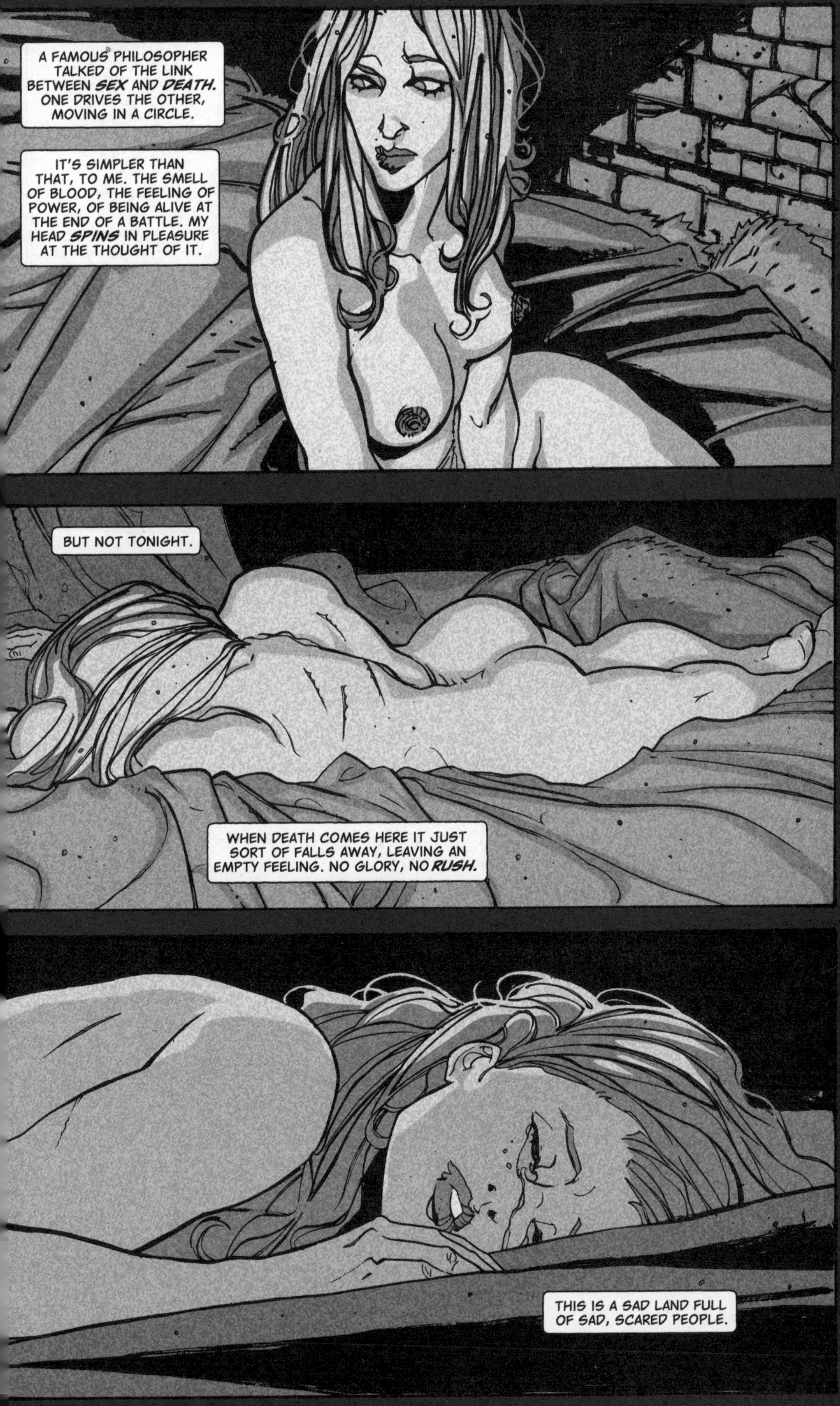
A FAMOUS PHILOSOPHER TALKED OF THE LINK BETWEEN SEX AND DEATH. ONE DRIVES THE OTHER, MOVING IN A CIRCLE.
IT'S SIMPLER THAN THAT, TO ME. THE SMELL OF BLOOD, THE FEELING OF POWER, OF BEING ALIVE AT THE END OF A BATTLE. MY HEAD SPINS IN PLEASURE AT THE THOUGHT OF IT.
BUT NOT TONIGHT.
WHEN DEATH COMES HERE IT JUST SORT OF FALLS AWAY, LEAVING AN EMPTY FEELING. NO GLORY, NO RUSH.
THIS IS A SAD LAND FULL OF SAD, SCARED PEOPLE.

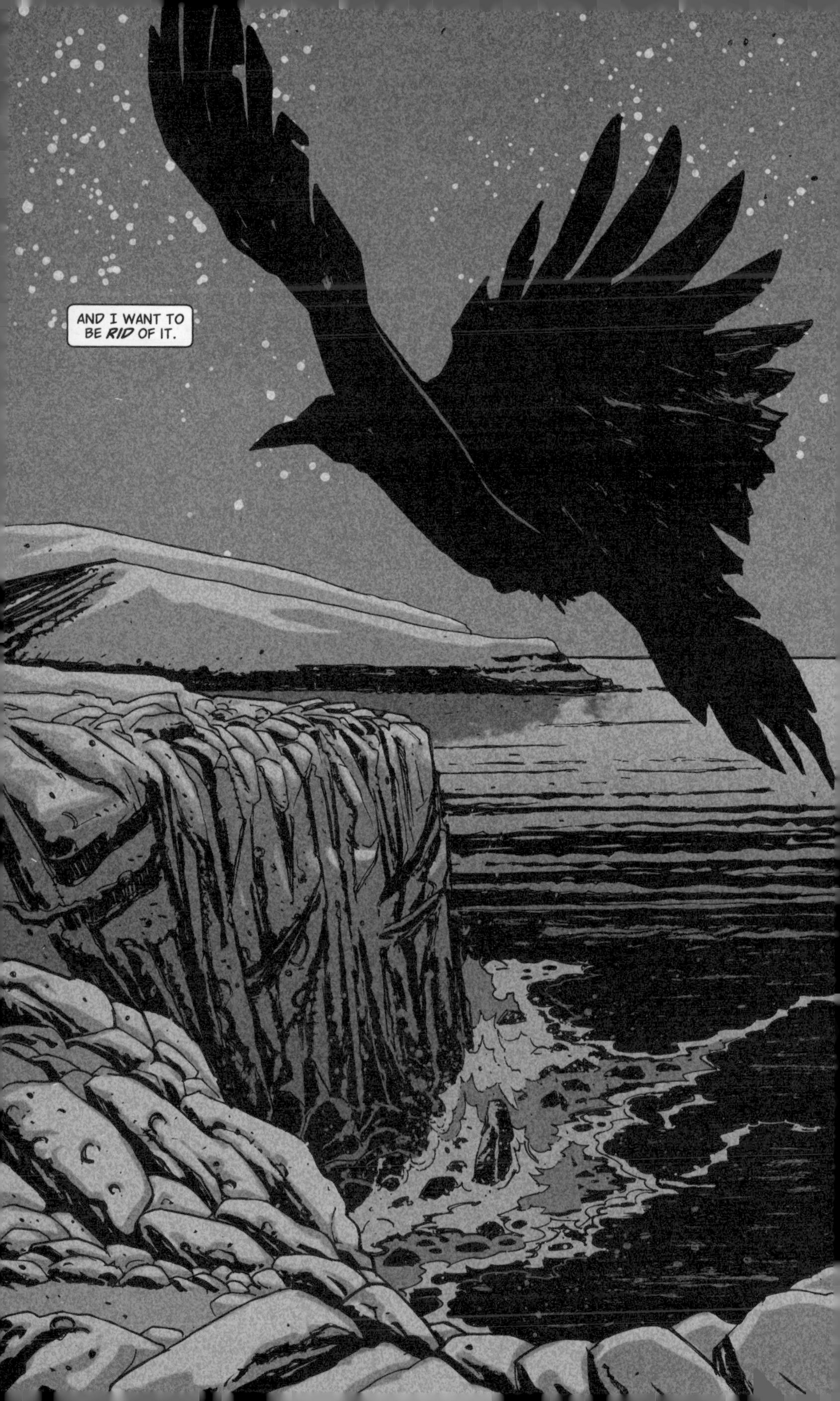
AND I WANT TO BE RID OF IT.

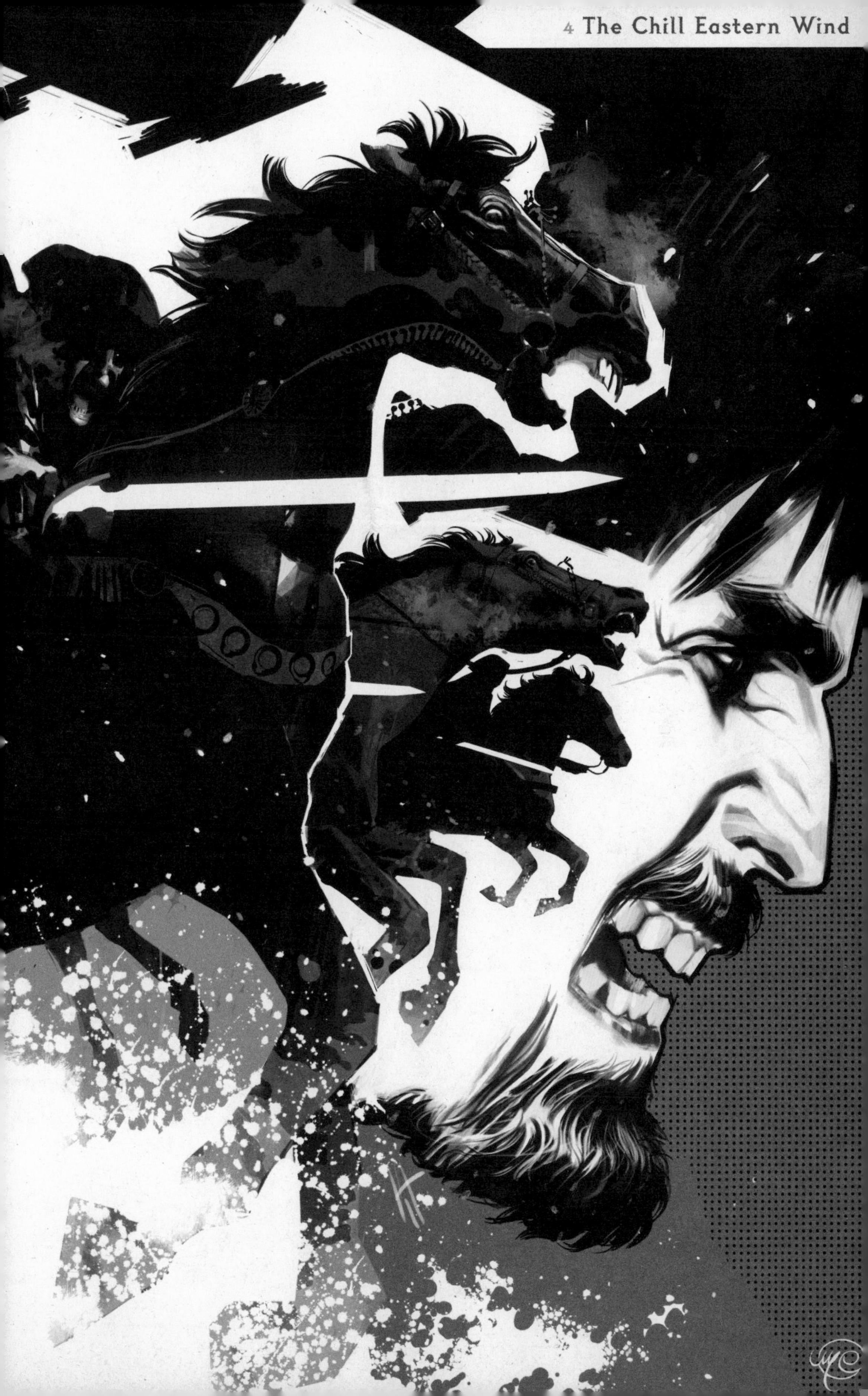

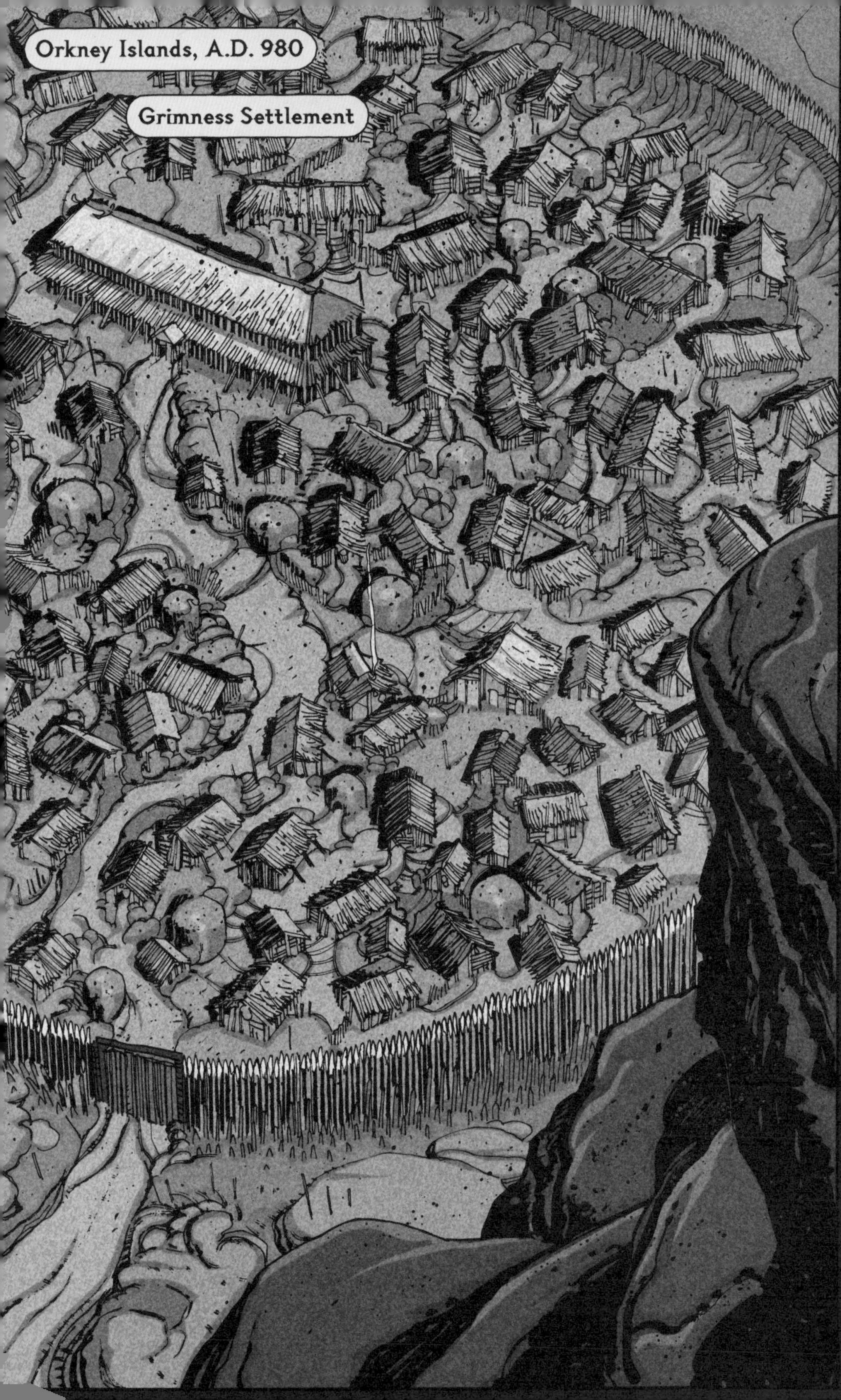
Orkney Islands, A.D. 980
Grimness Settlement

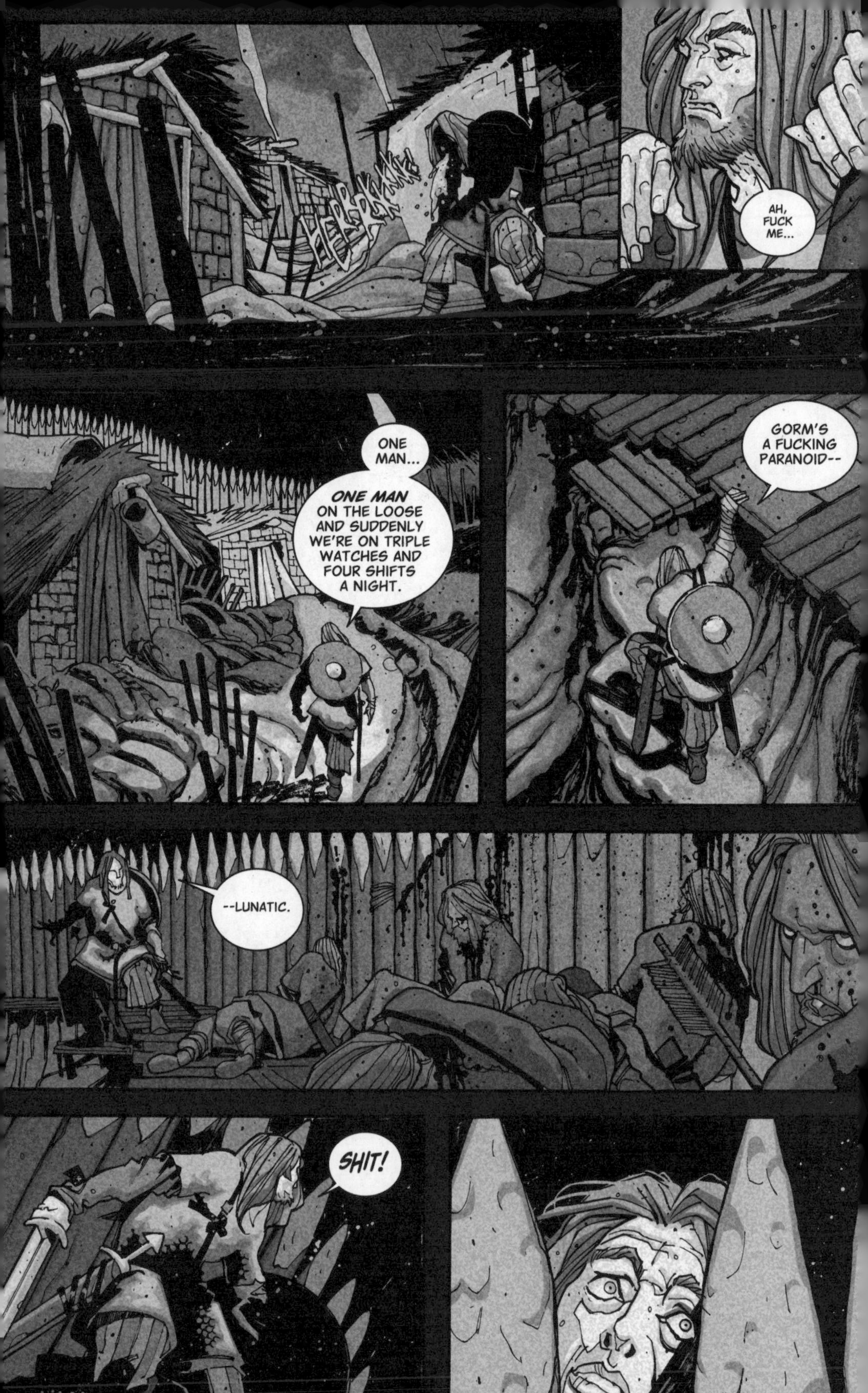
AH, FUCK ME...
ONE MAN...
ONE MAN ON THE LOOSE AND SUDDENLY WE'RE ON TRIPLE WATCHES AND FOUR SHIFTS A NIGHT.
GORM'S A FUCKING PARANOID--
--LUNATIC.
SHIT!

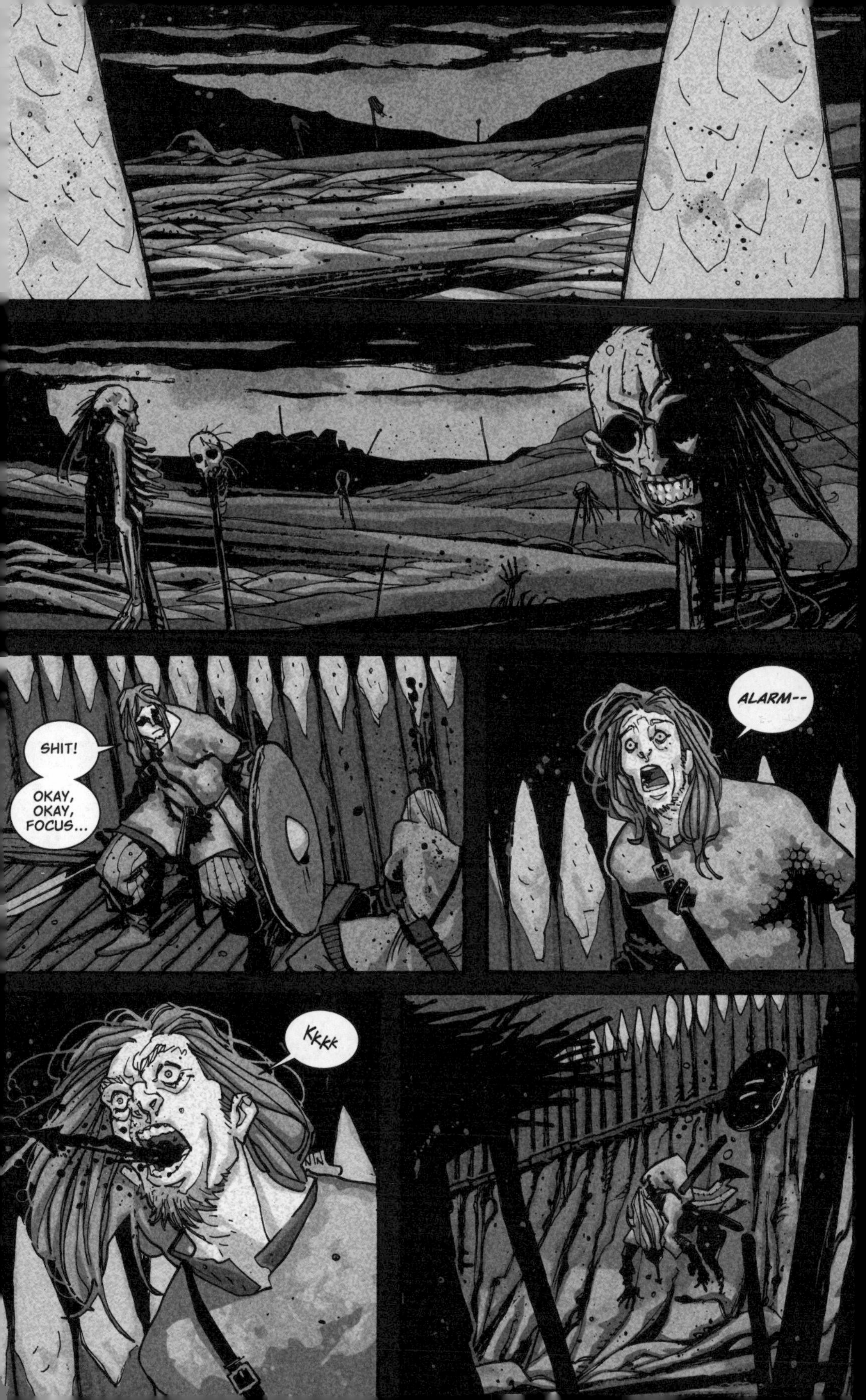
SHIT!
OKAY, OKAY, FOCUS...
ALARM--
KKKK

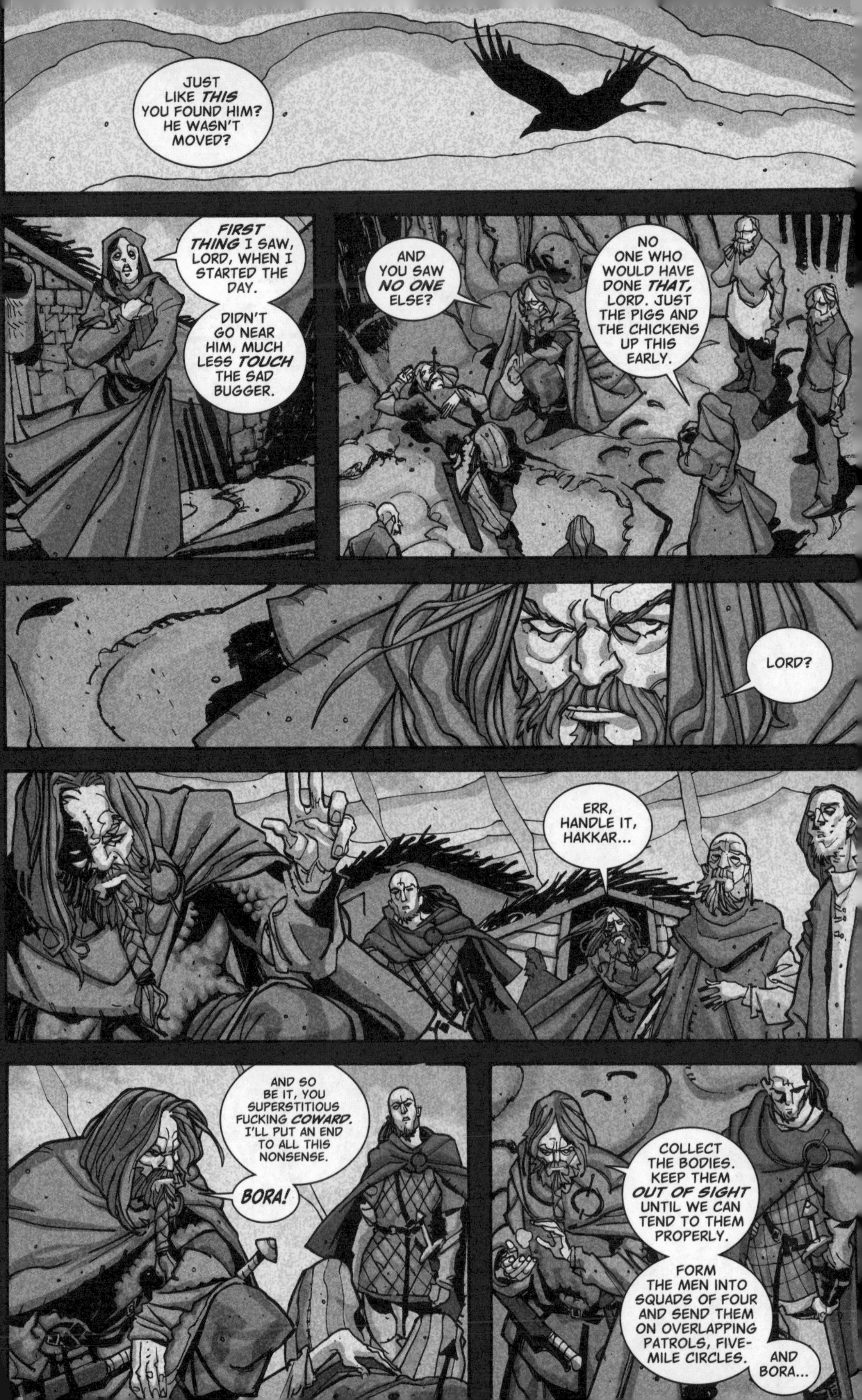
JUST LIKE *THIS* YOU FOUND HIM? HE WASN'T MOVED?
FIRST THING I SAW, LORD, WHEN I STARTED THE DAY.
DIDN'T GO NEAR HIM, MUCH LESS *TOUCH* THE SAD BUGGER.
AND YOU SAW *NO ONE* ELSE?
NO ONE WHO WOULD HAVE DONE *THAT,* LORD. JUST THE PIGS AND THE CHICKENS UP THIS EARLY.
LORD?
ERR, HANDLE IT, HAKKAR...
AND SO BE IT, YOU SUPERSTITIOUS FUCKING *COWARD.* I'LL PUT AN END TO ALL THIS NONSENSE.
BORA!
COLLECT THE BODIES. KEEP THEM *OUT OF SIGHT* UNTIL WE CAN TEND TO THEM PROPERLY.
FORM THE MEN INTO SQUADS OF FOUR AND SEND THEM ON OVERLAPPING PATROLS, FIVE-MILE CIRCLES.
AND BORA...

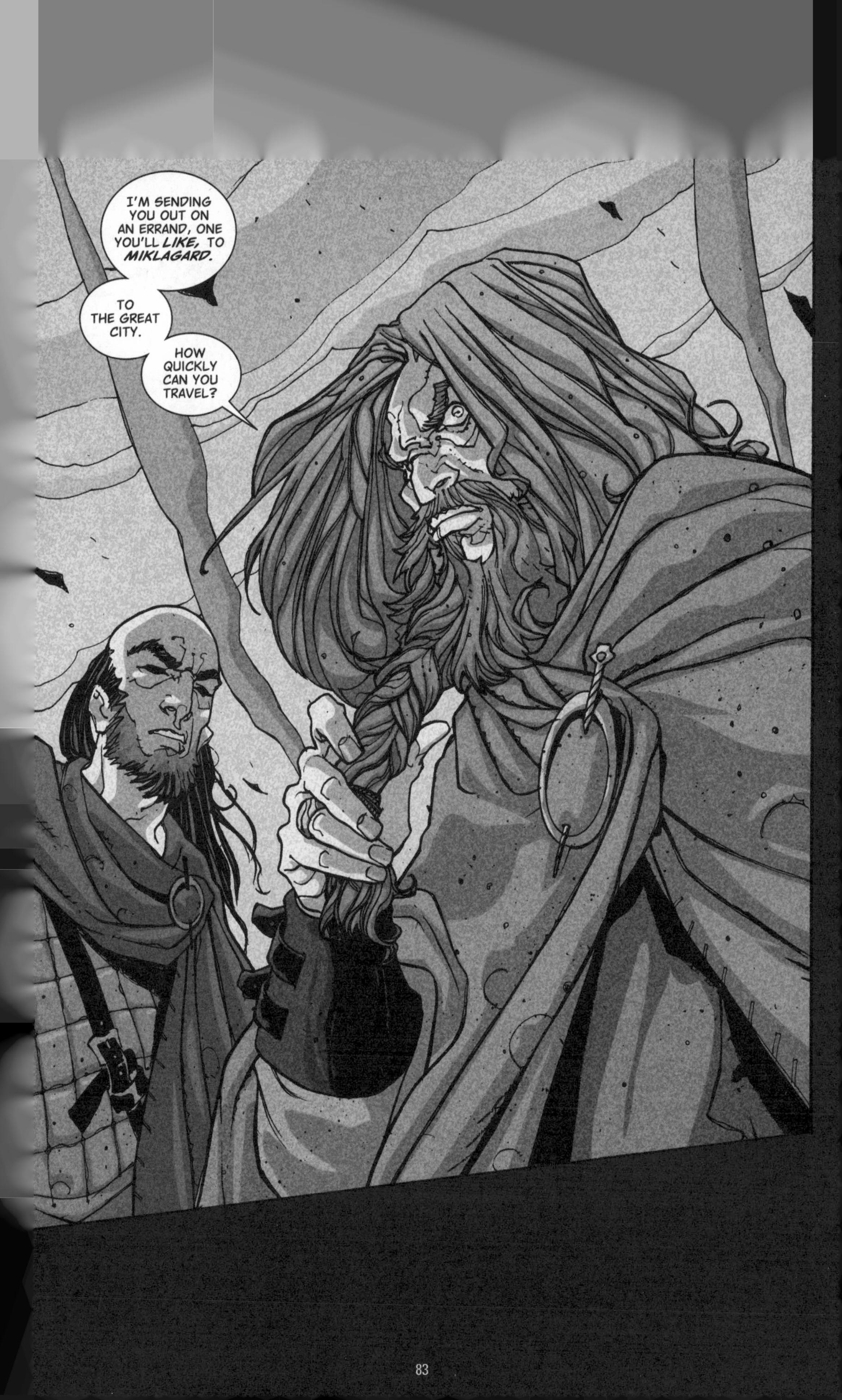
I'M SENDING YOU OUT ON AN ERRAND, ONE YOU'LL *LIKE,* TO ***MIKLAGARD.***
TO THE GREAT CITY.
HOW QUICKLY CAN YOU TRAVEL?

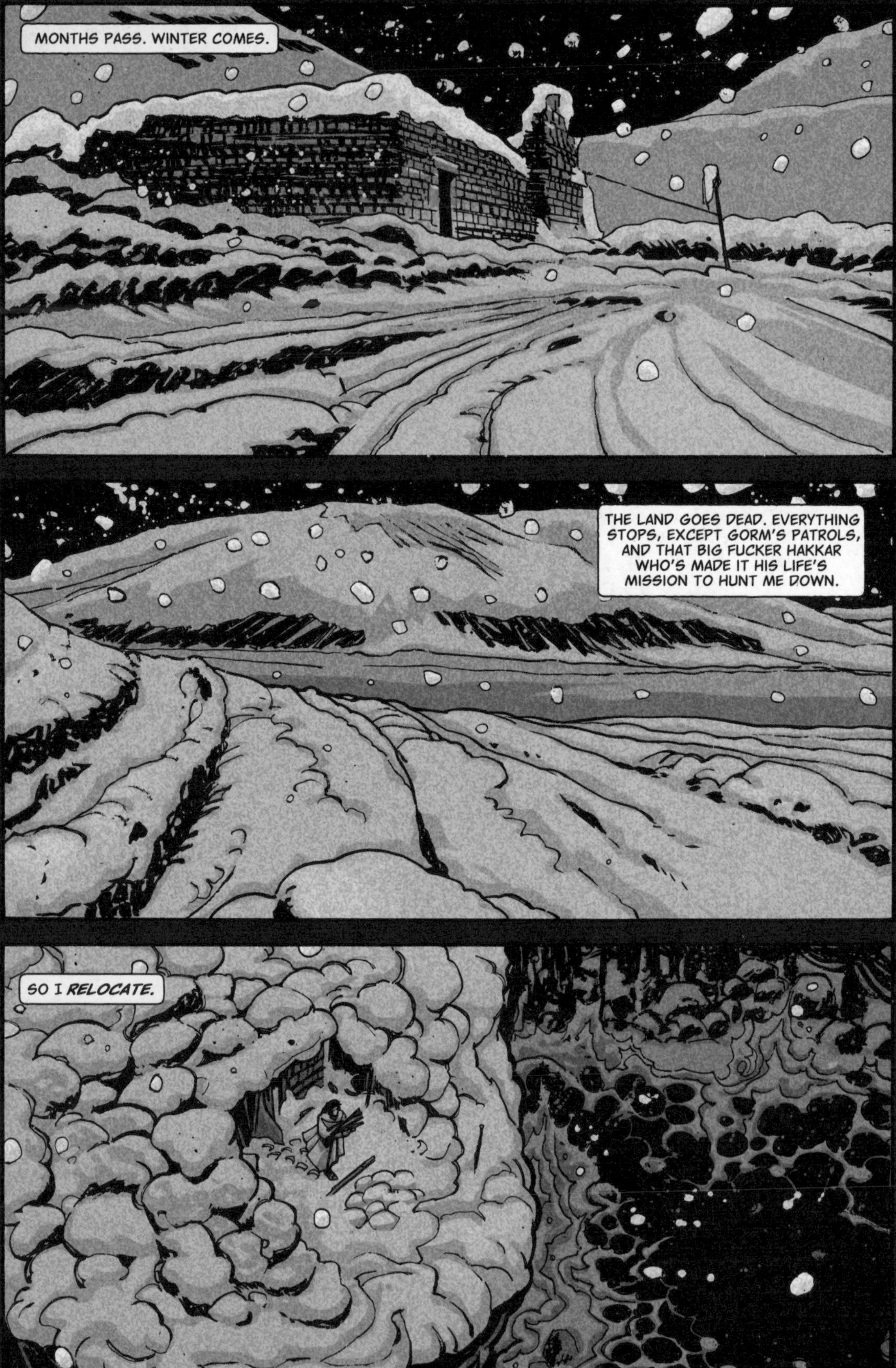
MONTHS PASS. WINTER COMES.
THE LAND GOES DEAD. EVERYTHING STOPS, EXCEPT GORM'S PATROLS, AND THAT BIG FUCKER HAKKAR WHO'S MADE IT HIS LIFE'S MISSION TO HUNT ME DOWN.
SO I *RELOCATE.*

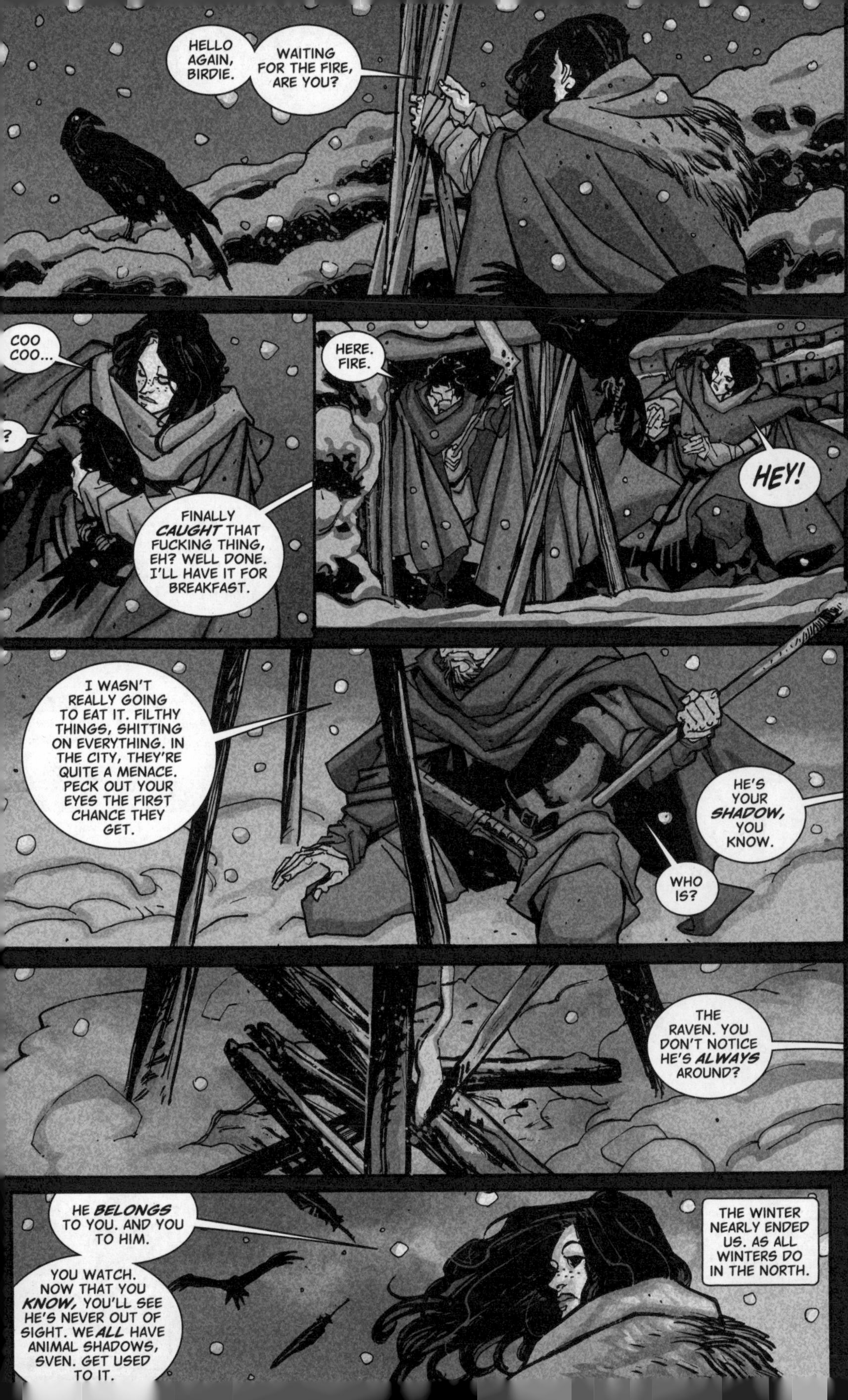
HELLO AGAIN, BIRDIE.
WAITING FOR THE FIRE, ARE YOU?
COO COO...
?
FINALLY CAUGHT THAT FUCKING THING, EH? WELL DONE. I'LL HAVE IT FOR BREAKFAST.
HERE. FIRE.
HEY!
I WASN'T REALLY GOING TO EAT IT. FILTHY THINGS, SHITTING ON EVERYTHING. IN THE CITY, THEY'RE QUITE A MENACE. PECK OUT YOUR EYES THE FIRST CHANCE THEY GET.
HE'S YOUR SHADOW, YOU KNOW.
WHO IS?
THE RAVEN. YOU DON'T NOTICE HE'S ALWAYS AROUND?
HE BELONGS TO YOU. AND YOU TO HIM.
YOU WATCH. NOW THAT YOU KNOW, YOU'LL SEE HE'S NEVER OUT OF SIGHT. WE ALL HAVE ANIMAL SHADOWS, SVEN. GET USED TO IT.
THE WINTER NEARLY ENDED US. AS ALL WINTERS DO IN THE NORTH.

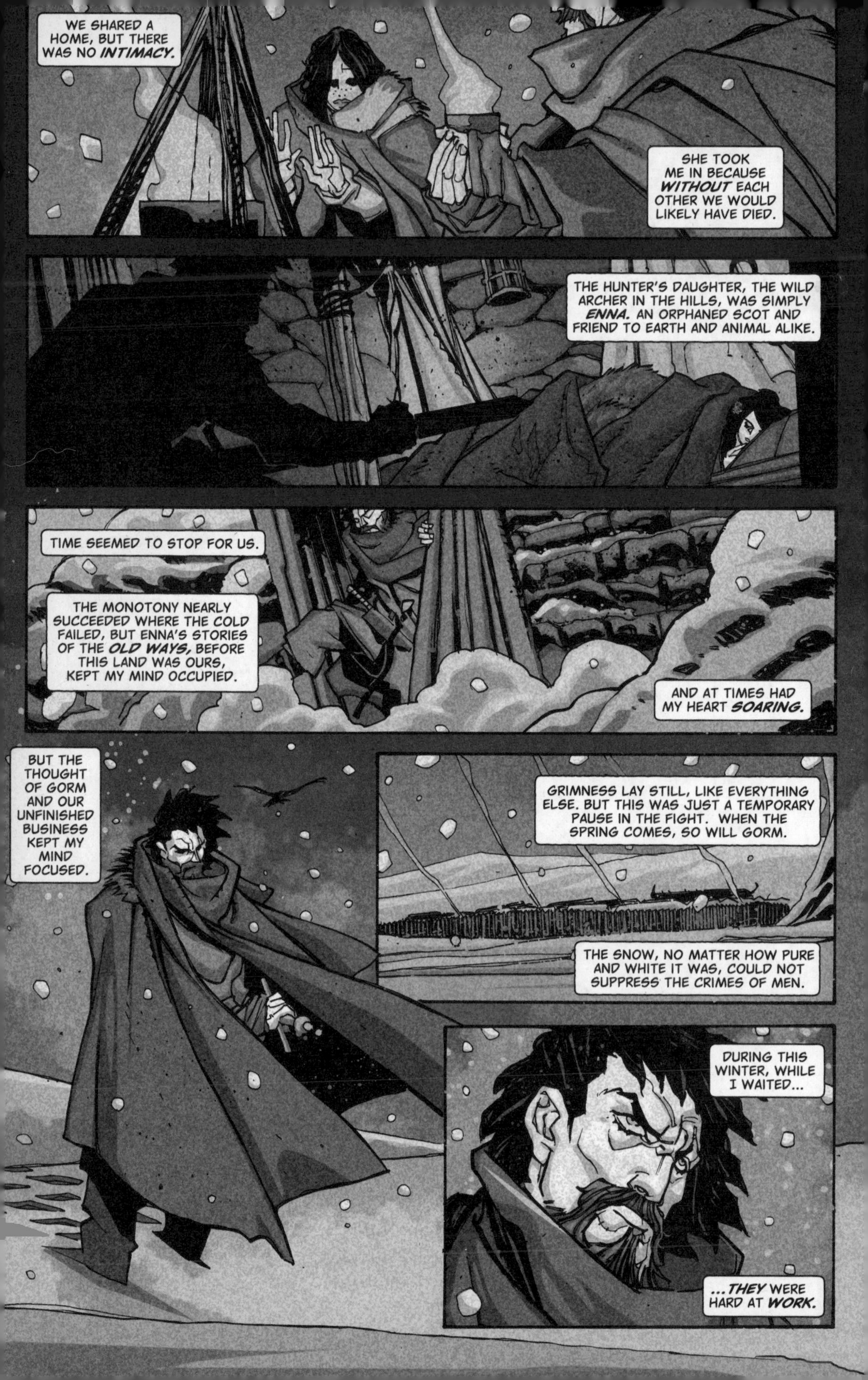
WE SHARED A HOME, BUT THERE WAS NO *INTIMACY.*
SHE TOOK ME IN BECAUSE *WITHOUT* EACH OTHER WE WOULD LIKELY HAVE DIED.
THE HUNTER'S DAUGHTER, THE WILD ARCHER IN THE HILLS, WAS SIMPLY *ENNA.* AN ORPHANED SCOT AND FRIEND TO EARTH AND ANIMAL ALIKE.
TIME SEEMED TO STOP FOR US.
THE MONOTONY NEARLY SUCCEEDED WHERE THE COLD FAILED, BUT ENNA'S STORIES OF THE *OLD WAYS,* BEFORE THIS LAND WAS OURS, KEPT MY MIND OCCUPIED.
AND AT TIMES HAD MY HEART *SOARING.*
BUT THE THOUGHT OF GORM AND OUR UNFINISHED BUSINESS KEPT MY MIND FOCUSED.
GRIMNESS LAY STILL, LIKE EVERYTHING ELSE. BUT THIS WAS JUST A TEMPORARY PAUSE IN THE FIGHT. WHEN THE SPRING COMES, SO WILL GORM.
THE SNOW, NO MATTER HOW PURE AND WHITE IT WAS, COULD NOT SUPPRESS THE CRIMES OF MEN.
DURING THIS WINTER, WHILE I WAITED...
...*THEY* WERE HARD AT *WORK.*

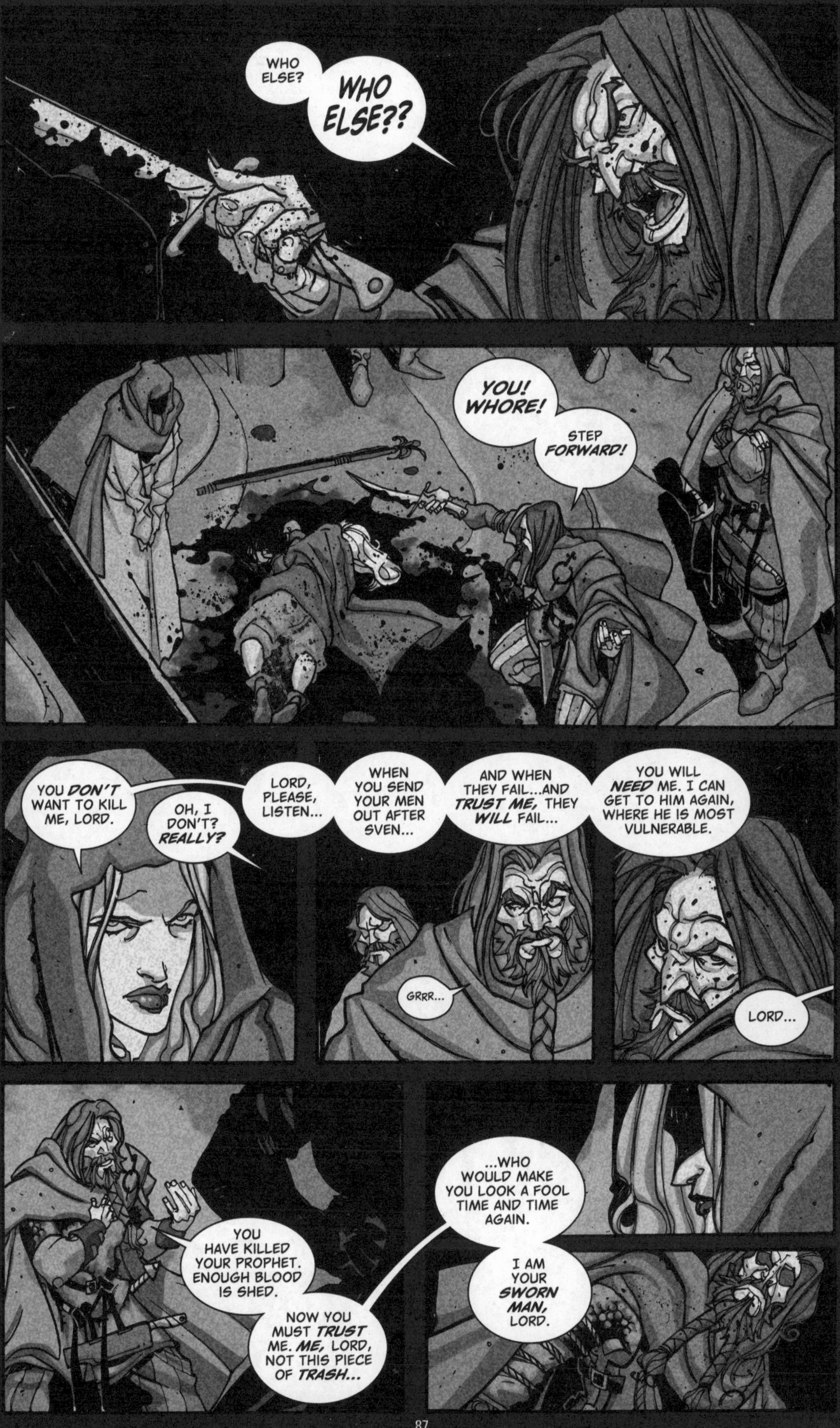
WHO ELSE?
WHO ELSE??
YOU! WHORE!
STEP FORWARD!
YOU DON'T WANT TO KILL ME, LORD.
OH, I DON'T? REALLY?
LORD, PLEASE, LISTEN...
WHEN YOU SEND YOUR MEN OUT AFTER SVEN...
AND WHEN THEY FAIL...AND TRUST ME, THEY WILL FAIL...
YOU WILL NEED ME. I CAN GET TO HIM AGAIN, WHERE HE IS MOST VULNERABLE.
GRRR...
LORD...
YOU HAVE KILLED YOUR PROPHET. ENOUGH BLOOD IS SHED.
NOW YOU MUST TRUST ME. ME, LORD, NOT THIS PIECE OF TRASH...
...WHO WOULD MAKE YOU LOOK A FOOL TIME AND TIME AGAIN.
I AM YOUR SWORN MAN, LORD.

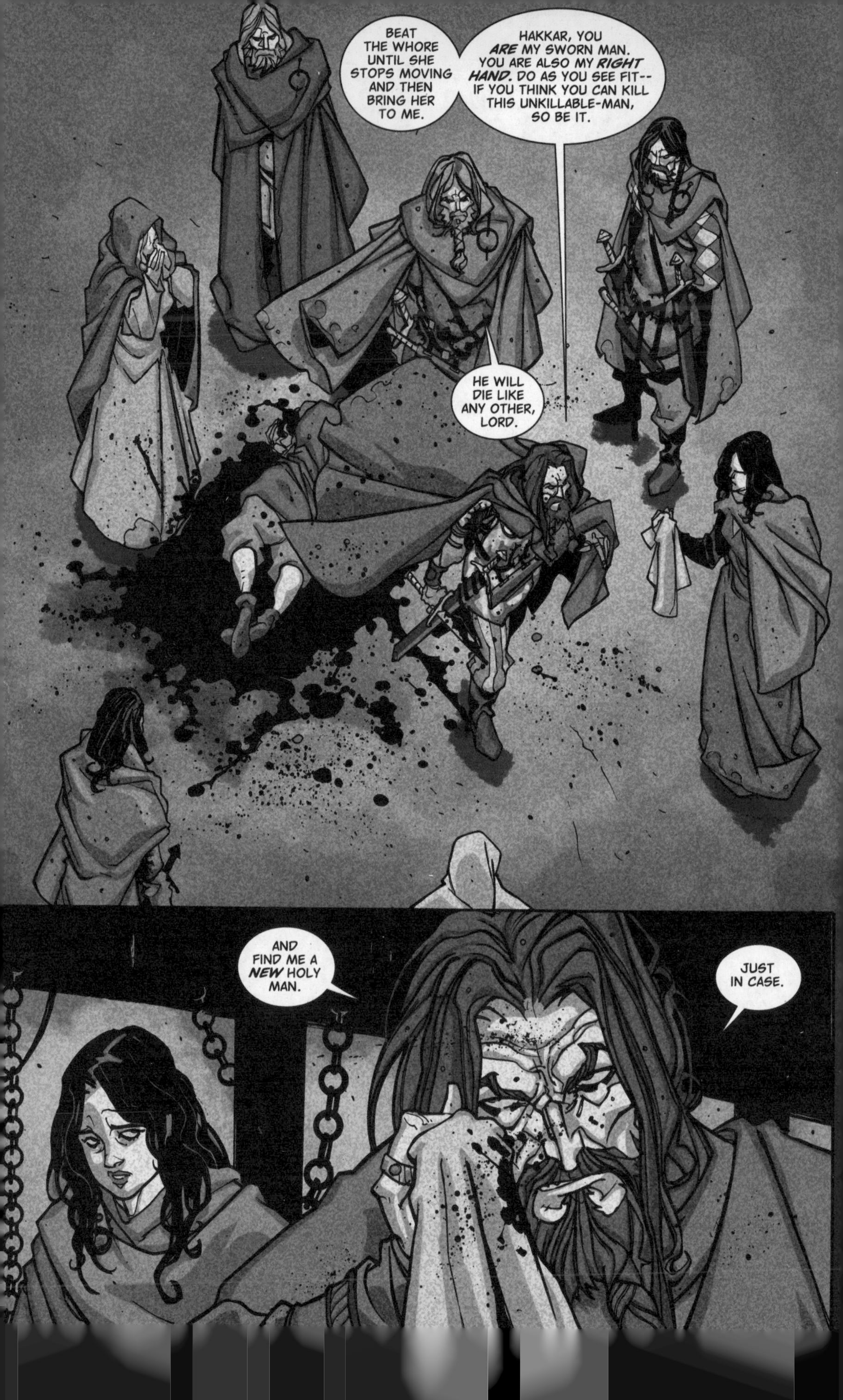
BEAT THE WHORE UNTIL SHE STOPS MOVING AND THEN BRING HER TO ME.
HAKKAR, YOU *ARE* MY SWORN MAN. YOU ARE ALSO MY *RIGHT HAND.* DO AS YOU SEE FIT-- IF YOU THINK YOU CAN KILL THIS UNKILLABLE-MAN, SO BE IT.
HE WILL DIE LIKE ANY OTHER, LORD.
AND FIND ME A *NEW* HOLY MAN.
JUST IN CASE.

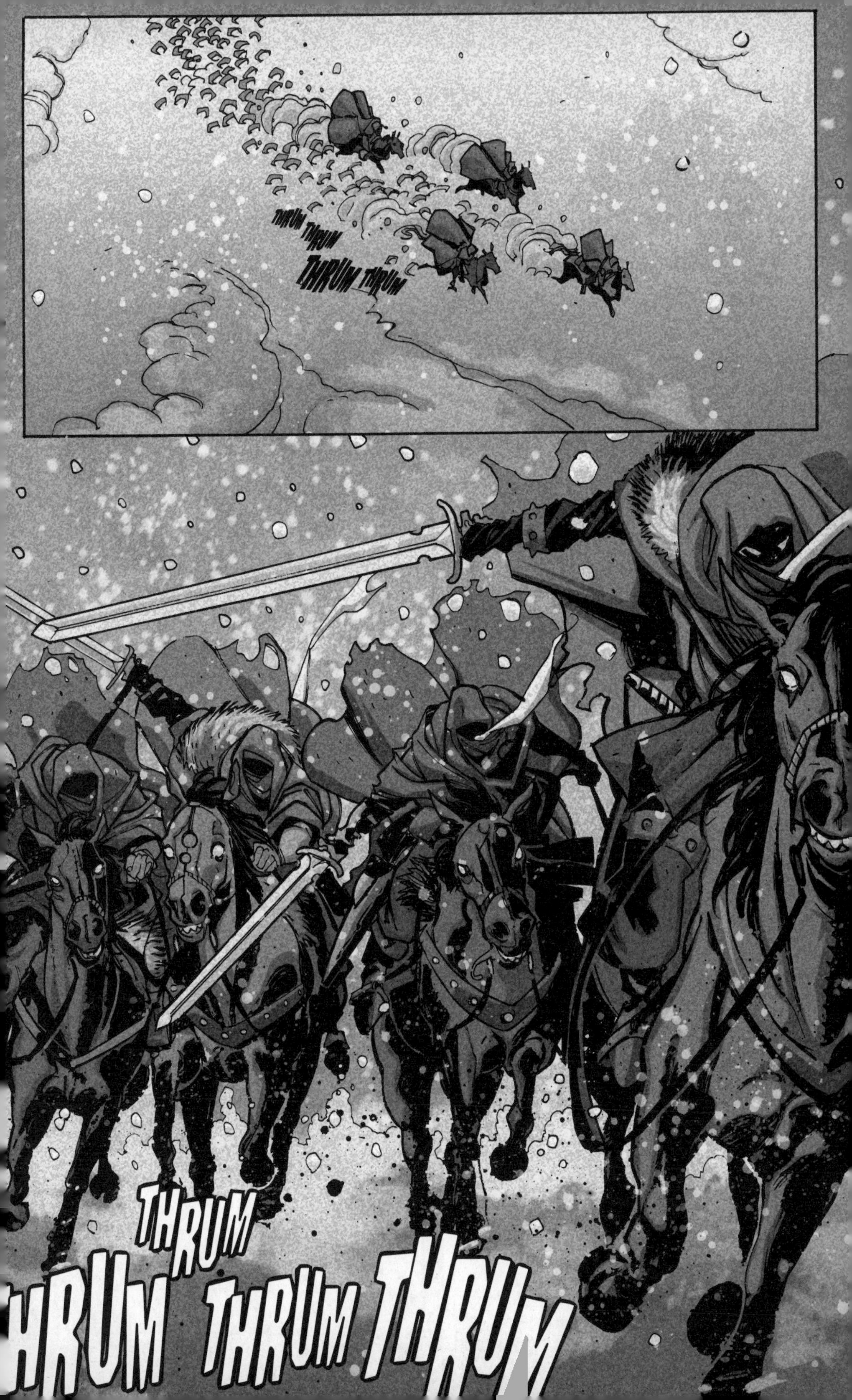
THRUM THRUM
THRUM THRUM
THRUM
THRUM THRUM THRUM

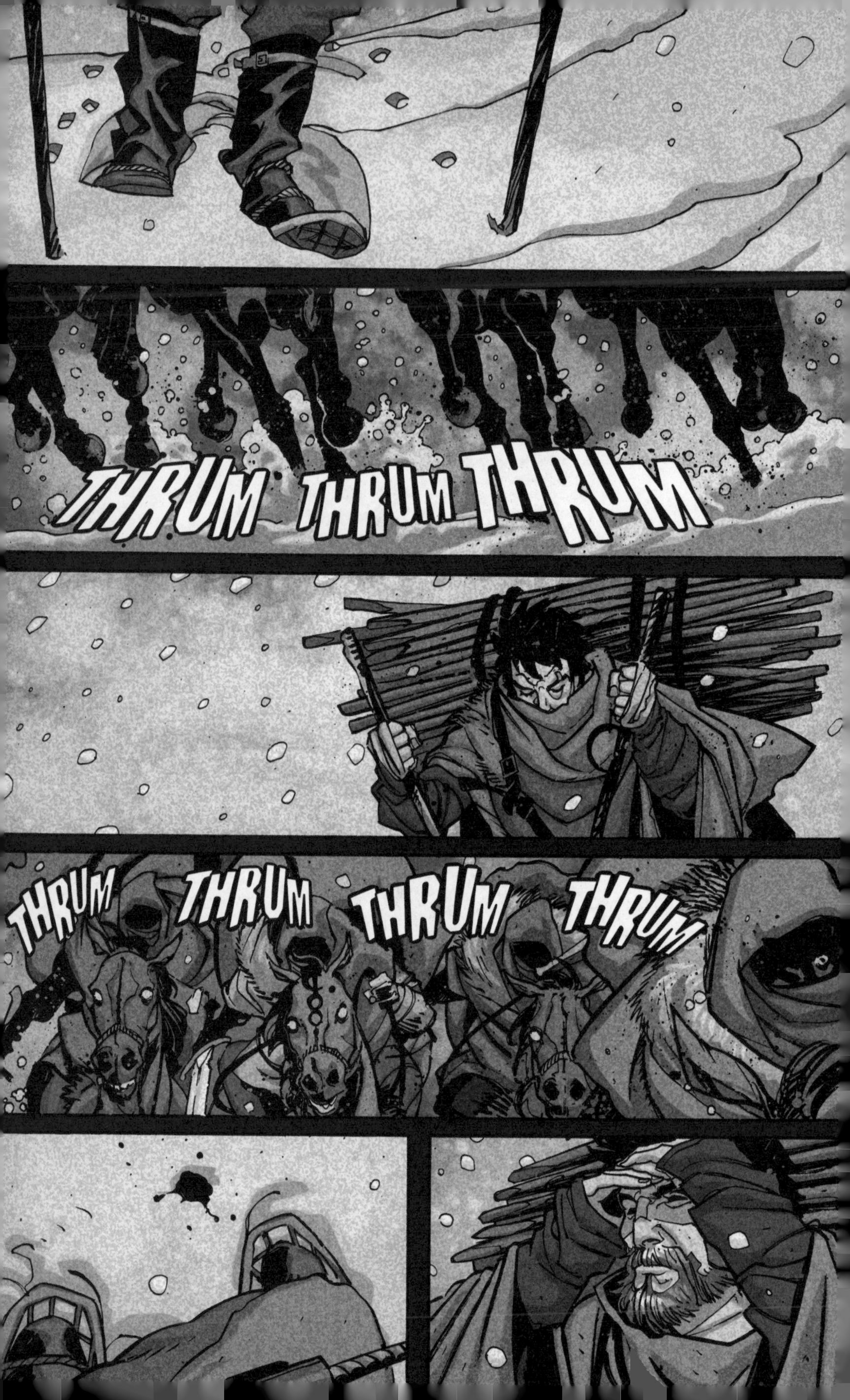
THRUM THRUM THRUM
THRUM THRUM THRUM THRUM

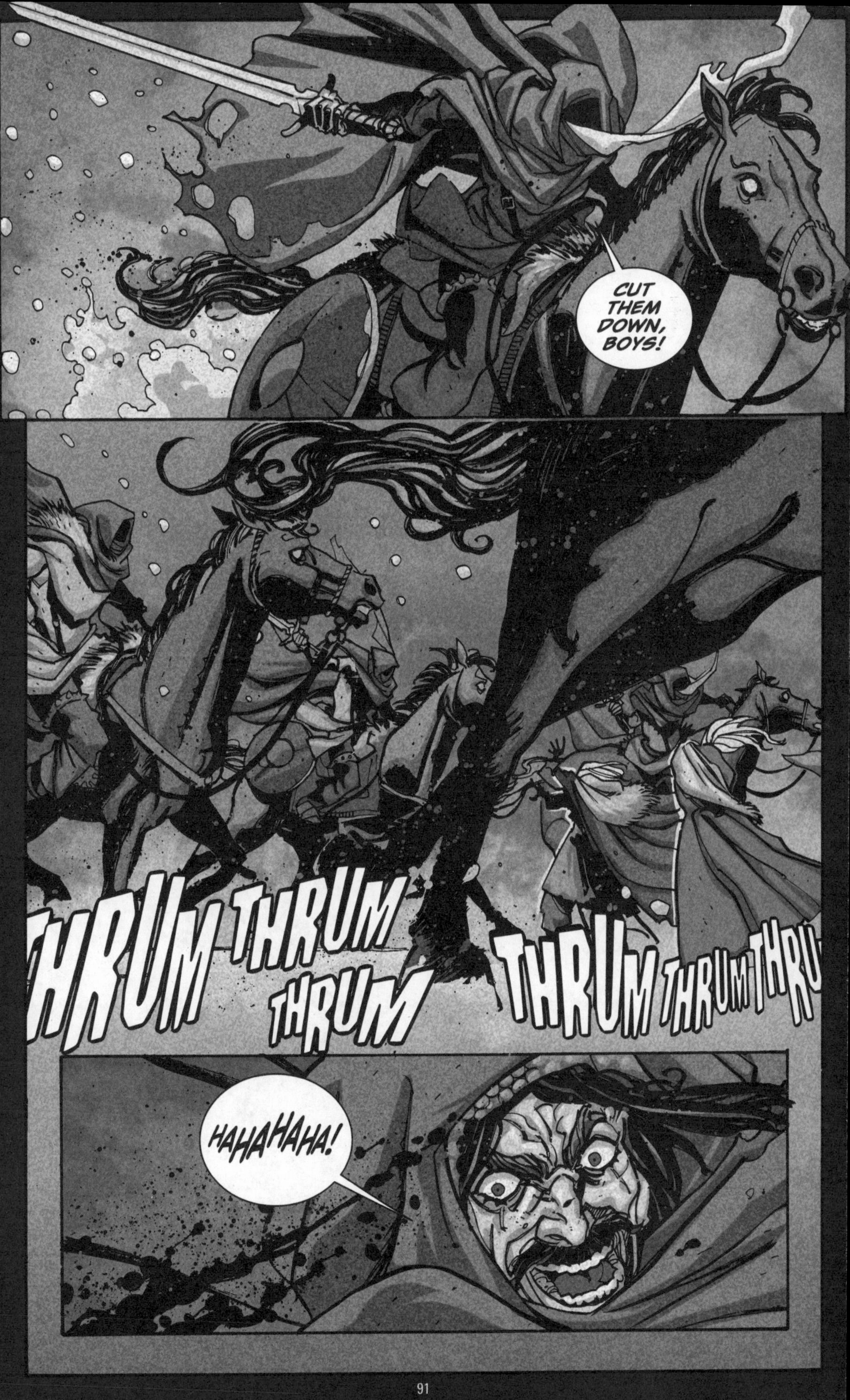
CUT THEM DOWN, BOYS!
THRUM THRUM THRUM THRUM THRUM THRU
HAHAHAHAHA!

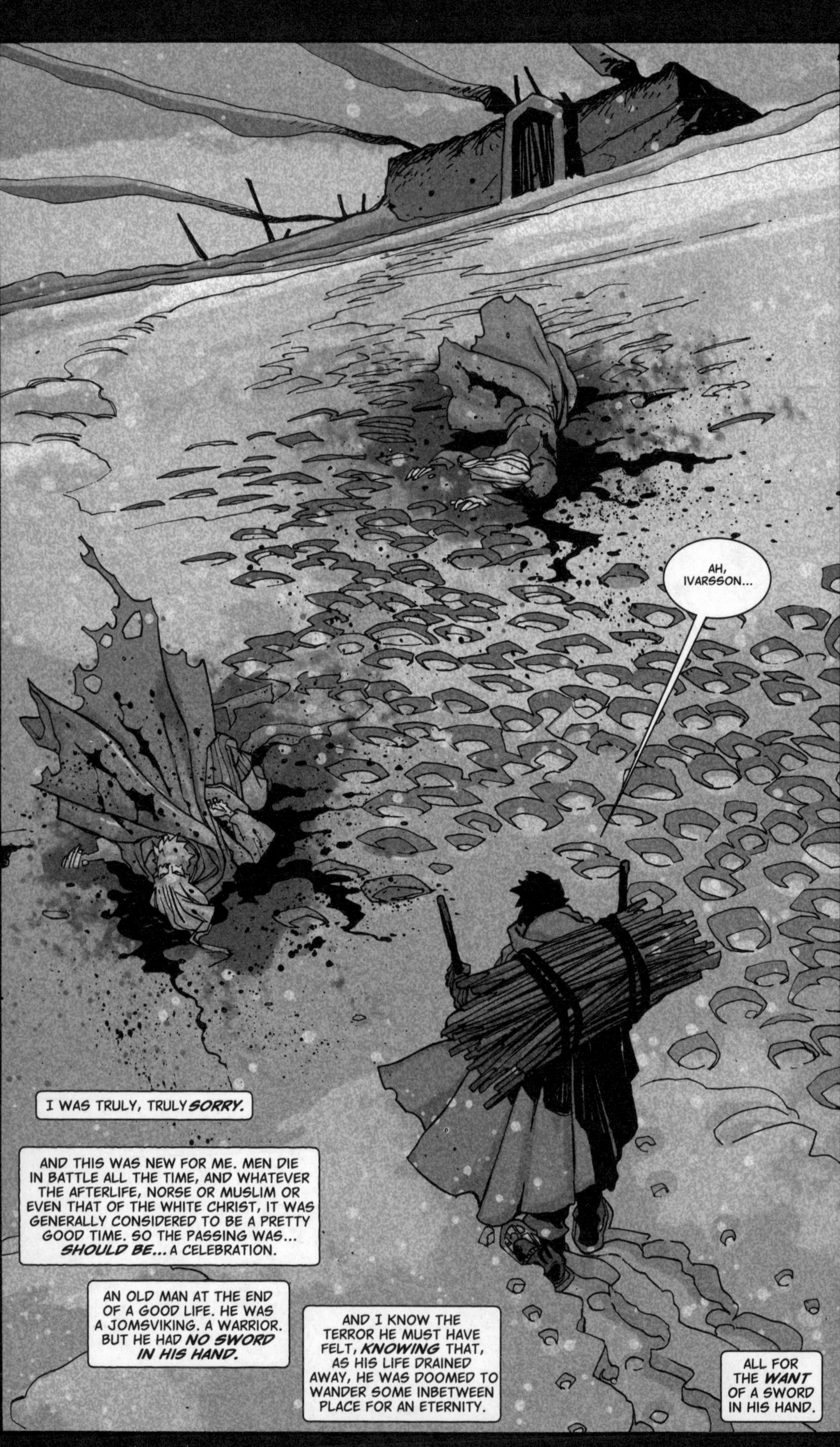
AH, IVARSSON...
I WAS TRULY, TRULY SORRY.
AND THIS WAS NEW FOR ME. MEN DIE IN BATTLE ALL THE TIME, AND WHATEVER THE AFTERLIFE, NORSE OR MUSLIM OR EVEN THAT OF THE WHITE CHRIST, IT WAS GENERALLY CONSIDERED TO BE A PRETTY GOOD TIME. SO THE PASSING WAS... SHOULD BE... A CELEBRATION.
AN OLD MAN AT THE END OF A GOOD LIFE. HE WAS A JOMSVIKING. A WARRIOR. BUT HE HAD NO SWORD IN HIS HAND.
AND I KNOW THE TERROR HE MUST HAVE FELT, KNOWING THAT, AS HIS LIFE DRAINED AWAY, HE WAS DOOMED TO WANDER SOME INBETWEEN PLACE FOR AN ETERNITY.
ALL FOR THE WANT OF A SWORD IN HIS HAND.

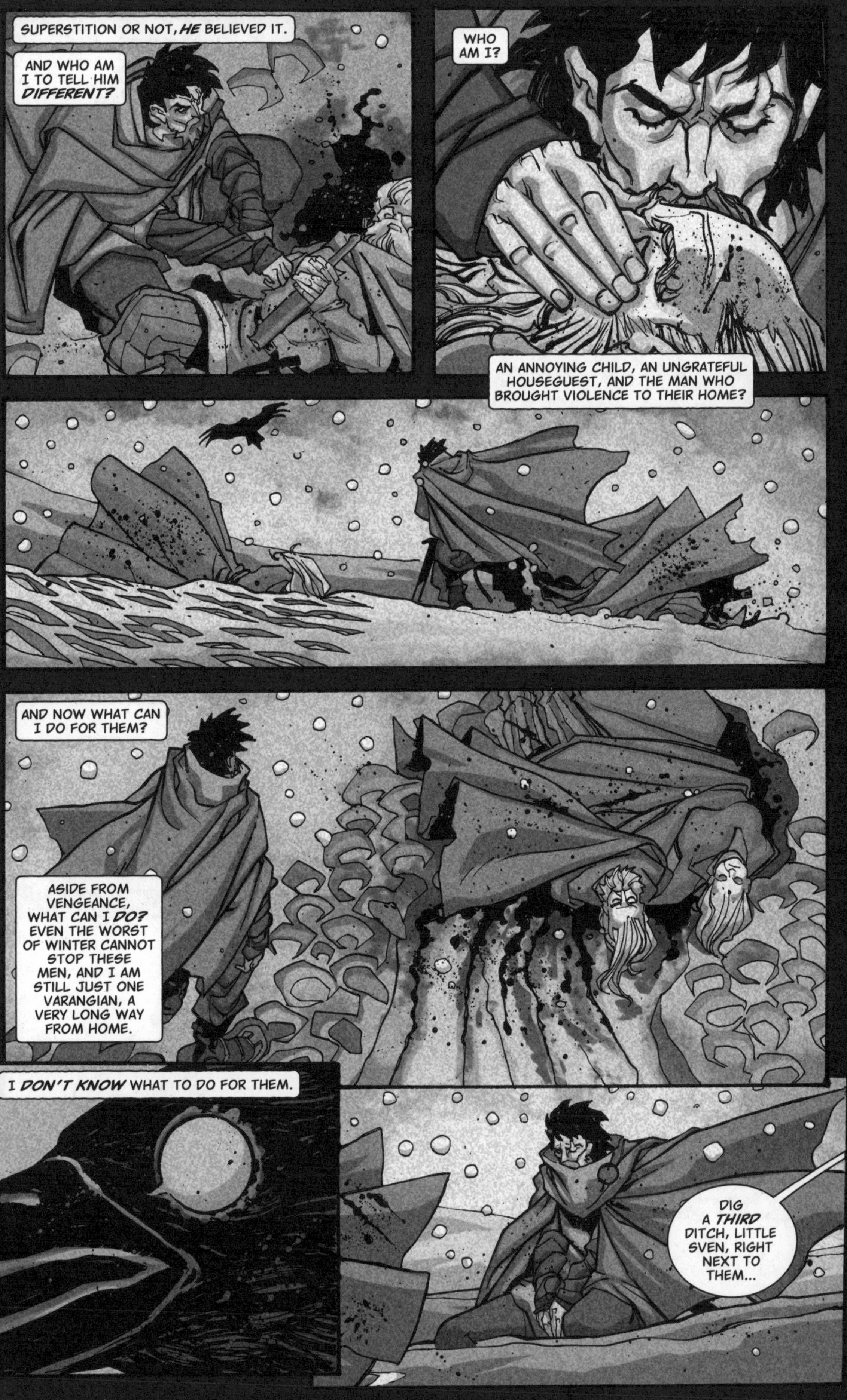
SUPERSTITION OR NOT, *HE* BELIEVED IT.
AND WHO AM I TO TELL HIM *DIFFERENT?*
WHO AM I?
AN ANNOYING CHILD, AN UNGRATEFUL HOUSEGUEST, AND THE MAN WHO BROUGHT VIOLENCE TO THEIR HOME?
AND NOW WHAT CAN I DO FOR THEM?
ASIDE FROM VENGEANCE, WHAT CAN I *DO?* EVEN THE WORST OF WINTER CANNOT STOP THESE MEN, AND I AM STILL JUST ONE VARANGIAN, A VERY LONG WAY FROM HOME.
I *DON'T KNOW* WHAT TO DO FOR THEM.
DIG A *THIRD* DITCH, LITTLE SVEN, RIGHT NEXT TO THEM...

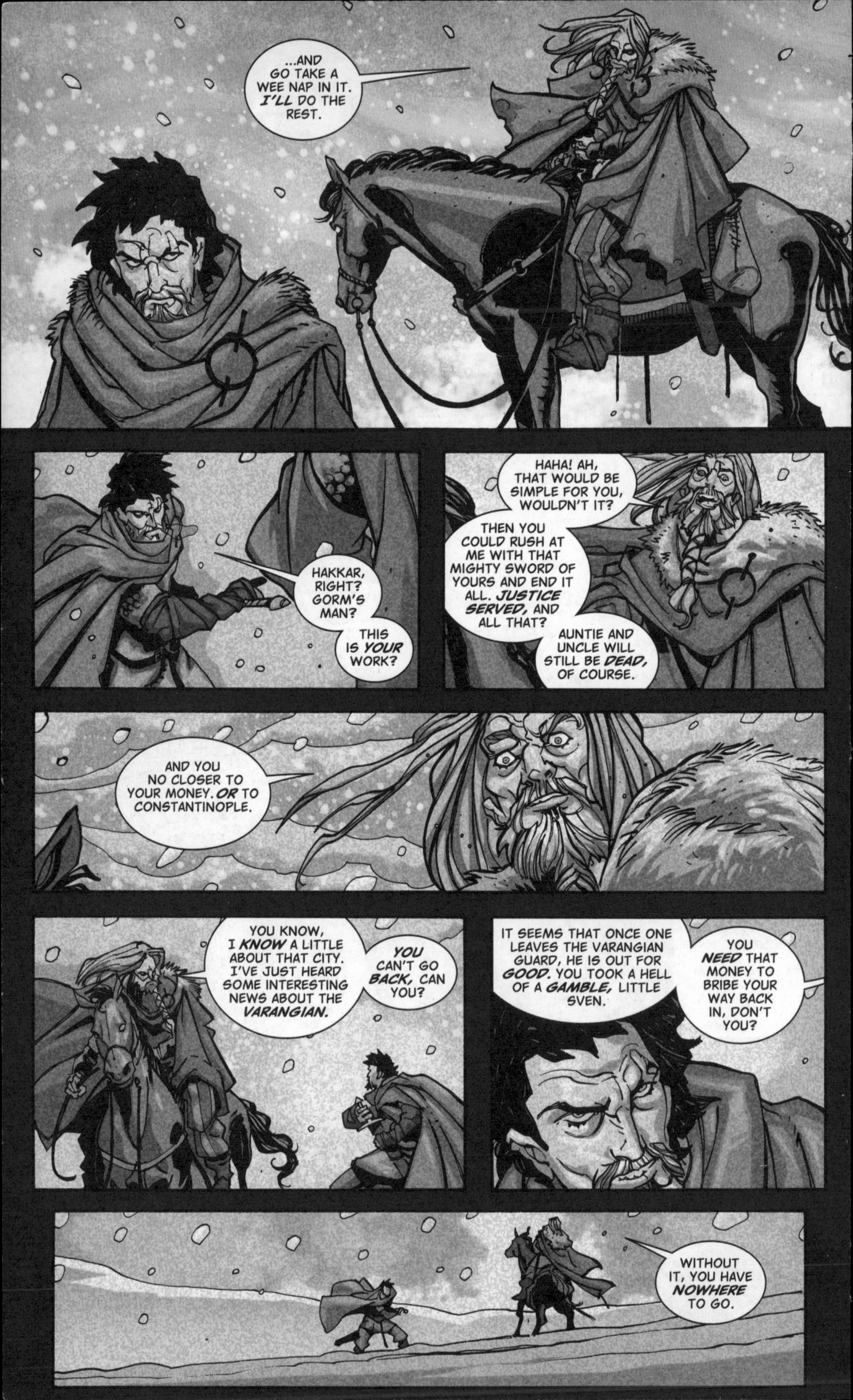

...AND GO TAKE A WEE NAP IN IT. *I'LL* DO THE REST.
HAKKAR, RIGHT? GORM'S MAN?
THIS IS *YOUR* WORK?
HAHA! AH, THAT WOULD BE SIMPLE FOR YOU, WOULDN'T IT?
THEN YOU COULD RUSH AT ME WITH THAT MIGHTY SWORD OF YOURS AND END IT ALL. *JUSTICE SERVED,* AND ALL THAT?
AUNTIE AND UNCLE WILL STILL BE *DEAD,* OF COURSE.
AND YOU NO CLOSER TO YOUR MONEY. *OR* TO CONSTANTINOPLE.
YOU KNOW, I *KNOW* A LITTLE ABOUT THAT CITY. I'VE JUST HEARD SOME INTERESTING NEWS ABOUT THE *VARANGIAN.*
YOU CAN'T GO *BACK,* CAN YOU?
IT SEEMS THAT ONCE ONE LEAVES THE VARANGIAN GUARD, HE IS OUT FOR *GOOD.* YOU TOOK A HELL OF A *GAMBLE,* LITTLE SVEN.
YOU *NEED* THAT MONEY TO BRIBE YOUR WAY BACK IN, DON'T YOU?
WITHOUT IT, YOU HAVE *NOWHERE* TO GO.

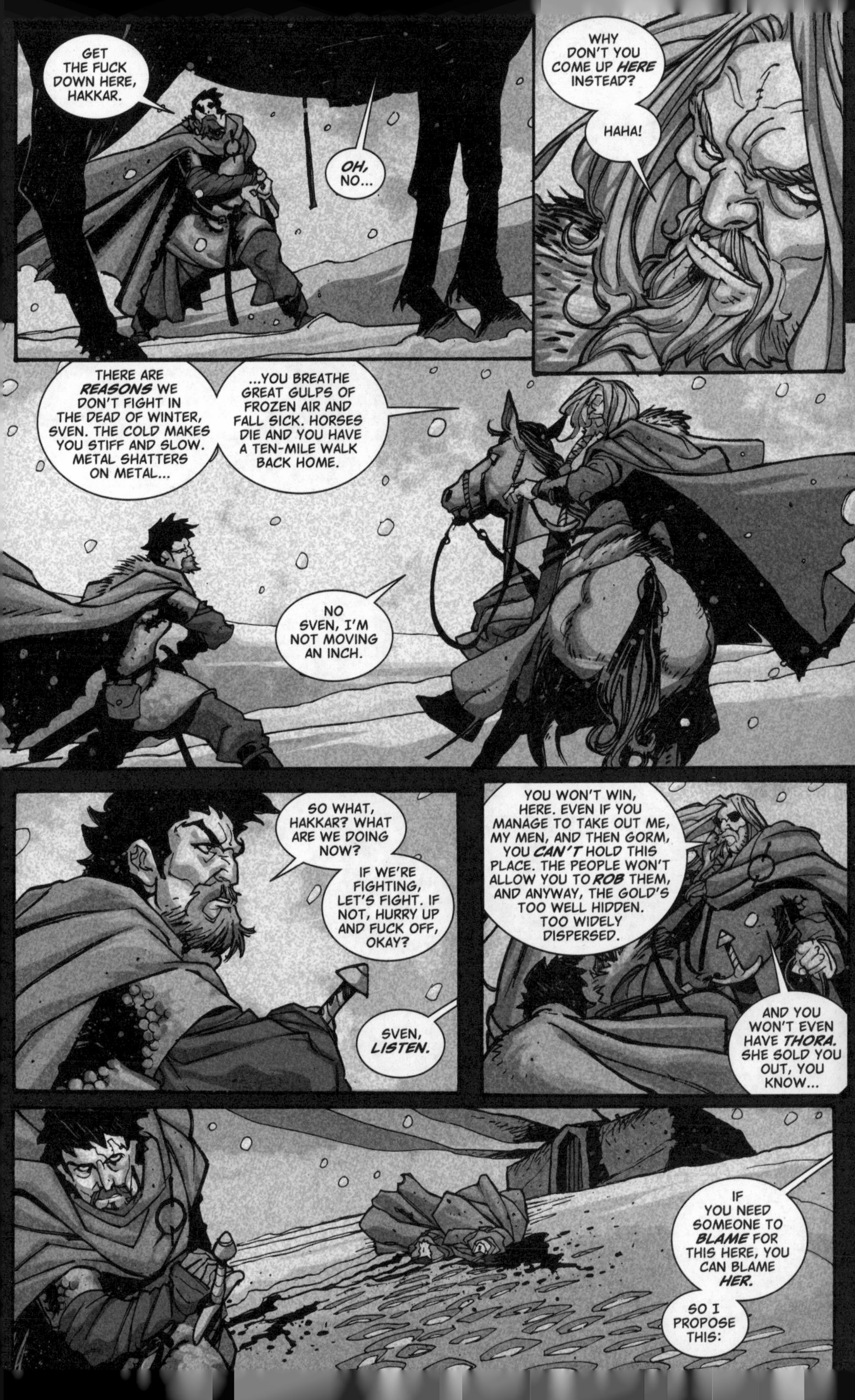
GET THE FUCK DOWN HERE, HAKKAR.
OH, NO...
WHY DON'T YOU COME UP HERE INSTEAD?
HAHA!
THERE ARE REASONS WE DON'T FIGHT IN THE DEAD OF WINTER, SVEN. THE COLD MAKES YOU STIFF AND SLOW. METAL SHATTERS ON METAL...
...YOU BREATHE GREAT GULPS OF FROZEN AIR AND FALL SICK. HORSES DIE AND YOU HAVE A TEN-MILE WALK BACK HOME.
NO SVEN, I'M NOT MOVING AN INCH.
SO WHAT, HAKKAR? WHAT ARE WE DOING NOW?
IF WE'RE FIGHTING, LET'S FIGHT. IF NOT, HURRY UP AND FUCK OFF, OKAY?
SVEN, LISTEN.
YOU WON'T WIN, HERE. EVEN IF YOU MANAGE TO TAKE OUT ME, MY MEN, AND THEN GORM, YOU CAN'T HOLD THIS PLACE. THE PEOPLE WON'T ALLOW YOU TO ROB THEM, AND ANYWAY, THE GOLD'S TOO WELL HIDDEN. TOO WIDELY DISPERSED.
AND YOU WON'T EVEN HAVE THORA. SHE SOLD YOU OUT, YOU KNOW...
IF YOU NEED SOMEONE TO BLAME FOR THIS HERE, YOU CAN BLAME HER.
SO I PROPOSE THIS:

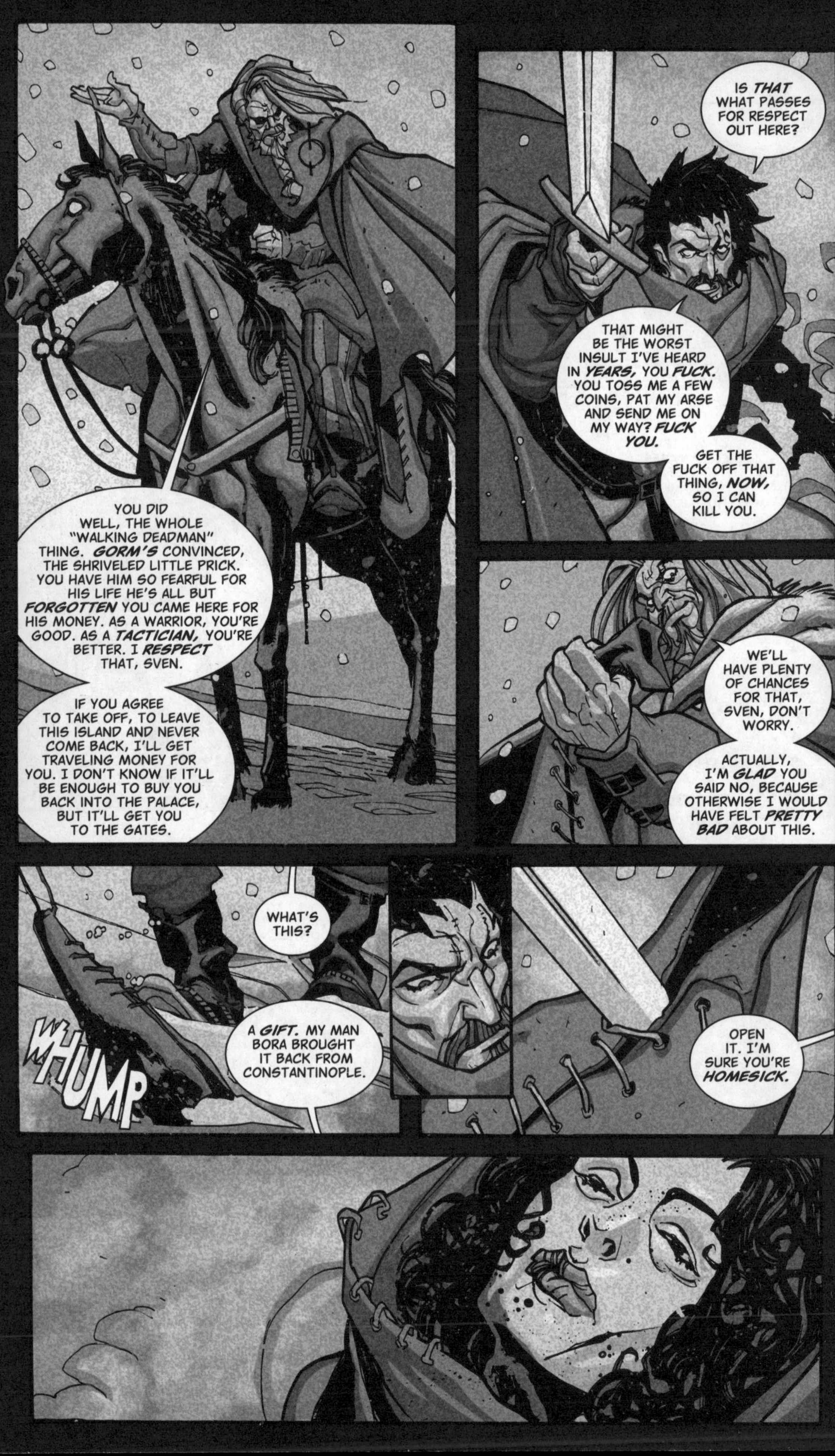
YOU DID WELL, THE WHOLE "WALKING DEADMAN" THING. GORM'S CONVINCED, THE SHRIVELED LITTLE PRICK. YOU HAVE HIM SO FEARFUL FOR HIS LIFE HE'S ALL BUT FORGOTTEN YOU CAME HERE FOR HIS MONEY. AS A WARRIOR, YOU'RE GOOD. AS A TACTICIAN, YOU'RE BETTER. I RESPECT THAT, SVEN.
IF YOU AGREE TO TAKE OFF, TO LEAVE THIS ISLAND AND NEVER COME BACK, I'LL GET TRAVELING MONEY FOR YOU. I DON'T KNOW IF IT'LL BE ENOUGH TO BUY YOU BACK INTO THE PALACE, BUT IT'LL GET YOU TO THE GATES.
IS THAT WHAT PASSES FOR RESPECT OUT HERE?
THAT MIGHT BE THE WORST INSULT I'VE HEARD IN YEARS, YOU FUCK. YOU TOSS ME A FEW COINS, PAT MY ARSE AND SEND ME ON MY WAY? FUCK YOU.
GET THE FUCK OFF THAT THING, NOW, SO I CAN KILL YOU.
WE'LL HAVE PLENTY OF CHANCES FOR THAT, SVEN, DON'T WORRY.
ACTUALLY, I'M GLAD YOU SAID NO, BECAUSE OTHERWISE I WOULD HAVE FELT PRETTY BAD ABOUT THIS.
WHUMP
WHAT'S THIS?
A GIFT. MY MAN BORA BROUGHT IT BACK FROM CONSTANTINOPLE.
OPEN IT. I'M SURE YOU'RE HOMESICK.

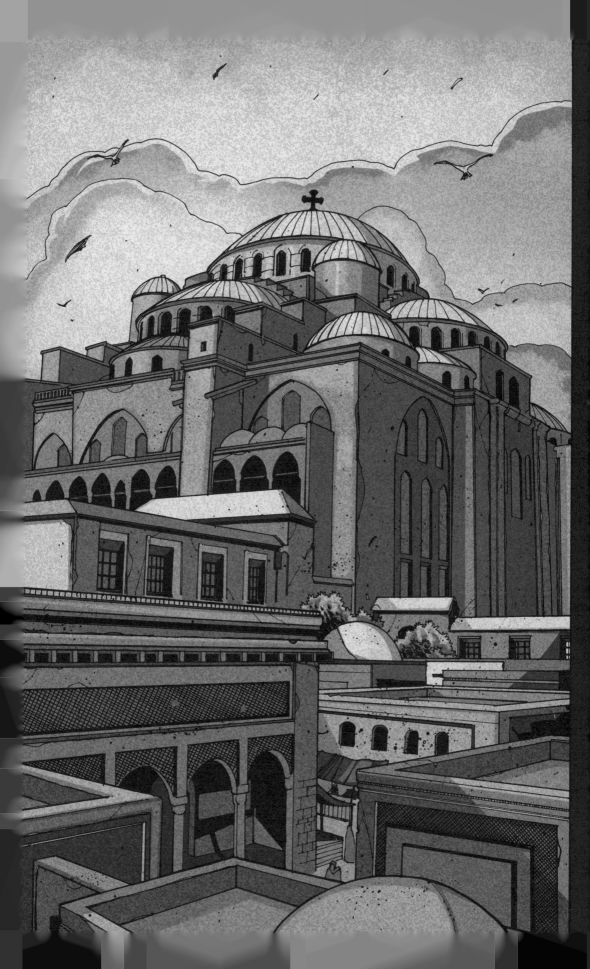

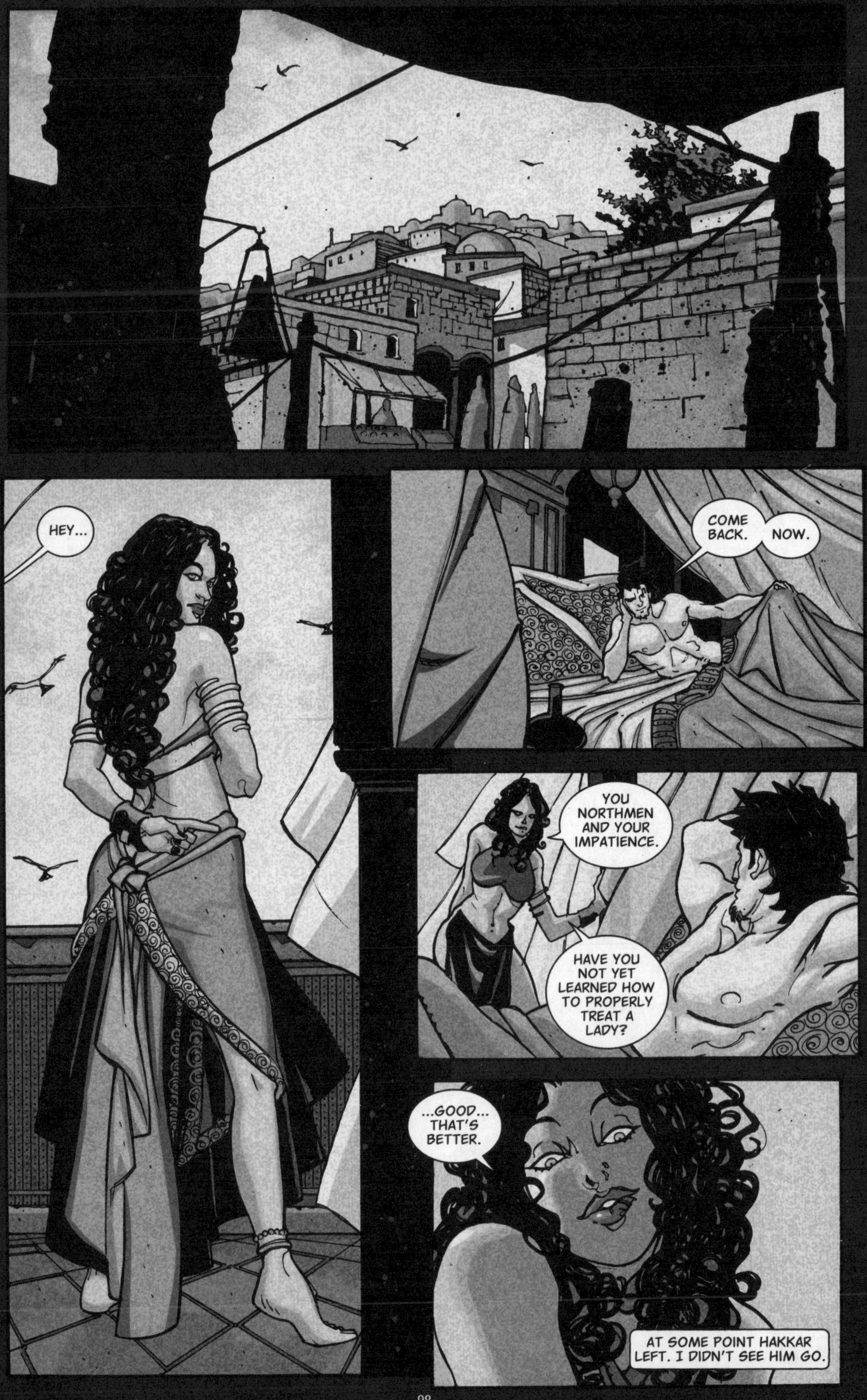
HEY...
COME BACK.
NOW.
YOU NORTHMEN AND YOUR IMPATIENCE.
HAVE YOU NOT YET LEARNED HOW TO PROPERLY TREAT A LADY?
...GOOD... THAT'S BETTER.
AT SOME POINT HAKKAR LEFT. I DIDN'T SEE HIM GO.

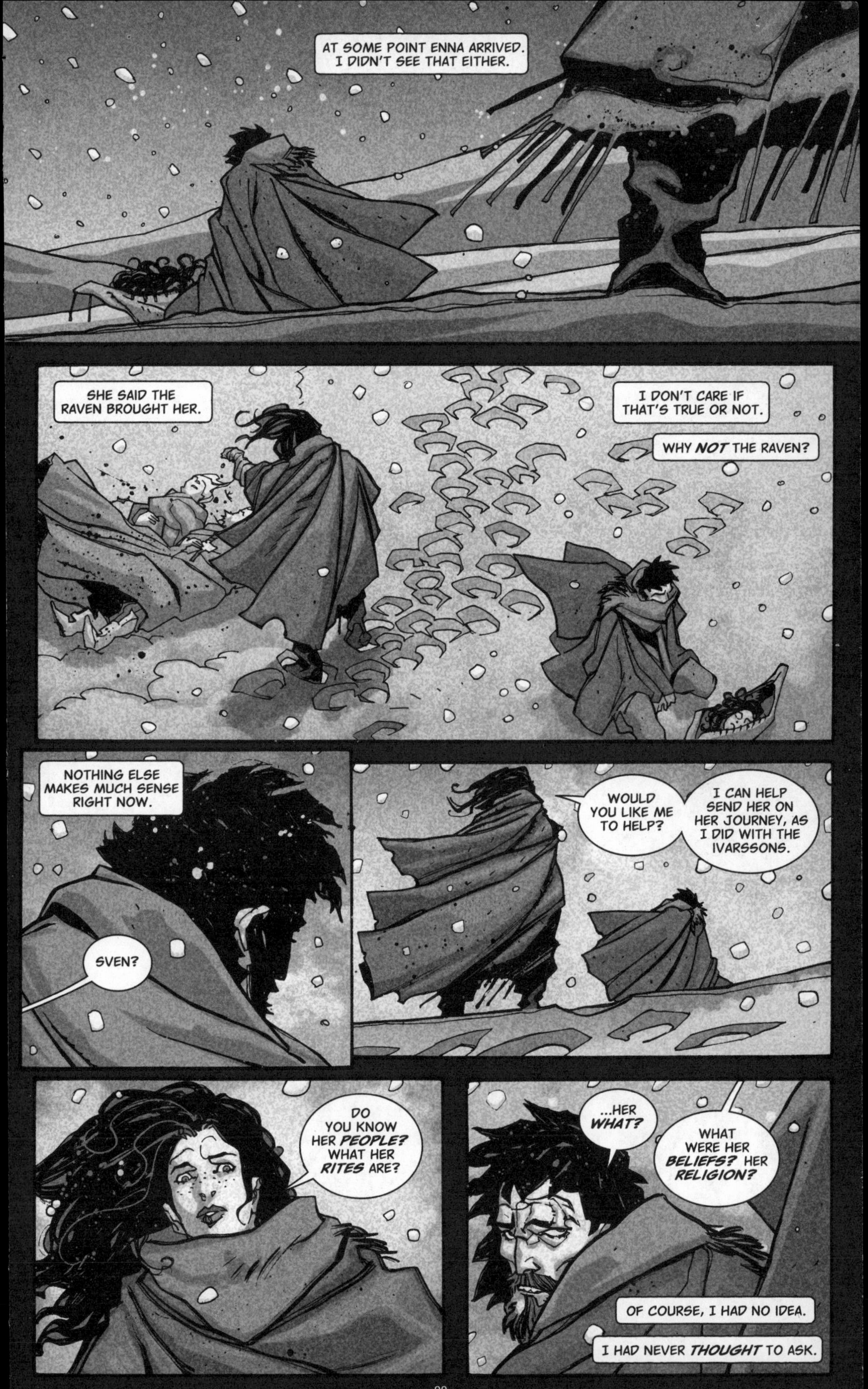
AT SOME POINT ENNA ARRIVED. I DIDN'T SEE THAT EITHER.
SHE SAID THE RAVEN BROUGHT HER.
I DON'T CARE IF THAT'S TRUE OR NOT.
WHY *NOT* THE RAVEN?
NOTHING ELSE MAKES MUCH SENSE RIGHT NOW.
SVEN?
WOULD YOU LIKE ME TO HELP?
I CAN HELP SEND HER ON HER JOURNEY, AS I DID WITH THE IVARSSONS.
DO YOU KNOW HER *PEOPLE?* WHAT HER *RITES* ARE?
...HER *WHAT?*
WHAT WERE HER *BELIEFS?* HER *RELIGION?*
OF COURSE, I HAD NO IDEA.
I HAD NEVER *THOUGHT* TO ASK.

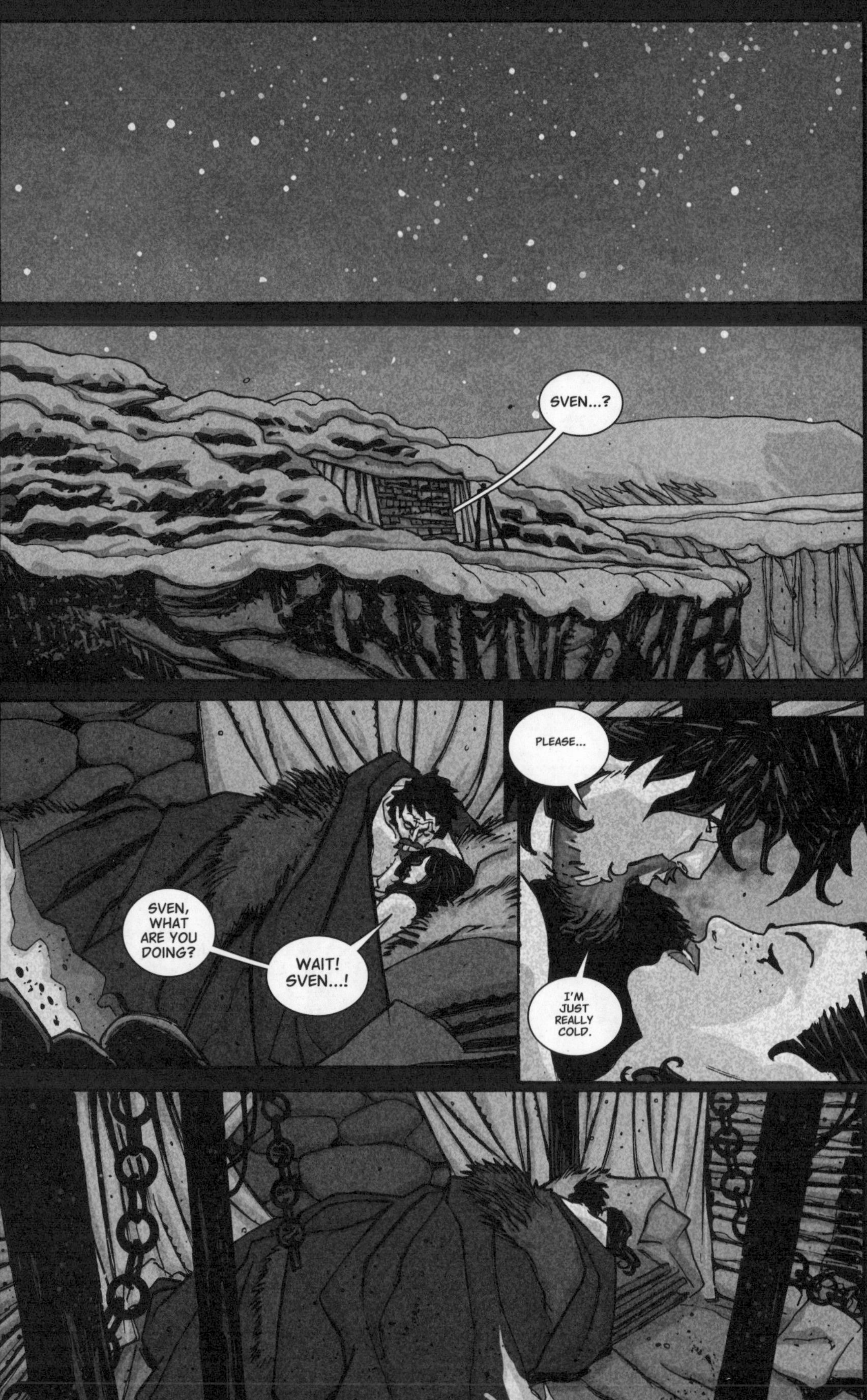
SVEN...?
SVEN, WHAT ARE YOU DOING?
WAIT! SVEN...!
PLEASE...
I'M JUST REALLY COLD.

5 The Land of the Leal

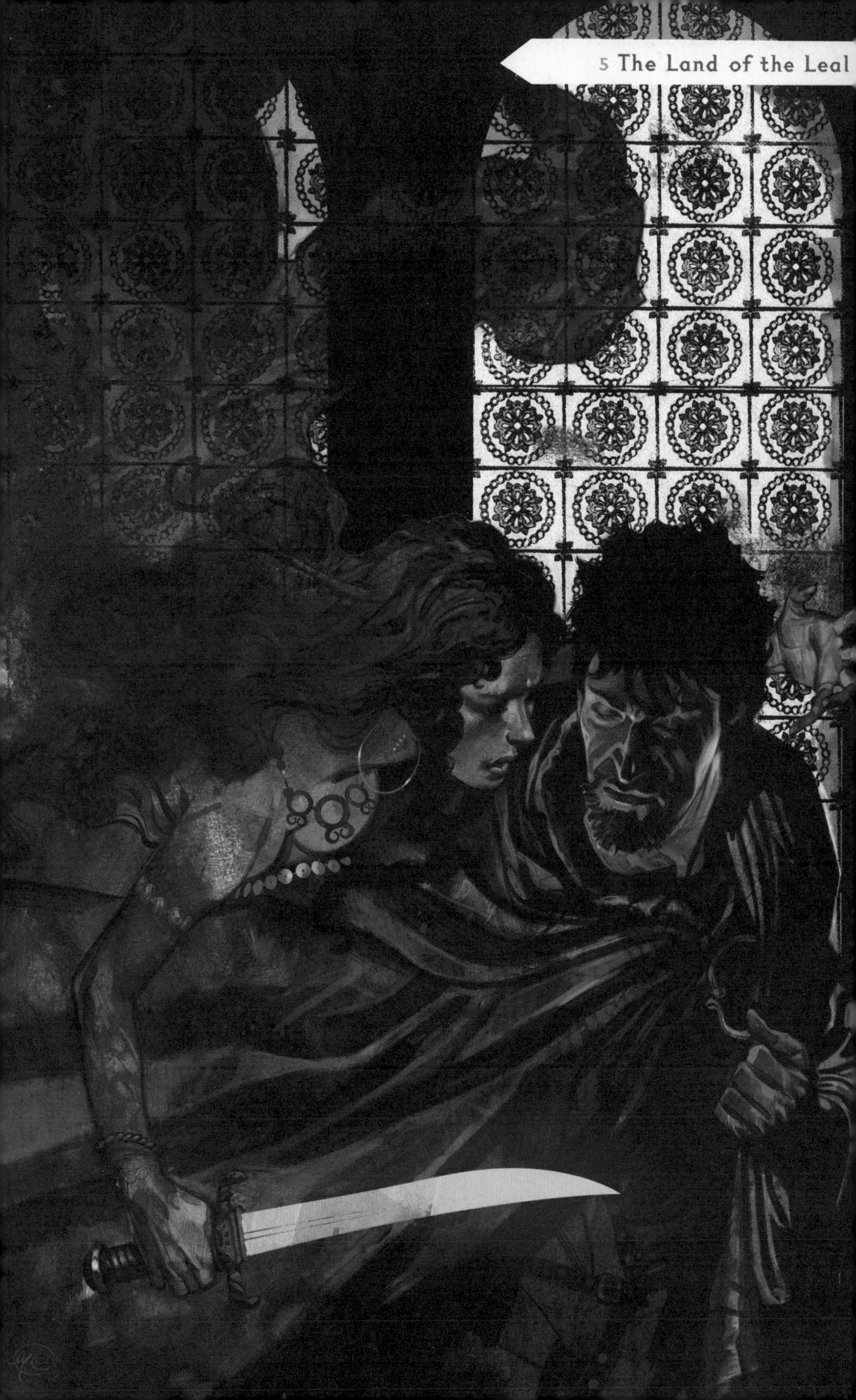

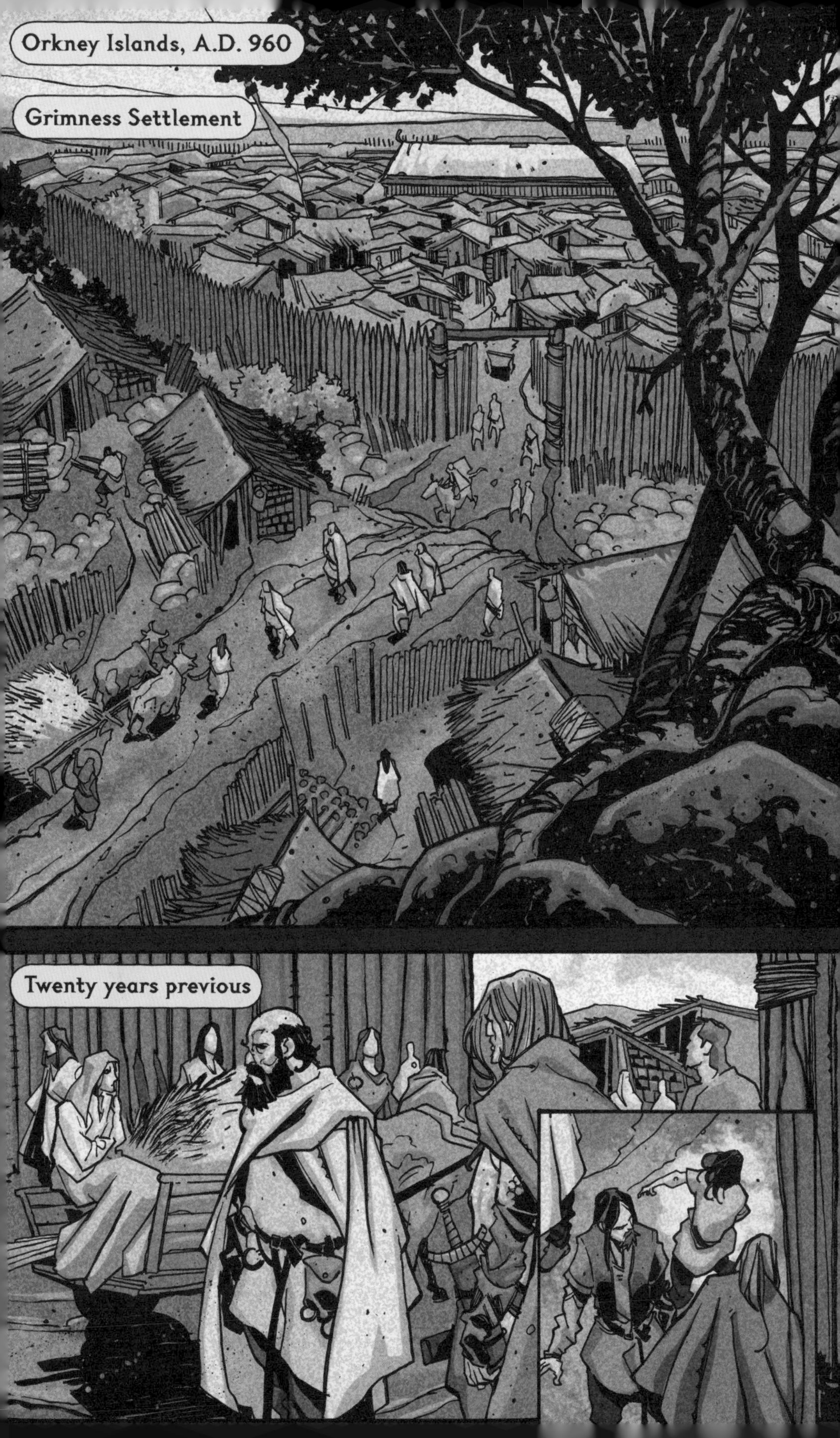
Orkney Islands, A.D. 960
Grimness Settlement
Twenty years previous

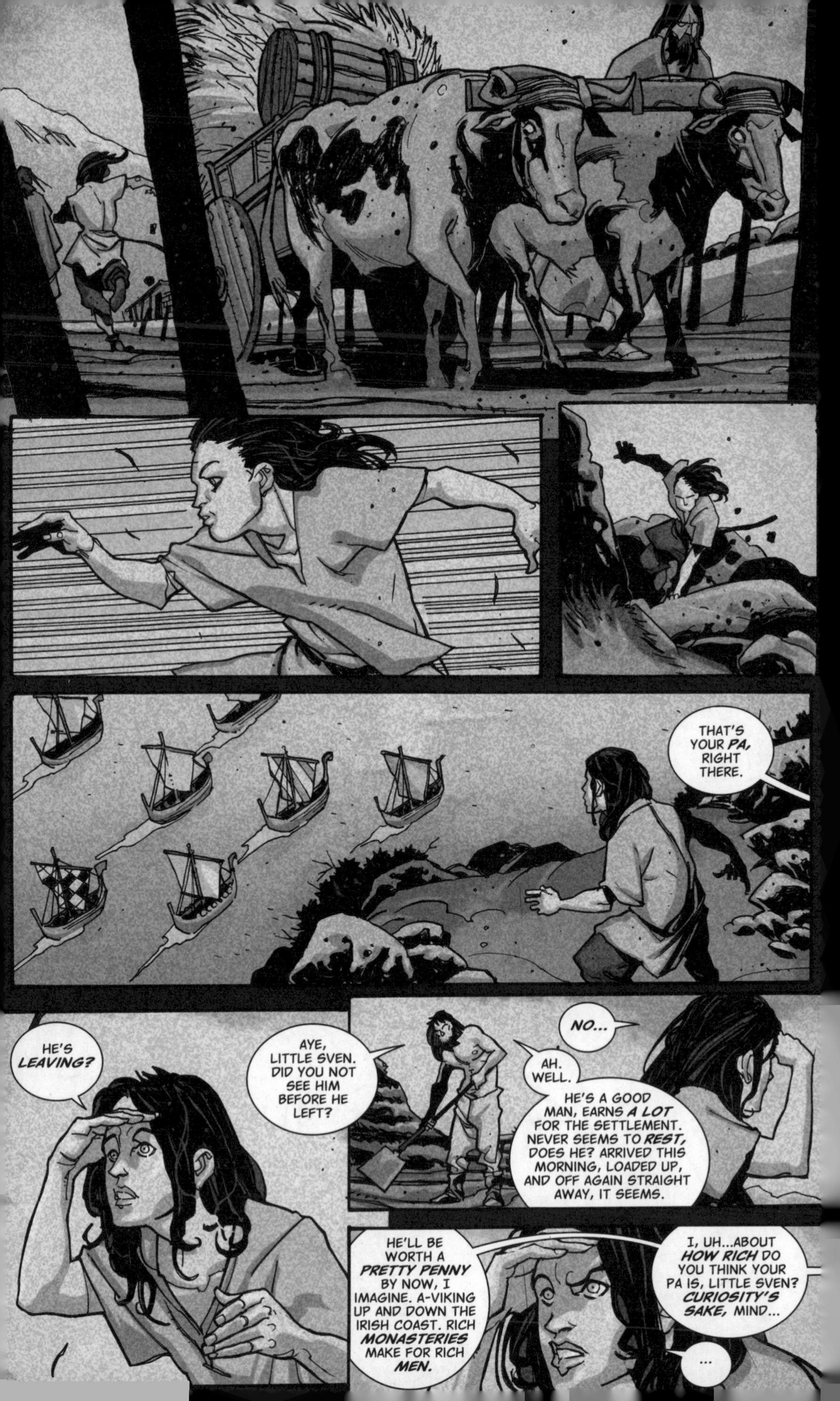
THAT'S YOUR PA, RIGHT THERE.
HE'S LEAVING?
AYE, LITTLE SVEN. DID YOU NOT SEE HIM BEFORE HE LEFT?
NO...
AH. WELL.
HE'S A GOOD MAN, EARNS A LOT FOR THE SETTLEMENT. NEVER SEEMS TO REST, DOES HE? ARRIVED THIS MORNING, LOADED UP, AND OFF AGAIN STRAIGHT AWAY, IT SEEMS.
HE'LL BE WORTH A PRETTY PENNY BY NOW, I IMAGINE. A-VIKING UP AND DOWN THE IRISH COAST. RICH MONASTERIES MAKE FOR RICH MEN.
I, UH...ABOUT HOW RICH DO YOU THINK YOUR PA IS, LITTLE SVEN? CURIOSITY'S SAKE, MIND...
...

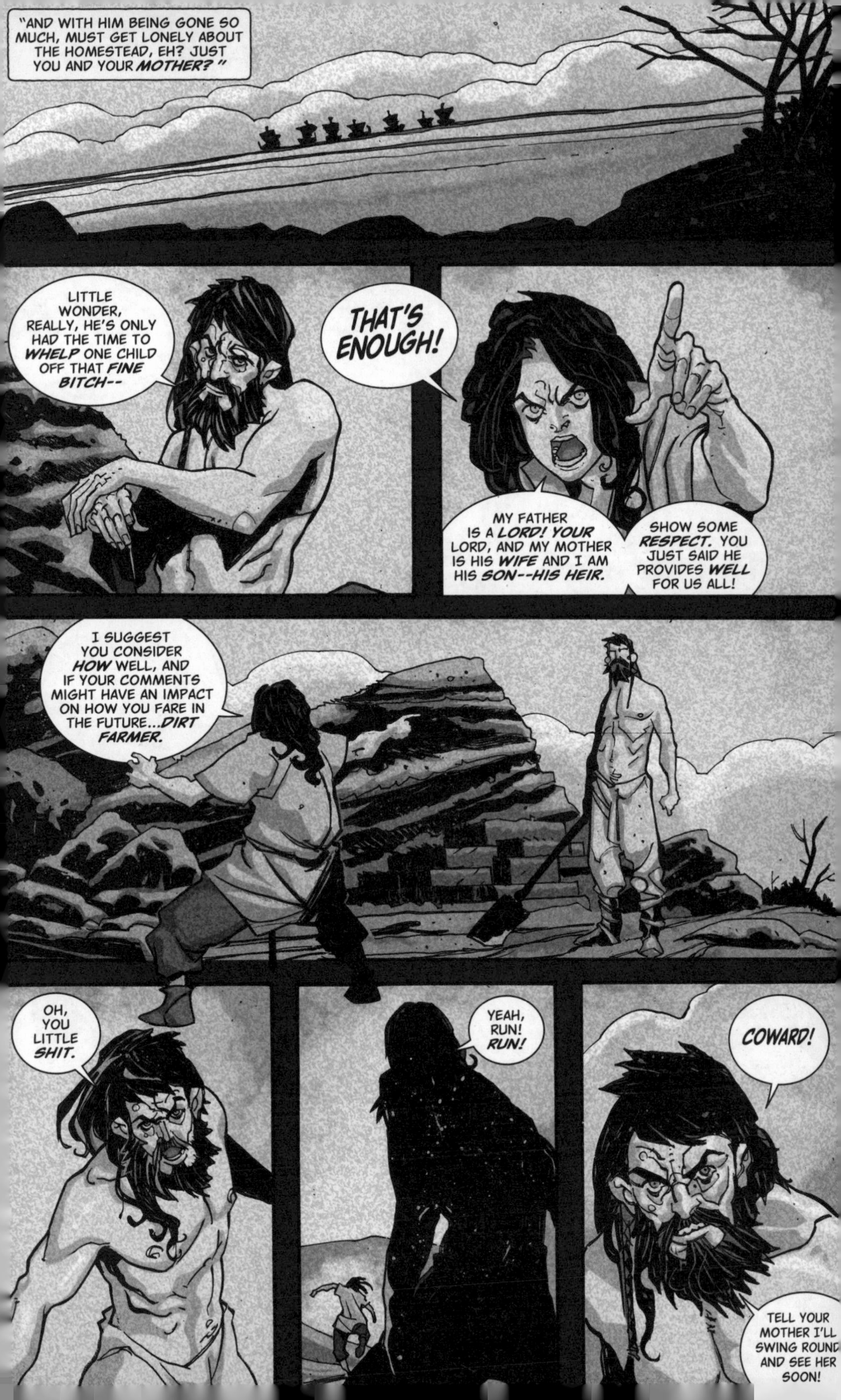
"AND WITH HIM BEING GONE SO MUCH, MUST GET LONELY ABOUT THE HOMESTEAD, EH? JUST YOU AND YOUR MOTHER?"
LITTLE WONDER, REALLY, HE'S ONLY HAD THE TIME TO WHELP ONE CHILD OFF THAT FINE BITCH--
THAT'S ENOUGH!
MY FATHER IS A LORD! YOUR LORD, AND MY MOTHER IS HIS WIFE AND I AM HIS SON--HIS HEIR.
SHOW SOME RESPECT. YOU JUST SAID HE PROVIDES WELL FOR US ALL!
I SUGGEST YOU CONSIDER HOW WELL, AND IF YOUR COMMENTS MIGHT HAVE AN IMPACT ON HOW YOU FARE IN THE FUTURE...DIRT FARMER.
OH, YOU LITTLE SHIT.
YEAH, RUN! RUN!
COWARD!
TELL YOUR MOTHER I'LL SWING ROUND AND SEE HER SOON!

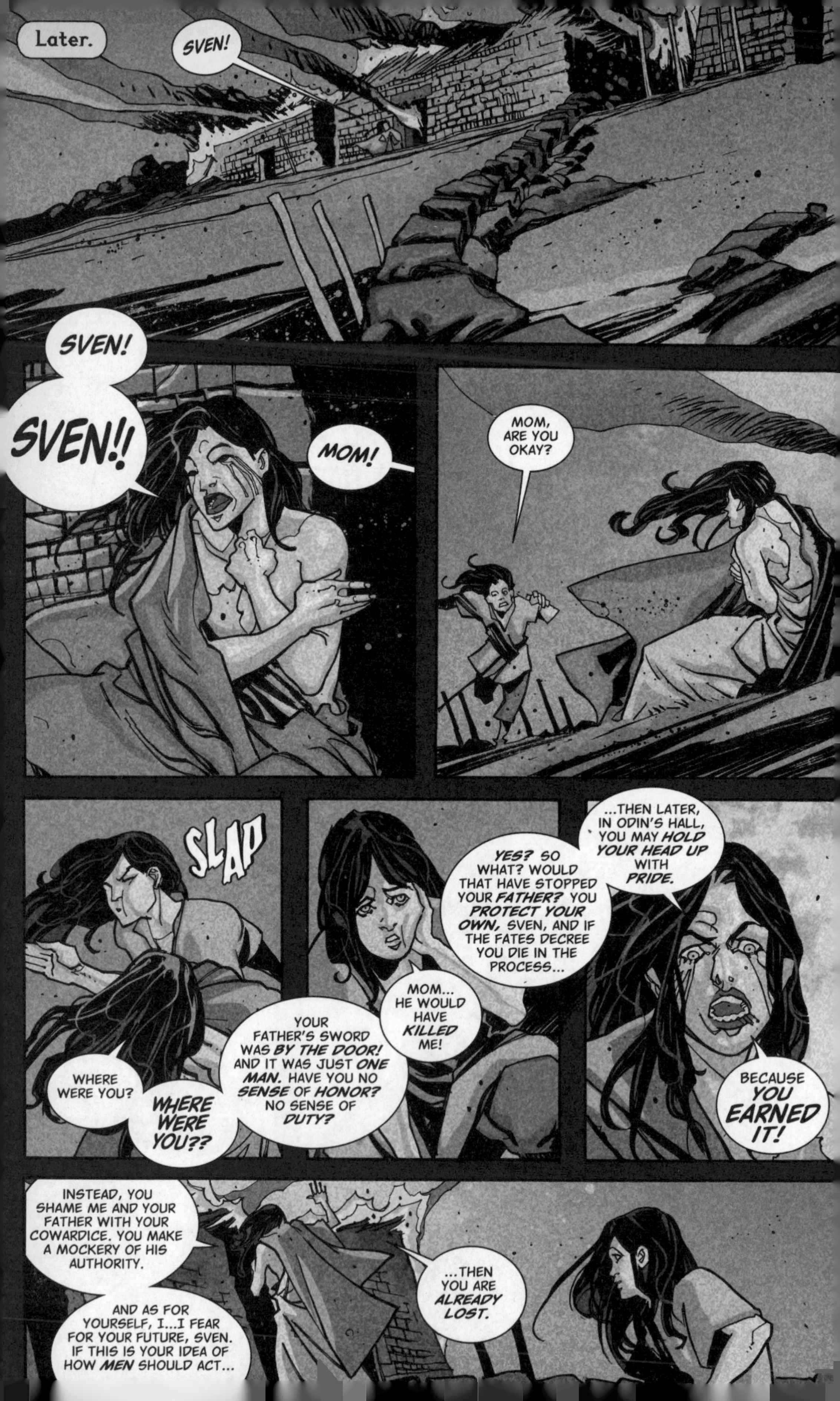
Later.
SVEN!
SVEN!
SVEN!!
MOM!
MOM, ARE YOU OKAY?
SLAP
WHERE WERE YOU?
WHERE WERE YOU??
YOUR FATHER'S SWORD WAS BY THE DOOR! AND IT WAS JUST ONE MAN. HAVE YOU NO SENSE OF HONOR? NO SENSE OF DUTY?
MOM... HE WOULD HAVE KILLED ME!
YES? SO WHAT? WOULD THAT HAVE STOPPED YOUR FATHER? YOU PROTECT YOUR OWN, SVEN, AND IF THE FATES DECREE YOU DIE IN THE PROCESS...
...THEN LATER, IN ODIN'S HALL, YOU MAY HOLD YOUR HEAD UP WITH PRIDE.
BECAUSE YOU EARNED IT!
INSTEAD, YOU SHAME ME AND YOUR FATHER WITH YOUR COWARDICE. YOU MAKE A MOCKERY OF HIS AUTHORITY.
AND AS FOR YOURSELF, I...I FEAR FOR YOUR FUTURE, SVEN. IF THIS IS YOUR IDEA OF HOW MEN SHOULD ACT...
...THEN YOU ARE ALREADY LOST.

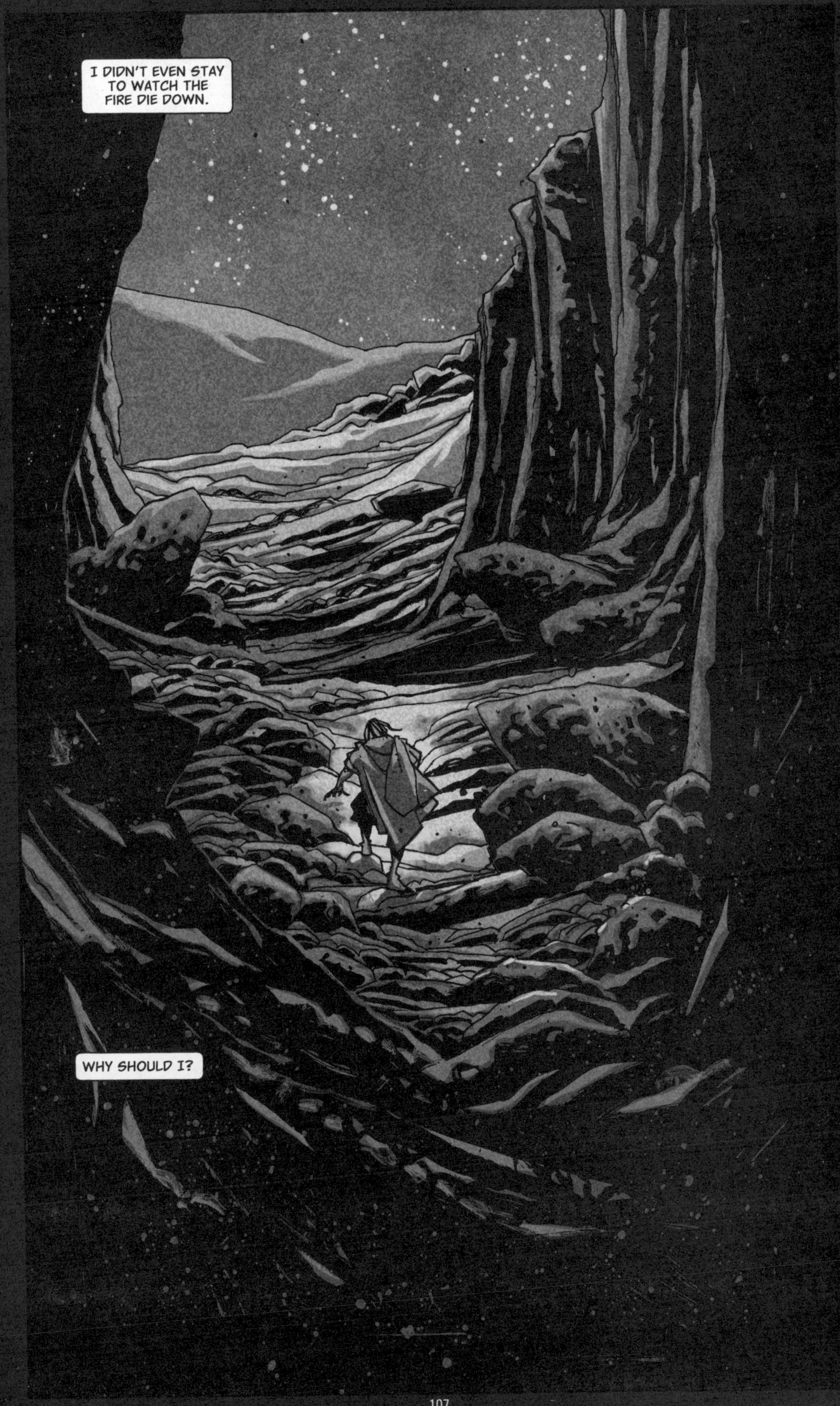
I DIDN'T EVEN STAY TO WATCH THE FIRE DIE DOWN.
WHY SHOULD I?

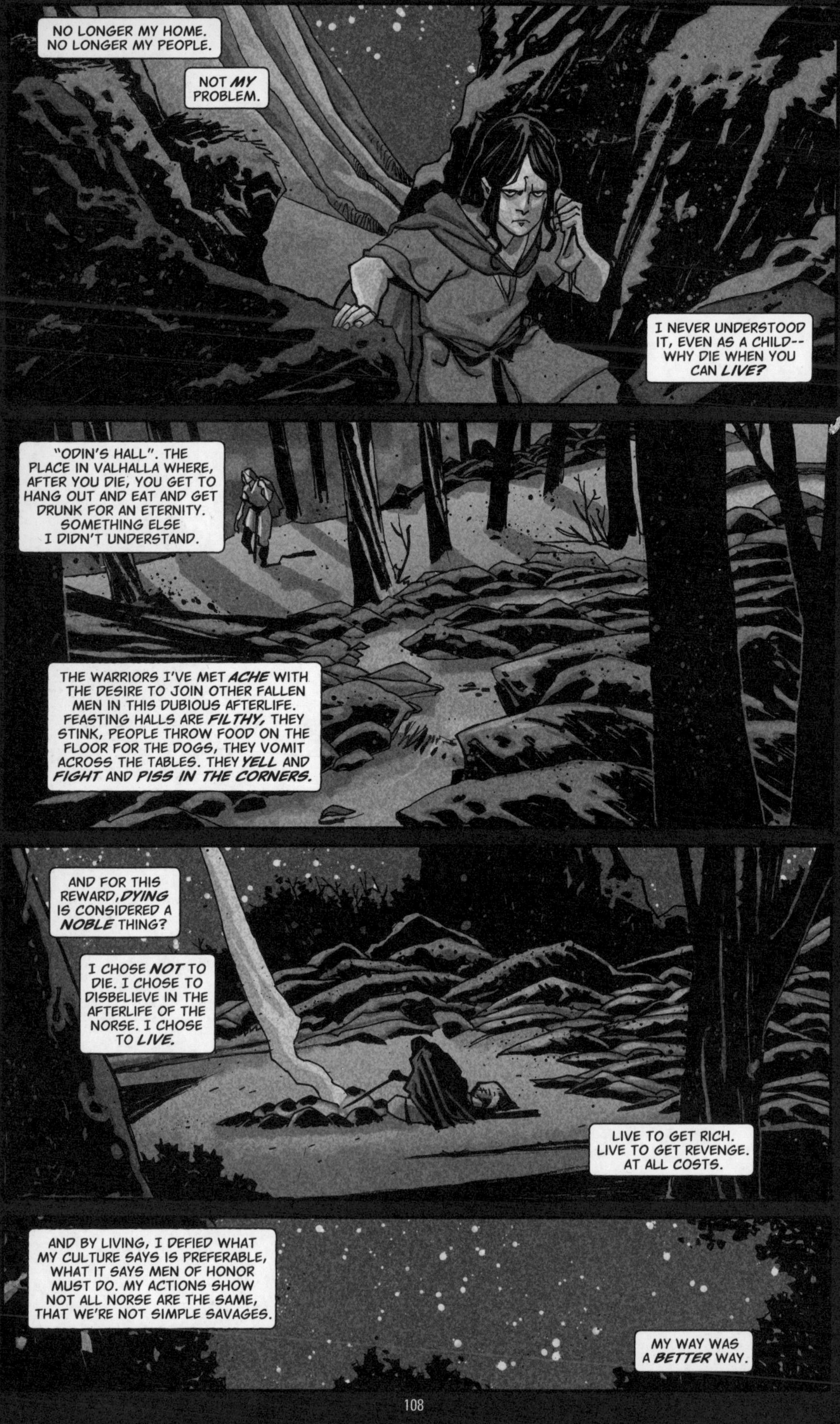
NO LONGER MY HOME.
NO LONGER MY PEOPLE.
NOT *MY* PROBLEM.
I NEVER UNDERSTOOD IT, EVEN AS A CHILD-- WHY DIE WHEN YOU CAN *LIVE?*
"ODIN'S HALL". THE PLACE IN VALHALLA WHERE, AFTER YOU DIE, YOU GET TO HANG OUT AND EAT AND GET DRUNK FOR AN ETERNITY. SOMETHING ELSE I DIDN'T UNDERSTAND.
THE WARRIORS I'VE MET *ACHE* WITH THE DESIRE TO JOIN OTHER FALLEN MEN IN THIS DUBIOUS AFTERLIFE. FEASTING HALLS ARE *FILTHY,* THEY STINK, PEOPLE THROW FOOD ON THE FLOOR FOR THE DOGS, THEY VOMIT ACROSS THE TABLES. THEY *YELL* AND *FIGHT* AND *PISS IN THE CORNERS.*
AND FOR THIS REWARD, *DYING* IS CONSIDERED A *NOBLE* THING?
I CHOSE *NOT* TO DIE. I CHOSE TO DISBELIEVE IN THE AFTERLIFE OF THE NORSE. I CHOSE TO *LIVE.*
LIVE TO GET RICH. LIVE TO GET REVENGE. AT ALL COSTS.
AND BY LIVING, I DEFIED WHAT MY CULTURE SAYS IS PREFERABLE, WHAT IT SAYS MEN OF HONOR MUST DO. MY ACTIONS SHOW NOT ALL NORSE ARE THE SAME, THAT WE'RE NOT SIMPLE SAVAGES.
MY WAY WAS A *BETTER* WAY.

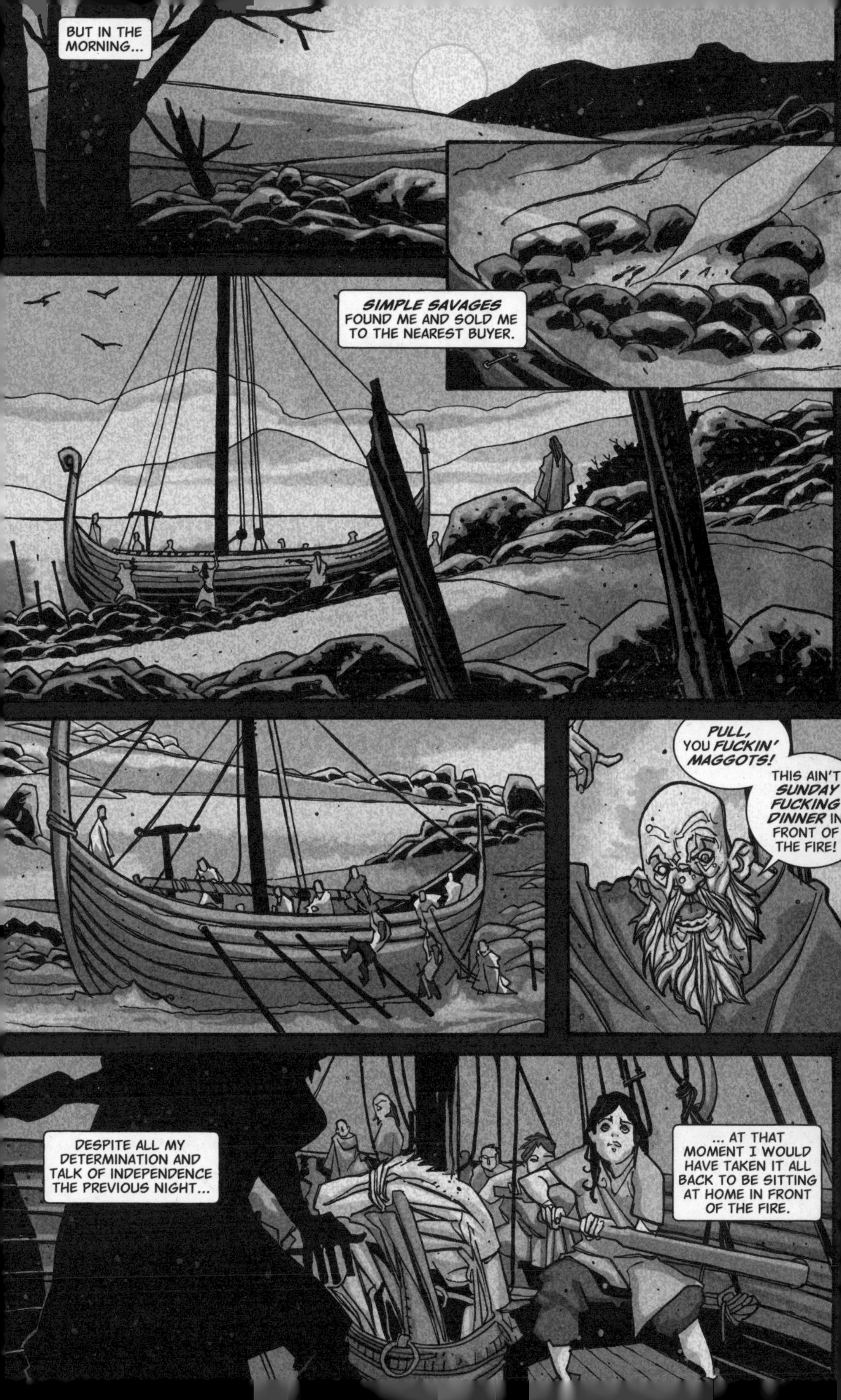
BUT IN THE MORNING...
SIMPLE SAVAGES FOUND ME AND SOLD ME TO THE NEAREST BUYER.
PULL, YOU FUCKIN' MAGGOTS!
THIS AIN'T SUNDAY FUCKING DINNER IN FRONT OF THE FIRE!
DESPITE ALL MY DETERMINATION AND TALK OF INDEPENDENCE THE PREVIOUS NIGHT...
... AT THAT MOMENT I WOULD HAVE TAKEN IT ALL BACK TO BE SITTING AT HOME IN FRONT OF THE FIRE.

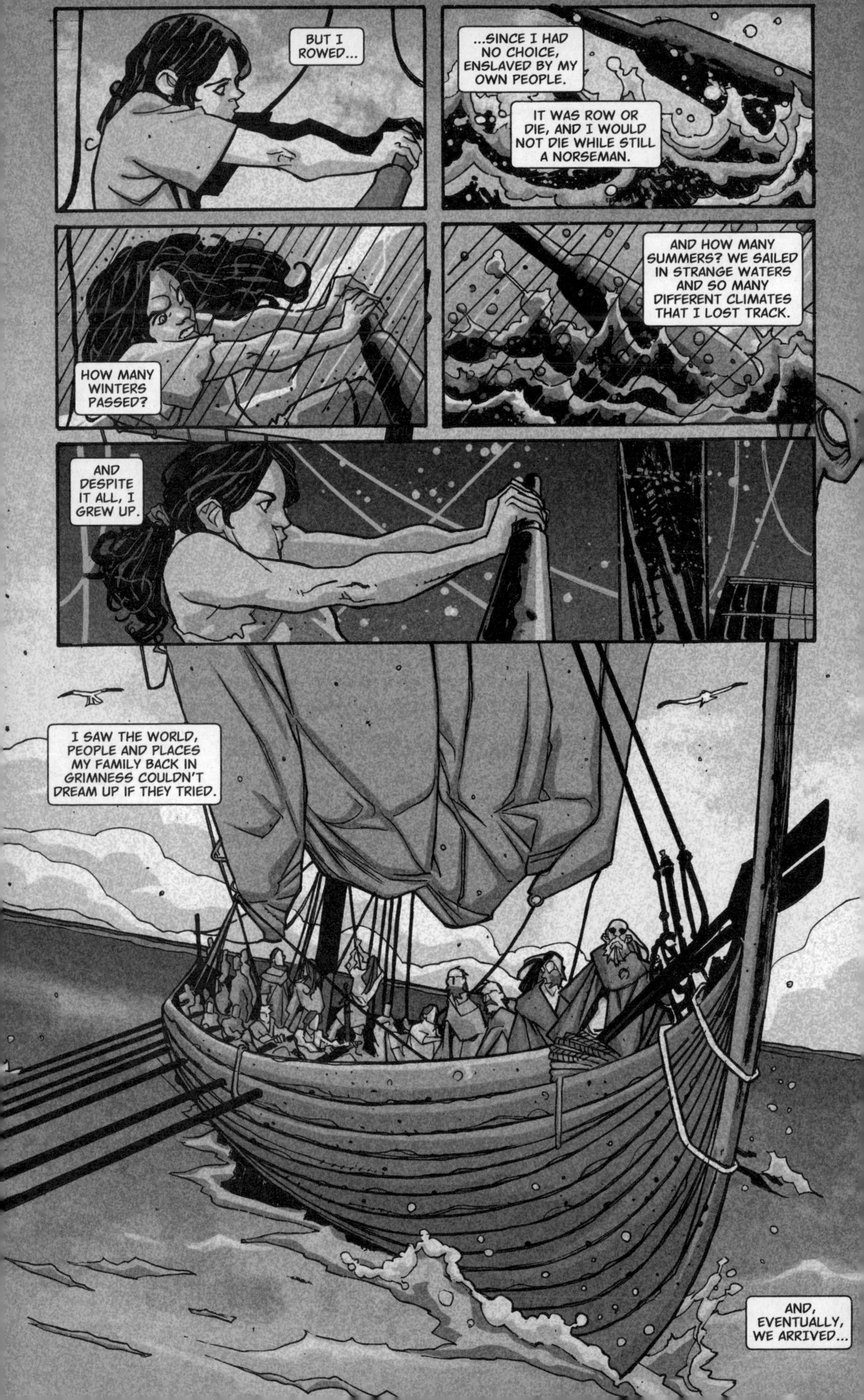
BUT I ROWED...
...SINCE I HAD NO CHOICE, ENSLAVED BY MY OWN PEOPLE.
IT WAS ROW OR DIE, AND I WOULD NOT DIE WHILE STILL A NORSEMAN.
HOW MANY WINTERS PASSED?
AND HOW MANY SUMMERS? WE SAILED IN STRANGE WATERS AND SO MANY DIFFERENT CLIMATES THAT I LOST TRACK.
AND DESPITE IT ALL, I GREW UP.
I SAW THE WORLD, PEOPLE AND PLACES MY FAMILY BACK IN GRIMNESS COULDN'T DREAM UP IF THEY TRIED.
AND, EVENTUALLY, WE ARRIVED...

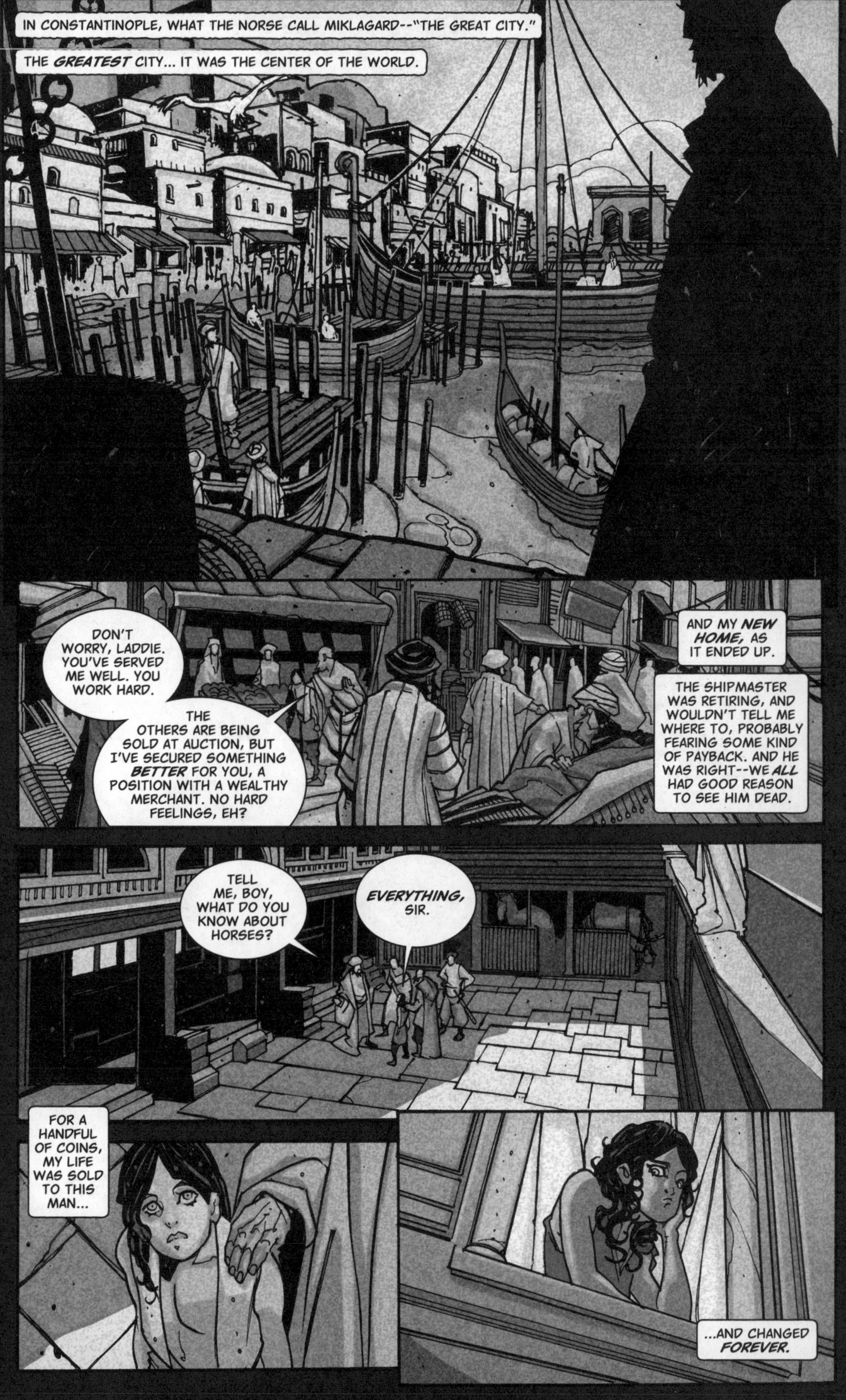

IN CONSTANTINOPLE, WHAT THE NORSE CALL MIKLAGARD--"THE GREAT CITY."
THE *GREATEST* CITY... IT WAS THE CENTER OF THE WORLD.
DON'T WORRY, LADDIE. YOU'VE SERVED ME WELL. YOU WORK HARD.
THE OTHERS ARE BEING SOLD AT AUCTION, BUT I'VE SECURED SOMETHING *BETTER* FOR YOU, A POSITION WITH A WEALTHY MERCHANT. NO HARD FEELINGS, EH?
AND MY *NEW HOME,* AS IT ENDED UP.
THE SHIPMASTER WAS RETIRING, AND WOULDN'T TELL ME WHERE TO, PROBABLY FEARING SOME KIND OF PAYBACK. AND HE WAS RIGHT--WE *ALL* HAD GOOD REASON TO SEE HIM DEAD.
TELL ME, BOY, WHAT DO YOU KNOW ABOUT HORSES?
EVERYTHING, SIR.
FOR A HANDFUL OF COINS, MY LIFE WAS SOLD TO THIS MAN...
...AND CHANGED *FOREVER.*

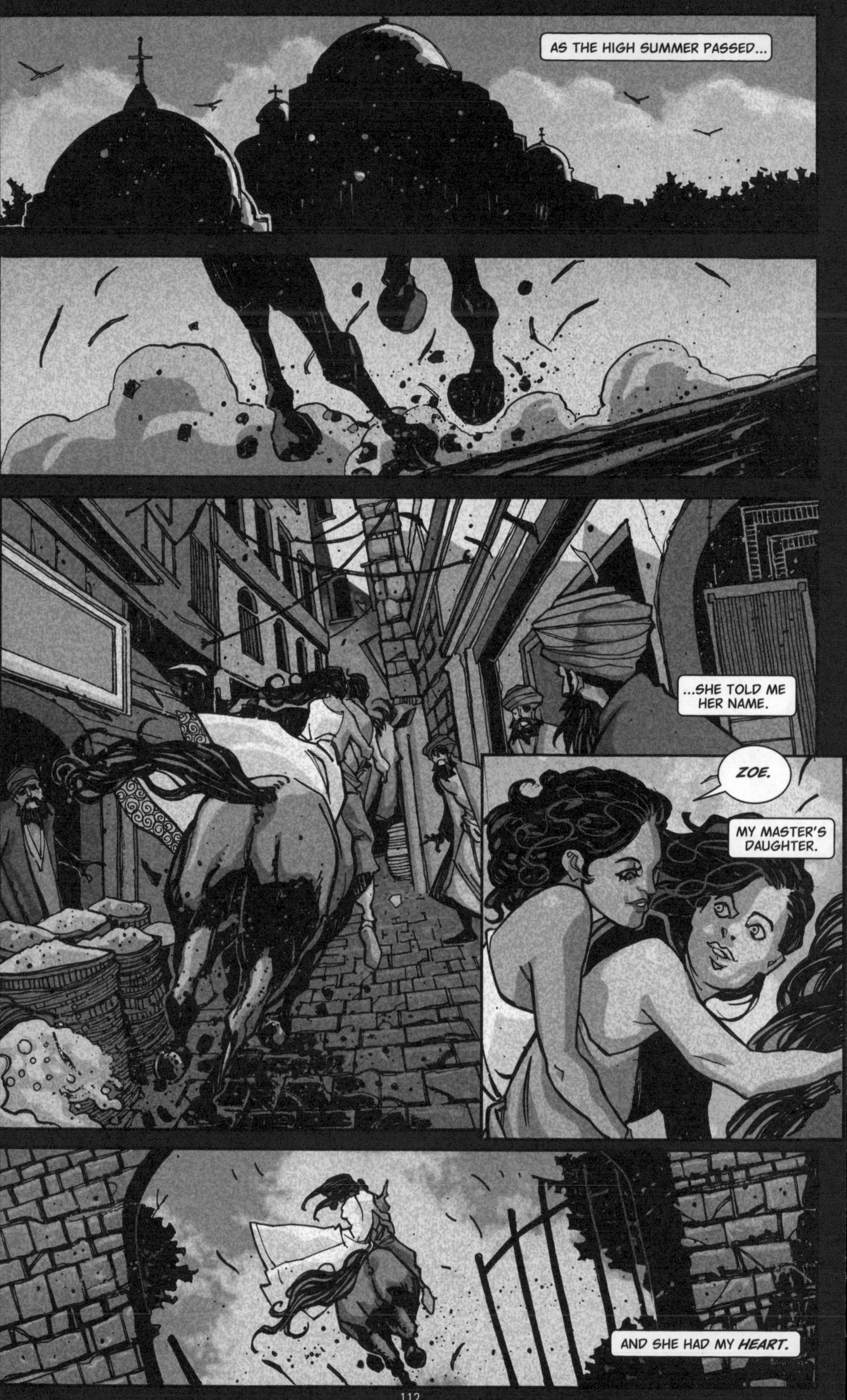
AS THE HIGH SUMMER PASSED...
...SHE TOLD ME HER NAME.
ZOE.
MY MASTER'S DAUGHTER.
AND SHE HAD MY HEART.

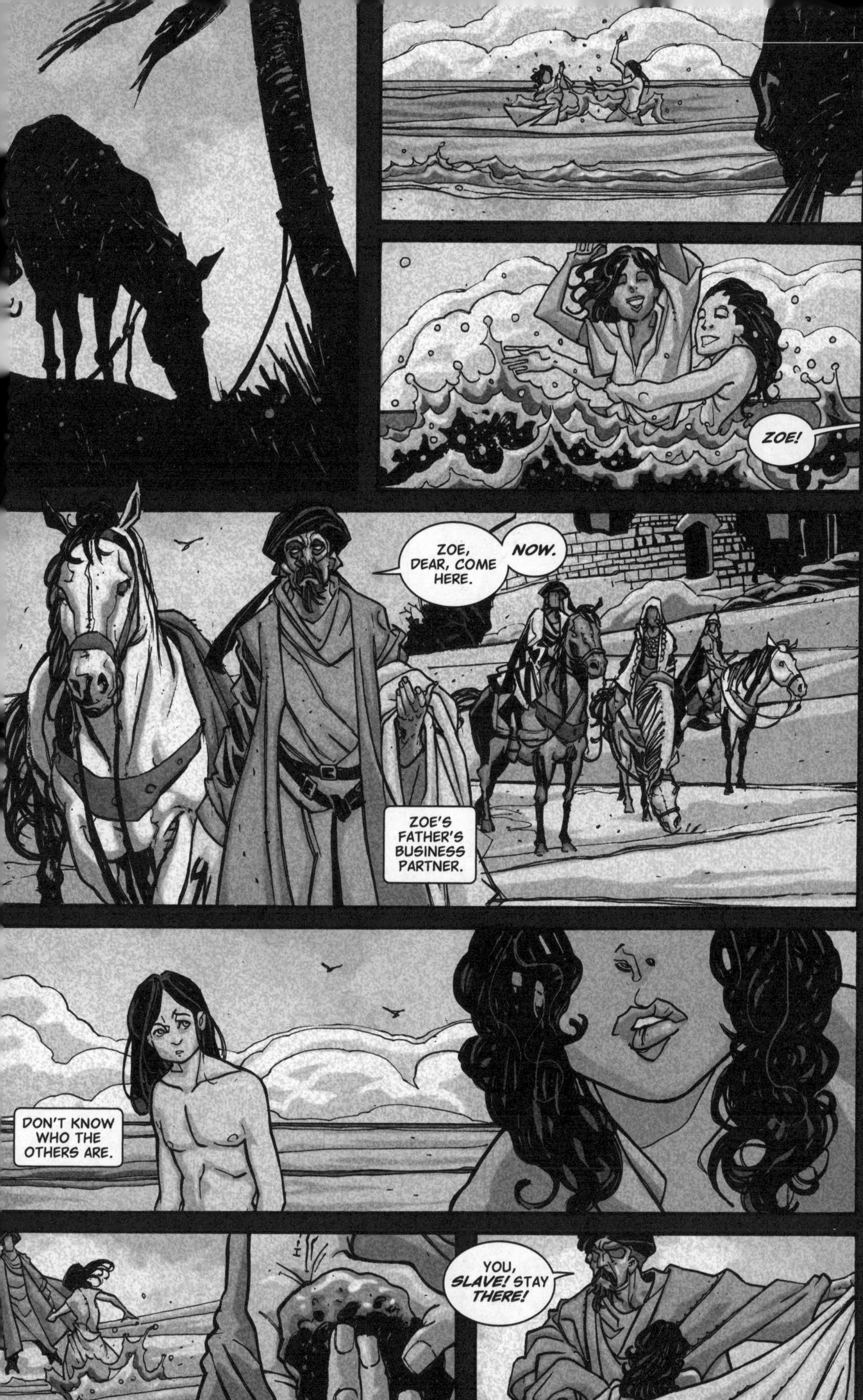
ZOE!
ZOE, DEAR, COME HERE.
NOW.
ZOE'S FATHER'S BUSINESS PARTNER.
DON'T KNOW WHO THE OTHERS ARE.
YOU, SLAVE! STAY THERE!

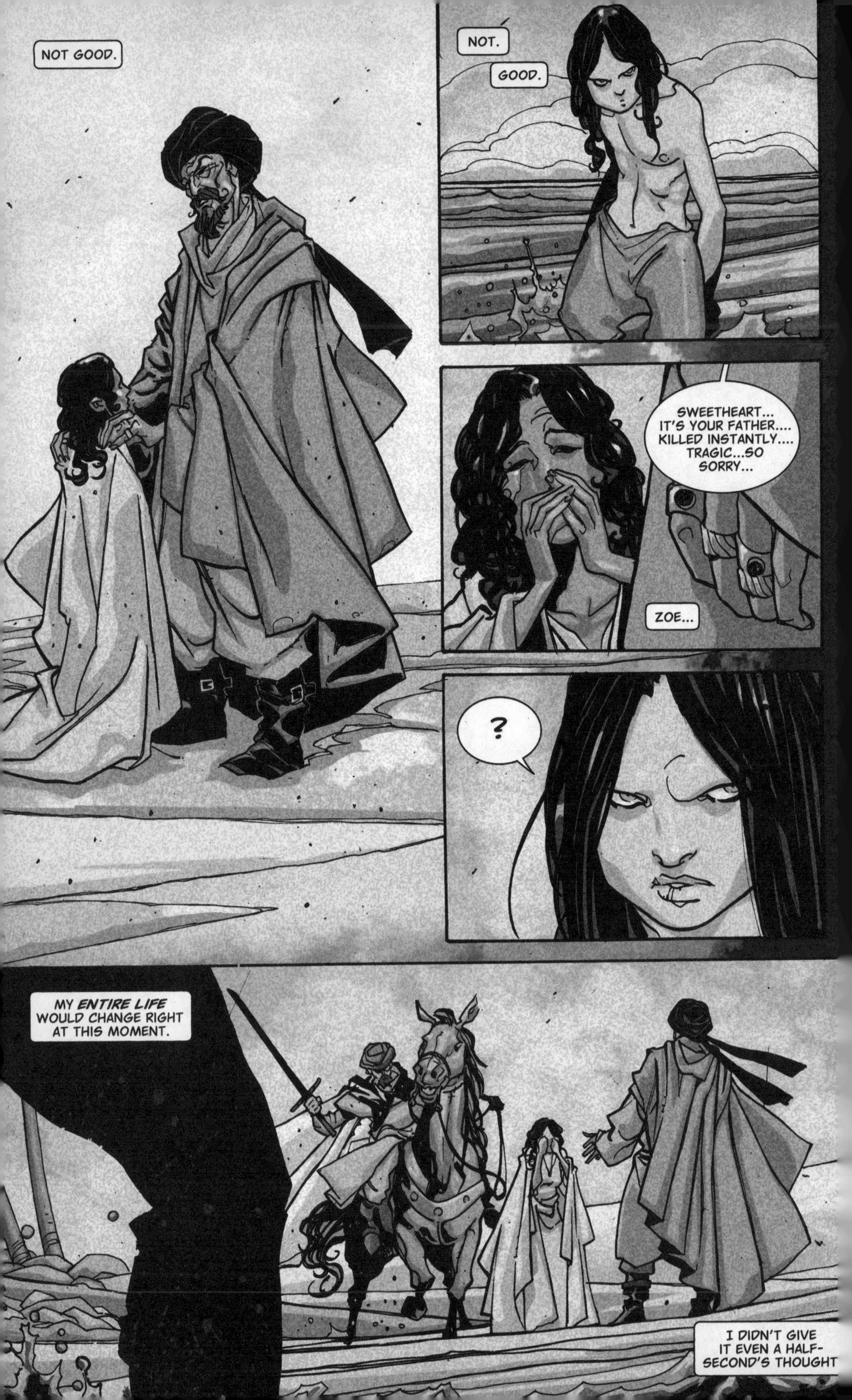
NOT GOOD.
NOT.
GOOD.
SWEETHEART... IT'S YOUR FATHER.... KILLED INSTANTLY.... TRAGIC...SO SORRY...
ZOE...
?
MY ENTIRE LIFE WOULD CHANGE RIGHT AT THIS MOMENT.
I DIDN'T GIVE IT EVEN A HALF-SECOND'S THOUGHT

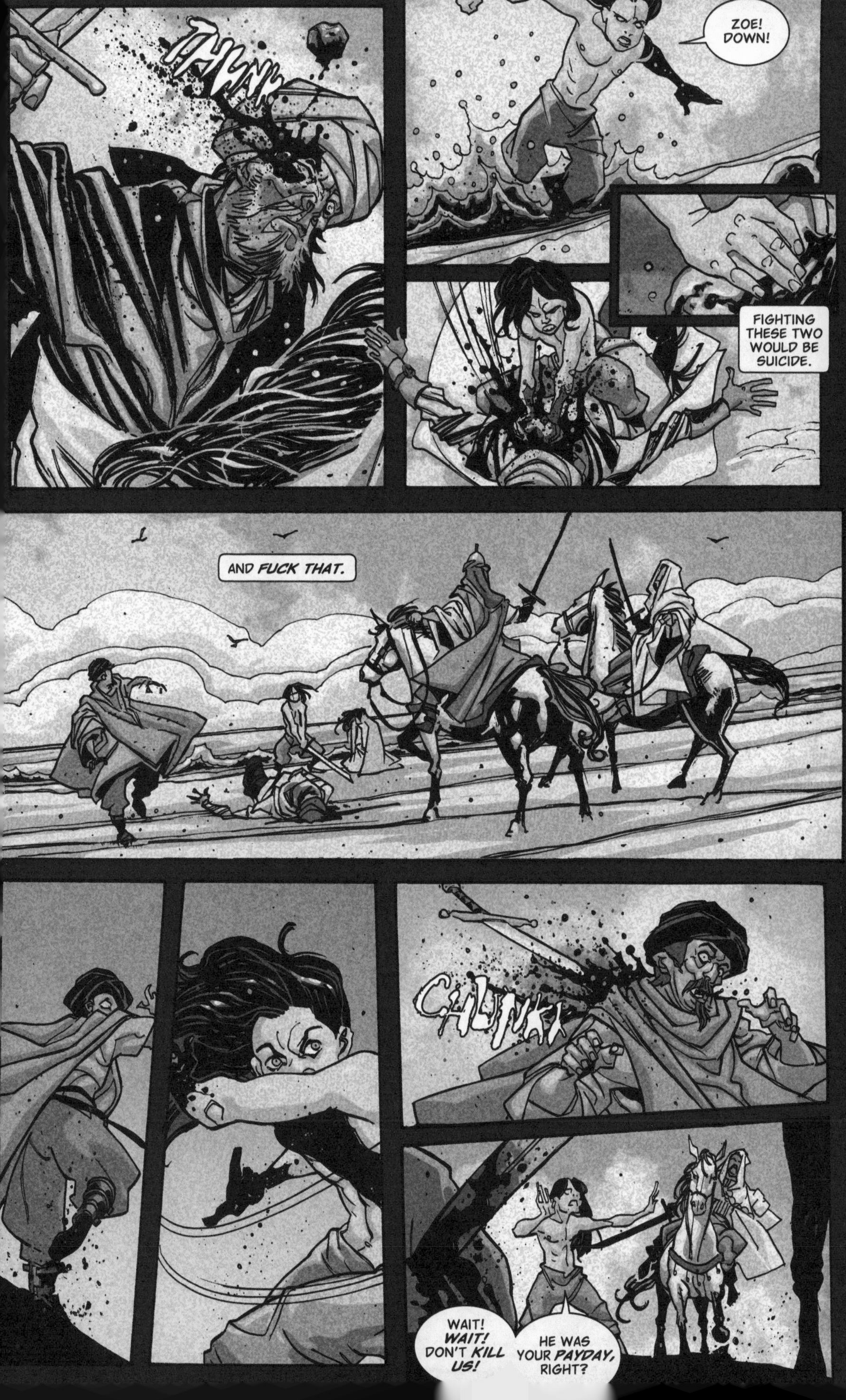
THUNK
ZOE! DOWN!
FIGHTING THESE TWO WOULD BE SUICIDE.
AND FUCK THAT.
CHUNKK
WAIT! WAIT! DON'T KILL US!
HE WAS YOUR PAYDAY, RIGHT?

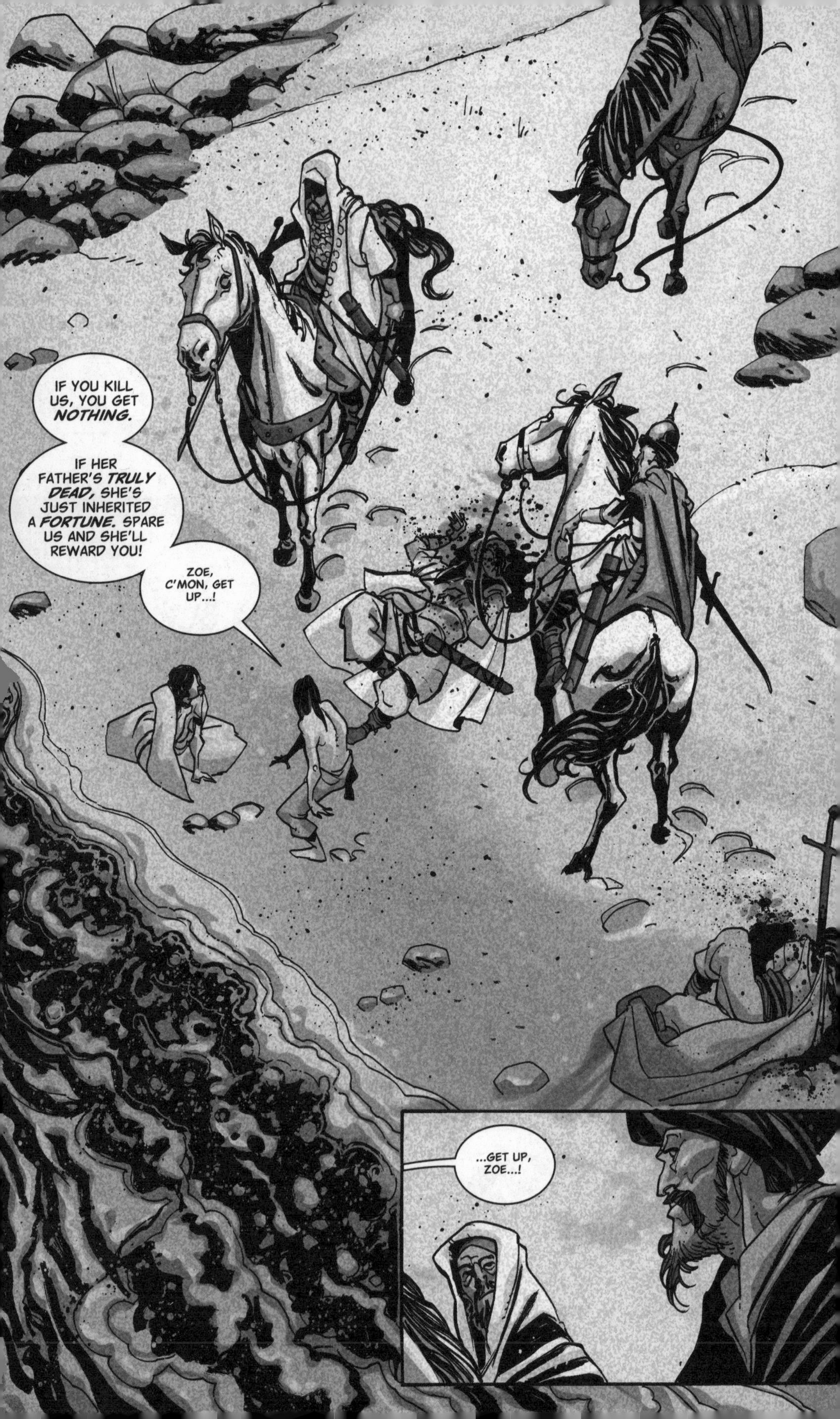
IF YOU KILL US, YOU GET *NOTHING.*
IF HER FATHER'S *TRULY DEAD,* SHE'S JUST INHERITED A *FORTUNE.* SPARE US AND SHE'LL REWARD YOU!
ZOE, C'MON, GET UP...!
...GET UP, ZOE...!

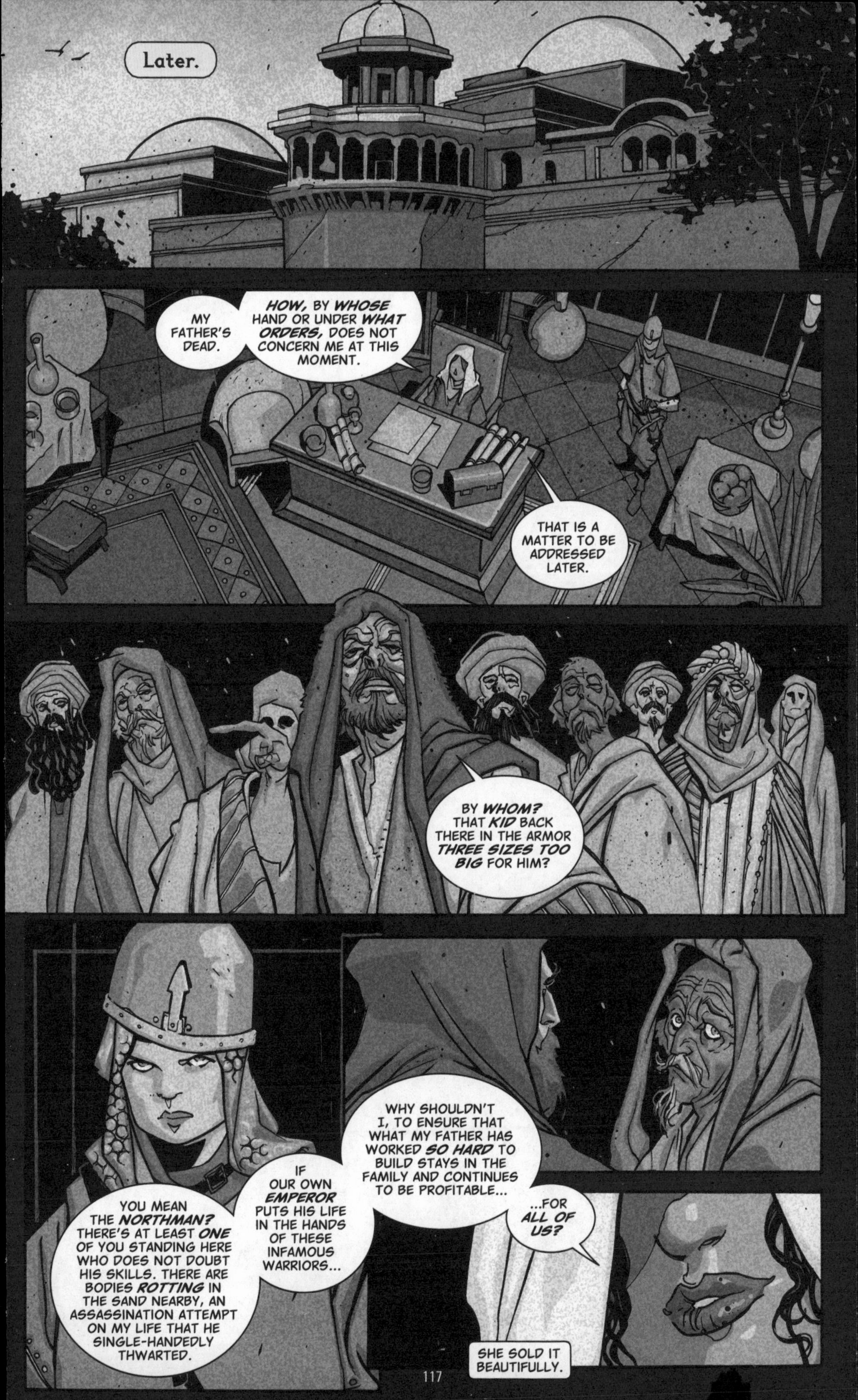
Later.
MY FATHER'S DEAD.
HOW, BY WHOSE HAND OR UNDER WHAT ORDERS, DOES NOT CONCERN ME AT THIS MOMENT.
THAT IS A MATTER TO BE ADDRESSED LATER.
BY WHOM? THAT KID BACK THERE IN THE ARMOR THREE SIZES TOO BIG FOR HIM?
YOU MEAN THE NORTHMAN? THERE'S AT LEAST ONE OF YOU STANDING HERE WHO DOES NOT DOUBT HIS SKILLS. THERE ARE BODIES ROTTING IN THE SAND NEARBY, AN ASSASSINATION ATTEMPT ON MY LIFE THAT HE SINGLE-HANDEDLY THWARTED.
IF OUR OWN EMPEROR PUTS HIS LIFE IN THE HANDS OF THESE INFAMOUS WARRIORS...
WHY SHOULDN'T I, TO ENSURE THAT WHAT MY FATHER HAS WORKED SO HARD TO BUILD STAYS IN THE FAMILY AND CONTINUES TO BE PROFITABLE...
...FOR ALL OF US?
SHE SOLD IT BEAUTIFULLY.

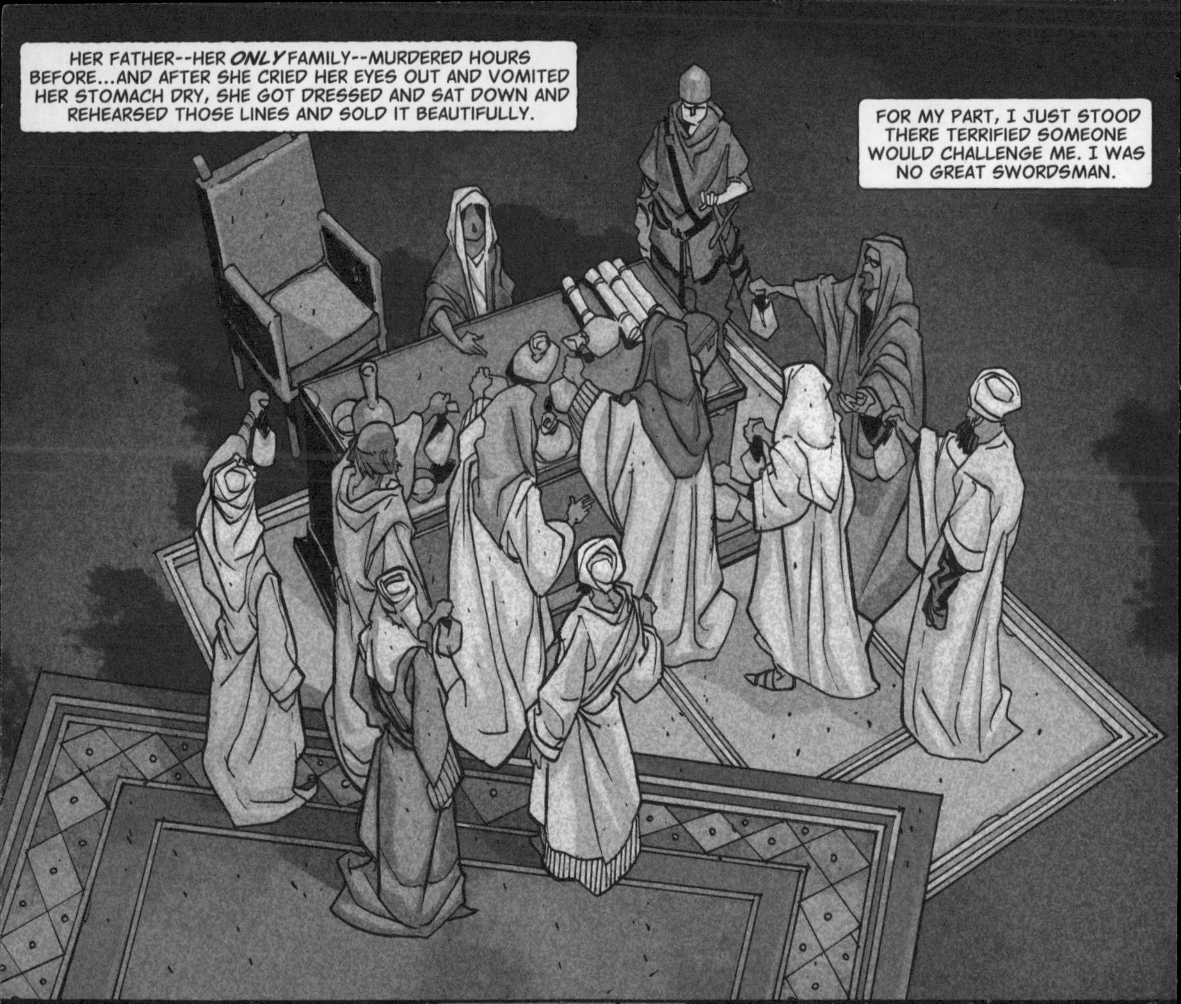
HER FATHER--HER ONLY FAMILY--MURDERED HOURS BEFORE...AND AFTER SHE CRIED HER EYES OUT AND VOMITED HER STOMACH DRY, SHE GOT DRESSED AND SAT DOWN AND REHEARSED THOSE LINES AND SOLD IT BEAUTIFULLY.
FOR MY PART, I JUST STOOD THERE TERRIFIED SOMEONE WOULD CHALLENGE ME. I WAS NO GREAT SWORDSMAN.

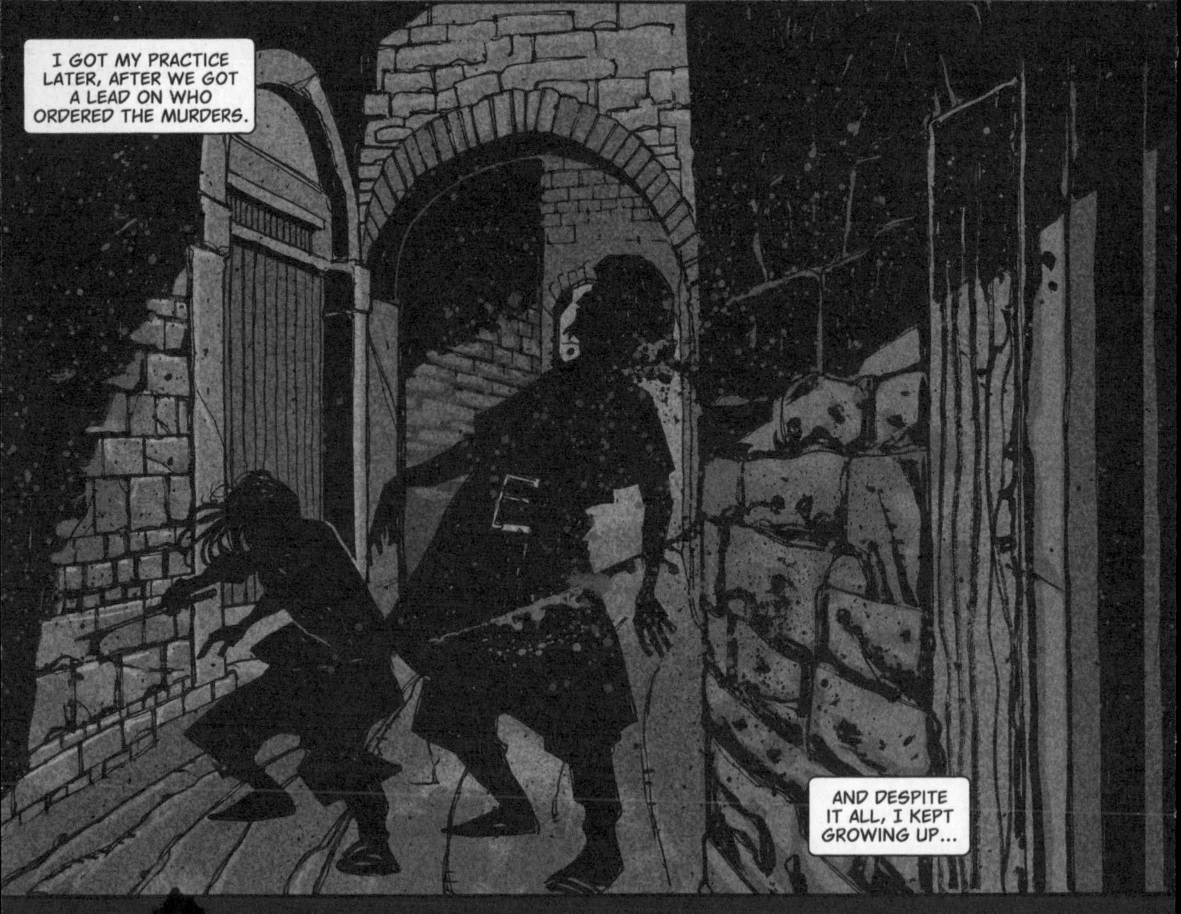
I GOT MY PRACTICE LATER, AFTER WE GOT A LEAD ON WHO ORDERED THE MURDERS.
AND DESPITE IT ALL, I KEPT GROWING UP...

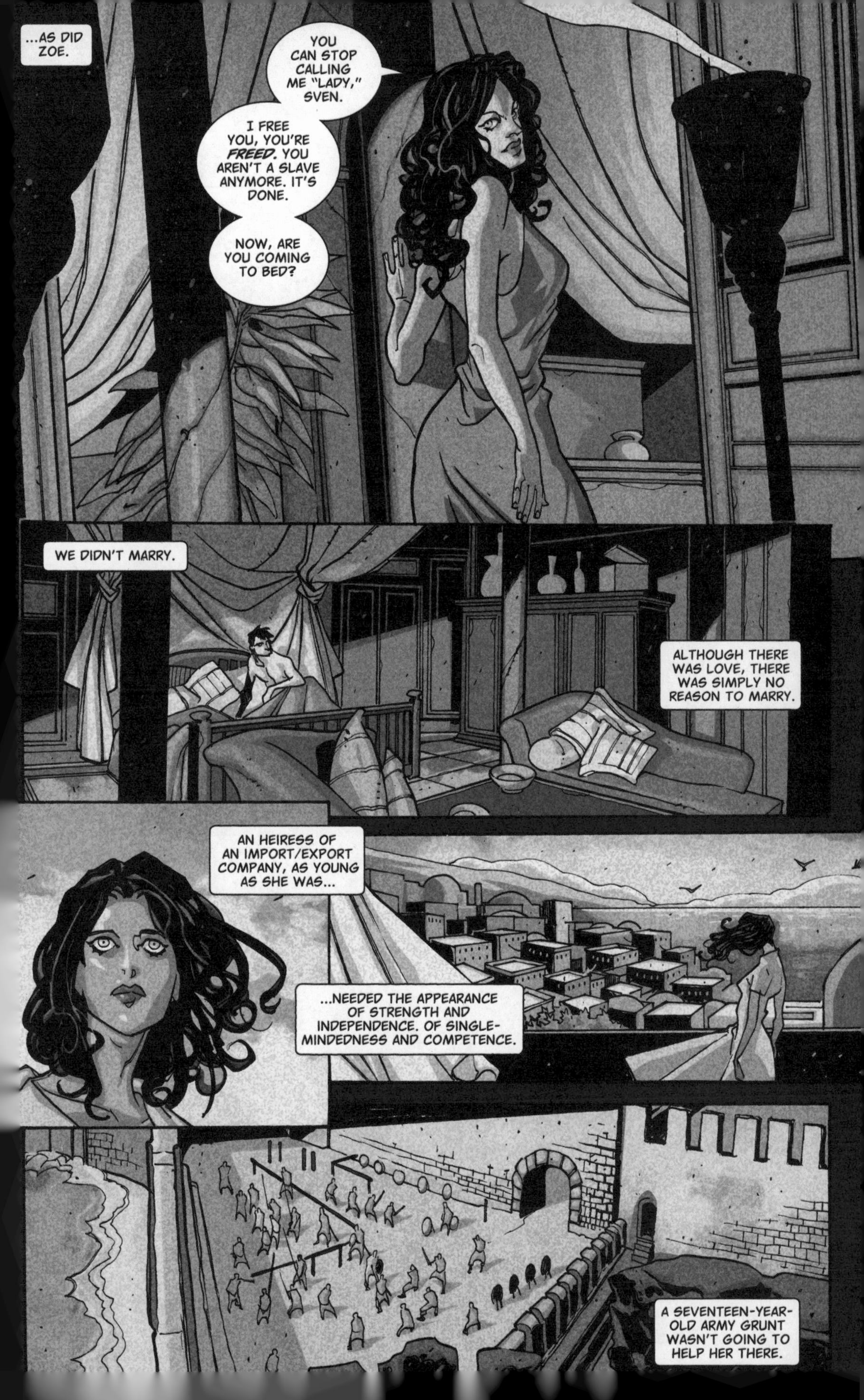
...AS DID ZOE.
YOU CAN STOP CALLING ME "LADY," SVEN.
I FREE YOU, YOU'RE *FREED*. YOU AREN'T A SLAVE ANYMORE. IT'S DONE.
NOW, ARE YOU COMING TO BED?
WE DIDN'T MARRY.
ALTHOUGH THERE WAS LOVE, THERE WAS SIMPLY NO REASON TO MARRY.
AN HEIRESS OF AN IMPORT/EXPORT COMPANY, AS YOUNG AS SHE WAS...
...NEEDED THE APPEARANCE OF STRENGTH AND INDEPENDENCE. OF SINGLE-MINDEDNESS AND COMPETENCE.
A SEVENTEEN-YEAR-OLD ARMY GRUNT WASN'T GOING TO HELP HER THERE.

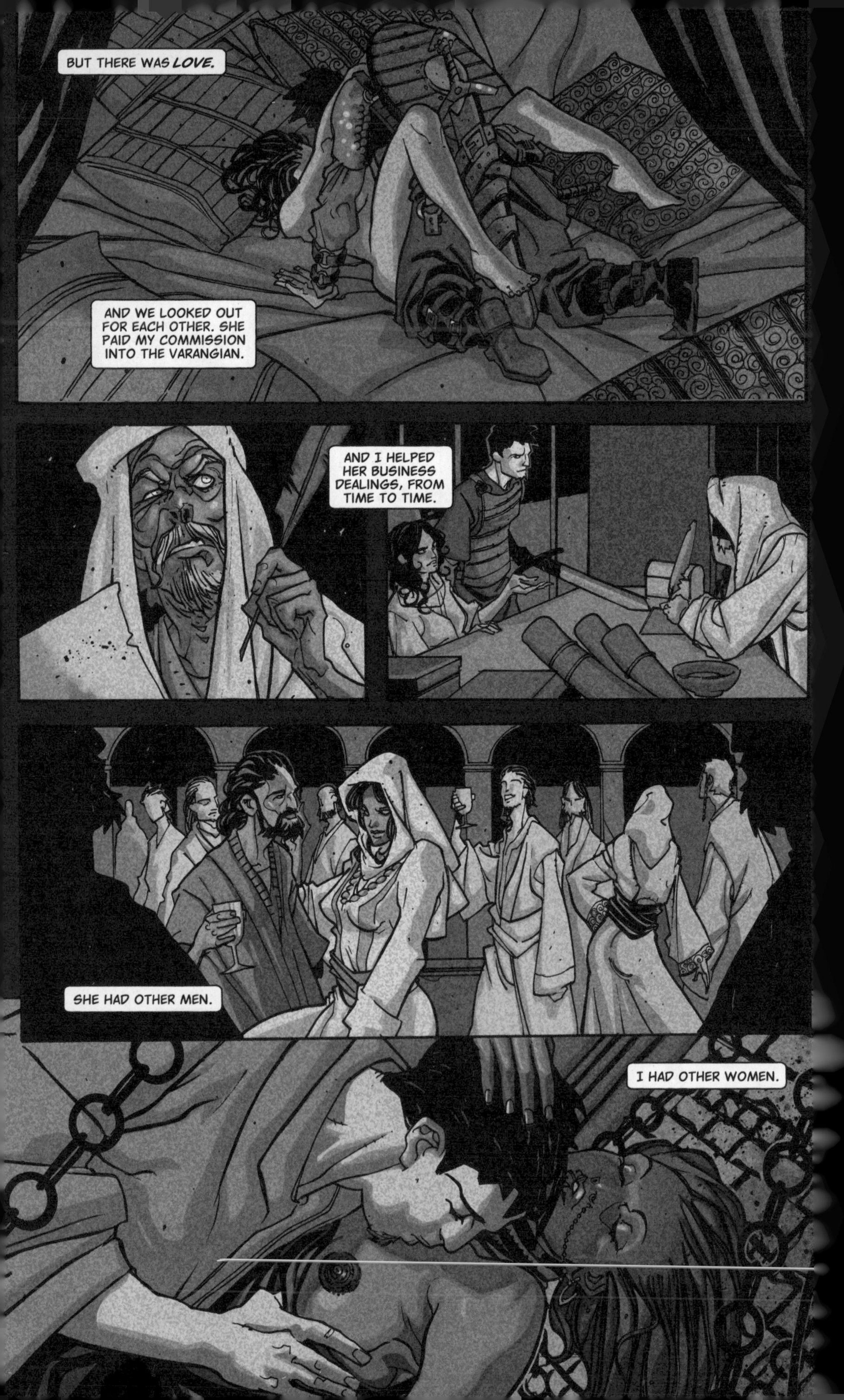
BUT THERE WAS LOVE.
AND WE LOOKED OUT FOR EACH OTHER. SHE PAID MY COMMISSION INTO THE VARANGIAN.
AND I HELPED HER BUSINESS DEALINGS, FROM TIME TO TIME.
SHE HAD OTHER MEN.
I HAD OTHER WOMEN.

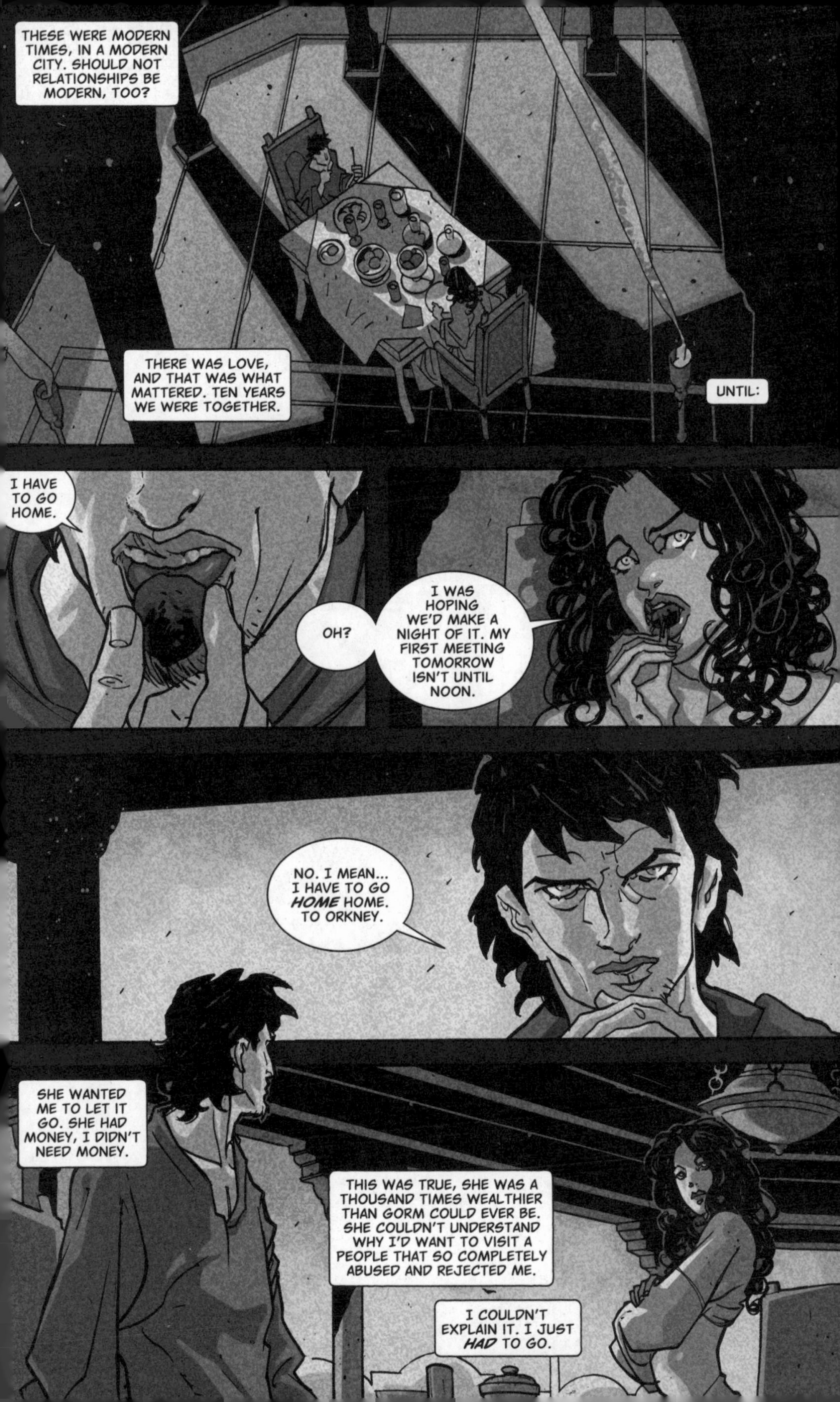
THESE WERE MODERN TIMES, IN A MODERN CITY. SHOULD NOT RELATIONSHIPS BE MODERN, TOO?
THERE WAS LOVE, AND THAT WAS WHAT MATTERED. TEN YEARS WE WERE TOGETHER.
UNTIL:
I HAVE TO GO HOME.
OH?
I WAS HOPING WE'D MAKE A NIGHT OF IT. MY FIRST MEETING TOMORROW ISN'T UNTIL NOON.
NO. I MEAN... I HAVE TO GO *HOME* HOME. TO ORKNEY.
SHE WANTED ME TO LET IT GO. SHE HAD MONEY, I DIDN'T NEED MONEY.
THIS WAS TRUE, SHE WAS A THOUSAND TIMES WEALTHIER THAN GORM COULD EVER BE. SHE COULDN'T UNDERSTAND WHY I'D WANT TO VISIT A PEOPLE THAT SO COMPLETELY ABUSED AND REJECTED ME.
I COULDN'T EXPLAIN IT. I JUST *HAD* TO GO.

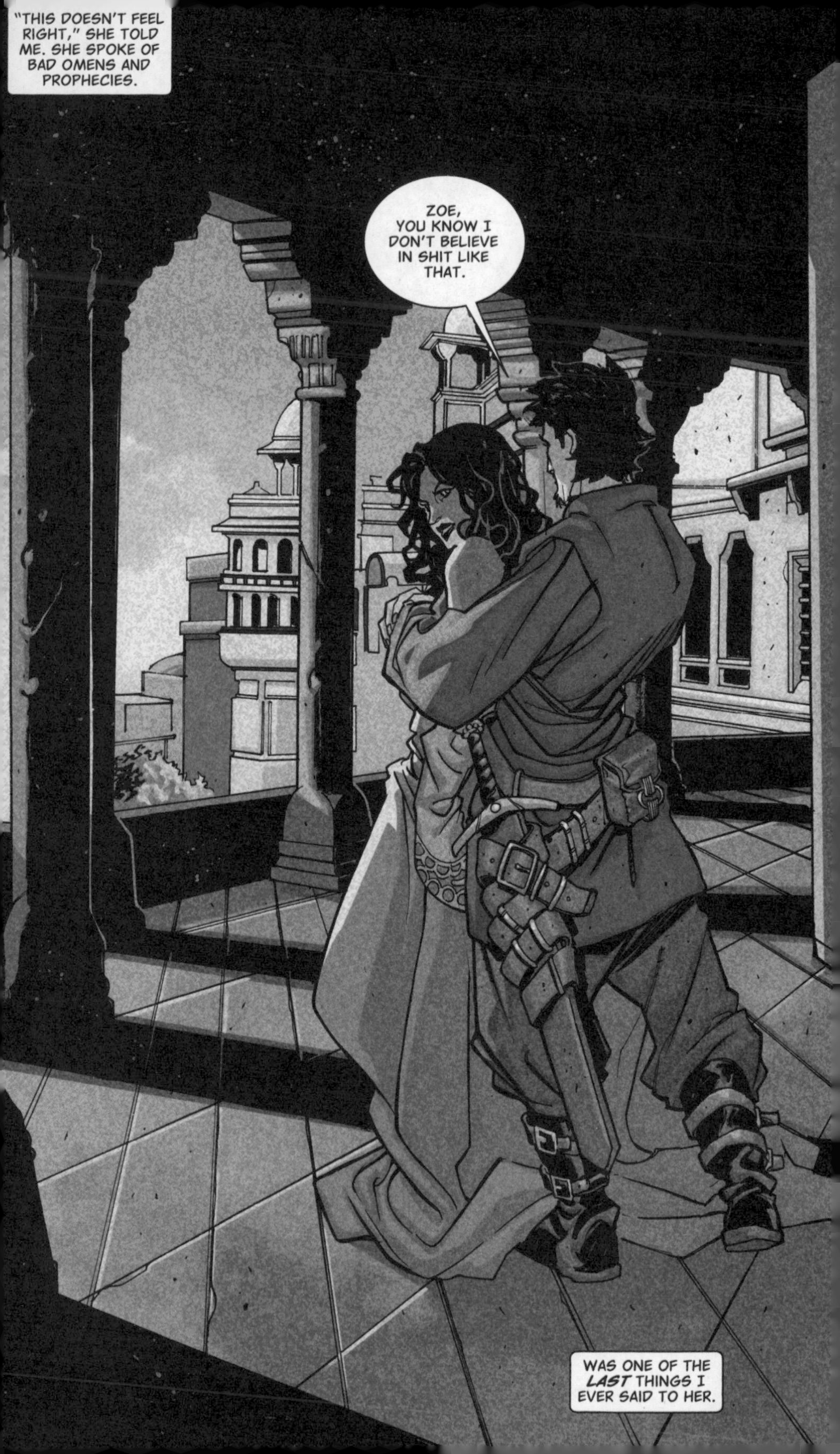
"THIS DOESN'T FEEL RIGHT," SHE TOLD ME. SHE SPOKE OF BAD OMENS AND PROPHECIES.
ZOE, YOU KNOW I DON'T BELIEVE IN SHIT LIKE THAT.
WAS ONE OF THE *LAST* THINGS I EVER SAID TO HER.

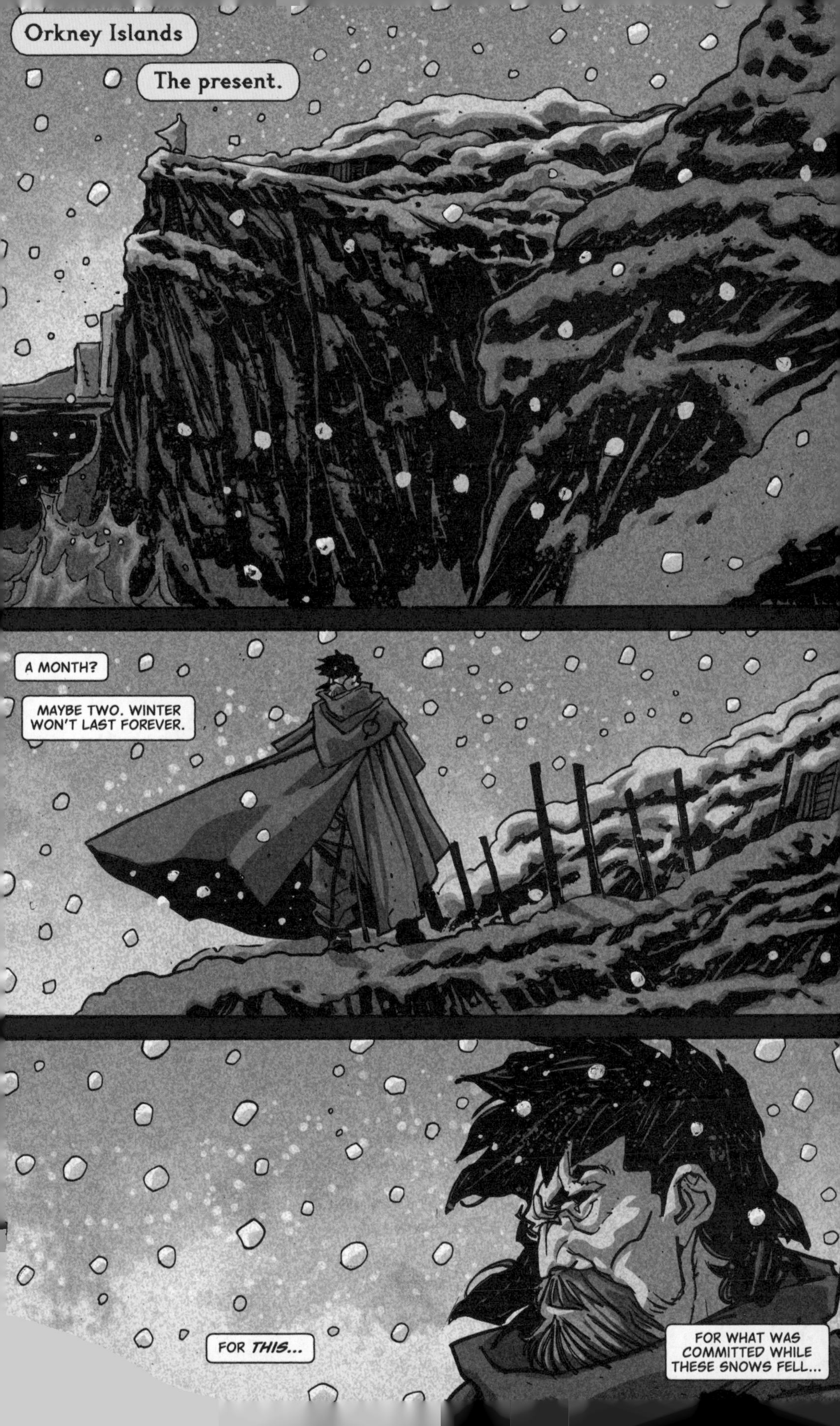
Orkney Islands
The present.
A MONTH?
MAYBE TWO. WINTER WON'T LAST FOREVER.
FOR *THIS*...
FOR WHAT WAS COMMITTED WHILE THESE SNOWS FELL...

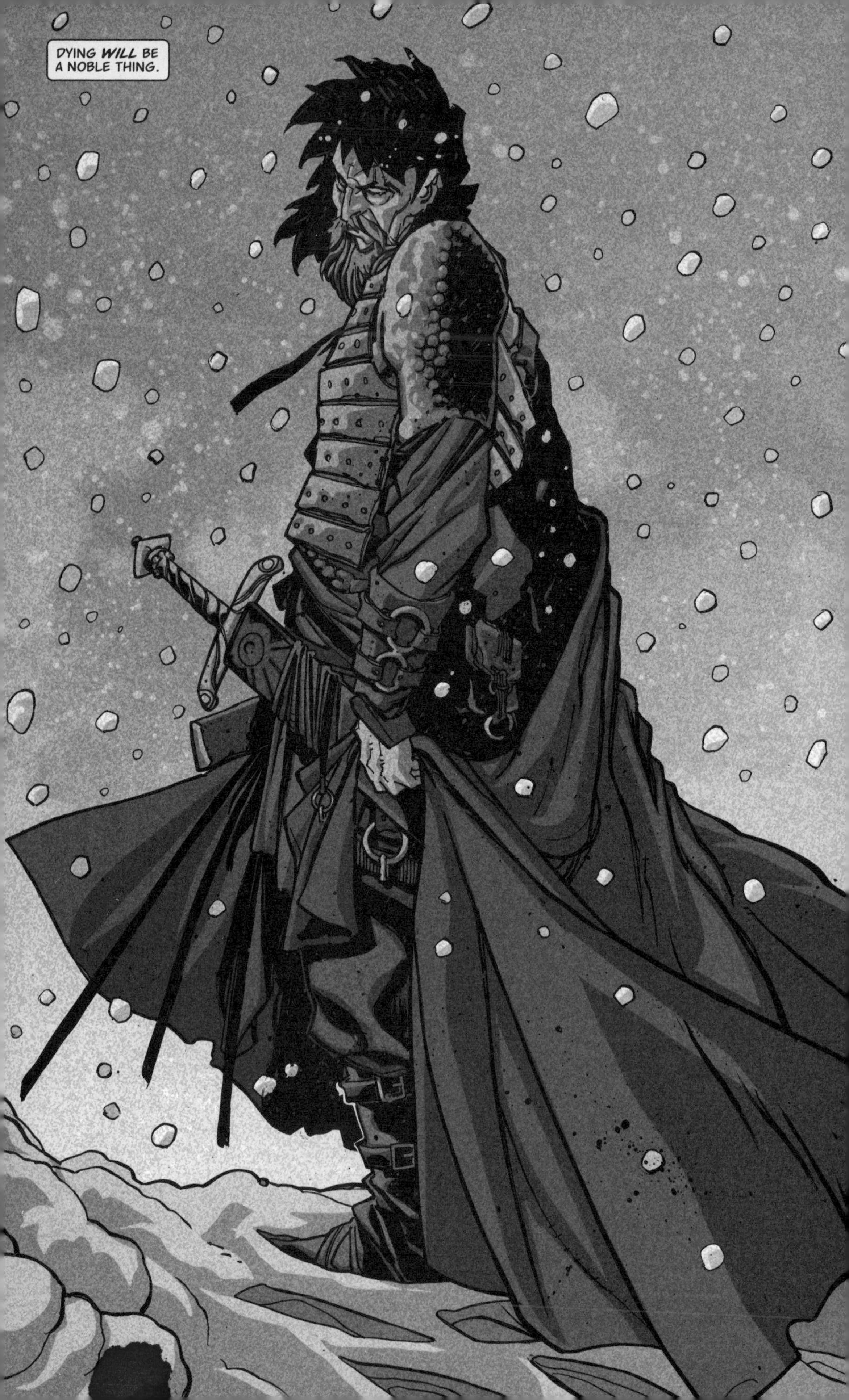
DYING WILL BE A NOBLE THING.

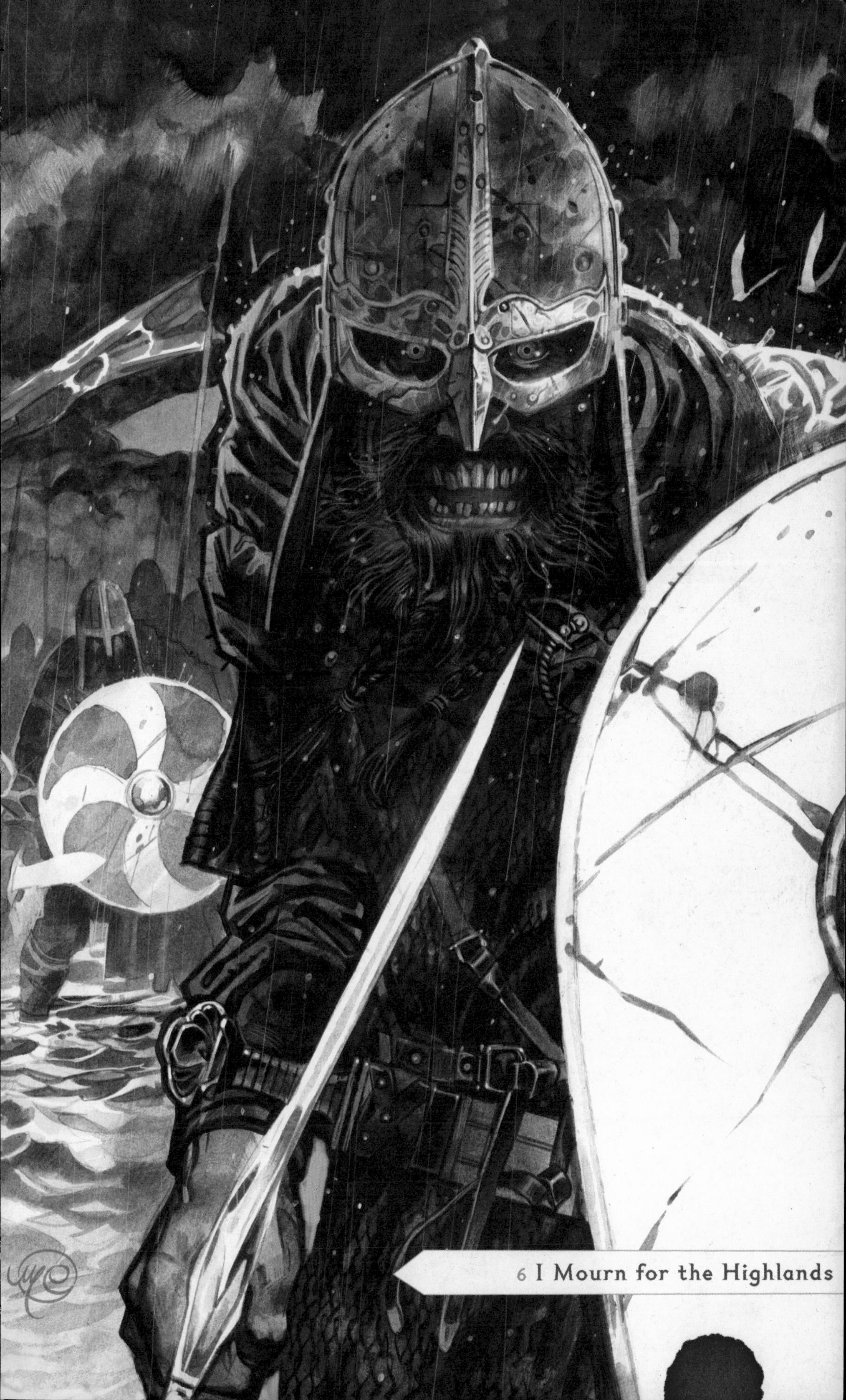

6 I Mourn for the Highlands

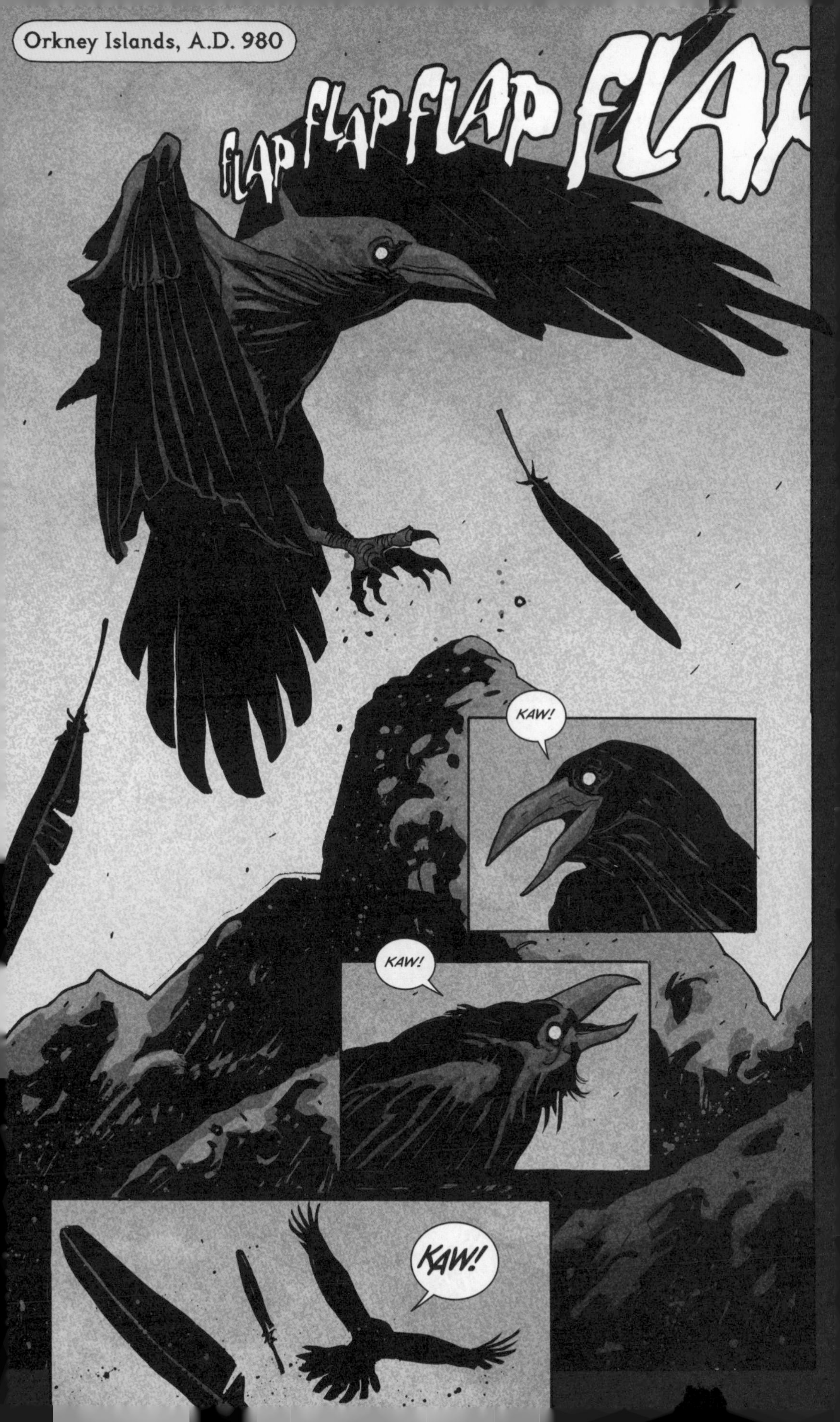
Orkney Islands, A.D. 980
FLAP FLAP FLAP FLAP FLAP
KAW!
KAW!
KAW!

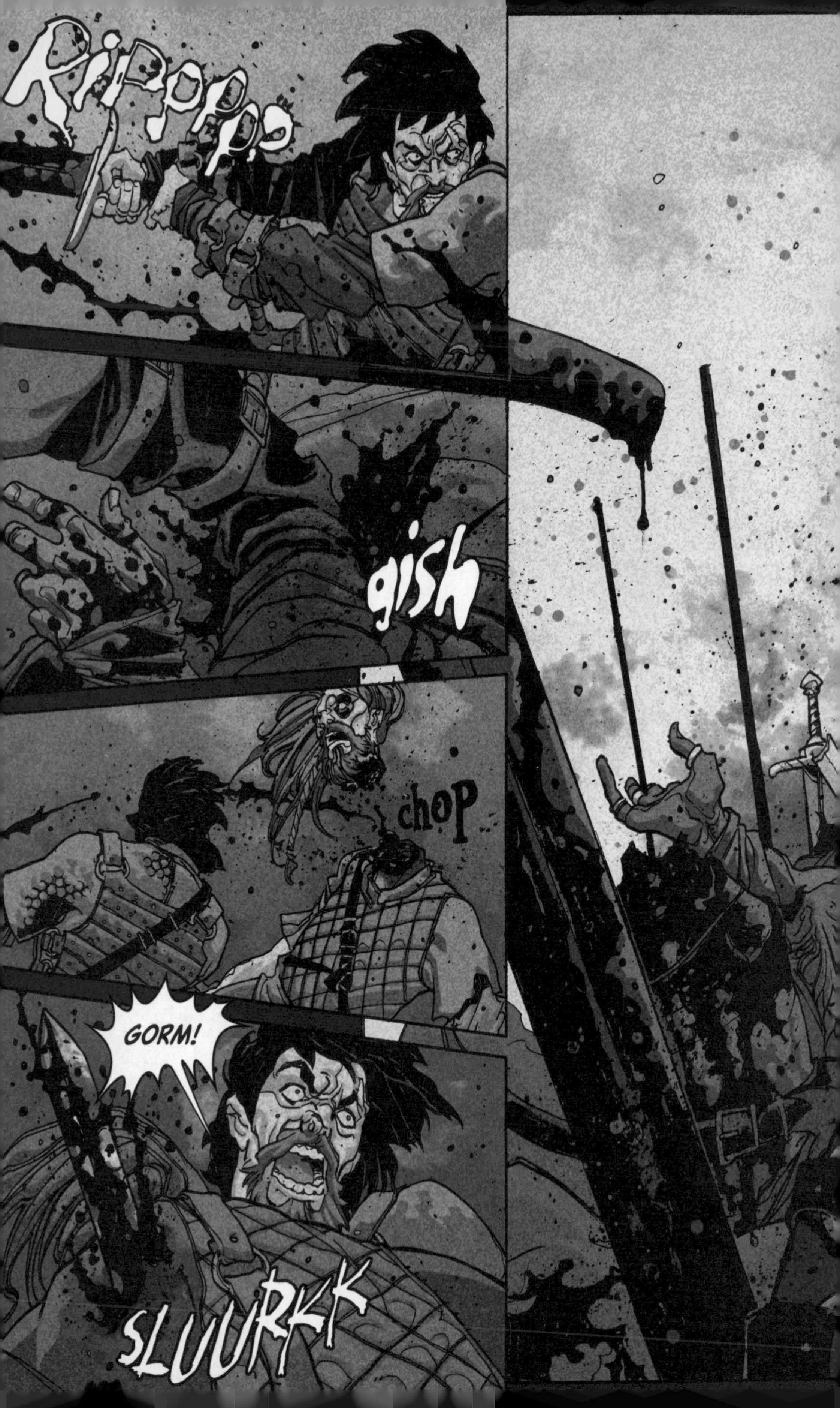
RIPPPP
gish
chop
GORM!
SLUURKK

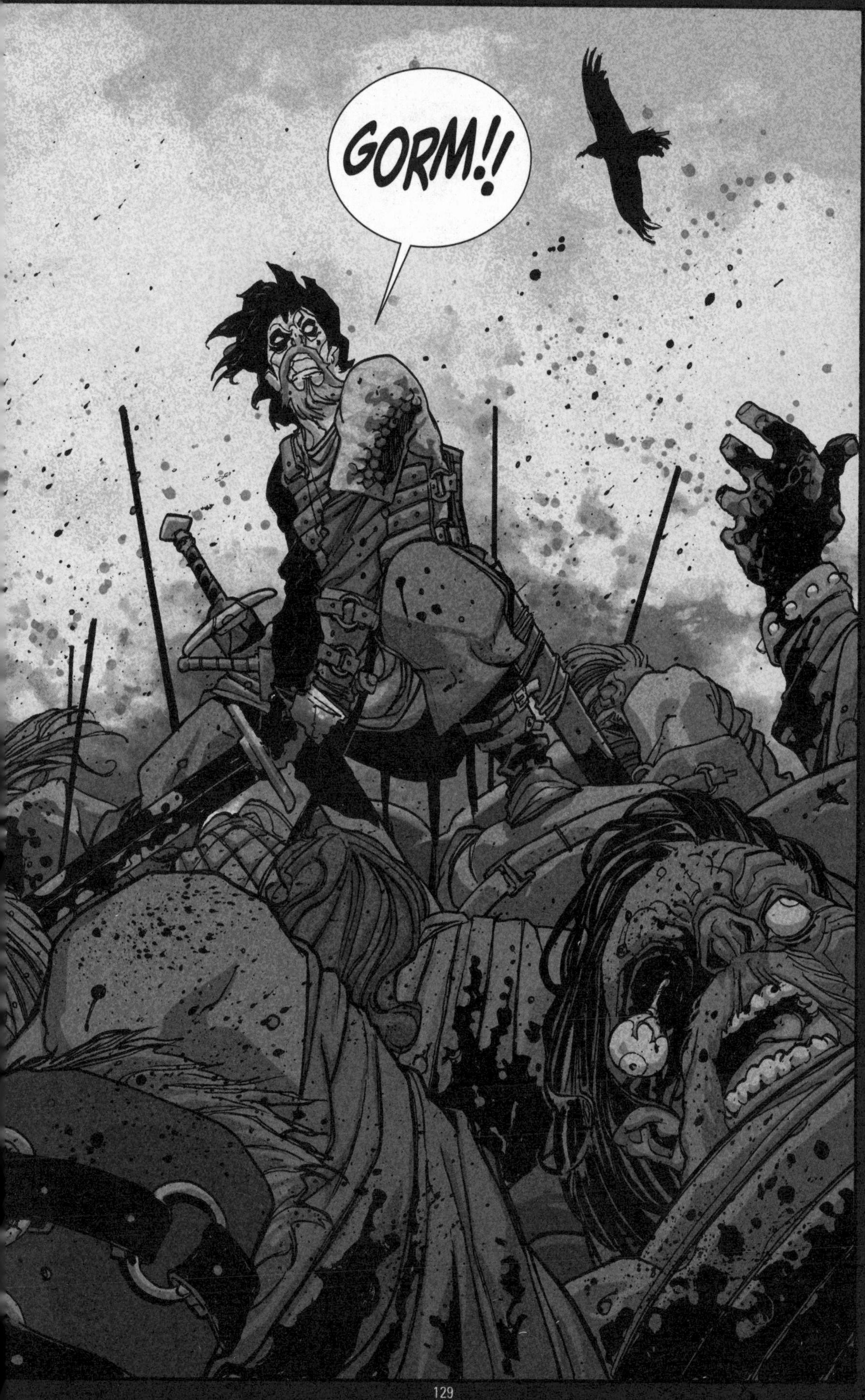
GORM!!

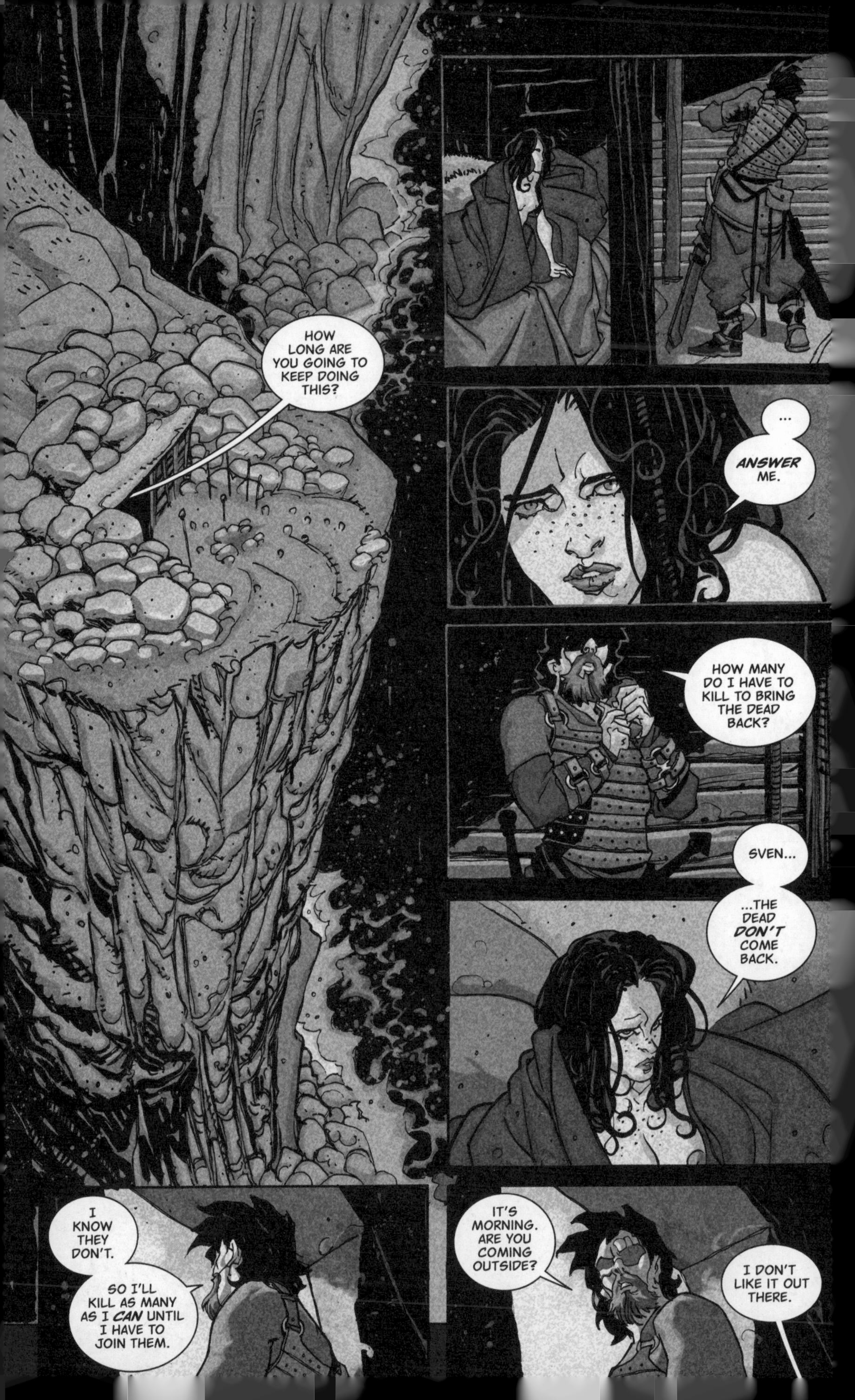
HOW LONG ARE YOU GOING TO KEEP DOING THIS?
...
ANSWER ME.
HOW MANY DO I HAVE TO KILL TO BRING THE DEAD BACK?
SVEN...
...THE DEAD DON'T COME BACK.
I KNOW THEY DON'T.
SO I'LL KILL AS MANY AS I CAN UNTIL I HAVE TO JOIN THEM.
IT'S MORNING. ARE YOU COMING OUTSIDE?
I DON'T LIKE IT OUT THERE.

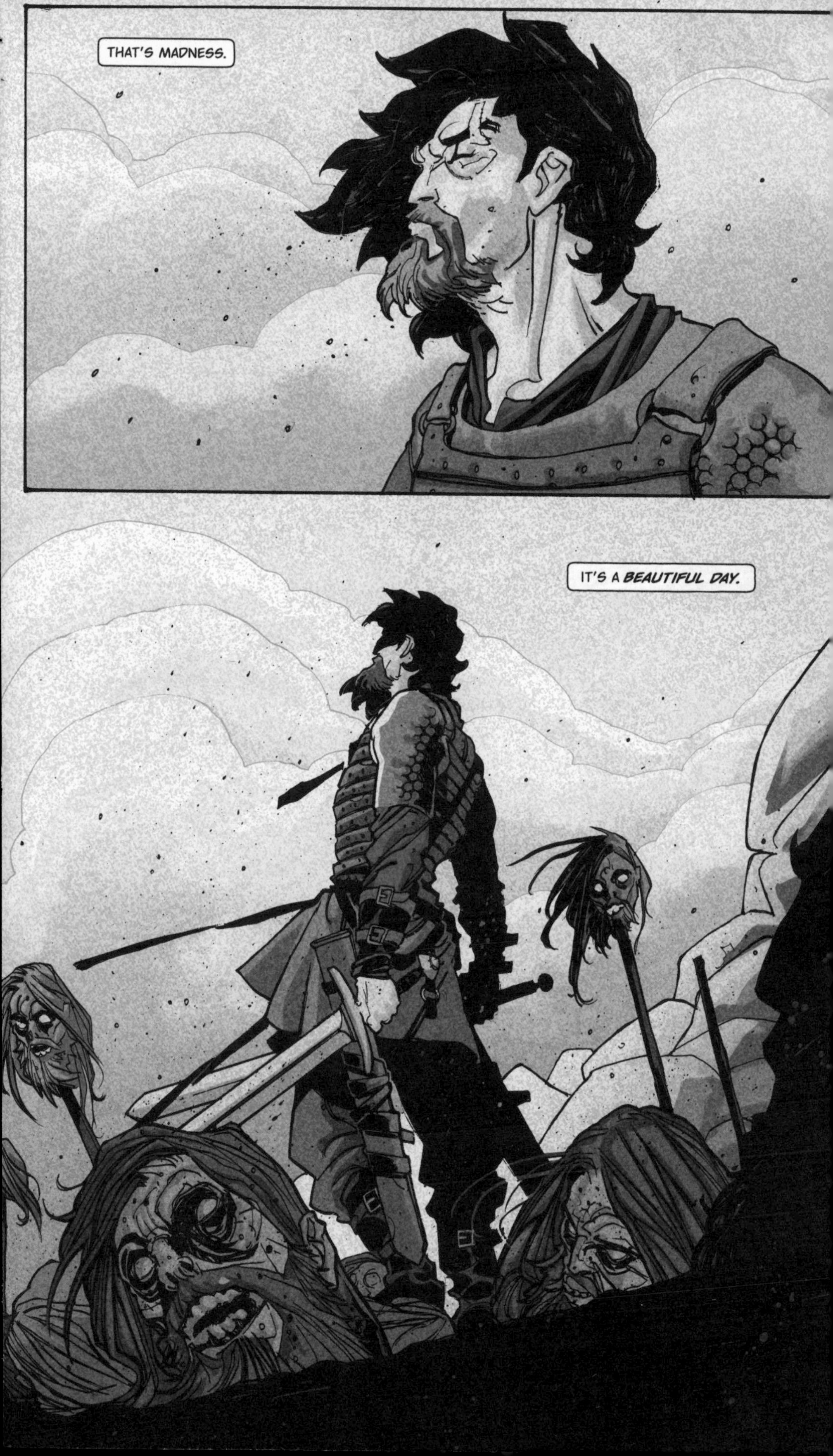
THAT'S MADNESS.
IT'S A BEAUTIFUL DAY.

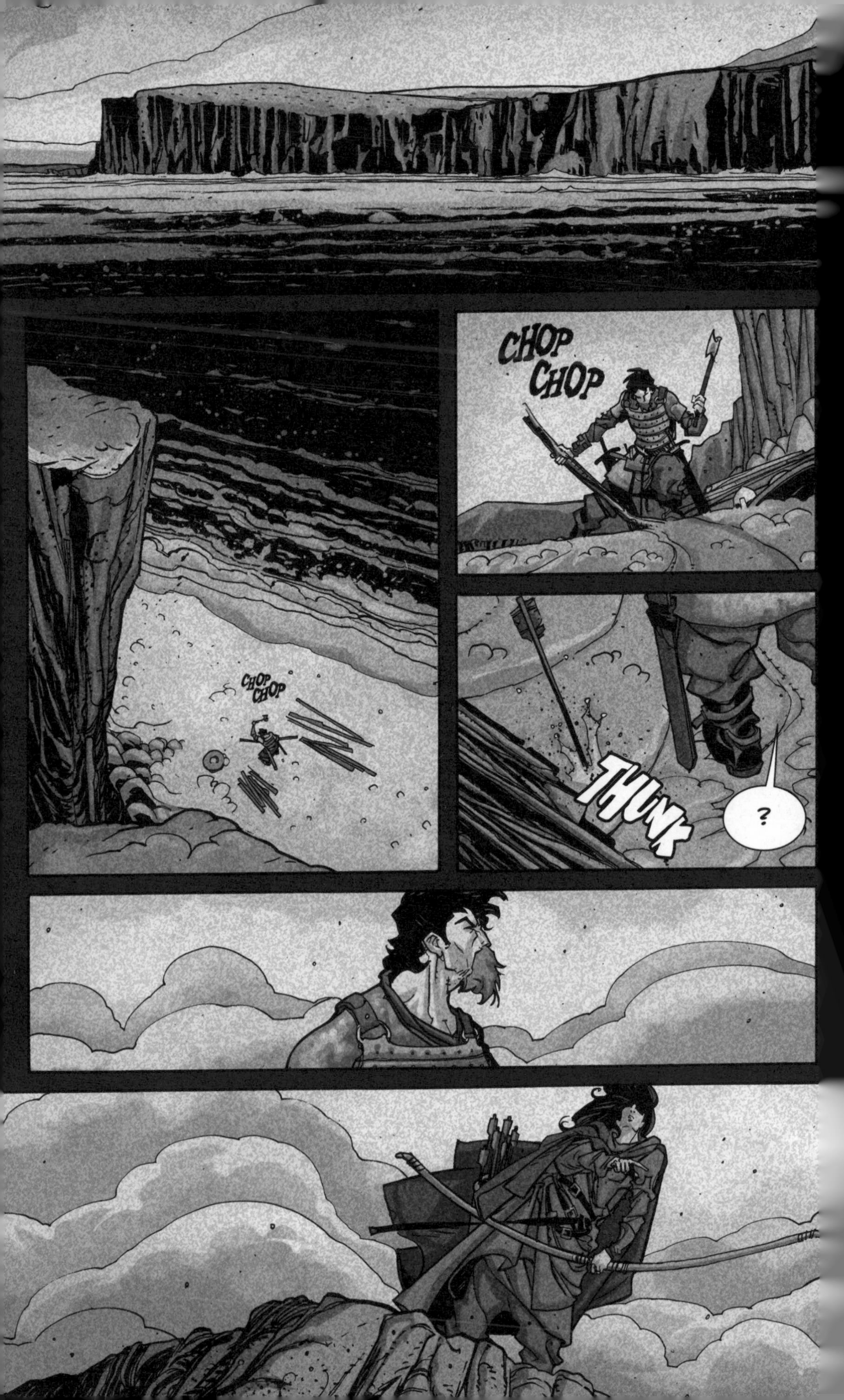
CHOP CHOP
CHOP
CHOP
THUNK
?

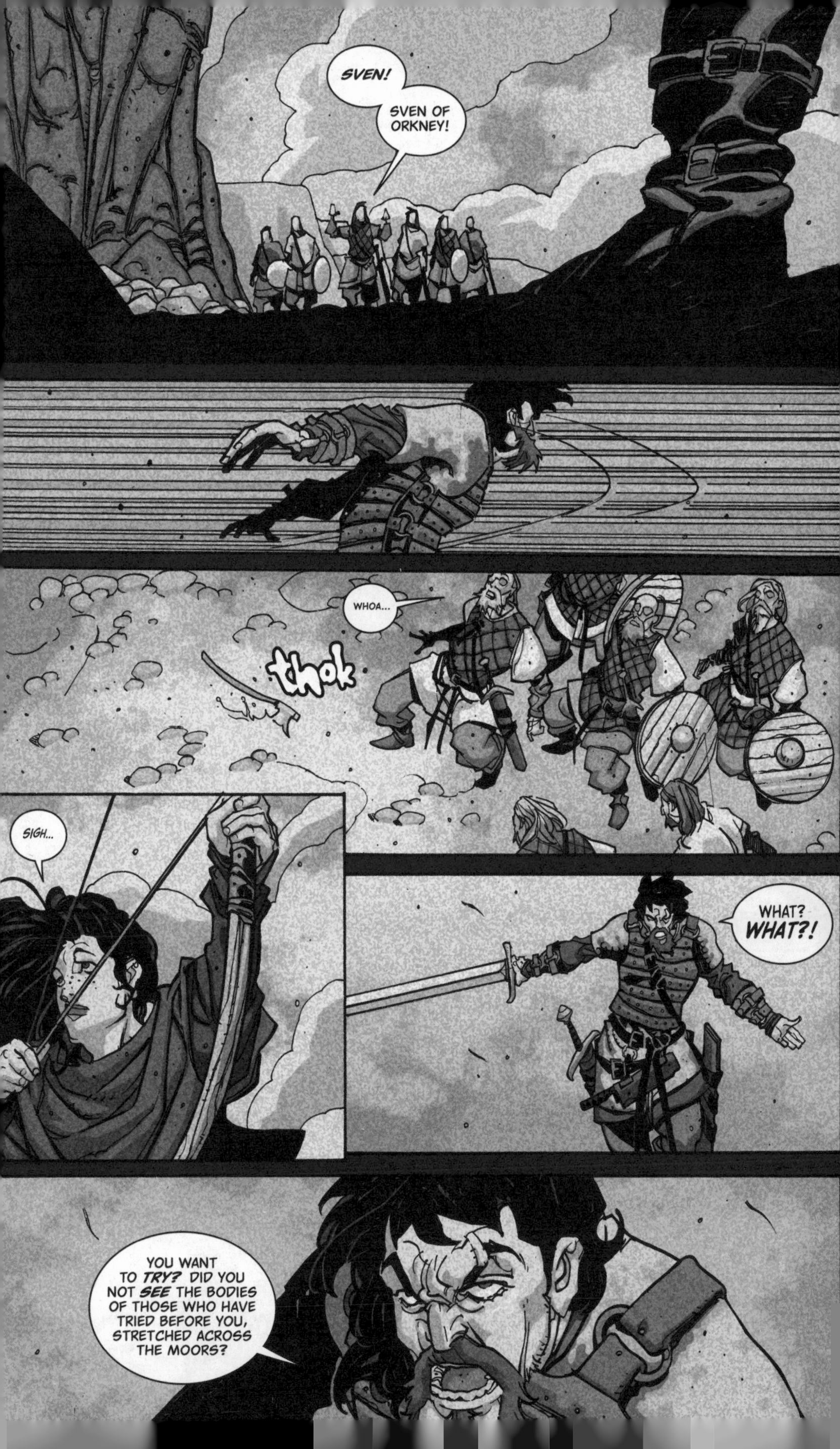
SVEN!
SVEN OF ORKNEY!
WHOA...
thok
SIGH...
WHAT? WHAT?!
YOU WANT TO TRY? DID YOU NOT SEE THE BODIES OF THOSE WHO HAVE TRIED BEFORE YOU, STRETCHED ACROSS THE MOORS?

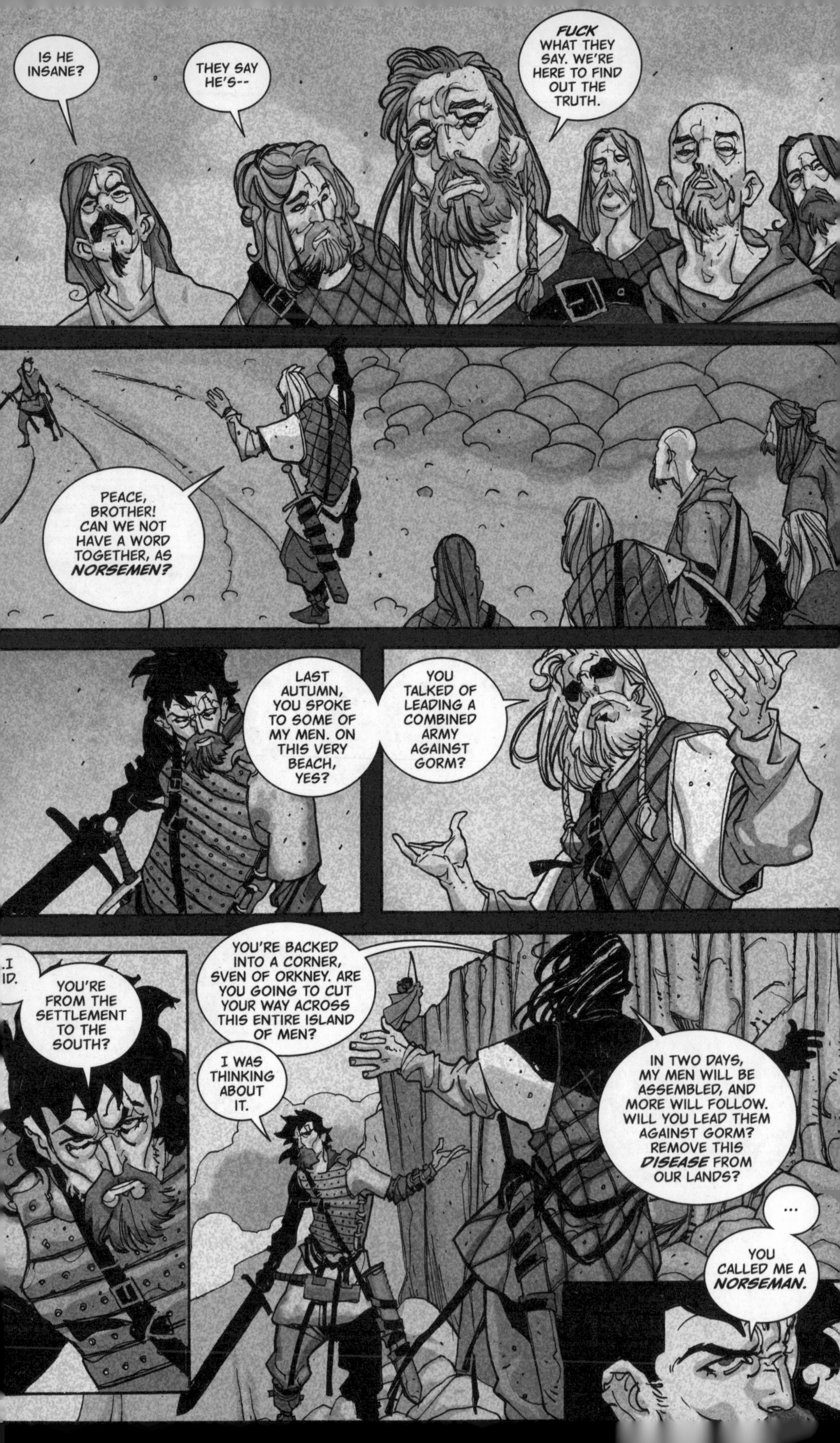
IS HE INSANE?
THEY SAY HE'S--
FUCK WHAT THEY SAY. WE'RE HERE TO FIND OUT THE TRUTH.
PEACE, BROTHER! CAN WE NOT HAVE A WORD TOGETHER, AS NORSEMEN?
LAST AUTUMN, YOU SPOKE TO SOME OF MY MEN. ON THIS VERY BEACH, YES?
YOU TALKED OF LEADING A COMBINED ARMY AGAINST GORM?
YOU'RE FROM THE SETTLEMENT TO THE SOUTH?
YOU'RE BACKED INTO A CORNER, SVEN OF ORKNEY. ARE YOU GOING TO CUT YOUR WAY ACROSS THIS ENTIRE ISLAND OF MEN?
I WAS THINKING ABOUT IT.
IN TWO DAYS, MY MEN WILL BE ASSEMBLED, AND MORE WILL FOLLOW. WILL YOU LEAD THEM AGAINST GORM? REMOVE THIS DISEASE FROM OUR LANDS?
...
YOU CALLED ME A NORSEMAN.

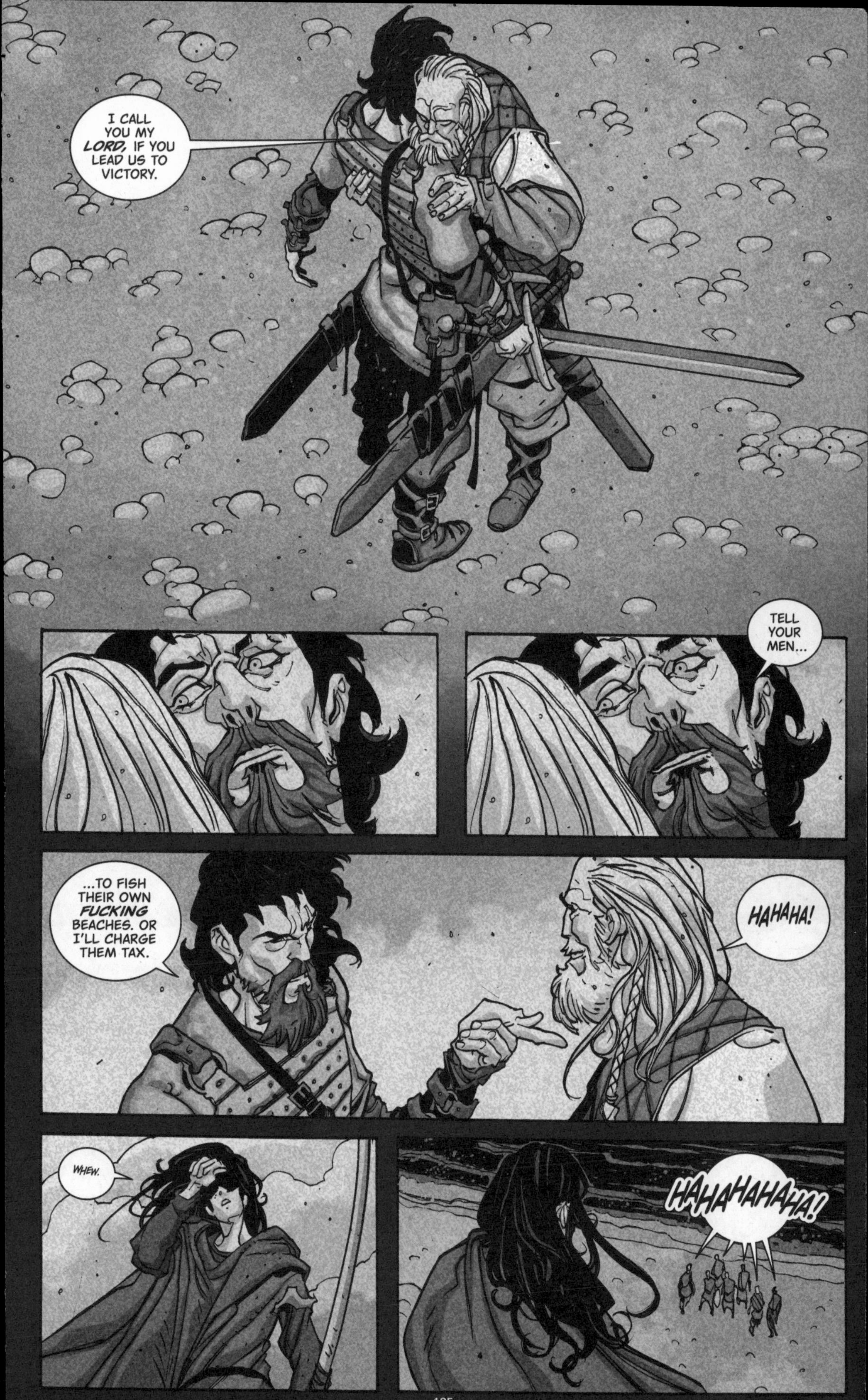
I CALL YOU MY LORD, IF YOU LEAD US TO VICTORY.
TELL YOUR MEN...
...TO FISH THEIR OWN FUCKING BEACHES. OR I'LL CHARGE THEM TAX.
HAHAHA!
WHEW.
HAHAHAHAHAHA!

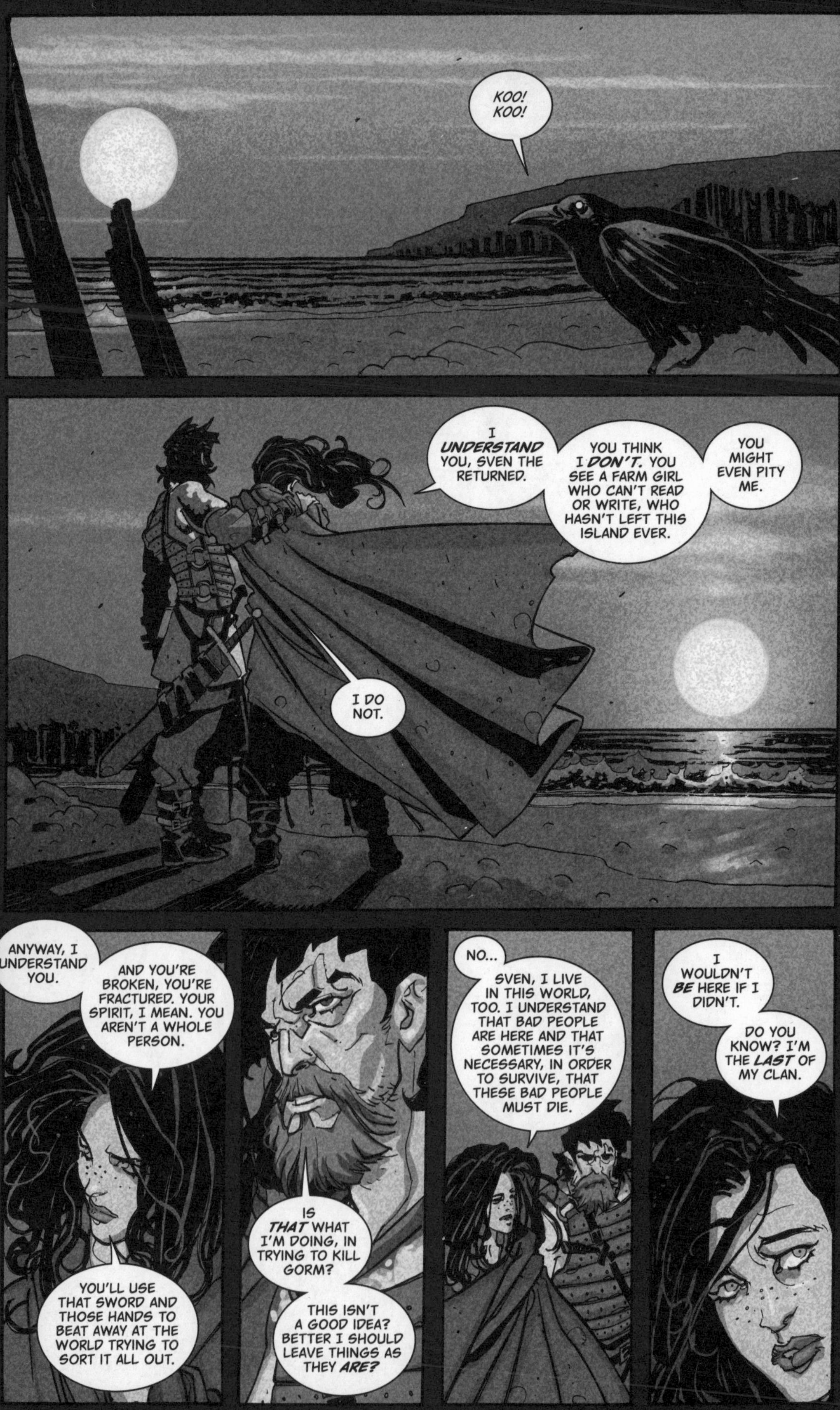
KOO! KOO!
I UNDERSTAND YOU, SVEN THE RETURNED.
YOU THINK I DON'T. YOU SEE A FARM GIRL WHO CAN'T READ OR WRITE, WHO HASN'T LEFT THIS ISLAND EVER.
YOU MIGHT EVEN PITY ME.
I DO NOT.
ANYWAY, I UNDERSTAND YOU.
AND YOU'RE BROKEN, YOU'RE FRACTURED. YOUR SPIRIT, I MEAN. YOU AREN'T A WHOLE PERSON.
YOU'LL USE THAT SWORD AND THOSE HANDS TO BEAT AWAY AT THE WORLD TRYING TO SORT IT ALL OUT.
IS THAT WHAT I'M DOING, IN TRYING TO KILL GORM?
THIS ISN'T A GOOD IDEA? BETTER I SHOULD LEAVE THINGS AS THEY ARE?
NO...
SVEN, I LIVE IN THIS WORLD, TOO. I UNDERSTAND THAT BAD PEOPLE ARE HERE AND THAT SOMETIMES IT'S NECESSARY, IN ORDER TO SURVIVE, THAT THESE BAD PEOPLE MUST DIE.
I WOULDN'T BE HERE IF I DIDN'T.
DO YOU KNOW? I'M THE LAST OF MY CLAN.

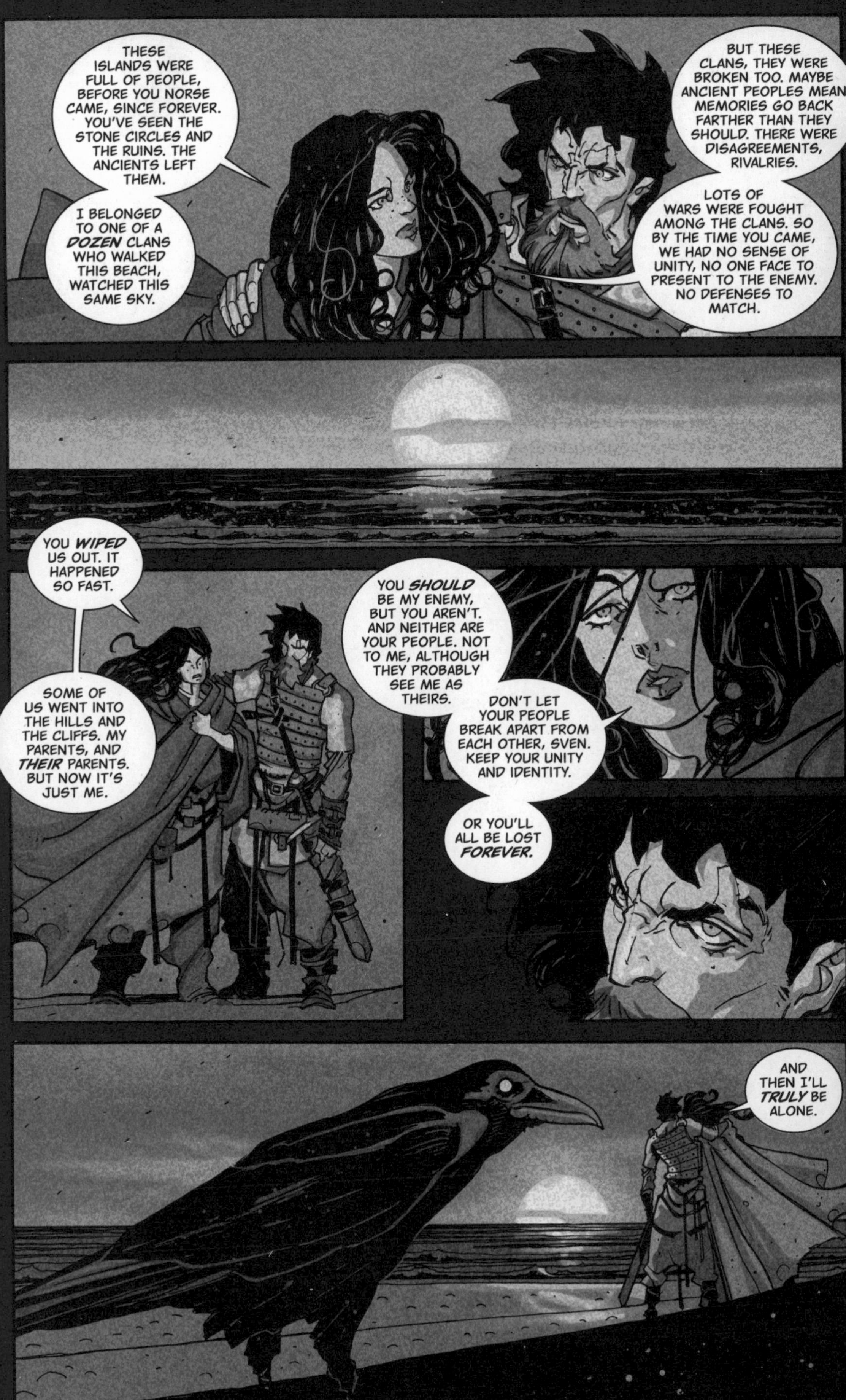
THESE ISLANDS WERE FULL OF PEOPLE, BEFORE YOU NORSE CAME, SINCE FOREVER. YOU'VE SEEN THE STONE CIRCLES AND THE RUINS. THE ANCIENTS LEFT THEM.
I BELONGED TO ONE OF A *DOZEN* CLANS WHO WALKED THIS BEACH, WATCHED THIS SAME SKY.
BUT THESE CLANS, THEY WERE BROKEN TOO. MAYBE ANCIENT PEOPLES MEAN MEMORIES GO BACK FARTHER THAN THEY SHOULD. THERE WERE DISAGREEMENTS, RIVALRIES.
LOTS OF WARS WERE FOUGHT AMONG THE CLANS. SO BY THE TIME YOU CAME, WE HAD NO SENSE OF UNITY, NO ONE FACE TO PRESENT TO THE ENEMY. NO DEFENSES TO MATCH.
YOU *WIPED* US OUT. IT HAPPENED SO FAST.
SOME OF US WENT INTO THE HILLS AND THE CLIFFS. MY PARENTS, AND *THEIR* PARENTS. BUT NOW IT'S JUST ME.
YOU *SHOULD* BE MY ENEMY, BUT YOU AREN'T. AND NEITHER ARE YOUR PEOPLE. NOT TO ME, ALTHOUGH THEY PROBABLY SEE ME AS THEIRS.
DON'T LET YOUR PEOPLE BREAK APART FROM EACH OTHER, SVEN. KEEP YOUR UNITY AND IDENTITY.
OR YOU'LL ALL BE LOST *FOREVER.*
AND THEN I'LL *TRULY* BE ALONE.

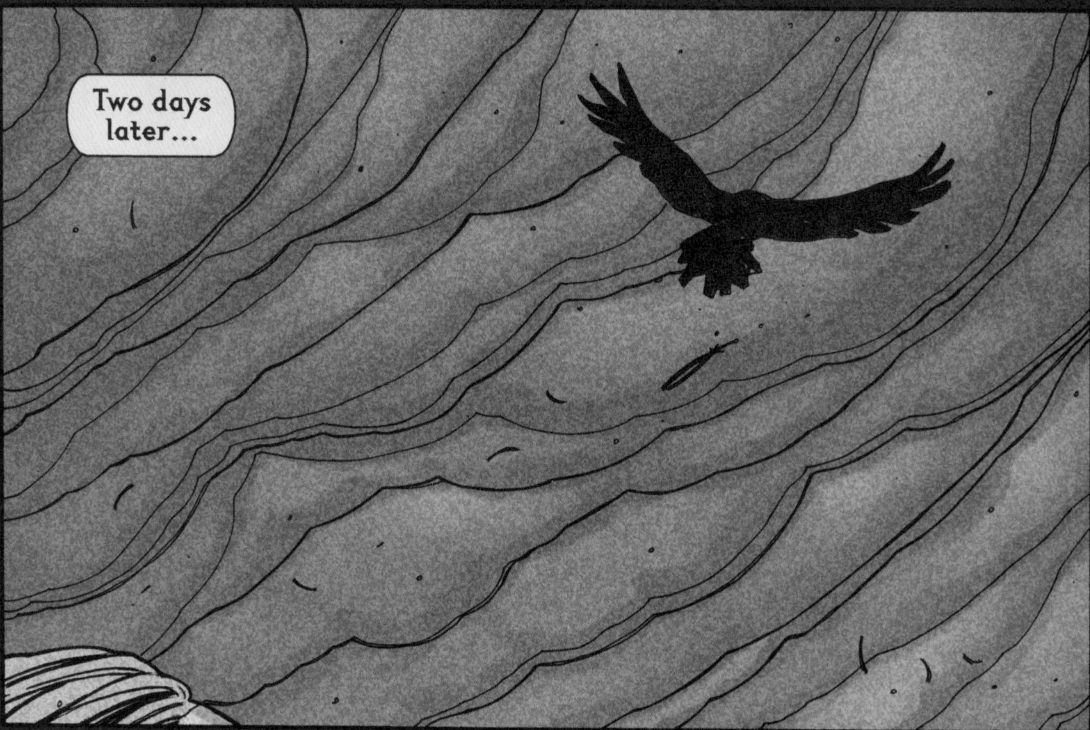
Two days later...

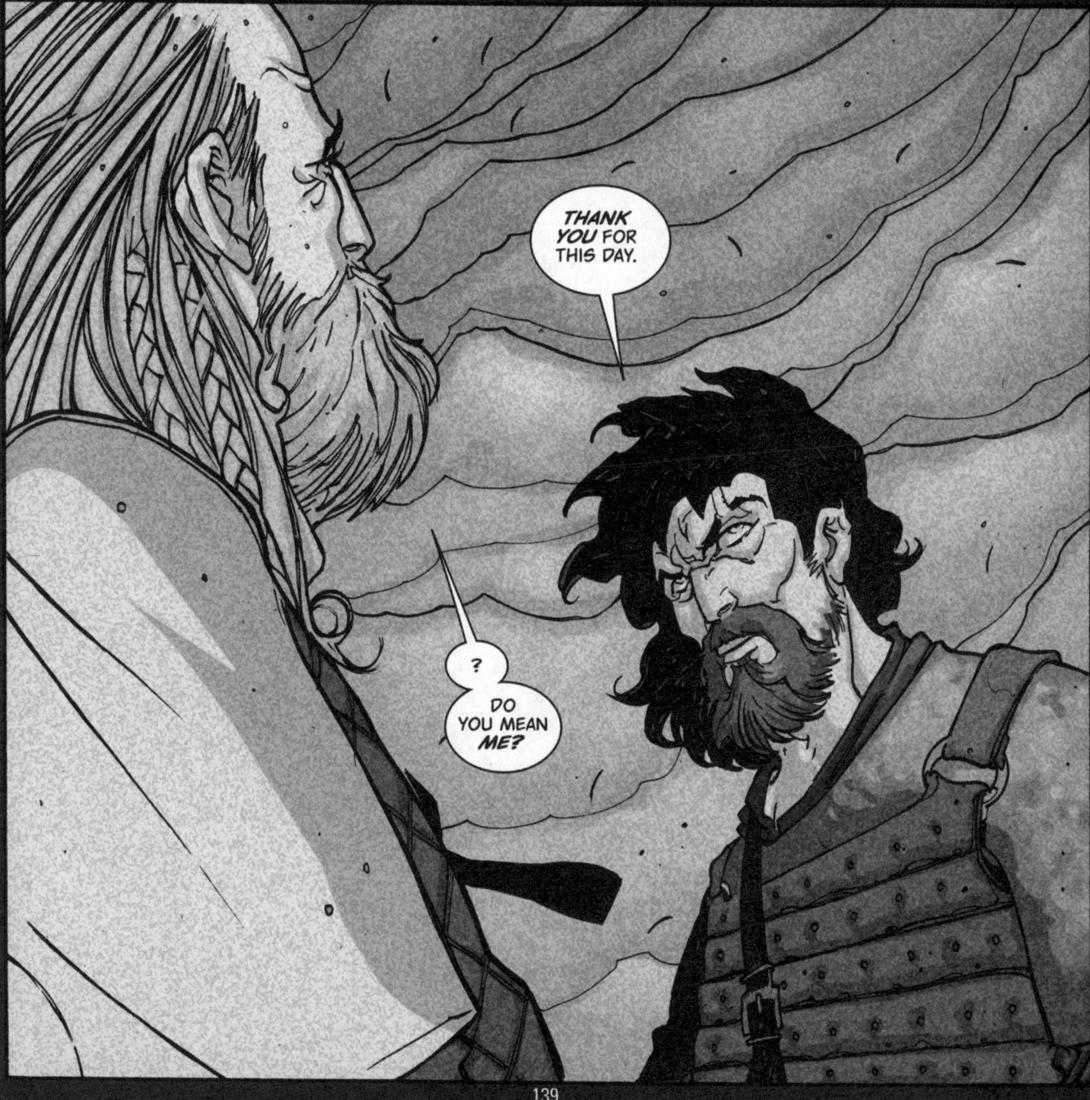
THANK YOU FOR THIS DAY.
?
DO YOU MEAN ME?

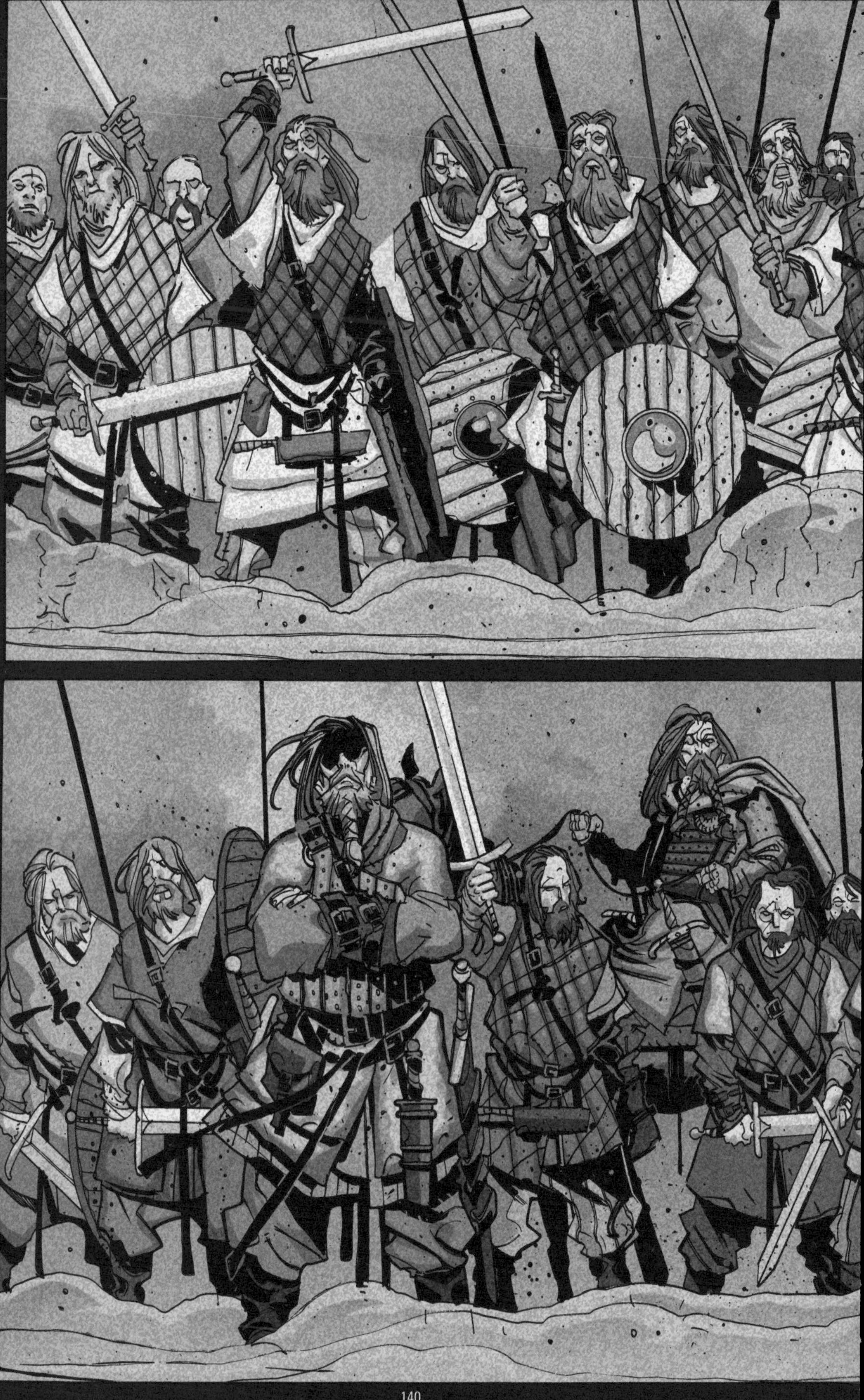

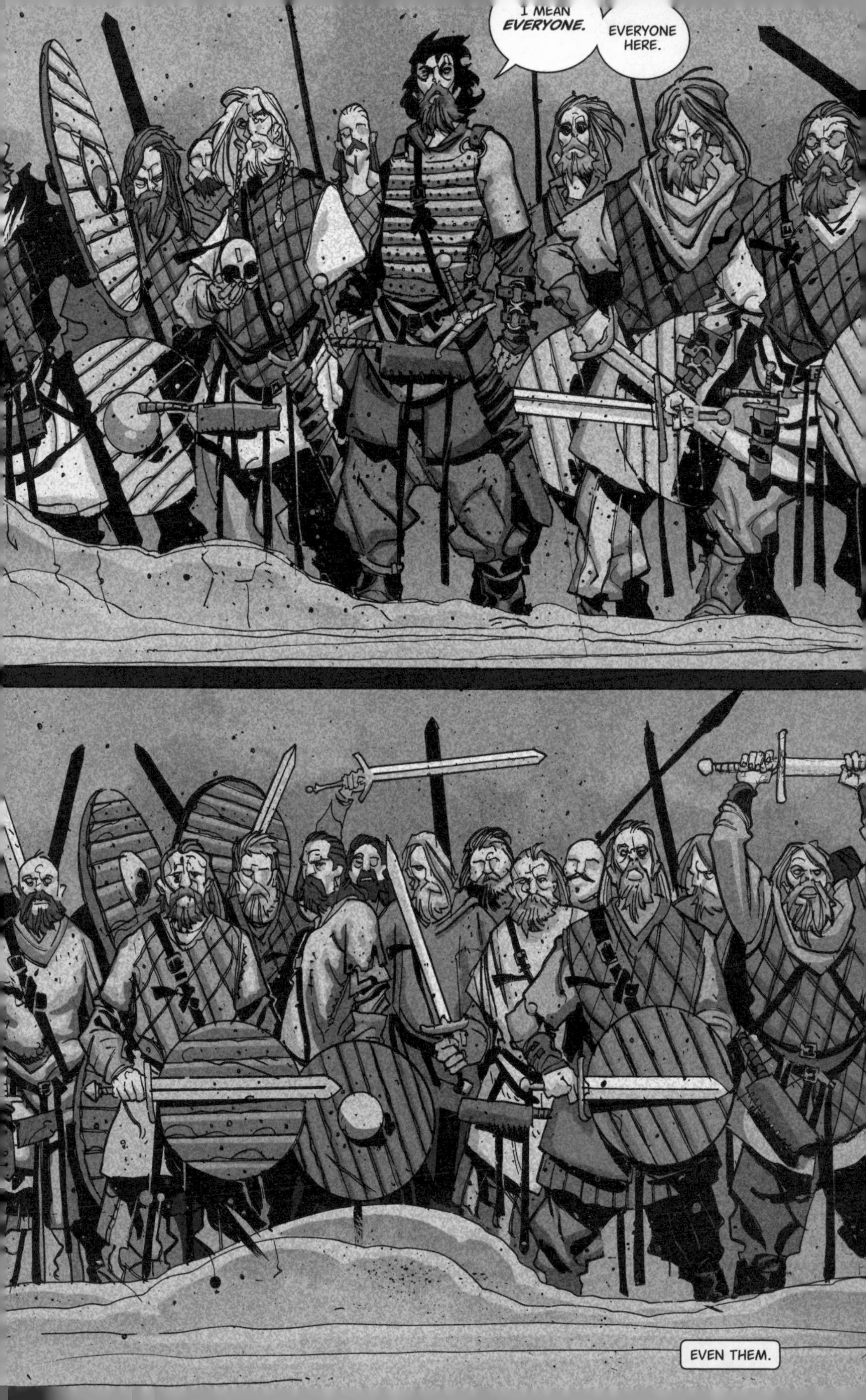
I MEAN *EVERYONE.*
EVERYONE HERE.
EVEN THEM.

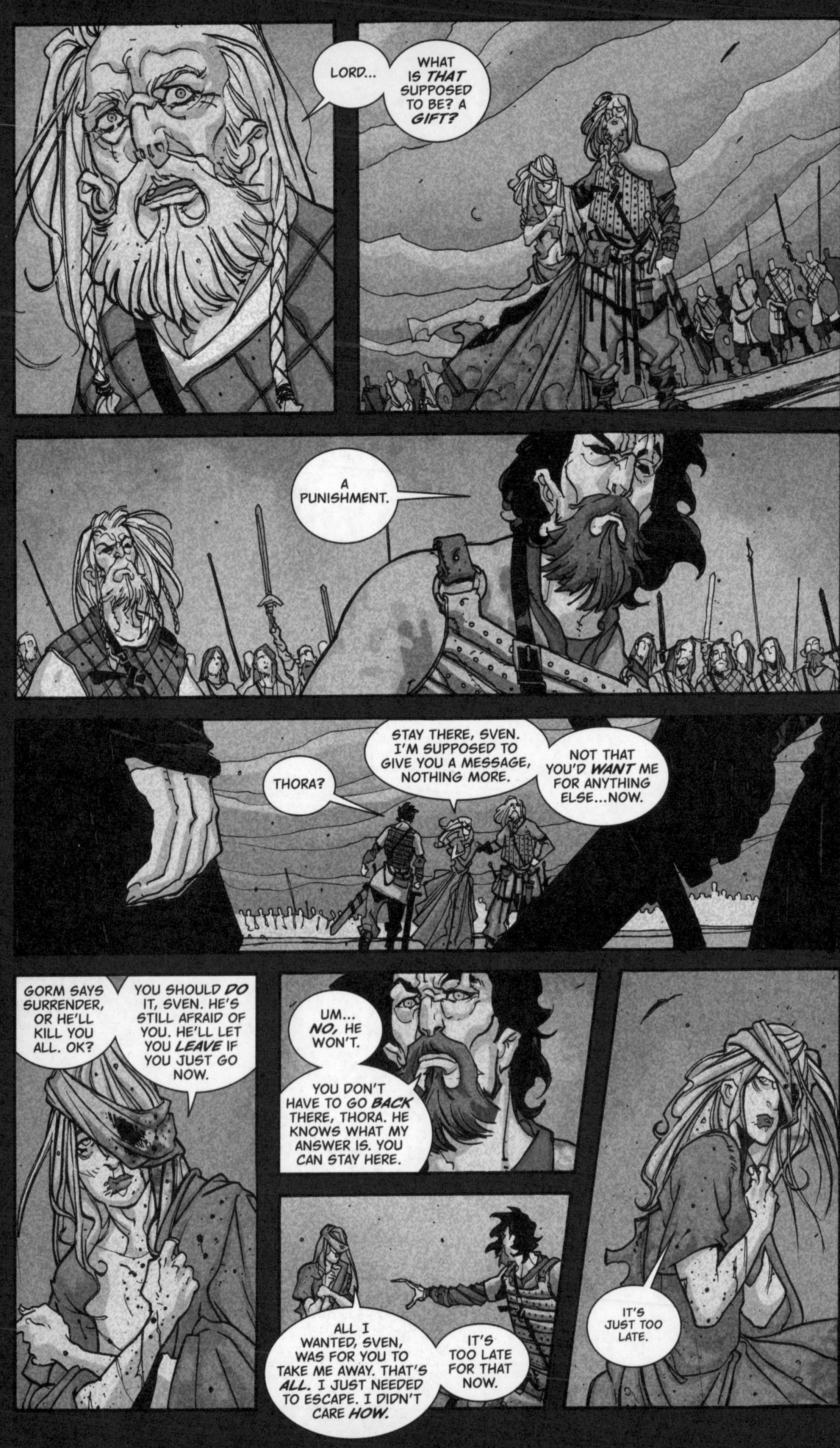

LORD...
WHAT IS *THAT* SUPPOSED TO BE? A *GIFT?*
A PUNISHMENT.
THORA?
STAY THERE, SVEN. I'M SUPPOSED TO GIVE YOU A MESSAGE, NOTHING MORE.
NOT THAT YOU'D *WANT* ME FOR ANYTHING ELSE...NOW.
GORM SAYS SURRENDER, OR HE'LL KILL YOU ALL. OK?
YOU SHOULD *DO* IT, SVEN. HE'S STILL AFRAID OF YOU. HE'LL LET YOU *LEAVE* IF YOU JUST GO NOW.
UM... *NO,* HE WON'T.
YOU DON'T HAVE TO GO *BACK* THERE, THORA. HE KNOWS WHAT MY ANSWER IS. YOU CAN STAY HERE.
ALL I WANTED, SVEN, WAS FOR YOU TO TAKE ME AWAY. THAT'S *ALL.* I JUST NEEDED TO ESCAPE. I DIDN'T CARE *HOW.*
IT'S TOO LATE FOR THAT NOW.
IT'S JUST TOO LATE.

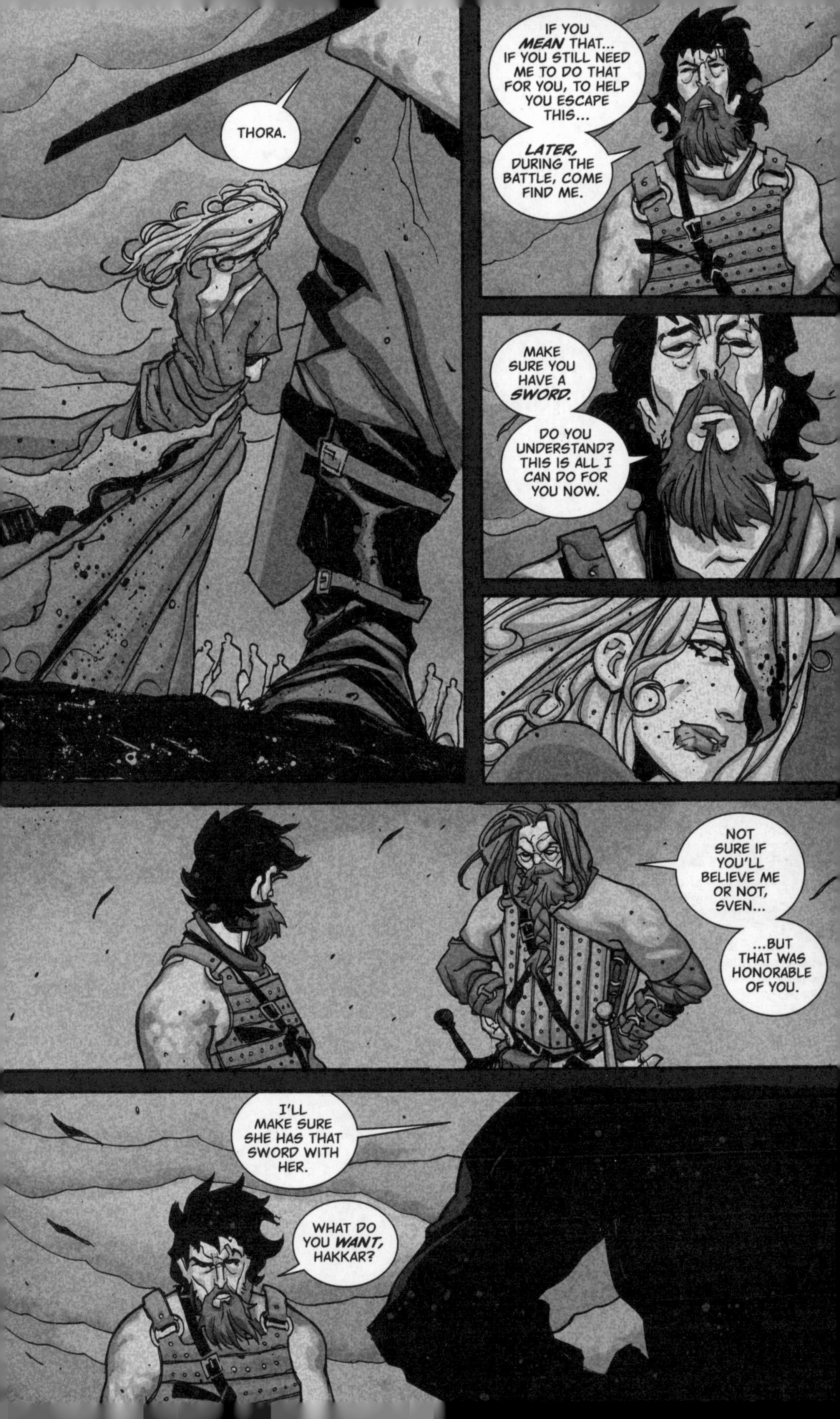
THORA.
IF YOU MEAN THAT... IF YOU STILL NEED ME TO DO THAT FOR YOU, TO HELP YOU ESCAPE THIS...
LATER, DURING THE BATTLE, COME FIND ME.
MAKE SURE YOU HAVE A SWORD.
DO YOU UNDERSTAND? THIS IS ALL I CAN DO FOR YOU NOW.
NOT SURE IF YOU'LL BELIEVE ME OR NOT, SVEN...
...BUT THAT WAS HONORABLE OF YOU.
I'LL MAKE SURE SHE HAS THAT SWORD WITH HER.
WHAT DO YOU WANT, HAKKAR?

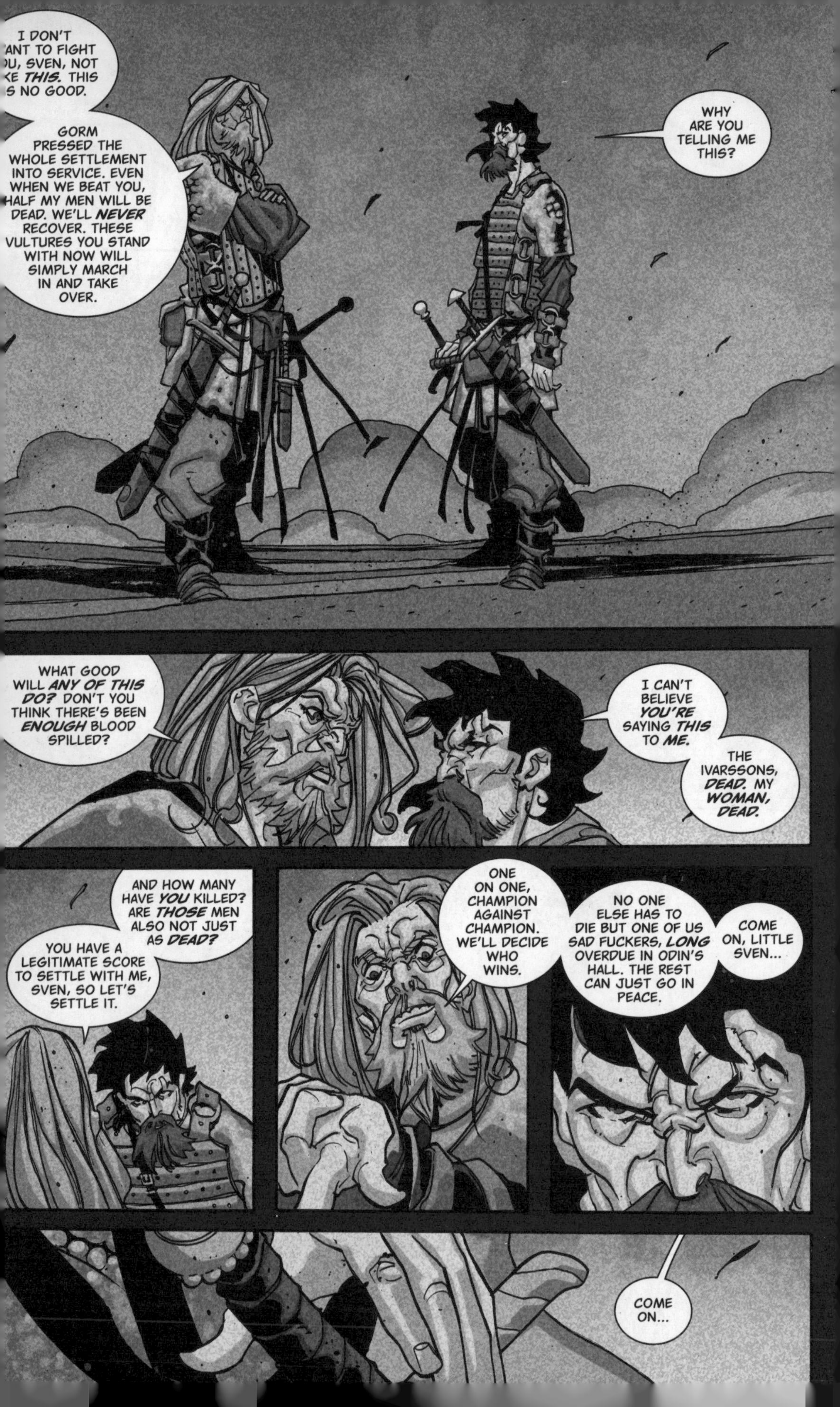
I DON'T ANT TO FIGHT OU, SVEN, NOT KE THIS. THIS S NO GOOD.
GORM PRESSED THE WHOLE SETTLEMENT INTO SERVICE. EVEN WHEN WE BEAT YOU, HALF MY MEN WILL BE DEAD. WE'LL NEVER RECOVER. THESE VULTURES YOU STAND WITH NOW WILL SIMPLY MARCH IN AND TAKE OVER.
WHY ARE YOU TELLING ME THIS?
WHAT GOOD WILL ANY OF THIS DO? DON'T YOU THINK THERE'S BEEN ENOUGH BLOOD SPILLED?
I CAN'T BELIEVE YOU'RE SAYING THIS TO ME.
THE IVARSSONS, DEAD. MY WOMAN, DEAD.
AND HOW MANY HAVE YOU KILLED? ARE THOSE MEN ALSO NOT JUST AS DEAD?
YOU HAVE A LEGITIMATE SCORE TO SETTLE WITH ME, SVEN, SO LET'S SETTLE IT.
ONE ON ONE, CHAMPION AGAINST CHAMPION. WE'LL DECIDE WHO WINS.
NO ONE ELSE HAS TO DIE BUT ONE OF US SAD FUCKERS, LONG OVERDUE IN ODIN'S HALL. THE REST CAN JUST GO IN PEACE.
COME ON, LITTLE SVEN...
COME ON...

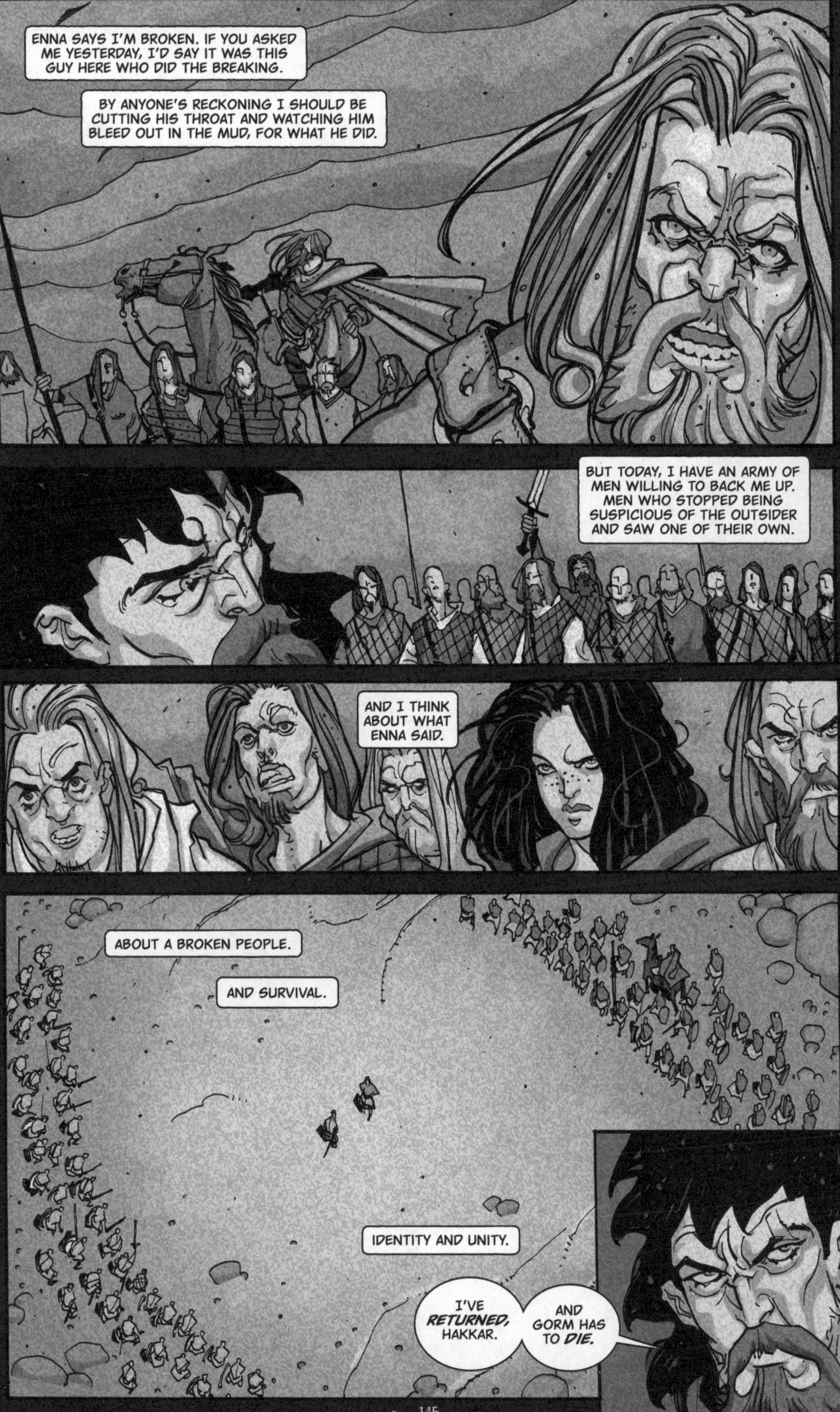
ENNA SAYS I'M BROKEN. IF YOU ASKED ME YESTERDAY, I'D SAY IT WAS THIS GUY HERE WHO DID THE BREAKING.
BY ANYONE'S RECKONING I SHOULD BE CUTTING HIS THROAT AND WATCHING HIM BLEED OUT IN THE MUD, FOR WHAT HE DID.
BUT TODAY, I HAVE AN ARMY OF MEN WILLING TO BACK ME UP. MEN WHO STOPPED BEING SUSPICIOUS OF THE OUTSIDER AND SAW ONE OF THEIR OWN.
AND I THINK ABOUT WHAT ENNA SAID.
ABOUT A BROKEN PEOPLE.
AND SURVIVAL.
IDENTITY AND UNITY.
I'VE *RETURNED,* HAKKAR.
AND GORM HAS TO *DIE.*

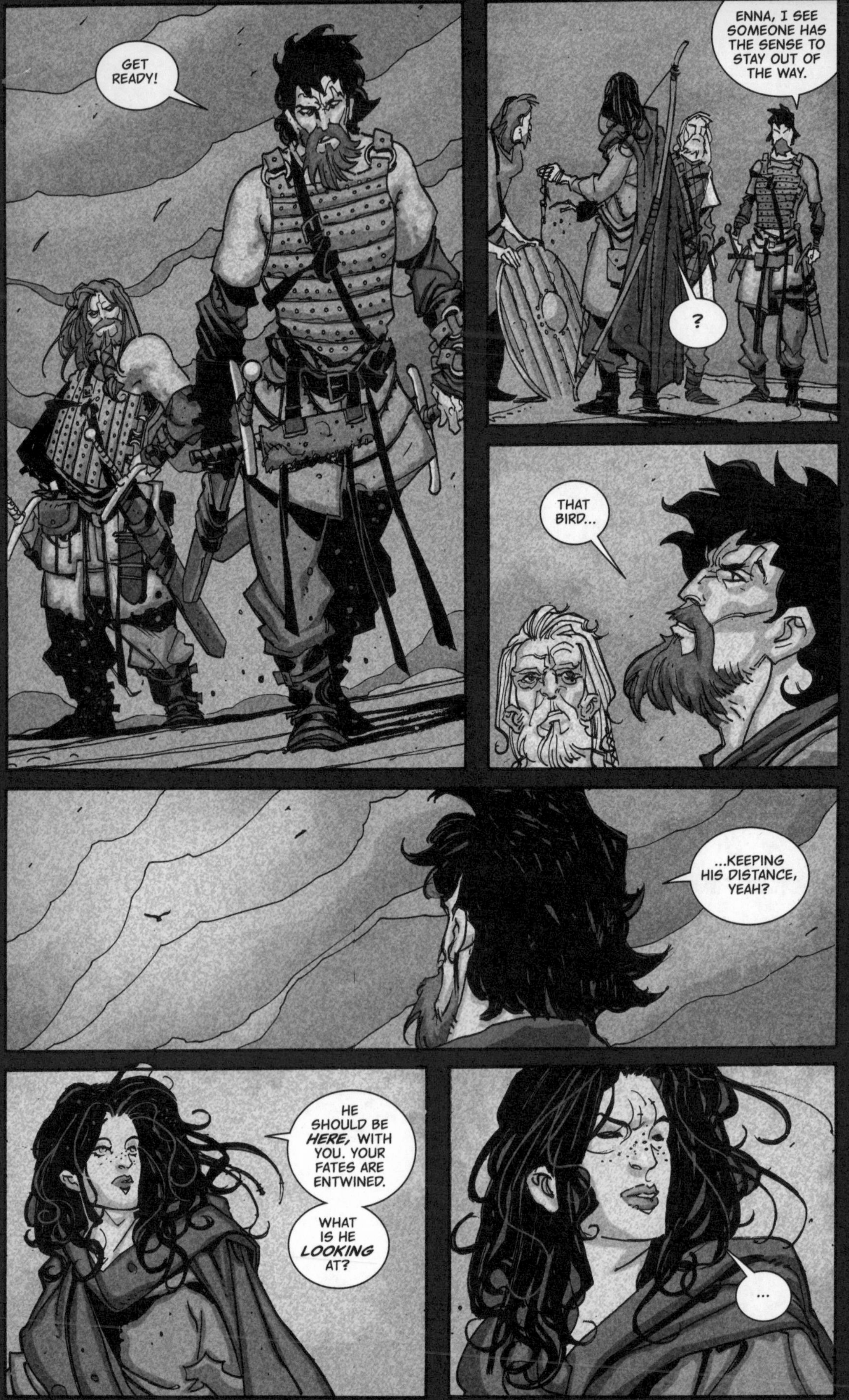
GET READY!
ENNA, I SEE SOMEONE HAS THE SENSE TO STAY OUT OF THE WAY.
?
THAT BIRD...
...KEEPING HIS DISTANCE, YEAH?
HE SHOULD BE *HERE,* WITH YOU. YOUR FATES ARE ENTWINED.
WHAT IS HE *LOOKING* AT?
...

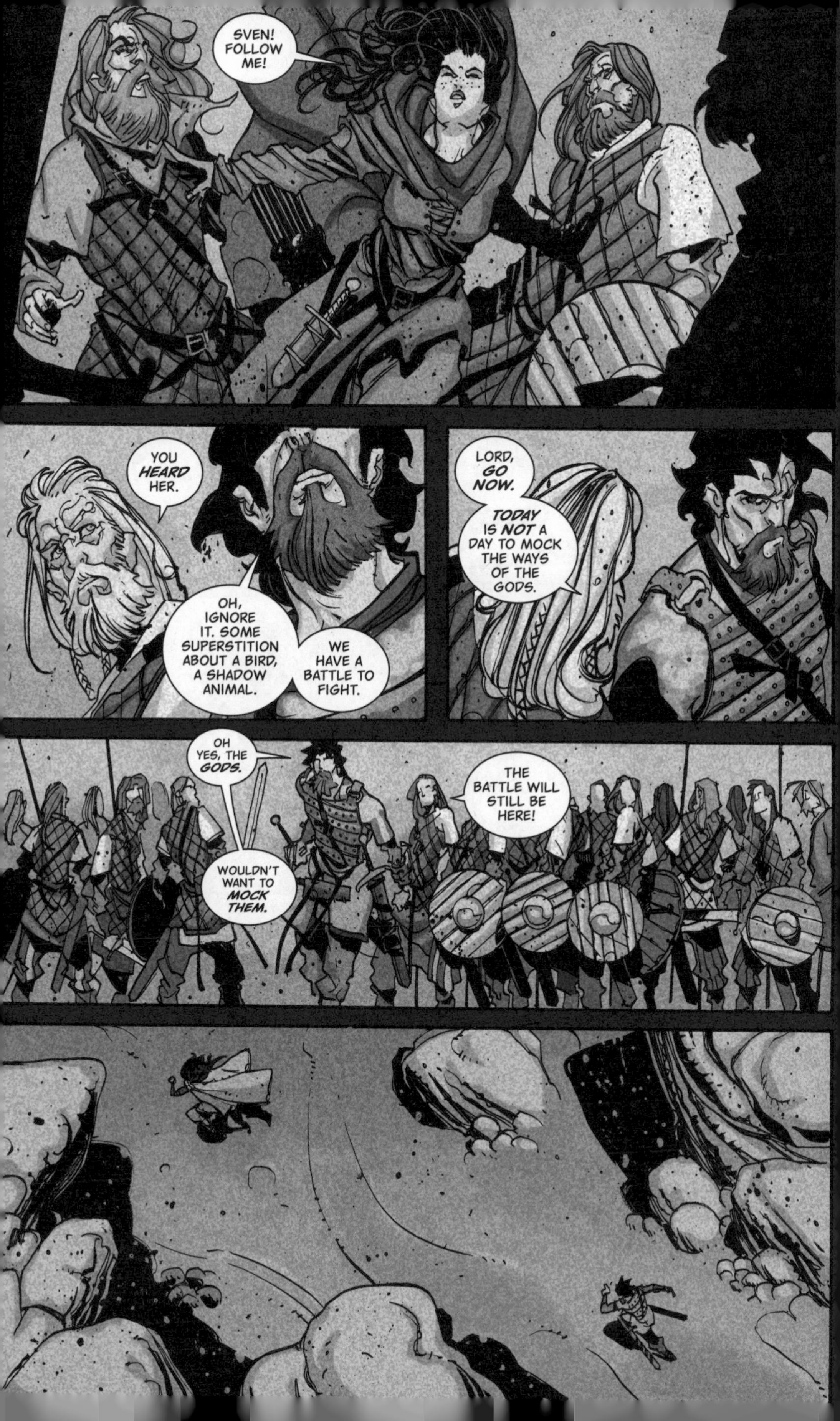
SVEN! FOLLOW ME!
YOU HEARD HER.
OH, IGNORE IT. SOME SUPERSTITION ABOUT A BIRD, A SHADOW ANIMAL.
WE HAVE A BATTLE TO FIGHT.
LORD, GO NOW.
TODAY IS NOT A DAY TO MOCK THE WAYS OF THE GODS.
OH YES, THE GODS.
WOULDN'T WANT TO MOCK THEM.
THE BATTLE WILL STILL BE HERE!

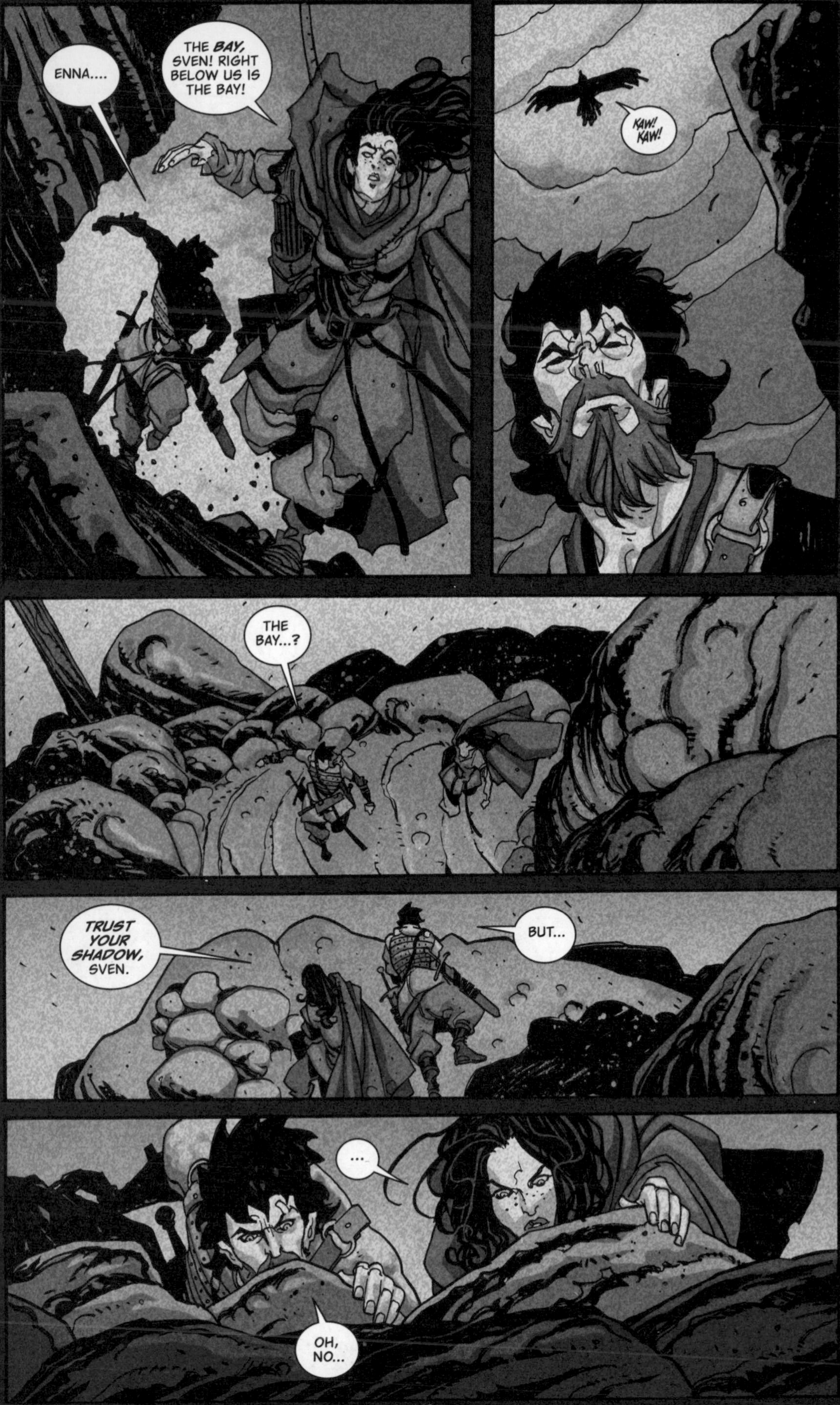
ENNA....
THE *BAY,* SVEN! RIGHT BELOW US IS THE BAY!
KAW! KAW!
THE BAY...?
TRUST YOUR SHADOW, SVEN.
BUT...
...
OH, NO...

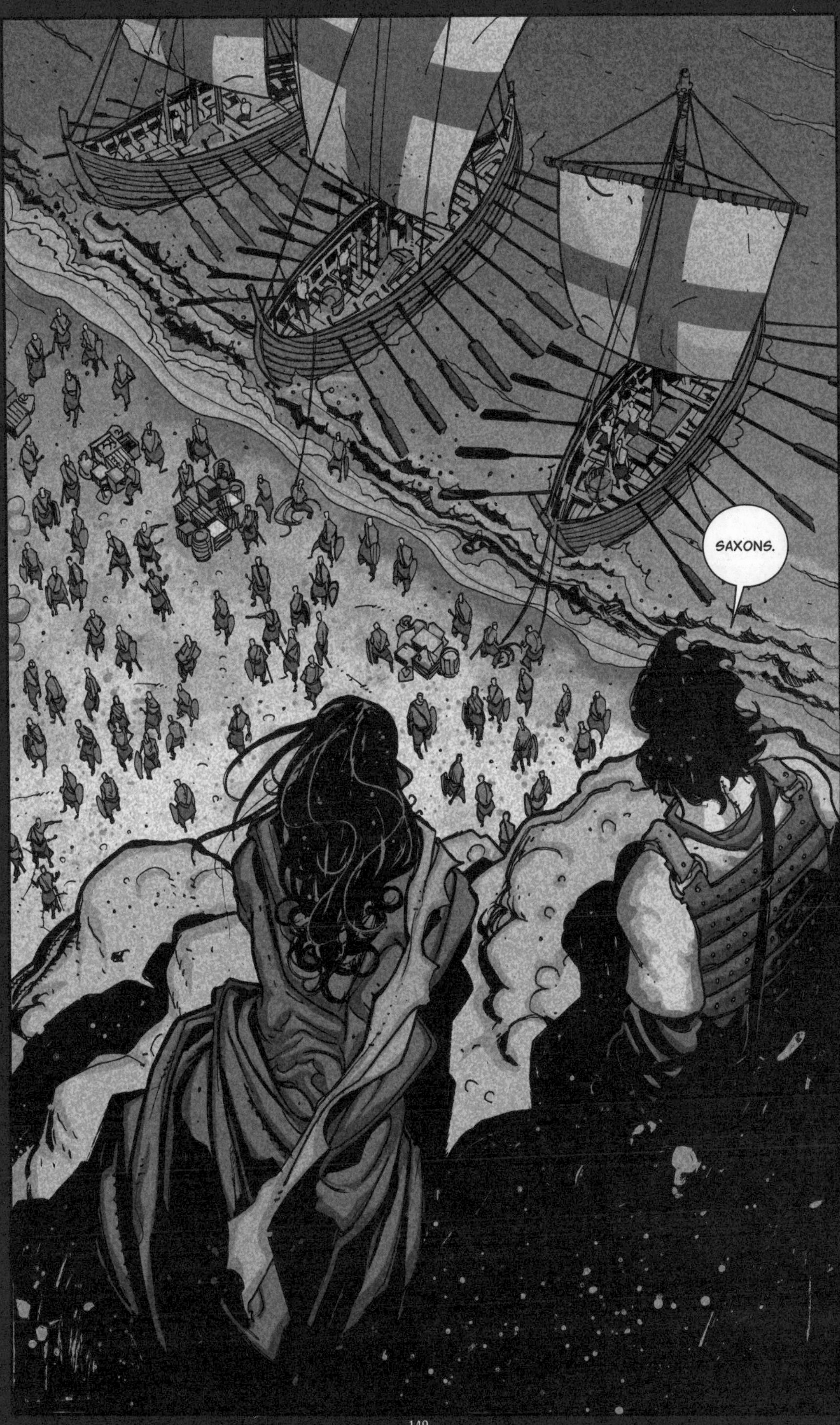
SAXONS.

7 Is Brônac Mo Cineamiun (Sad Is My Fate)

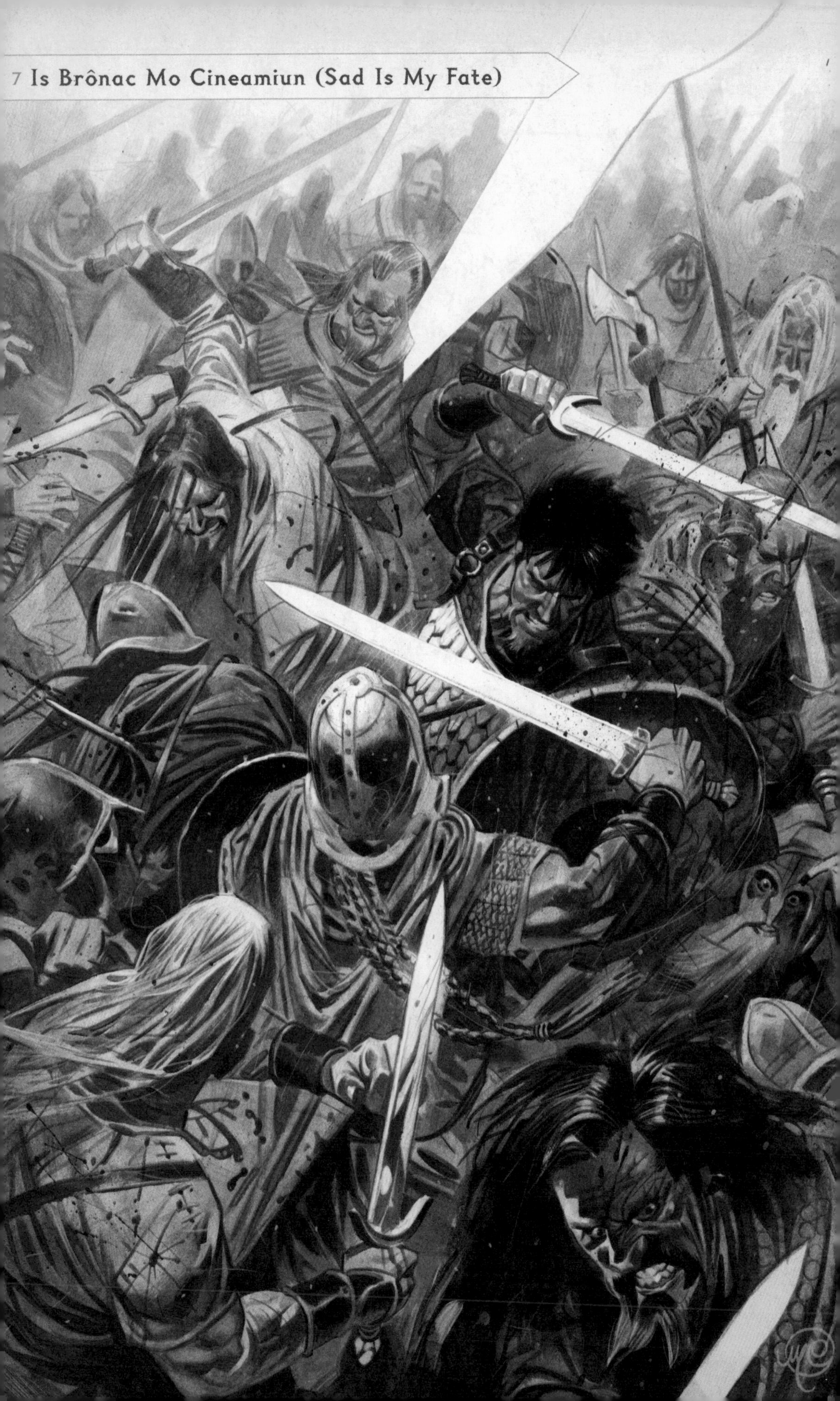

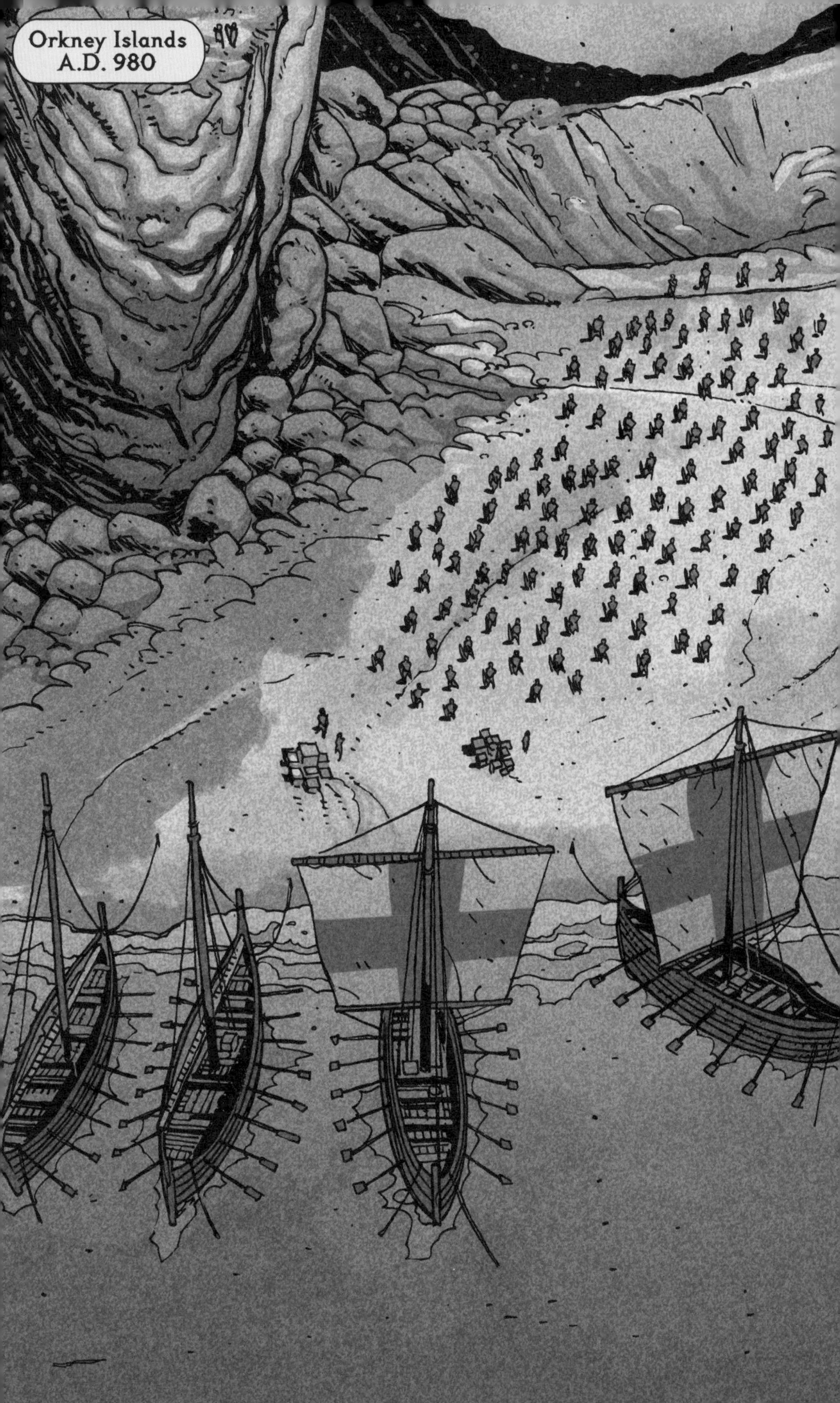
Orkney Islands
A.D. 980

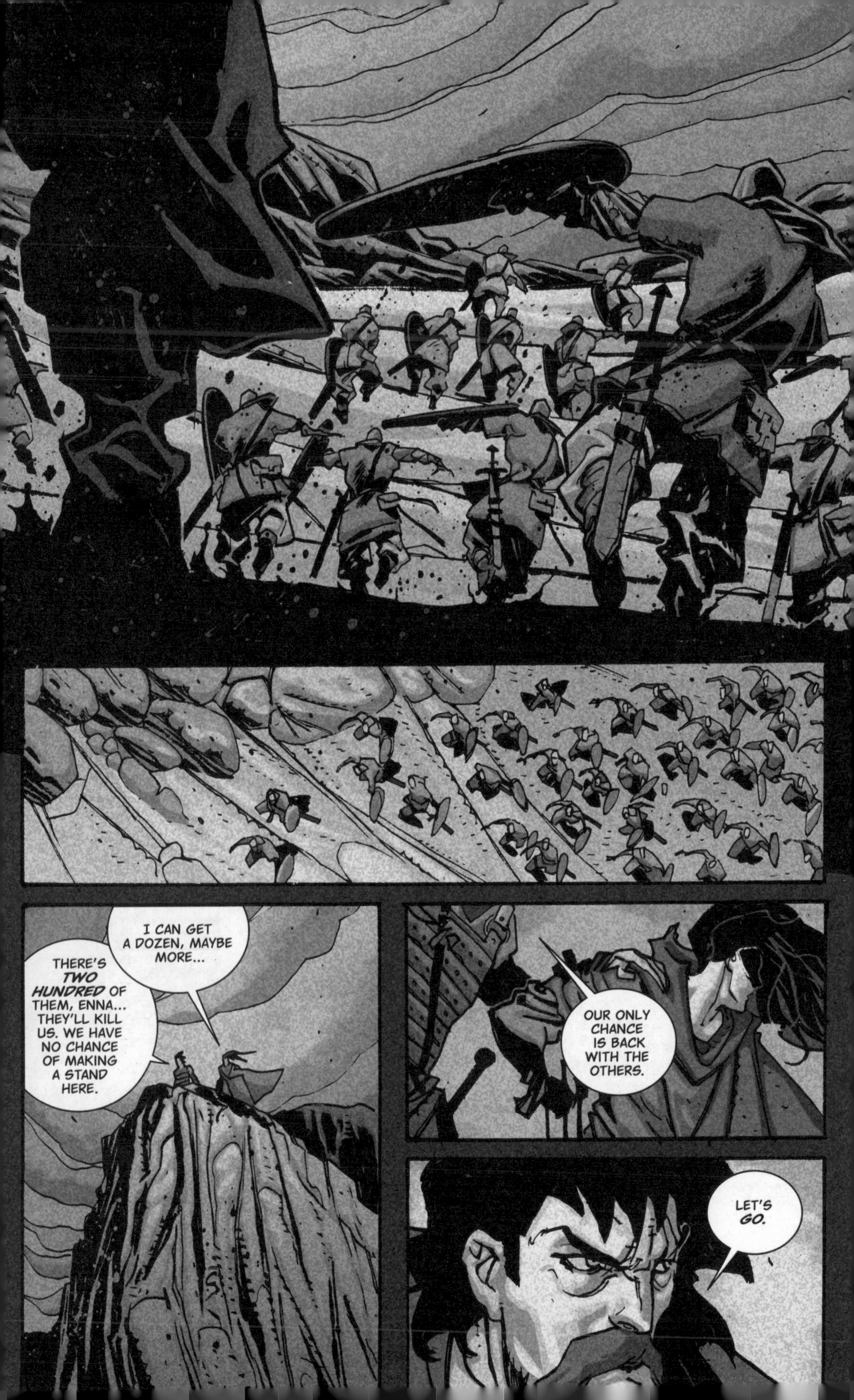

I CAN GET A DOZEN, MAYBE MORE...
THERE'S TWO HUNDRED OF THEM, ENNA... THEY'LL KILL US. WE HAVE NO CHANCE OF MAKING A STAND HERE.
OUR ONLY CHANCE IS BACK WITH THE OTHERS.
LET'S GO.

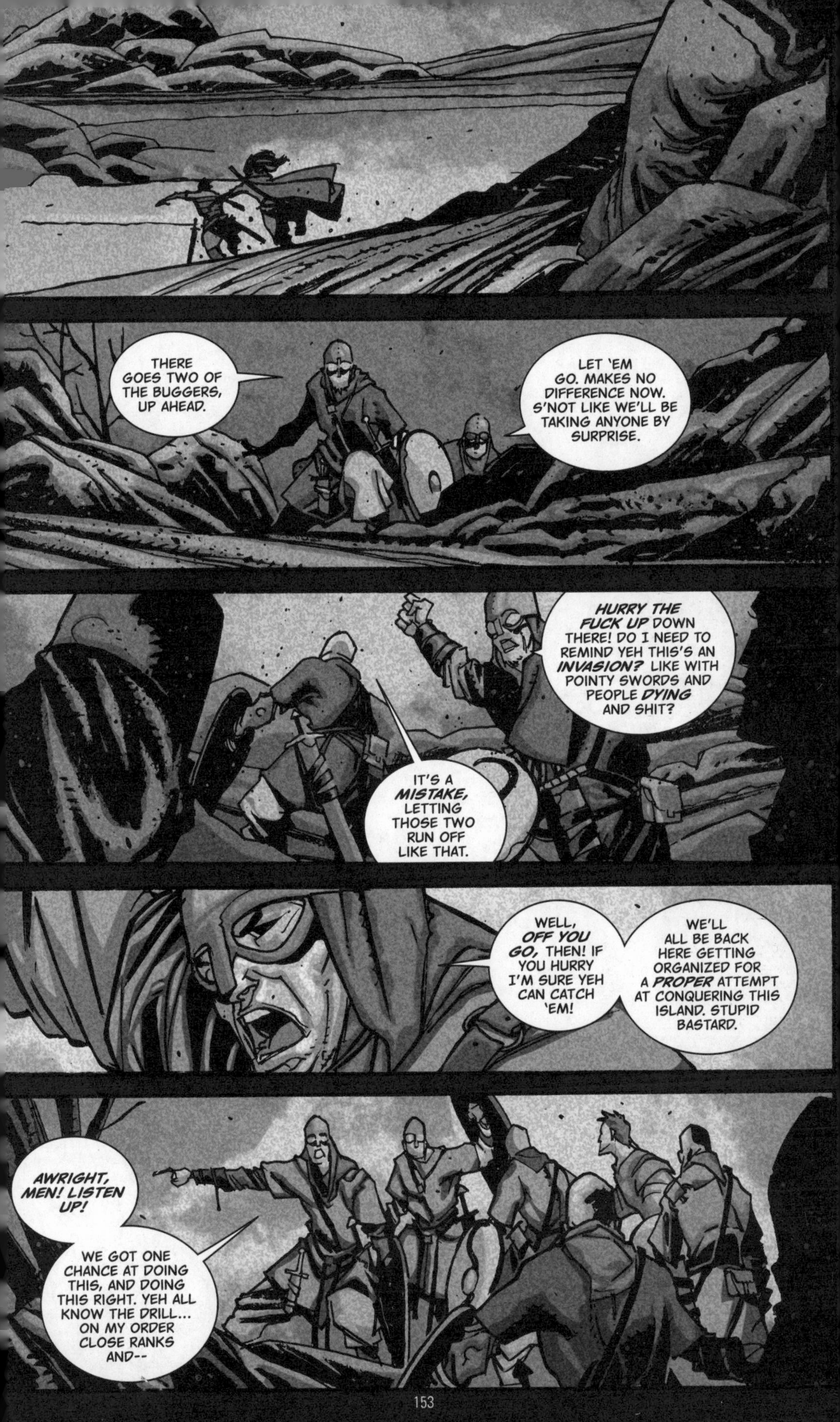

THERE GOES TWO OF THE BUGGERS, UP AHEAD.
LET 'EM GO. MAKES NO DIFFERENCE NOW. S'NOT LIKE WE'LL BE TAKING ANYONE BY SURPRISE.
HURRY THE FUCK UP DOWN THERE! DO I NEED TO REMIND YEH THIS'S AN INVASION? LIKE WITH POINTY SWORDS AND PEOPLE DYING AND SHIT?
IT'S A MISTAKE, LETTING THOSE TWO RUN OFF LIKE THAT.
WELL, OFF YOU GO, THEN! IF YOU HURRY I'M SURE YEH CAN CATCH 'EM!
WE'LL ALL BE BACK HERE GETTING ORGANIZED FOR A PROPER ATTEMPT AT CONQUERING THIS ISLAND. STUPID BASTARD.
AWRIGHT, MEN! LISTEN UP!
WE GOT ONE CHANCE AT DOING THIS, AND DOING THIS RIGHT. YEH ALL KNOW THE DRILL... ON MY ORDER CLOSE RANKS AND--

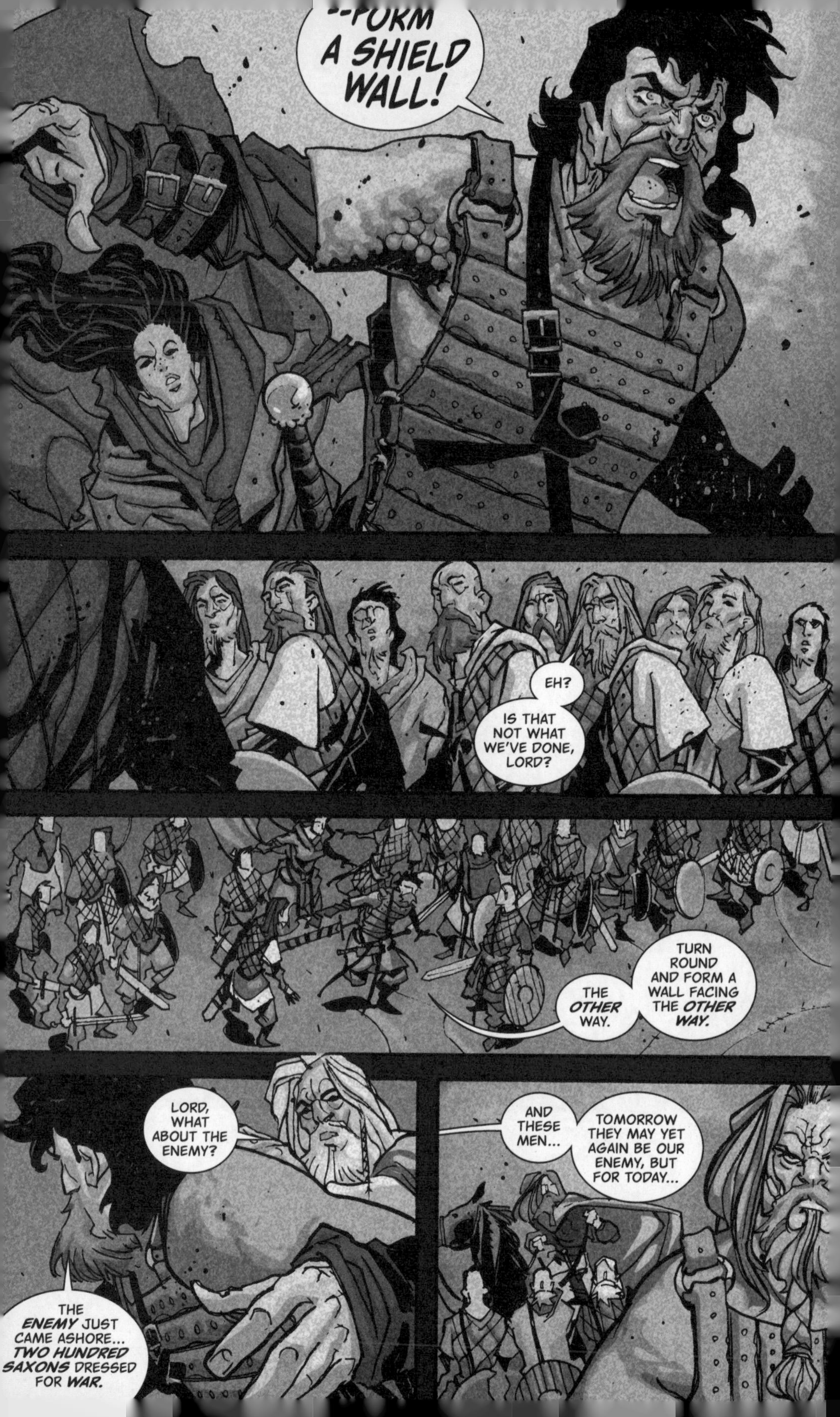
--FORM A SHIELD WALL!
EH?
IS THAT NOT WHAT WE'VE DONE, LORD?
THE OTHER WAY.
TURN ROUND AND FORM A WALL FACING THE OTHER WAY.
LORD, WHAT ABOUT THE ENEMY?
THE ENEMY JUST CAME ASHORE... TWO HUNDRED SAXONS DRESSED FOR WAR.
AND THESE MEN...
TOMORROW THEY MAY YET AGAIN BE OUR ENEMY, BUT FOR TODAY...

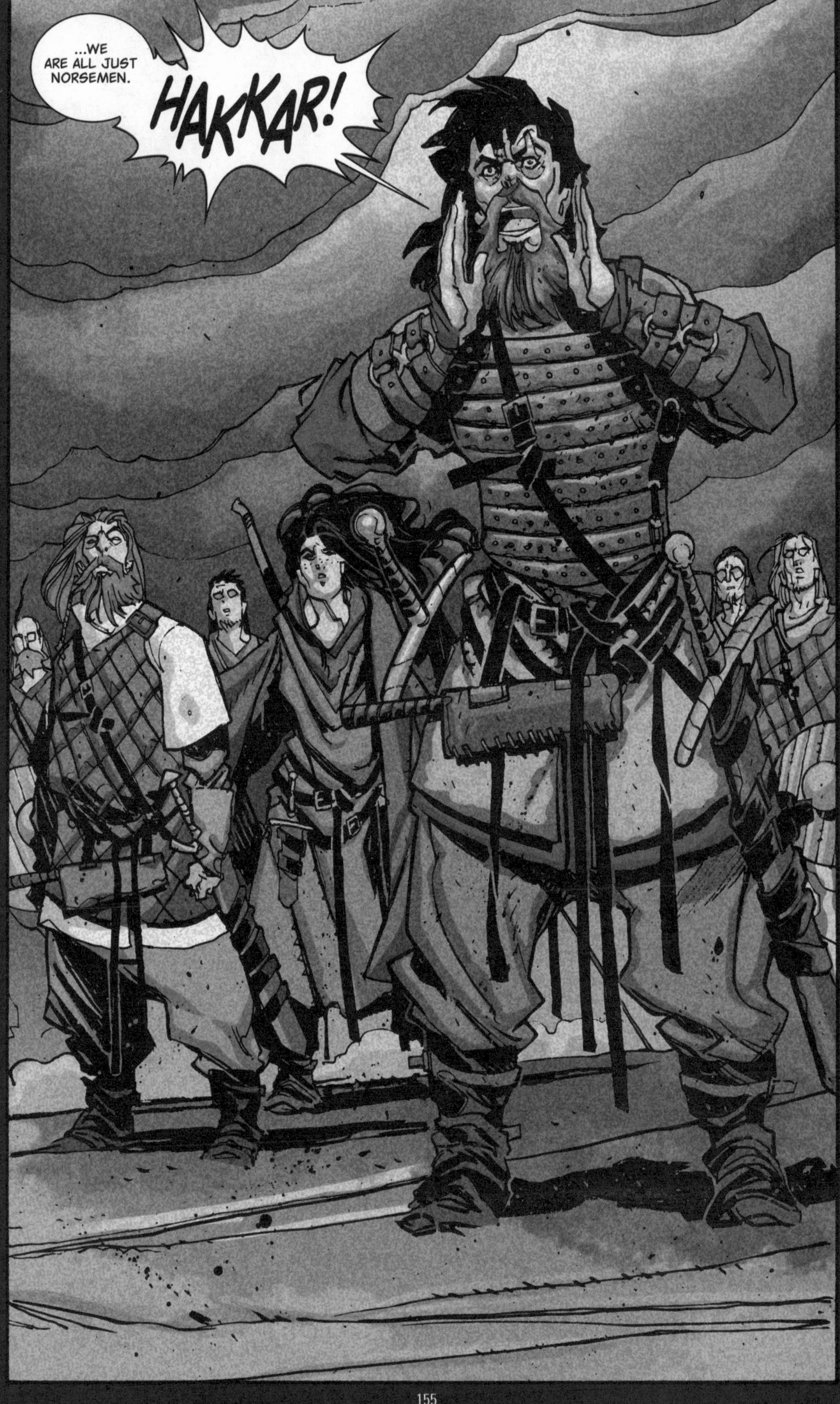
...WE ARE ALL JUST NORSEMEN.
HAKKAR!

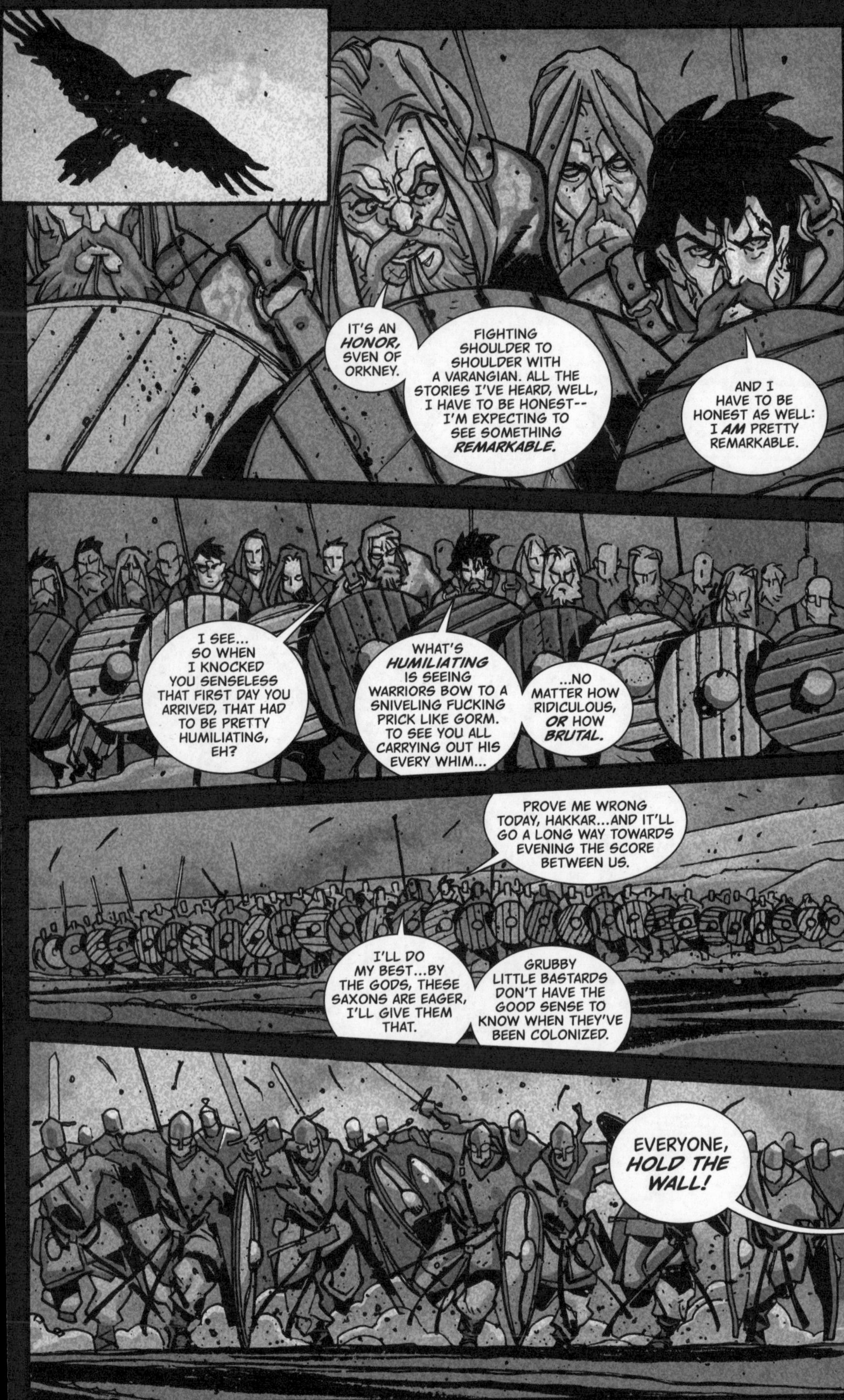
IT'S AN HONOR, SVEN OF ORKNEY.
FIGHTING SHOULDER TO SHOULDER WITH A VARANGIAN. ALL THE STORIES I'VE HEARD, WELL, I HAVE TO BE HONEST-- I'M EXPECTING TO SEE SOMETHING REMARKABLE.
AND I HAVE TO BE HONEST AS WELL: I AM PRETTY REMARKABLE.
I SEE... SO WHEN I KNOCKED YOU SENSELESS THAT FIRST DAY YOU ARRIVED, THAT HAD TO BE PRETTY HUMILIATING, EH?
WHAT'S HUMILIATING IS SEEING WARRIORS BOW TO A SNIVELING FUCKING PRICK LIKE GORM. TO SEE YOU ALL CARRYING OUT HIS EVERY WHIM...
...NO MATTER HOW RIDICULOUS, OR HOW BRUTAL.
PROVE ME WRONG TODAY, HAKKAR...AND IT'LL GO A LONG WAY TOWARDS EVENING THE SCORE BETWEEN US.
I'LL DO MY BEST...BY THE GODS, THESE SAXONS ARE EAGER, I'LL GIVE THEM THAT.
GRUBBY LITTLE BASTARDS DON'T HAVE THE GOOD SENSE TO KNOW WHEN THEY'VE BEEN COLONIZED.
EVERYONE, HOLD THE WALL!

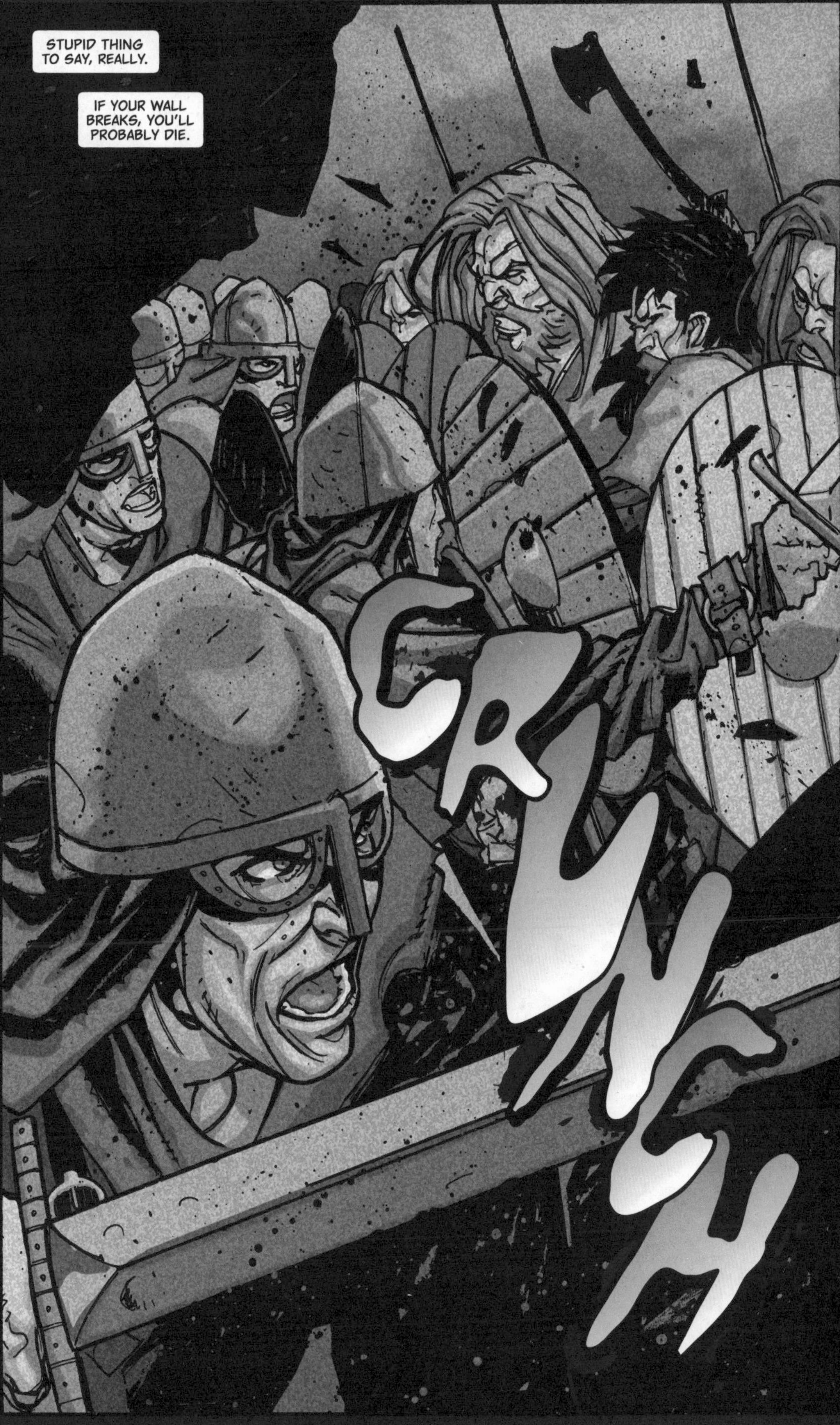
STUPID THING TO SAY, REALLY.
IF YOUR WALL BREAKS, YOU'LL PROBABLY DIE.
CRUNCH

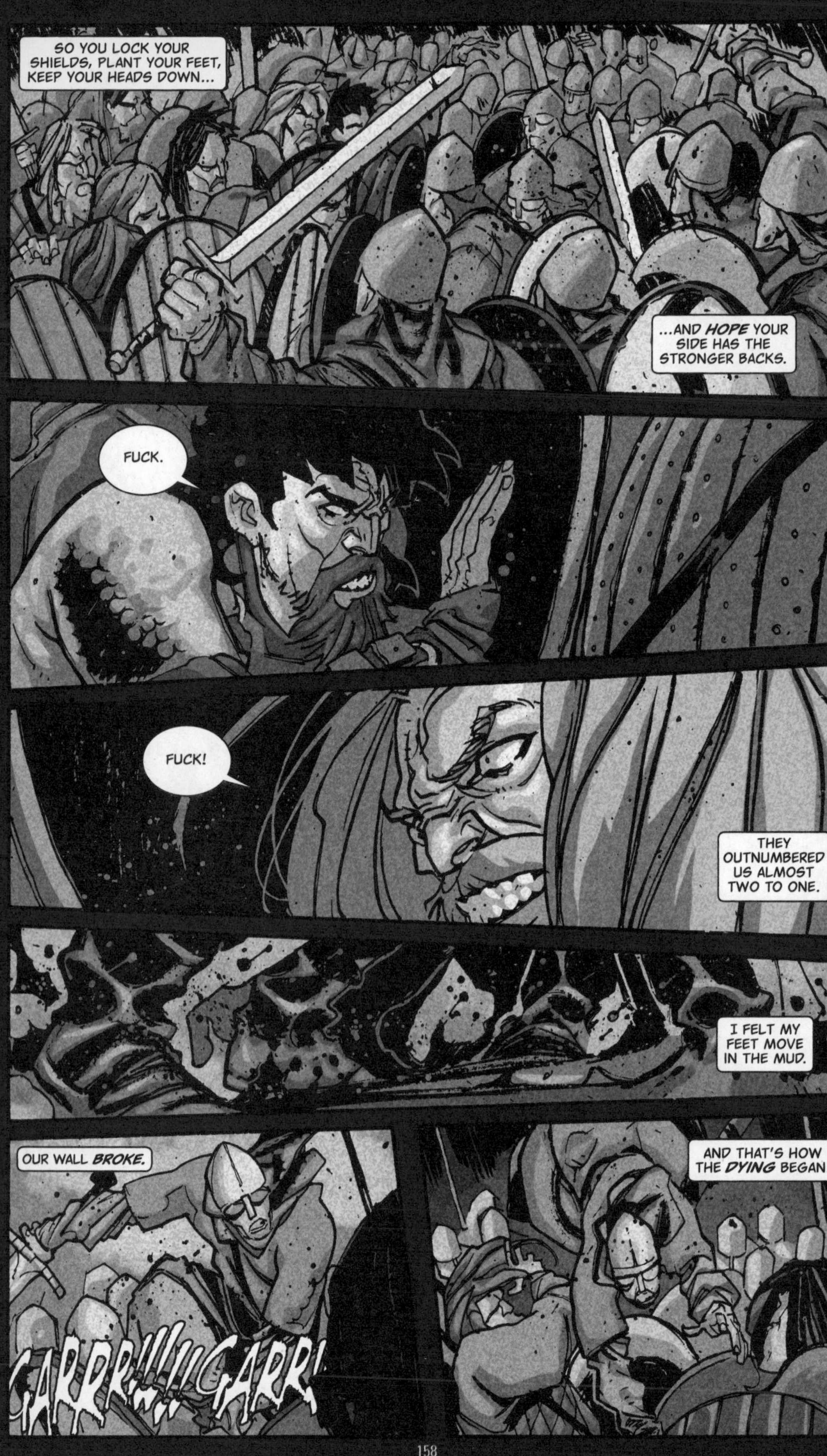
SO YOU LOCK YOUR SHIELDS, PLANT YOUR FEET, KEEP YOUR HEADS DOWN...
...AND HOPE YOUR SIDE HAS THE STRONGER BACKS.
FUCK.
FUCK!
THEY OUTNUMBERED US ALMOST TWO TO ONE.
I FELT MY FEET MOVE IN THE MUD.
OUR WALL BROKE.
AND THAT'S HOW THE DYING BEGAN.
GARRR!!!!GARR!

WHAT IT CAME DOWN TO WAS THE SAXONS *WANTING* IT MORE.

THEY WANTED IT *MORE* THE MOMENT THEY GOT ABOARD THEIR SHIPS, SAILING FROM WHEREVER THE FUCK THEY CAME FROM.

SLSSSH

AND HERE WE WERE, SQUABBLING AMONGST OURSELVES. WE CALLED THIS LAND CONQUERED AGES AGO AND GOT *LAZY*.

BMP

BUT SINCE WHEN IS LAND EVER *TRULY* CONQUERED?

ISN'T IT JUST SOMETHING THAT CHANGES OWNERS FROM TIME TO TIME?

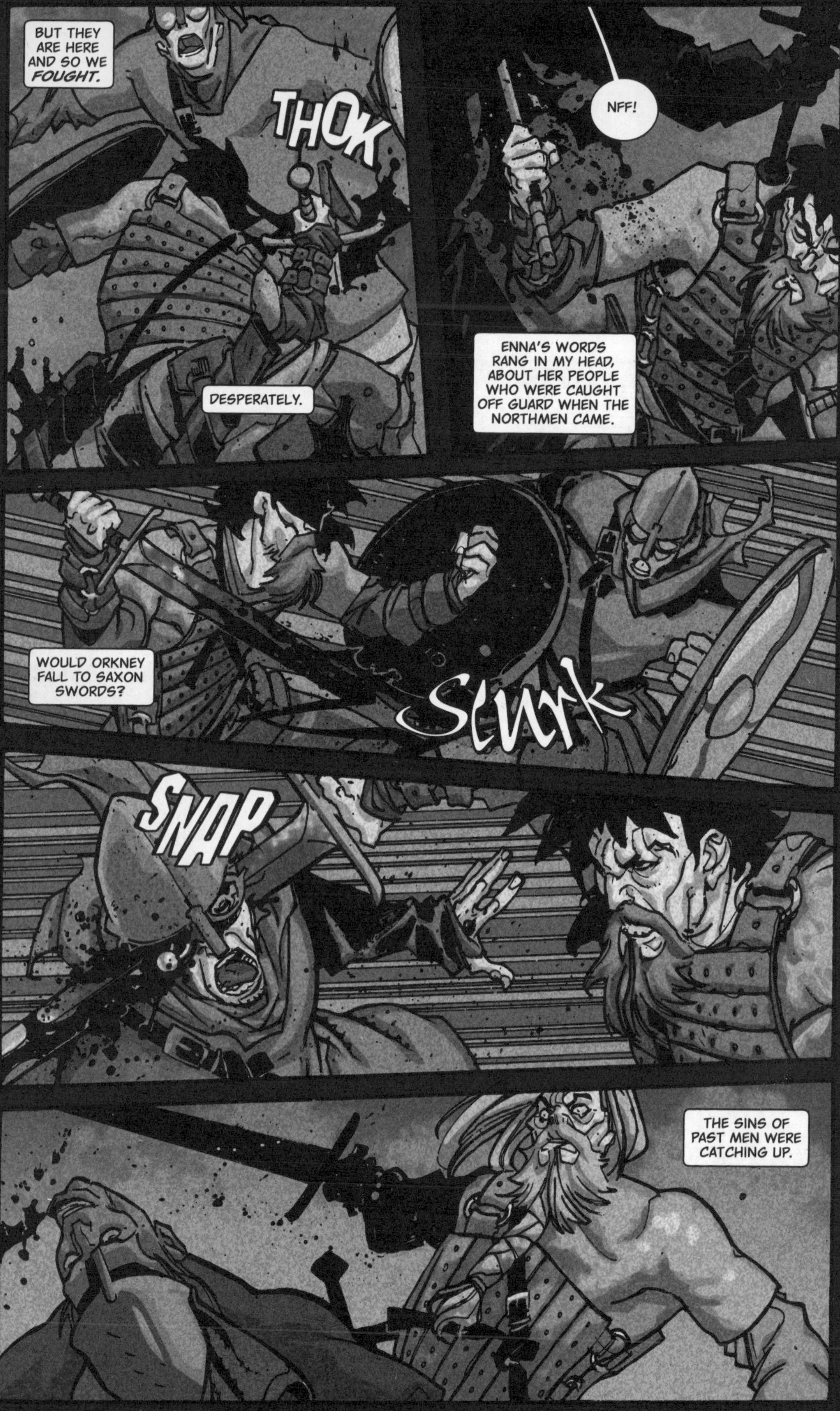
BUT THEY ARE HERE AND SO WE *FOUGHT*.
THOK
DESPERATELY.
NFF!
ENNA'S WORDS RANG IN MY HEAD, ABOUT HER PEOPLE WHO WERE CAUGHT OFF GUARD WHEN THE NORTHMEN CAME.
WOULD ORKNEY FALL TO SAXON SWORDS?
SLURK
SNAP
THE SINS OF PAST MEN WERE CATCHING UP.

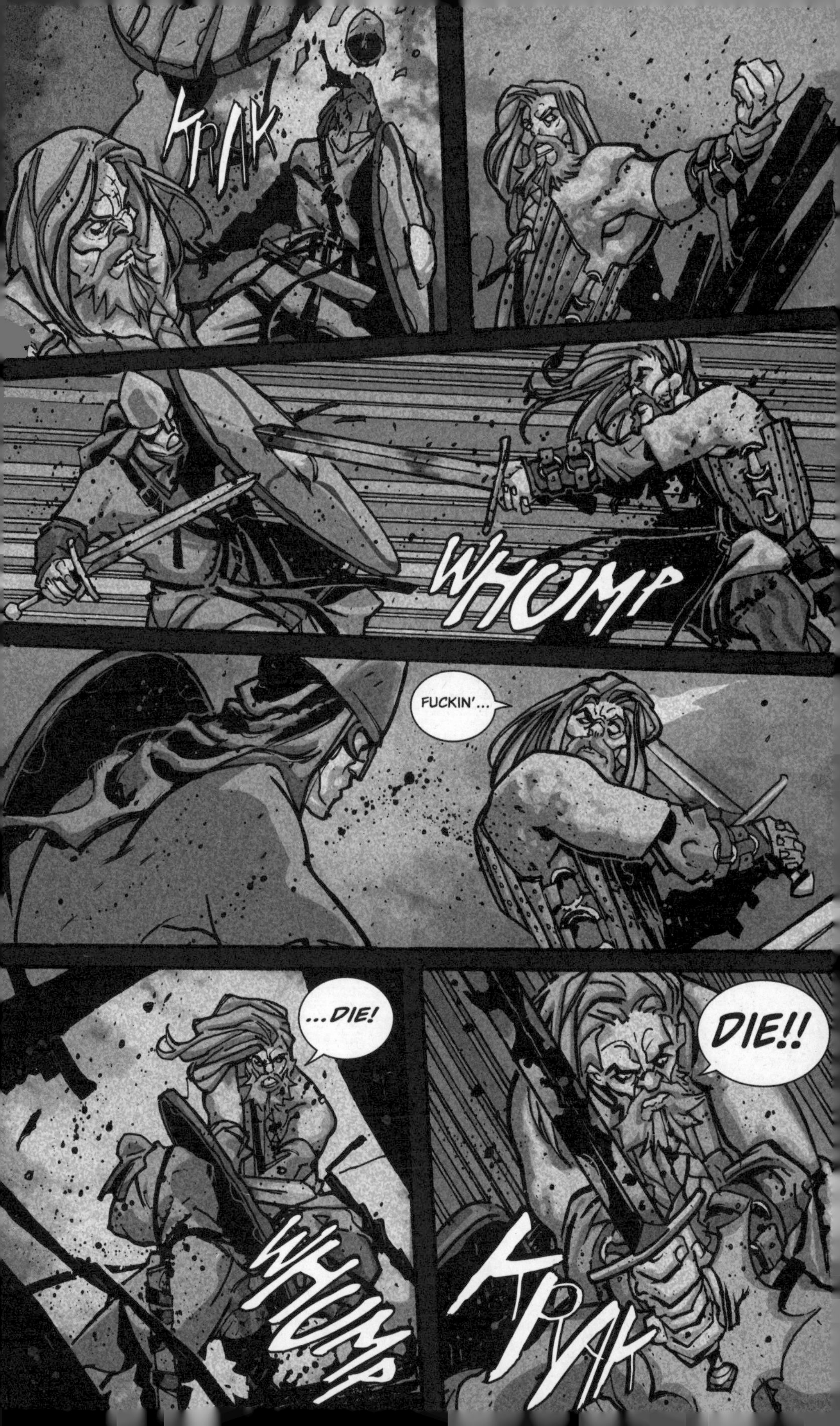
KRAK
WHUMP
FUCKIN'...
...DIE!
DIE!!
WHUMP
KRAK

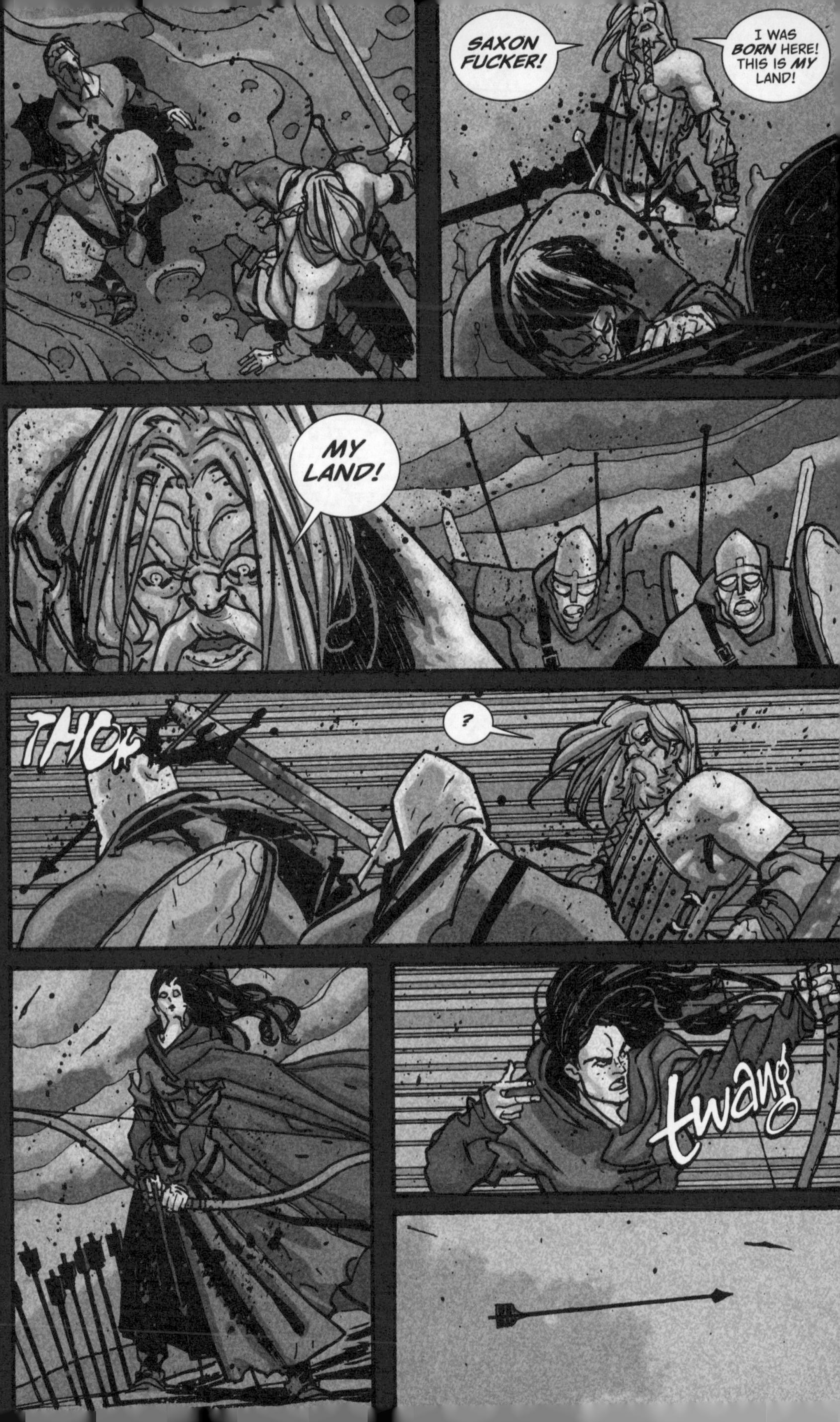
SAXON FUCKER!
I WAS BORN HERE! THIS IS MY LAND!
MY LAND!
THOK
?
twang

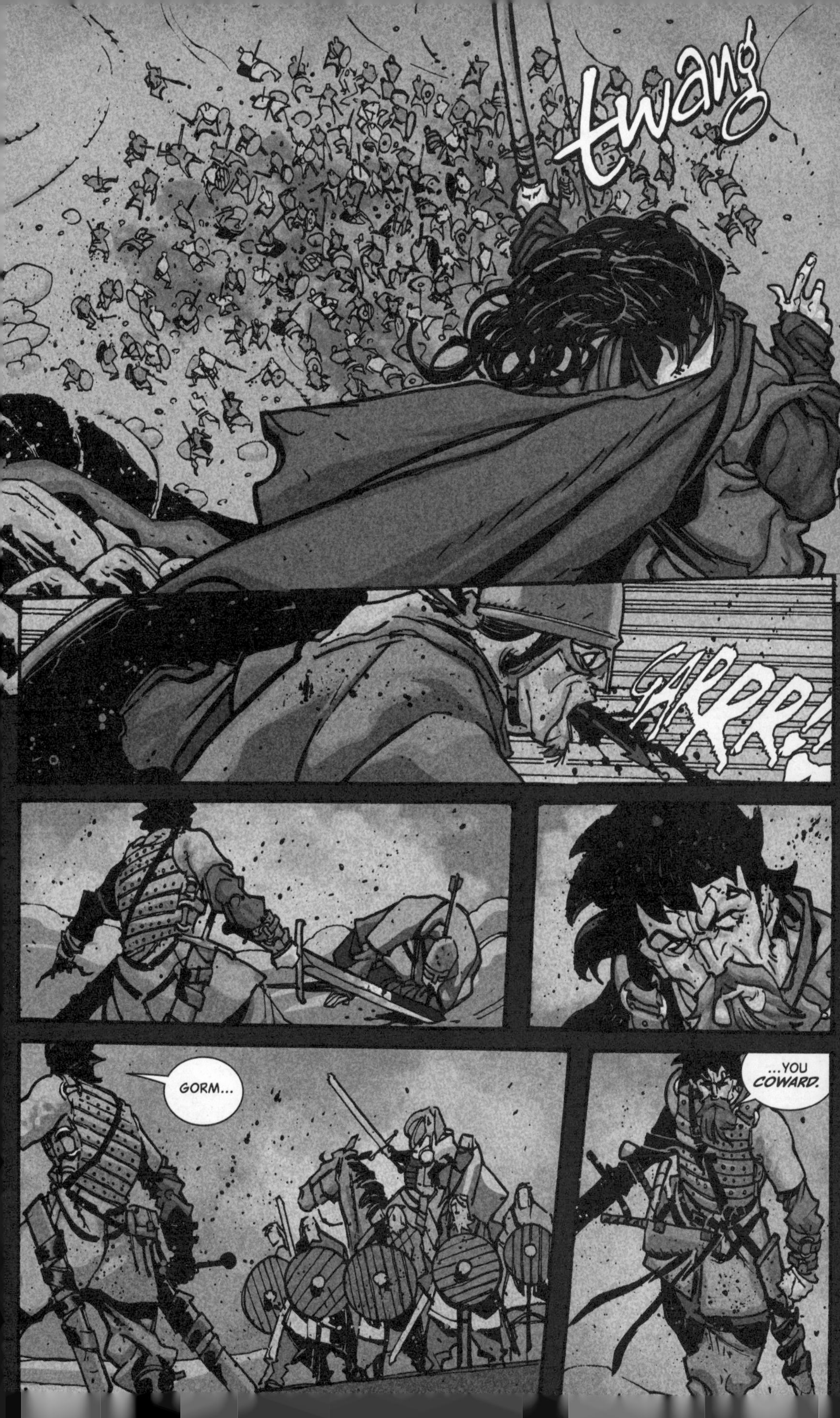
twang
GARRR!
GORM...
...YOU COWARD.

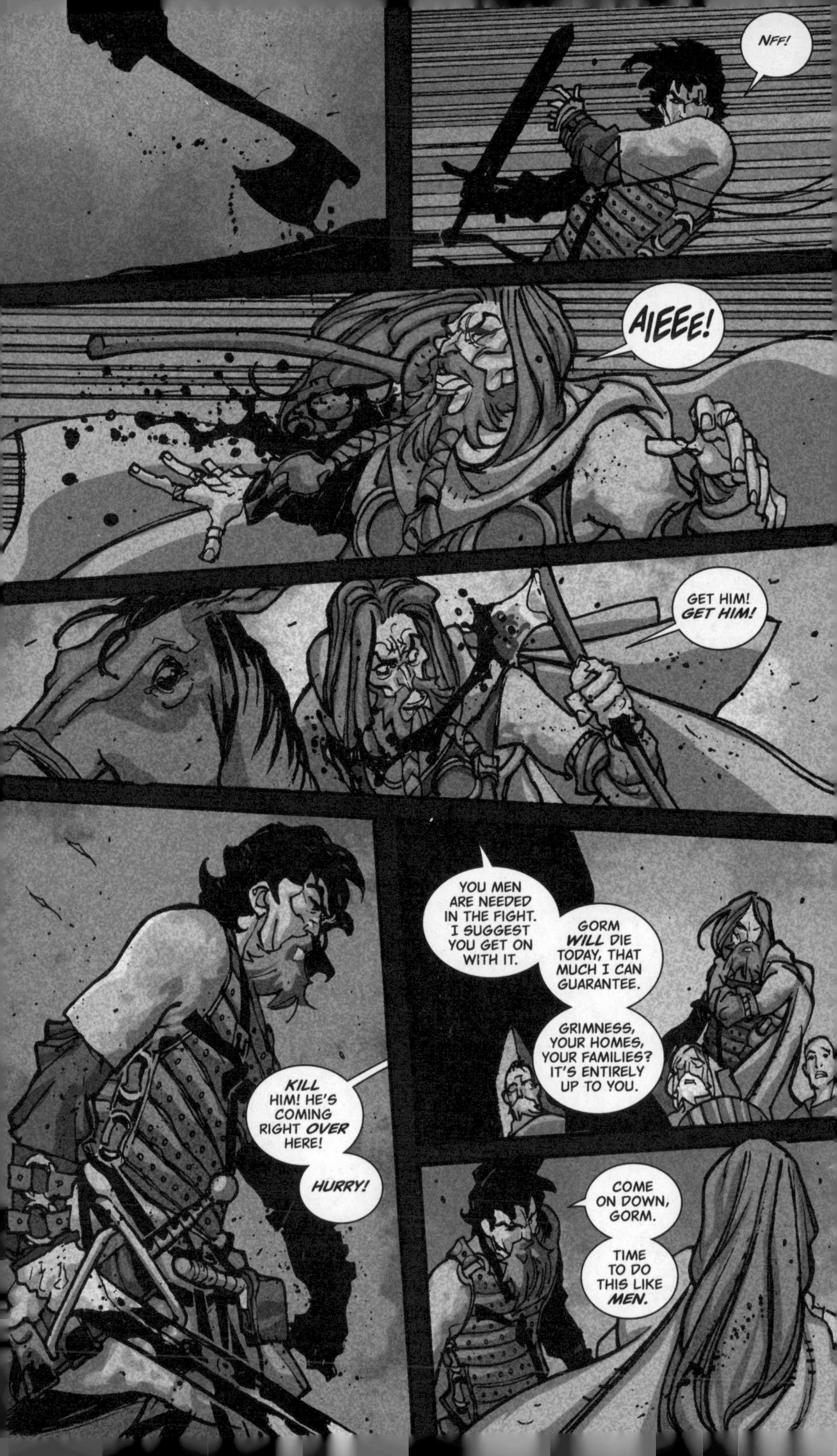
NFF!
AIEEE!
GET HIM! GET HIM!
KILL HIM! HE'S COMING RIGHT OVER HERE!
HURRY!
YOU MEN ARE NEEDED IN THE FIGHT. I SUGGEST YOU GET ON WITH IT.
GORM WILL DIE TODAY, THAT MUCH I CAN GUARANTEE.
GRIMNESS, YOUR HOMES, YOUR FAMILIES? IT'S ENTIRELY UP TO YOU.
COME ON DOWN, GORM.
TIME TO DO THIS LIKE MEN.

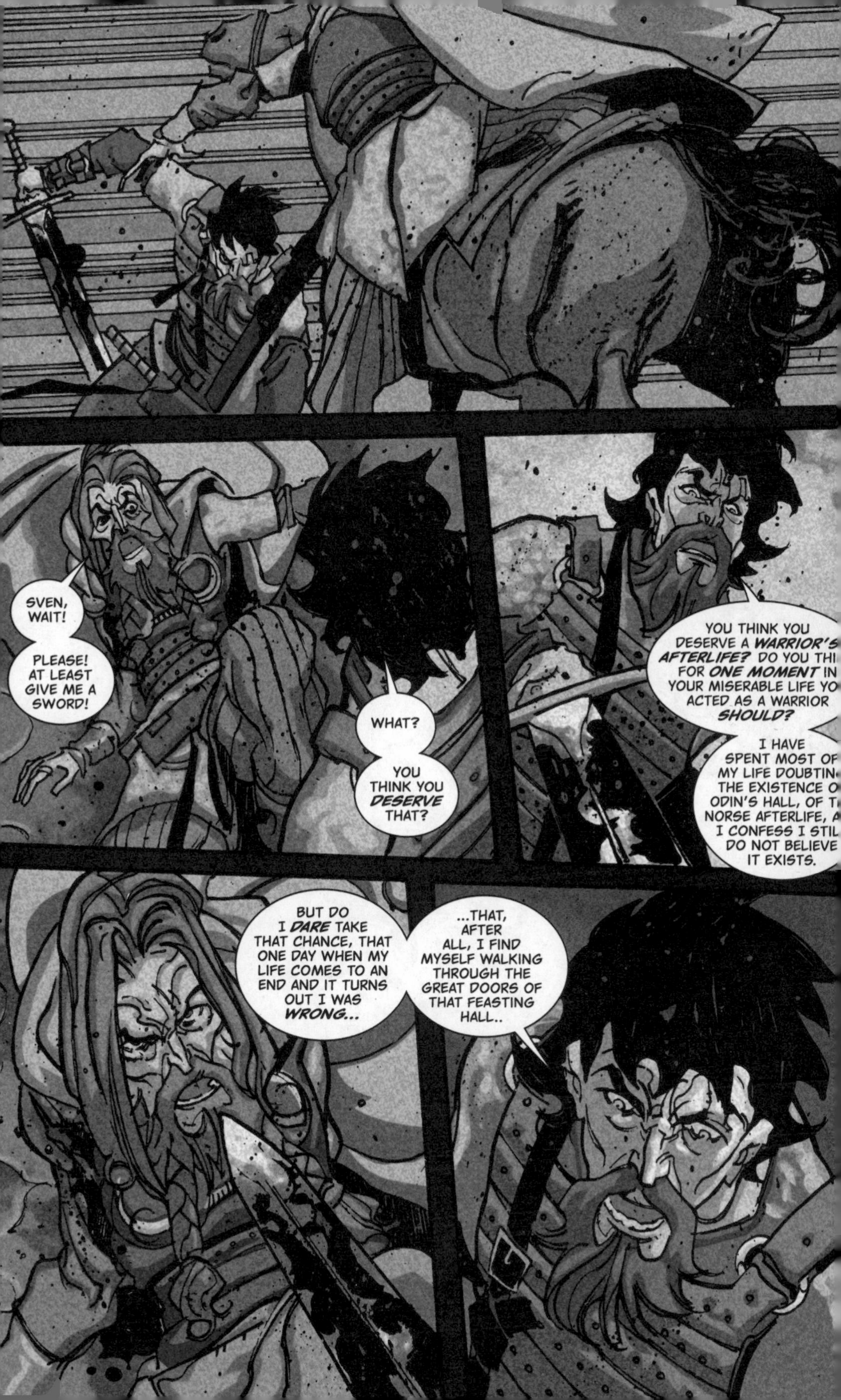
SVEN, WAIT!
PLEASE! AT LEAST GIVE ME A SWORD!
WHAT?
YOU THINK YOU *DESERVE* THAT?
YOU THINK YOU DESERVE A *WARRIOR'S AFTERLIFE?* DO YOU THI FOR *ONE MOMENT* IN YOUR MISERABLE LIFE YO ACTED AS A WARRIOR *SHOULD?*
I HAVE SPENT MOST OF MY LIFE DOUBTIN THE EXISTENCE O ODIN'S HALL, OF T NORSE AFTERLIFE, A I CONFESS I STIL DO NOT BELIEVE IT EXISTS.
BUT DO I *DARE* TAKE THAT CHANCE, THAT ONE DAY WHEN MY LIFE COMES TO AN END AND IT TURNS OUT I WAS *WRONG...*
...THAT, AFTER ALL, I FIND MYSELF WALKING THROUGH THE GREAT DOORS OF THAT FEASTING HALL..

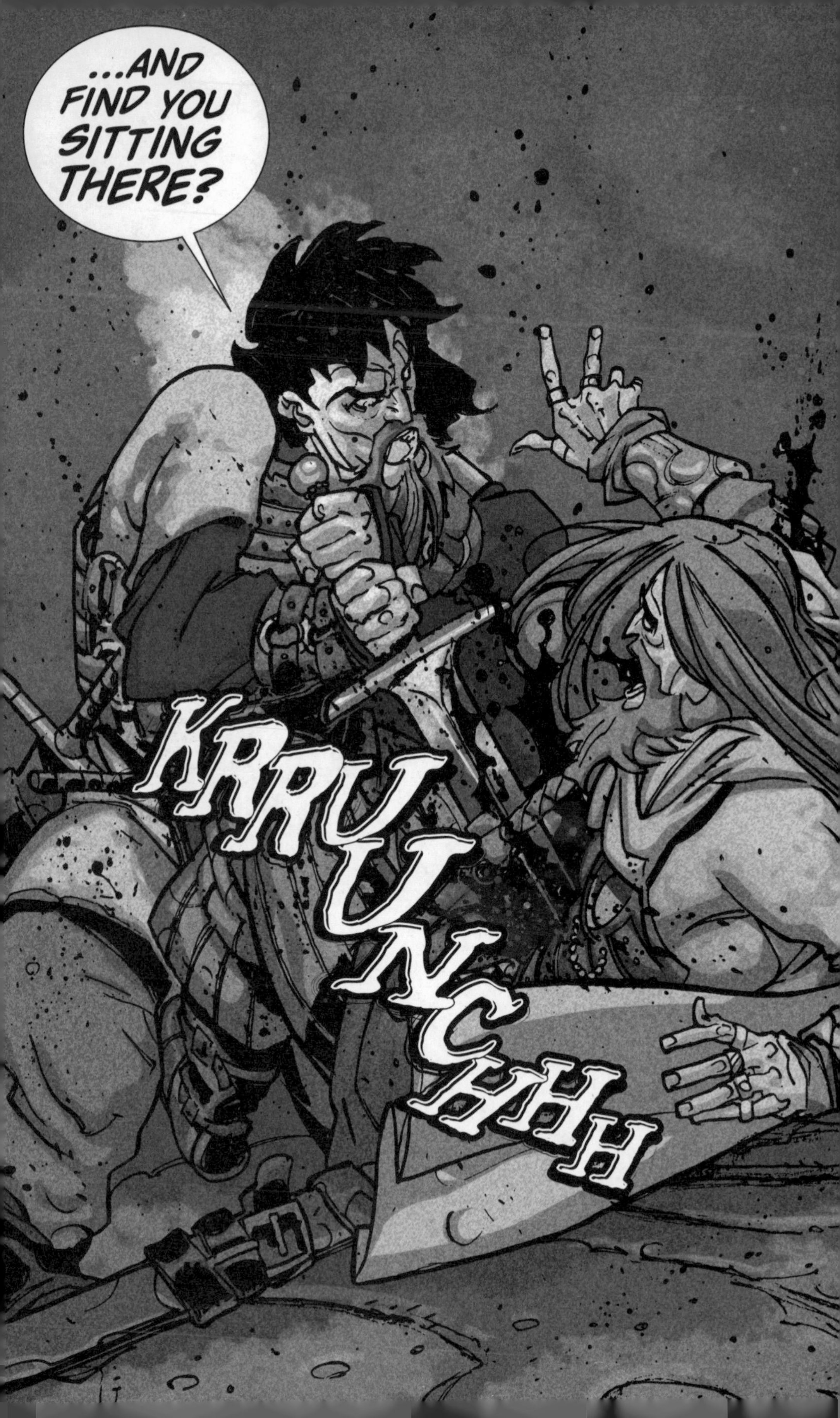
...AND FIND YOU SITTING THERE?
KRRUUNCHHH

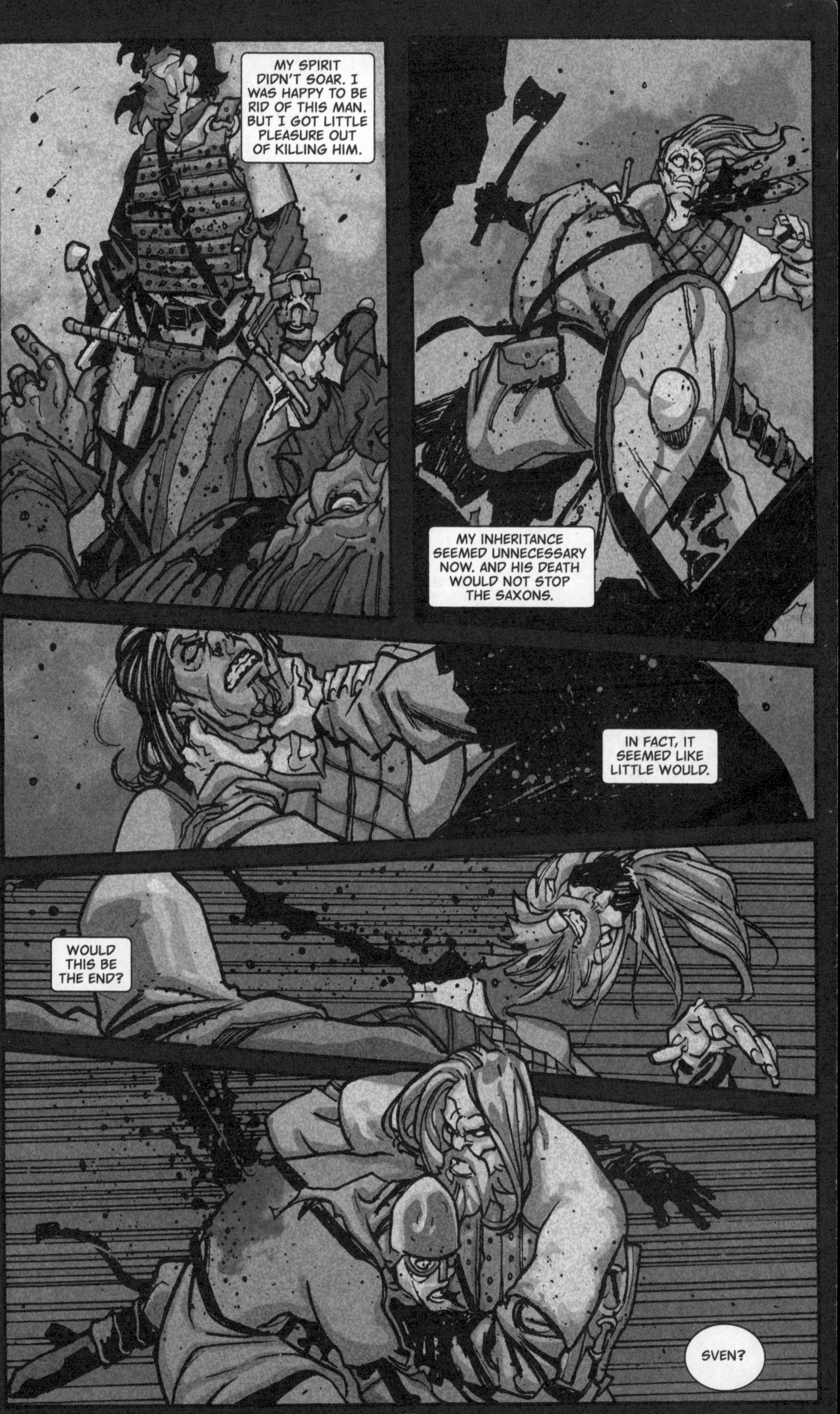
MY SPIRIT DIDN'T SOAR. I WAS HAPPY TO BE RID OF THIS MAN. BUT I GOT LITTLE PLEASURE OUT OF KILLING HIM.
MY INHERITANCE SEEMED UNNECESSARY NOW. AND HIS DEATH WOULD NOT STOP THE SAXONS.
IN FACT, IT SEEMED LIKE LITTLE WOULD.
WOULD THIS BE THE END?
SVEN?

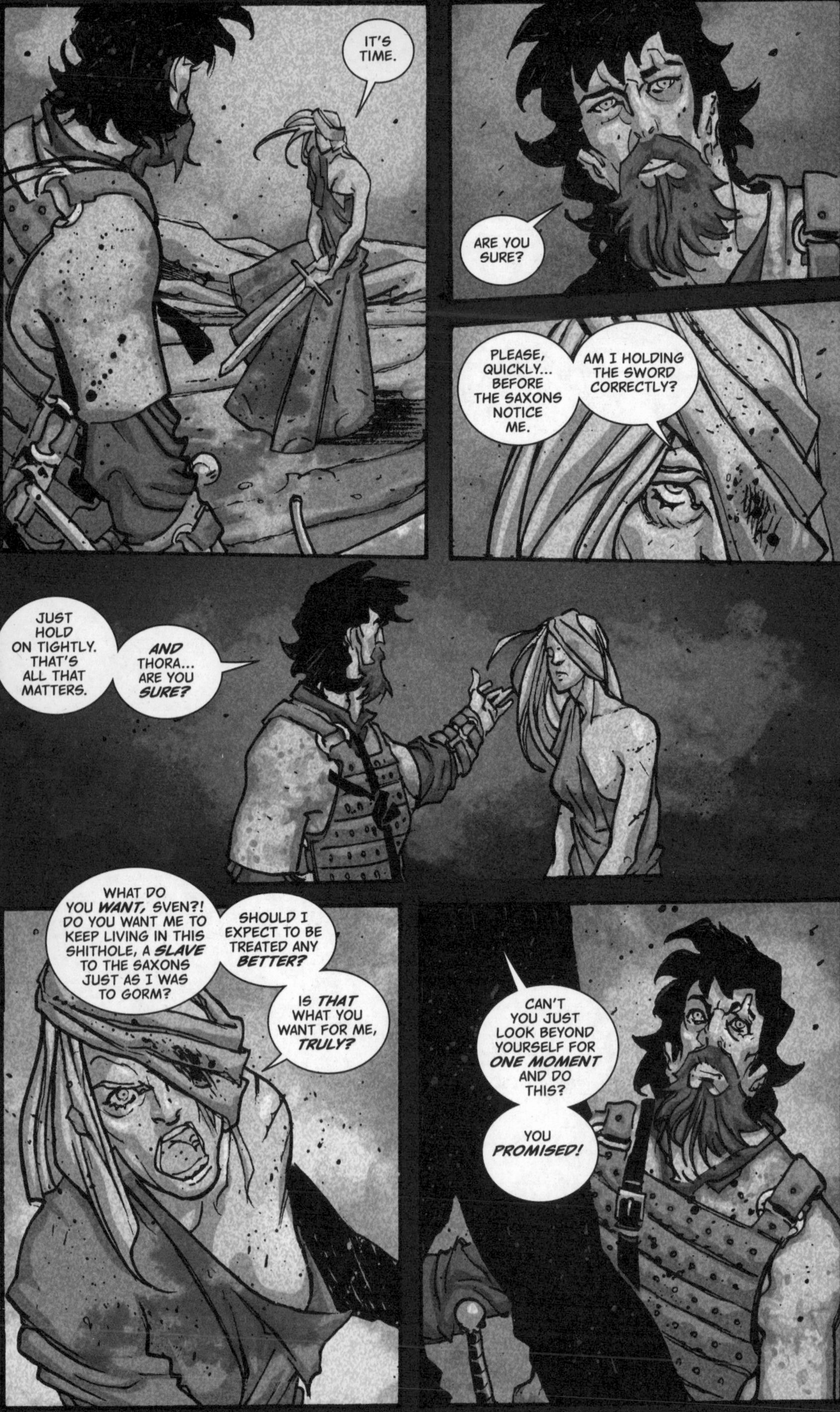
IT'S TIME.
ARE YOU SURE?
PLEASE, QUICKLY... BEFORE THE SAXONS NOTICE ME.
AM I HOLDING THE SWORD CORRECTLY?
JUST HOLD ON TIGHTLY. THAT'S ALL THAT MATTERS.
AND THORA... ARE YOU SURE?
WHAT DO YOU WANT, SVEN?! DO YOU WANT ME TO KEEP LIVING IN THIS SHITHOLE, A SLAVE TO THE SAXONS JUST AS I WAS TO GORM?
SHOULD I EXPECT TO BE TREATED ANY BETTER?
IS THAT WHAT YOU WANT FOR ME, TRULY?
CAN'T YOU JUST LOOK BEYOND YOURSELF FOR ONE MOMENT AND DO THIS?
YOU PROMISED!

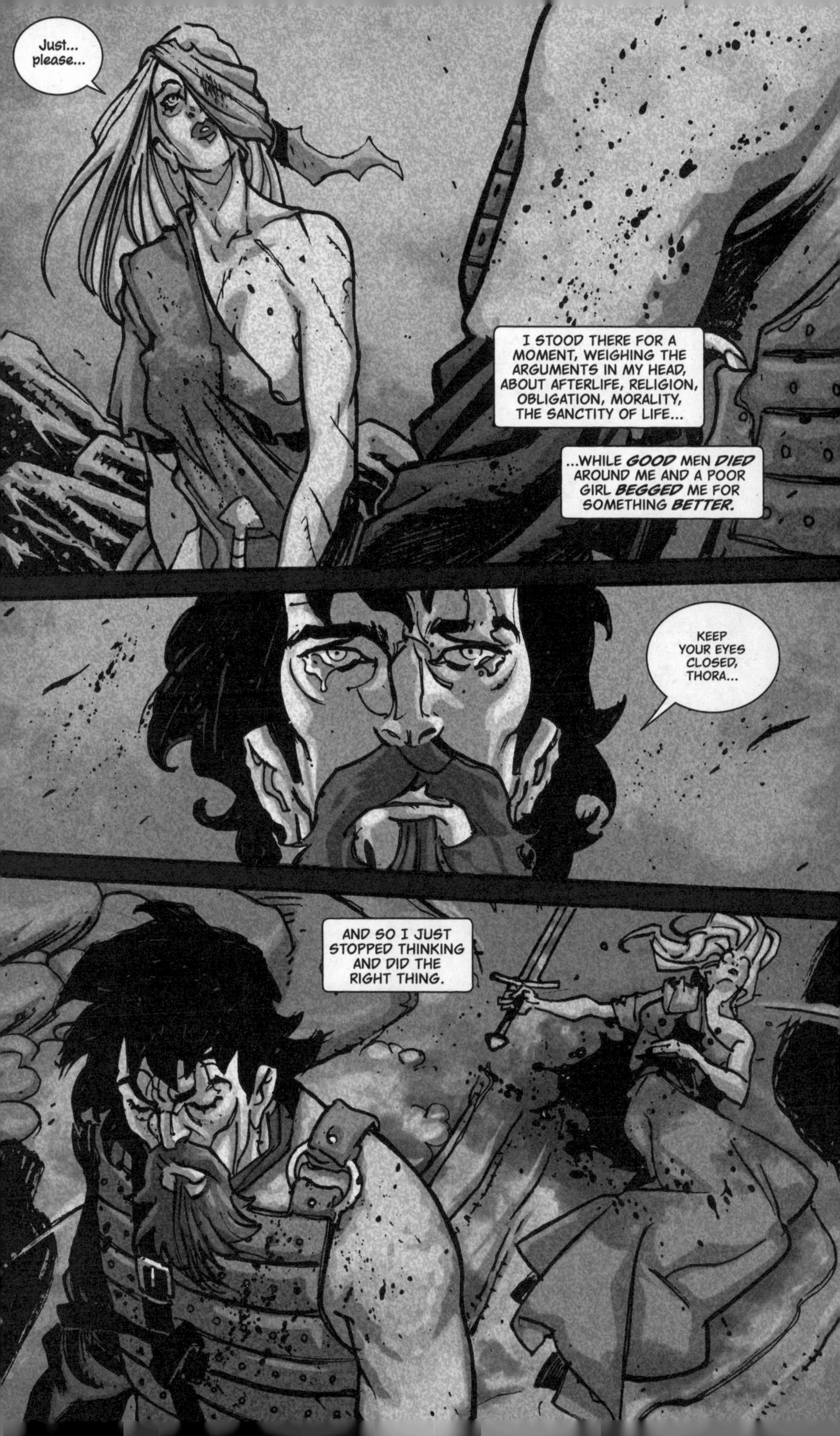
Just... please...
I STOOD THERE FOR A MOMENT, WEIGHING THE ARGUMENTS IN MY HEAD, ABOUT AFTERLIFE, RELIGION, OBLIGATION, MORALITY, THE SANCTITY OF LIFE...
...WHILE GOOD MEN DIED AROUND ME AND A POOR GIRL BEGGED ME FOR SOMETHING BETTER.
KEEP YOUR EYES CLOSED, THORA...
AND SO I JUST STOPPED THINKING AND DID THE RIGHT THING.

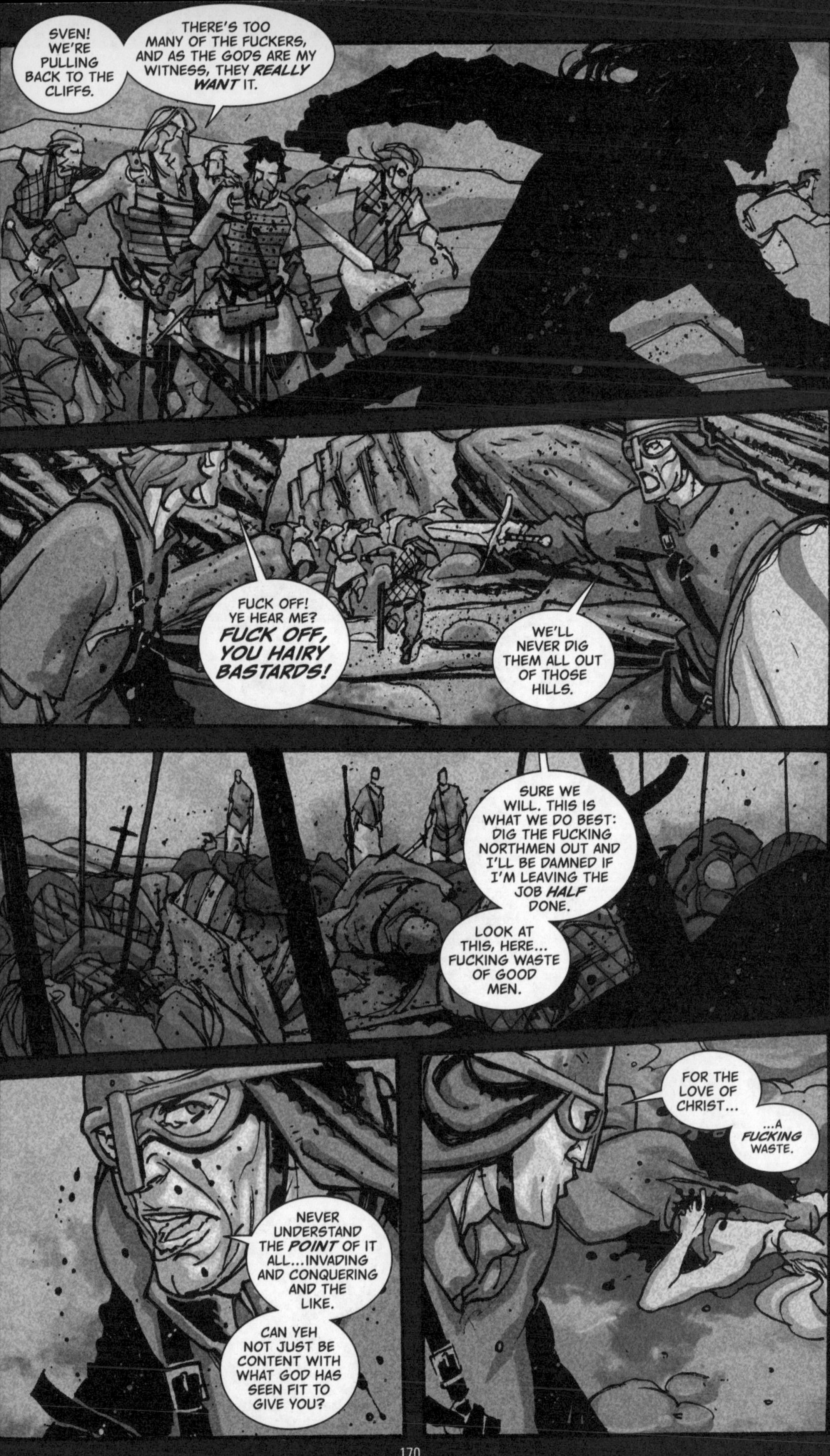
SVEN! WE'RE PULLING BACK TO THE CLIFFS.
THERE'S TOO MANY OF THE FUCKERS, AND AS THE GODS ARE MY WITNESS, THEY *REALLY WANT* IT.
FUCK OFF! YE HEAR ME? *FUCK OFF, YOU HAIRY BASTARDS!*
WE'LL NEVER DIG THEM ALL OUT OF THOSE HILLS.
SURE WE WILL. THIS IS WHAT WE DO BEST: DIG THE FUCKING NORTHMEN OUT AND I'LL BE DAMNED IF I'M LEAVING THE JOB *HALF* DONE.
LOOK AT THIS, HERE... FUCKING WASTE OF GOOD MEN.
NEVER UNDERSTAND THE *POINT* OF IT ALL...INVADING AND CONQUERING AND THE LIKE.
CAN YEH NOT JUST BE CONTENT WITH WHAT GOD HAS SEEN FIT TO GIVE YOU?
FOR THE LOVE OF CHRIST...
...A *FUCKING* WASTE.

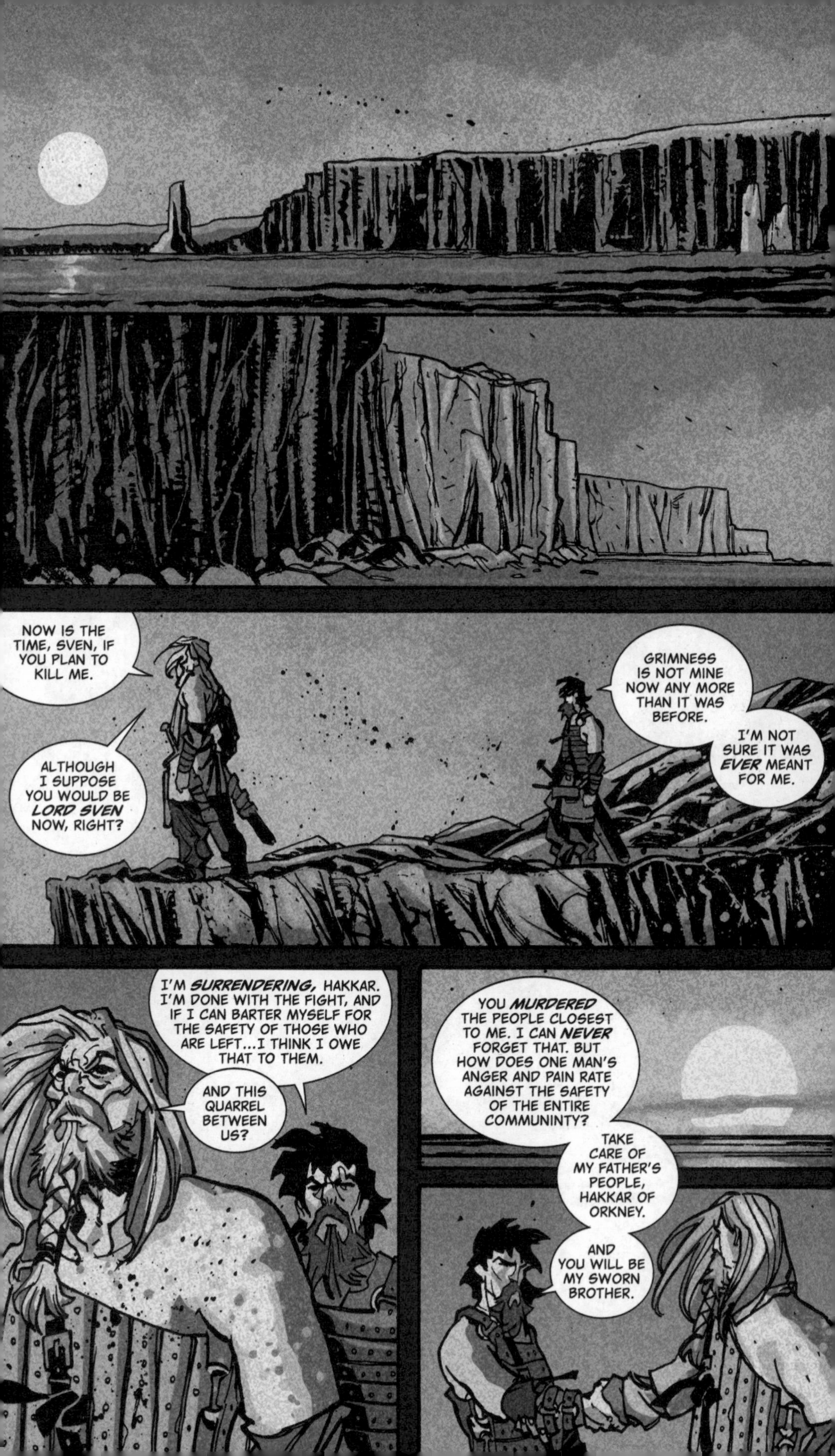
NOW IS THE TIME, SVEN, IF YOU PLAN TO KILL ME.
ALTHOUGH I SUPPOSE YOU WOULD BE LORD SVEN NOW, RIGHT?
GRIMNESS IS NOT MINE NOW ANY MORE THAN IT WAS BEFORE.
I'M NOT SURE IT WAS EVER MEANT FOR ME.
I'M SURRENDERING, HAKKAR. I'M DONE WITH THE FIGHT, AND IF I CAN BARTER MYSELF FOR THE SAFETY OF THOSE WHO ARE LEFT...I THINK I OWE THAT TO THEM.
AND THIS QUARREL BETWEEN US?
YOU MURDERED THE PEOPLE CLOSEST TO ME. I CAN NEVER FORGET THAT. BUT HOW DOES ONE MAN'S ANGER AND PAIN RATE AGAINST THE SAFETY OF THE ENTIRE COMMUNINTY?
TAKE CARE OF MY FATHER'S PEOPLE, HAKKAR OF ORKNEY.
AND YOU WILL BE MY SWORN BROTHER.

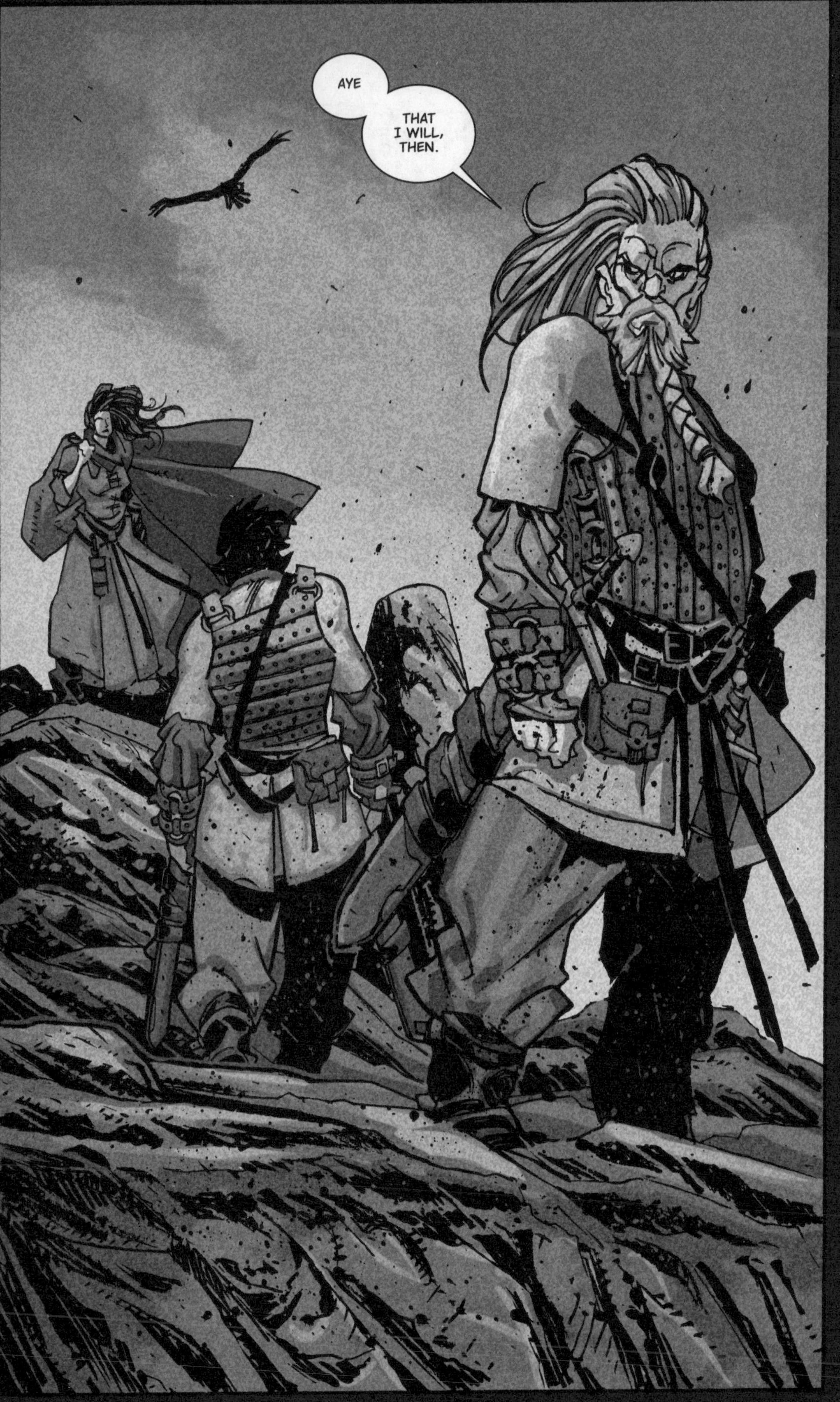
AYE
THAT I WILL, THEN.

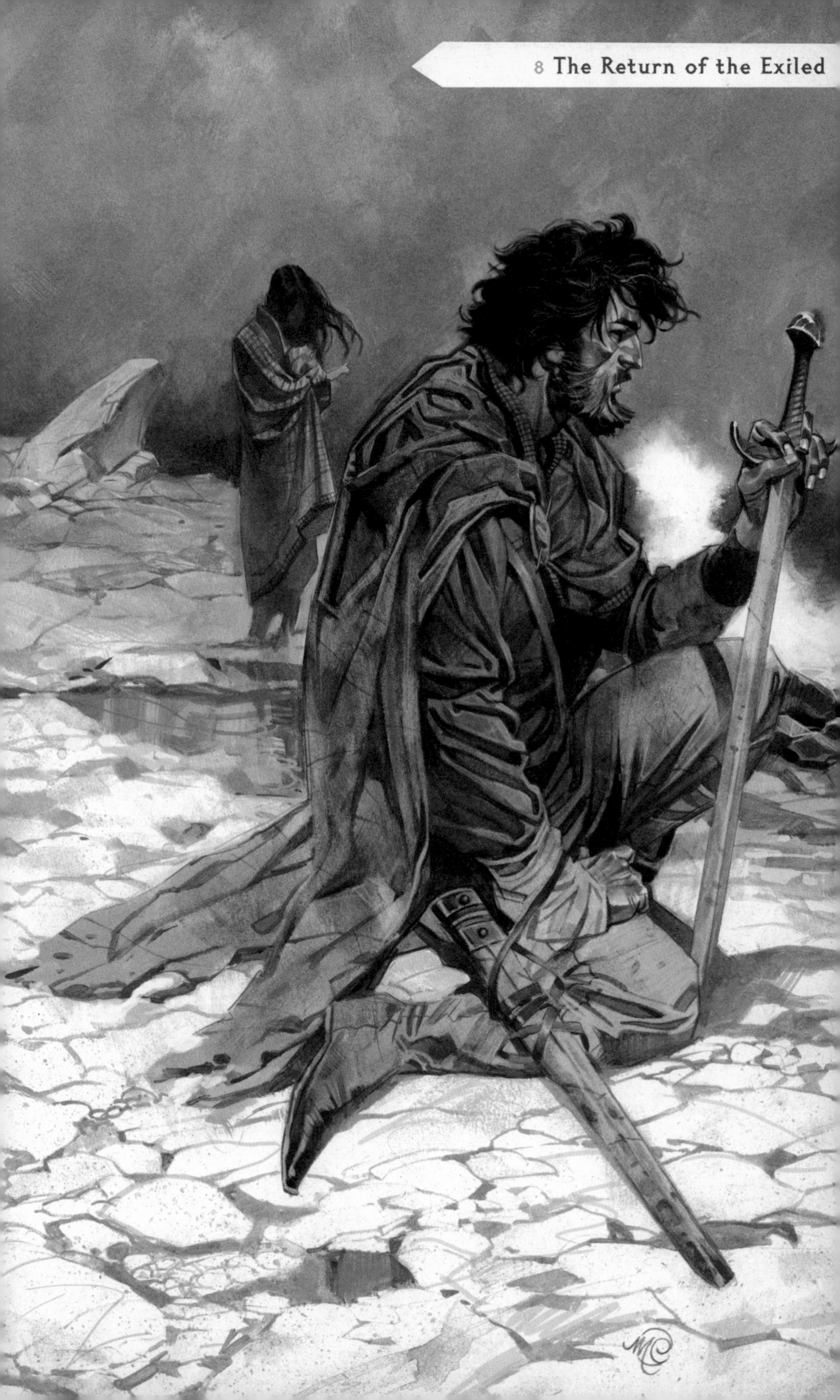

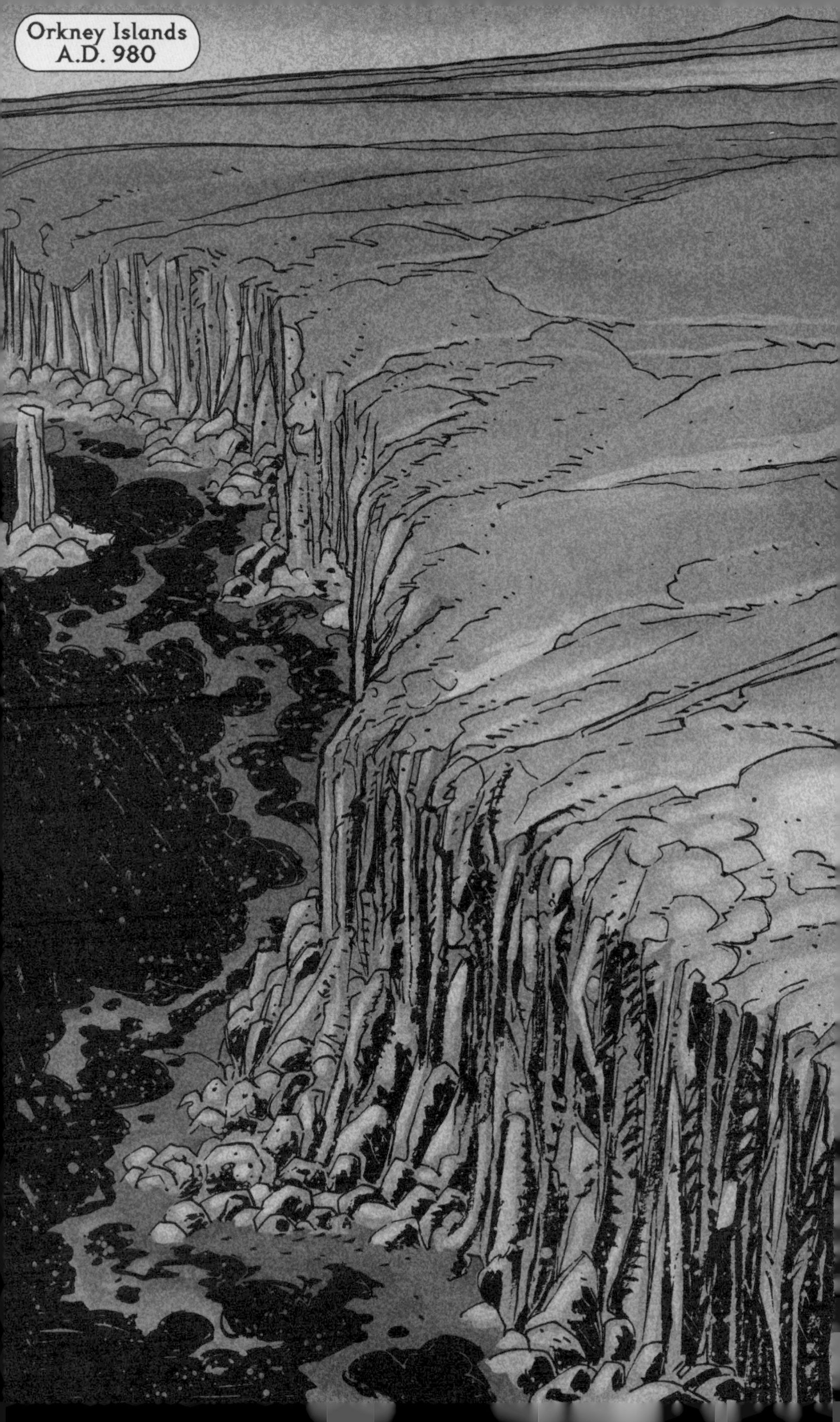
Orkney Islands
A.D. 980

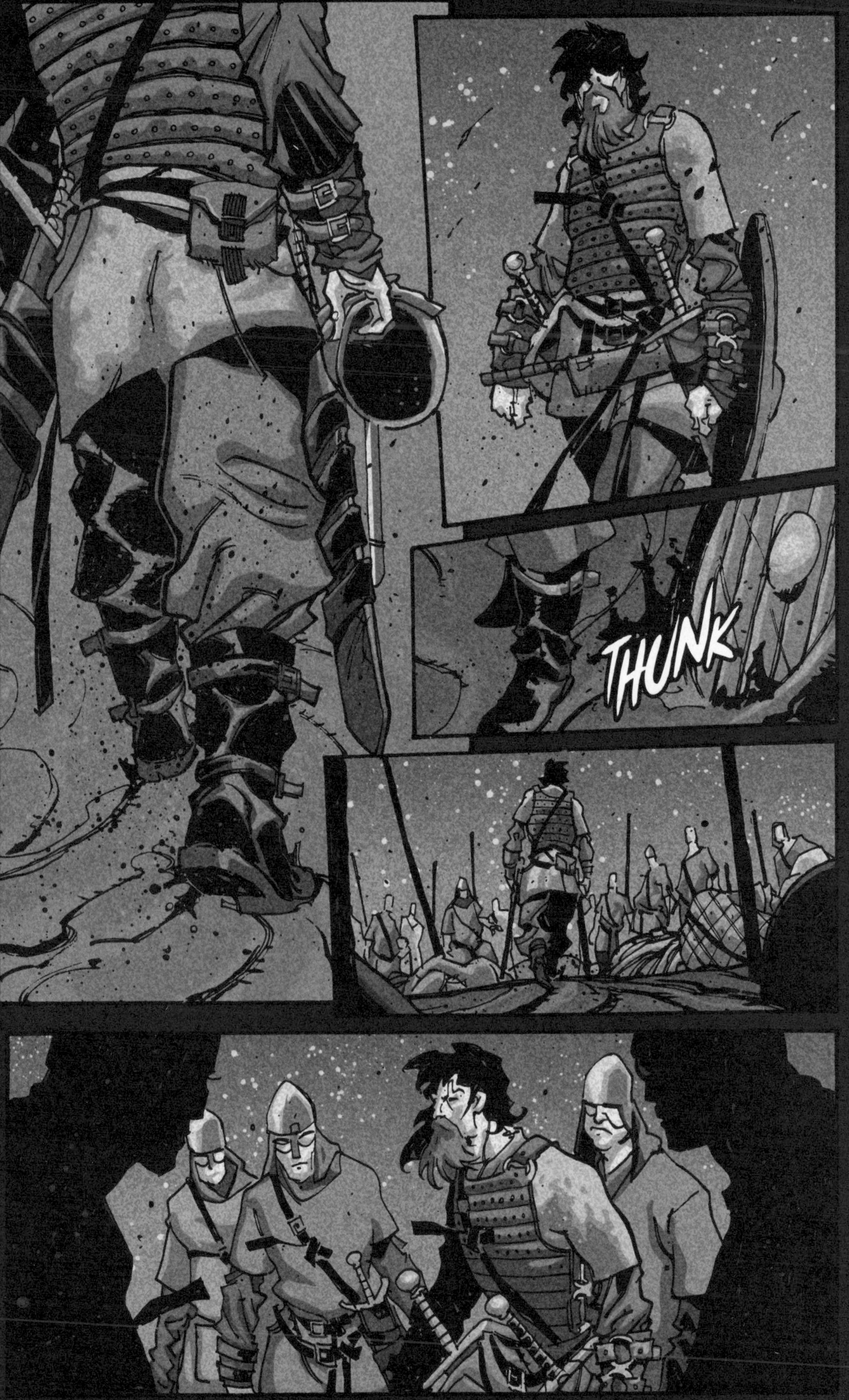
THUNK

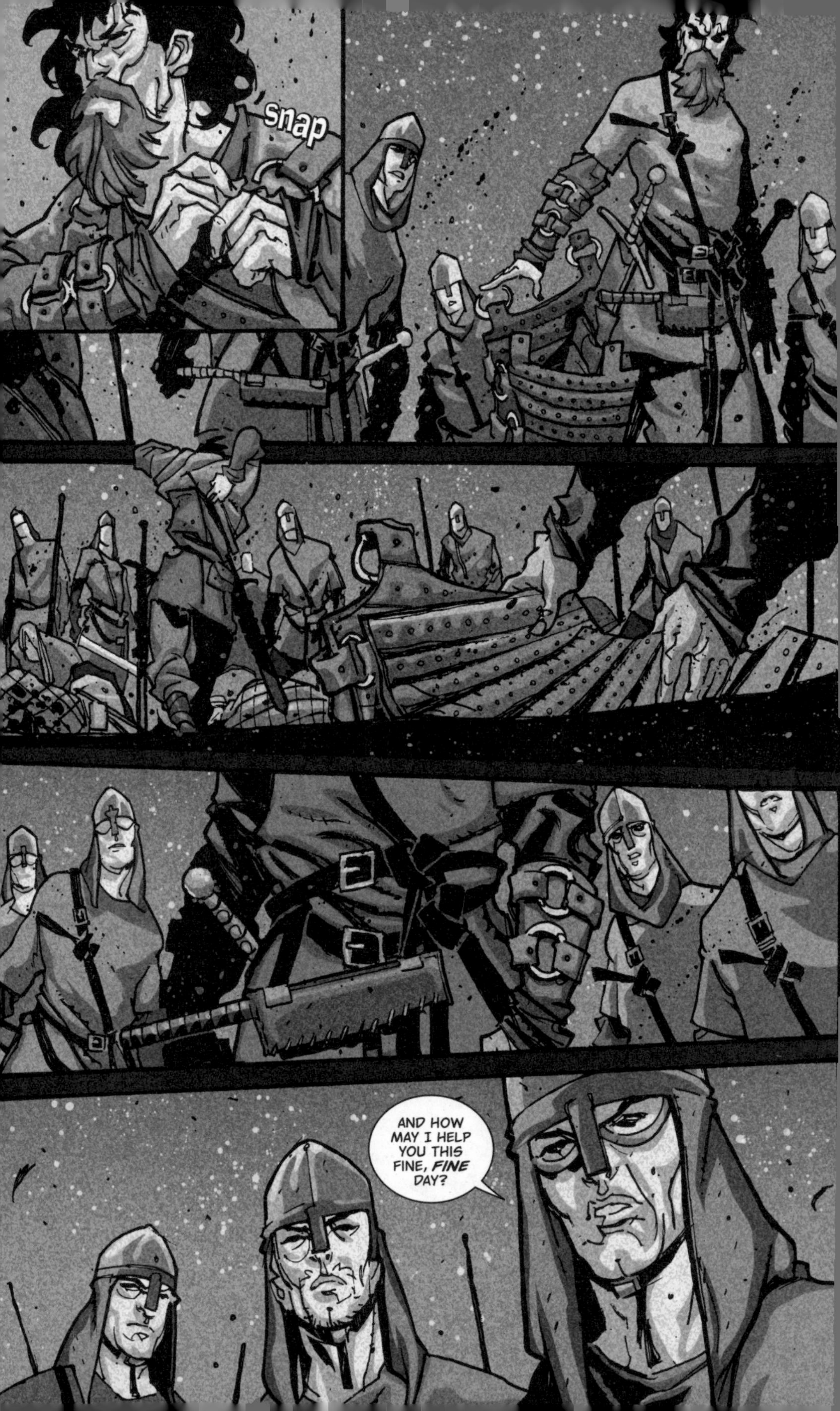
snap
AND HOW MAY I HELP YOU THIS FINE, *FINE* DAY?

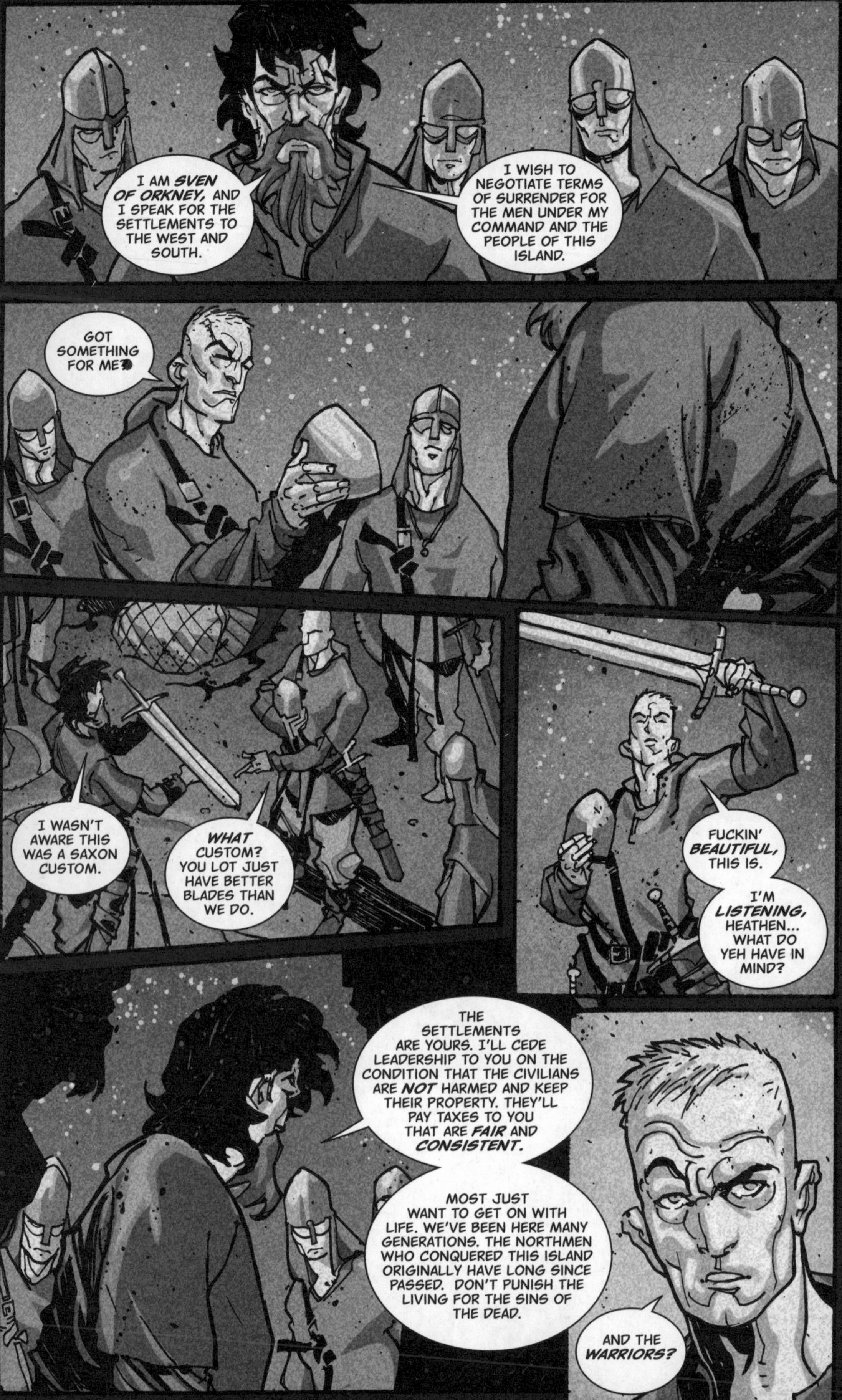
I AM SVEN OF ORKNEY, AND I SPEAK FOR THE SETTLEMENTS TO THE WEST AND SOUTH.
I WISH TO NEGOTIATE TERMS OF SURRENDER FOR THE MEN UNDER MY COMMAND AND THE PEOPLE OF THIS ISLAND.
GOT SOMETHING FOR ME?
I WASN'T AWARE THIS WAS A SAXON CUSTOM.
WHAT CUSTOM? YOU LOT JUST HAVE BETTER BLADES THAN WE DO.
FUCKIN' BEAUTIFUL, THIS IS.
I'M LISTENING, HEATHEN... WHAT DO YEH HAVE IN MIND?
THE SETTLEMENTS ARE YOURS. I'LL CEDE LEADERSHIP TO YOU ON THE CONDITION THAT THE CIVILIANS ARE NOT HARMED AND KEEP THEIR PROPERTY. THEY'LL PAY TAXES TO YOU THAT ARE FAIR AND CONSISTENT.
MOST JUST WANT TO GET ON WITH LIFE. WE'VE BEEN HERE MANY GENERATIONS. THE NORTHMEN WHO CONQUERED THIS ISLAND ORIGINALLY HAVE LONG SINCE PASSED. DON'T PUNISH THE LIVING FOR THE SINS OF THE DEAD.
AND THE WARRIORS?

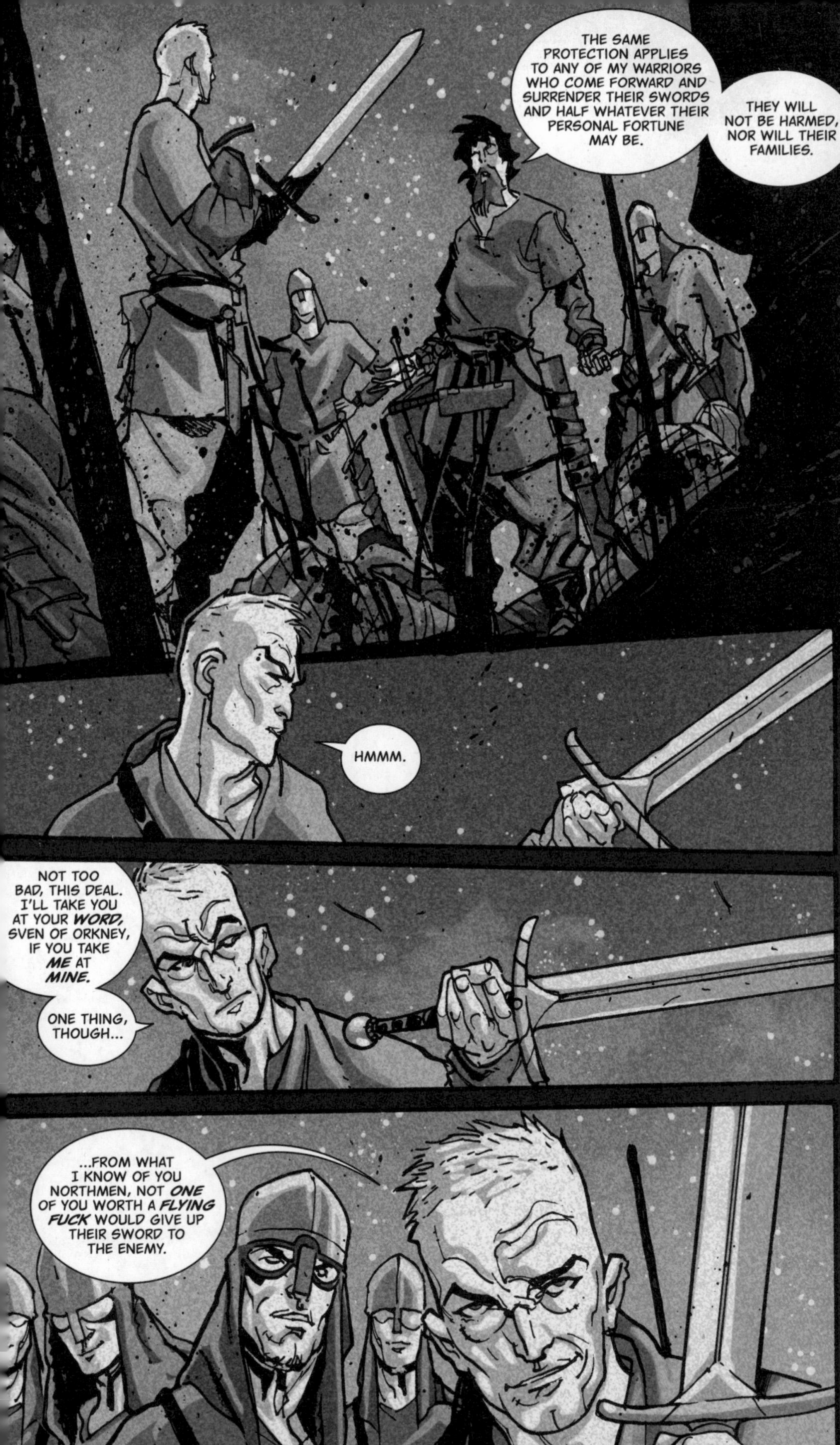
THE SAME PROTECTION APPLIES TO ANY OF MY WARRIORS WHO COME FORWARD AND SURRENDER THEIR SWORDS AND HALF WHATEVER THEIR PERSONAL FORTUNE MAY BE.
THEY WILL NOT BE HARMED, NOR WILL THEIR FAMILIES.
HMMM.
NOT TOO BAD, THIS DEAL. I'LL TAKE YOU AT YOUR *WORD,* SVEN OF ORKNEY, IF YOU TAKE *ME* AT *MINE.*
ONE THING, THOUGH...
...FROM WHAT I KNOW OF YOU NORTHMEN, NOT *ONE* OF YOU WORTH A *FLYING FUCK* WOULD GIVE UP THEIR SWORD TO THE ENEMY.

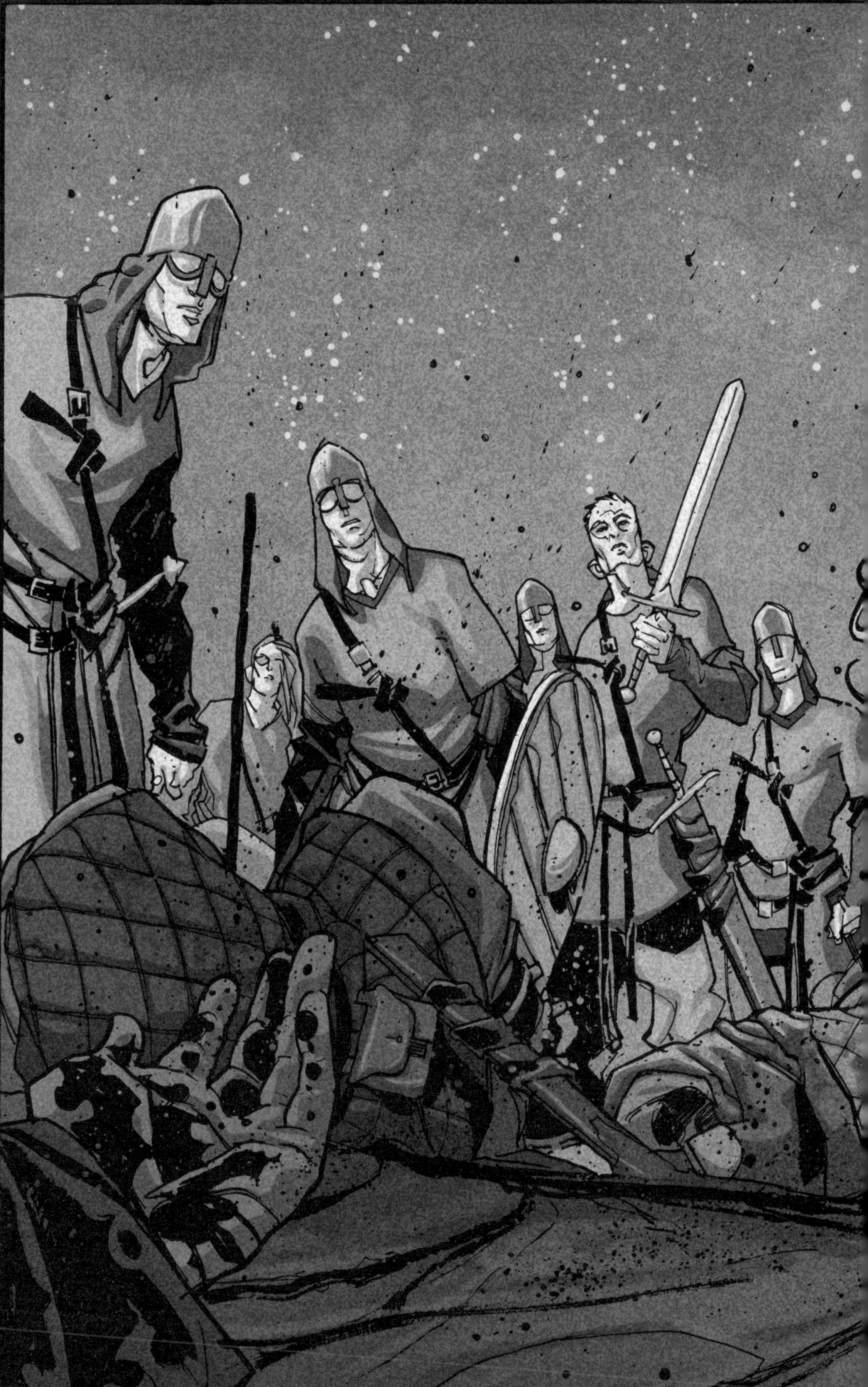

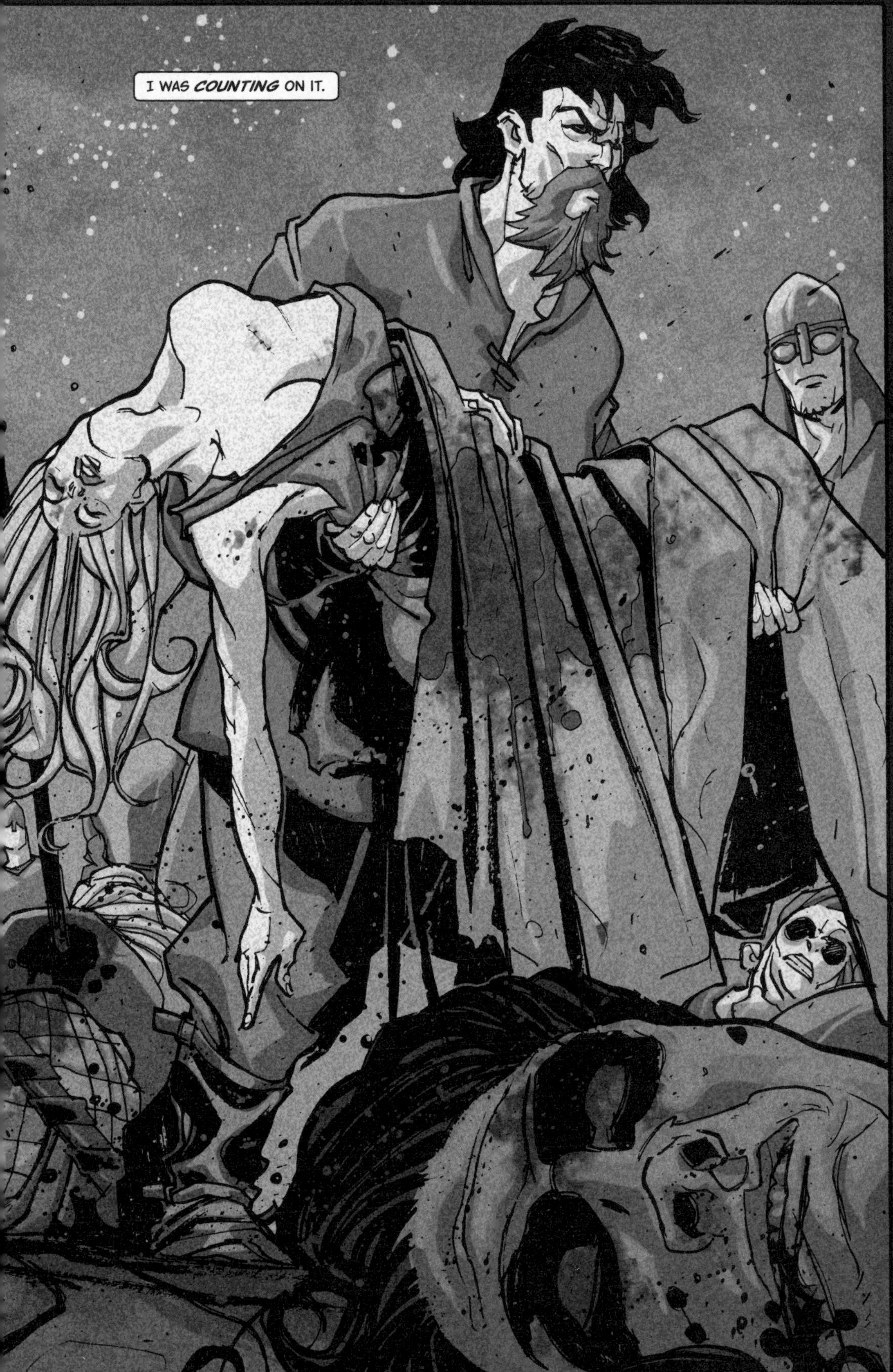
I WAS COUNTING ON IT.

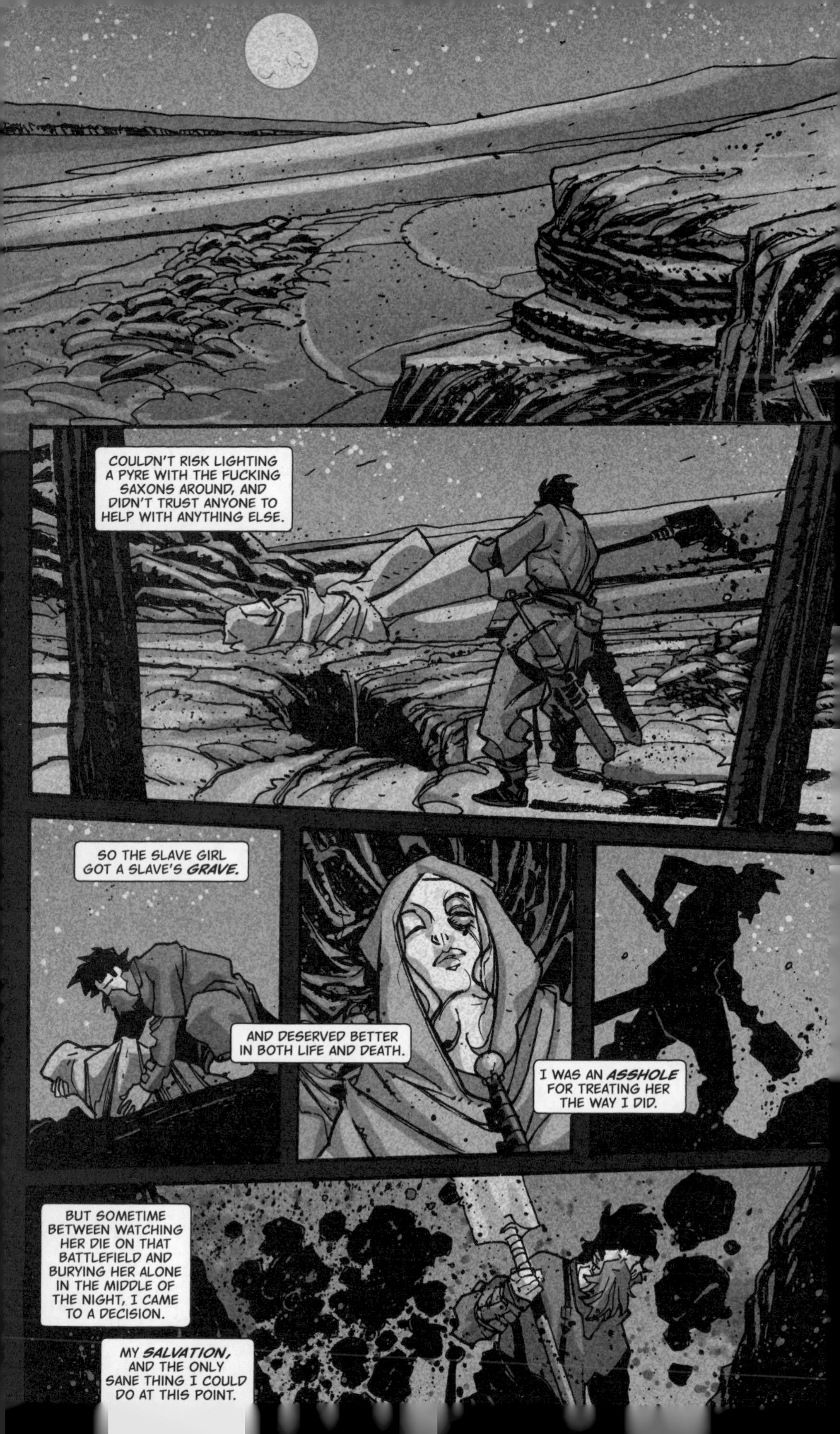
COULDN'T RISK LIGHTING A PYRE WITH THE FUCKING SAXONS AROUND, AND DIDN'T TRUST ANYONE TO HELP WITH ANYTHING ELSE.
SO THE SLAVE GIRL GOT A SLAVE'S *GRAVE.*
AND DESERVED BETTER IN BOTH LIFE AND DEATH.
I WAS AN *ASSHOLE* FOR TREATING HER THE WAY I DID.
BUT SOMETIME BETWEEN WATCHING HER DIE ON THAT BATTLEFIELD AND BURYING HER ALONE IN THE MIDDLE OF THE NIGHT, I CAME TO A DECISION.
MY *SALVATION,* AND THE ONLY SANE THING I COULD DO AT THIS POINT.

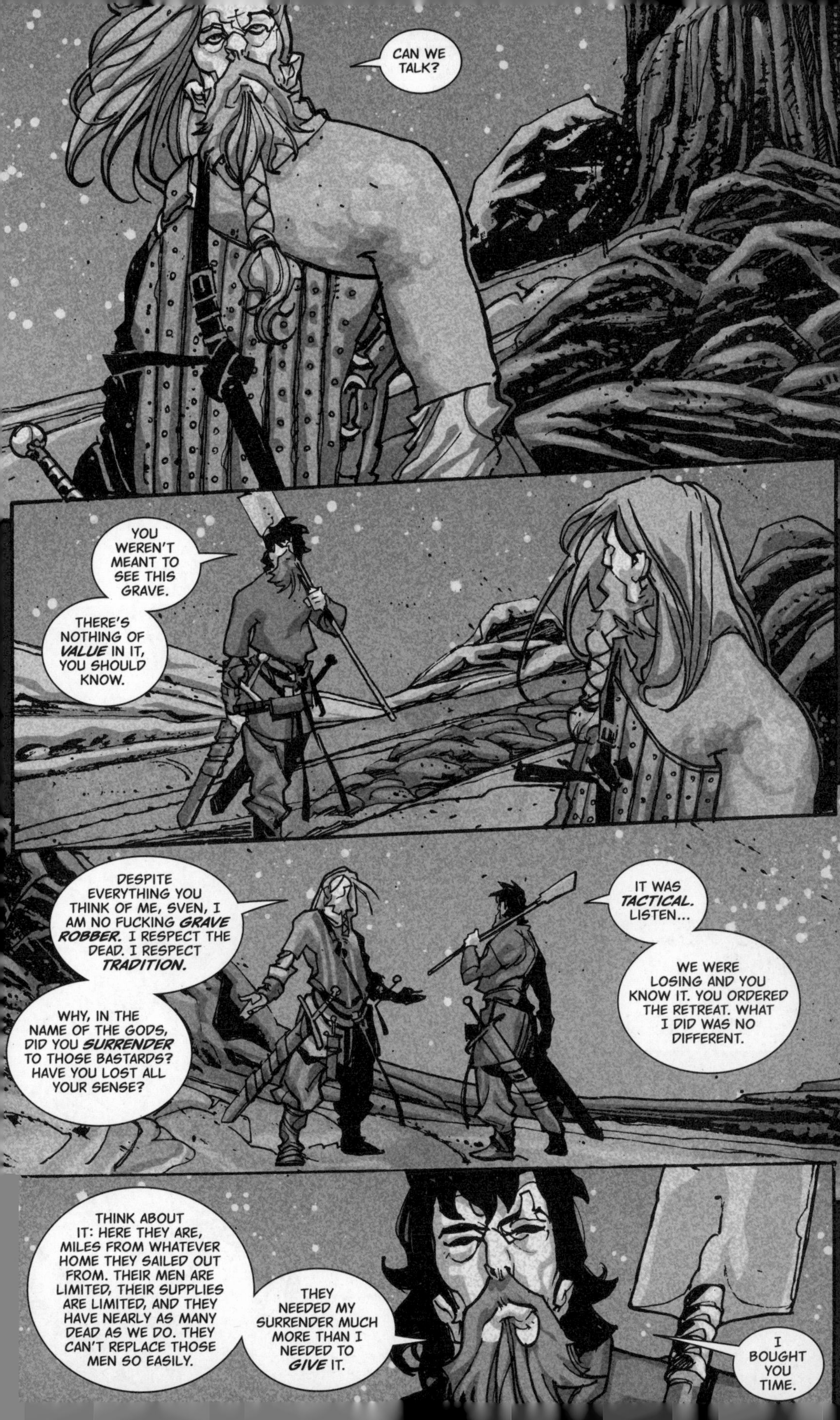
CAN WE TALK?
YOU WEREN'T MEANT TO SEE THIS GRAVE.
THERE'S NOTHING OF *VALUE* IN IT, YOU SHOULD KNOW.
DESPITE EVERYTHING YOU THINK OF ME, SVEN, I AM NO FUCKING *GRAVE ROBBER.* I RESPECT THE DEAD. I RESPECT *TRADITION.*
WHY, IN THE NAME OF THE GODS, DID YOU *SURRENDER* TO THOSE BASTARDS? HAVE YOU LOST ALL YOUR SENSE?
IT WAS *TACTICAL.* LISTEN...
WE WERE LOSING AND YOU KNOW IT. YOU ORDERED THE RETREAT. WHAT I DID WAS NO DIFFERENT.
THINK ABOUT IT: HERE THEY ARE, MILES FROM WHATEVER HOME THEY SAILED OUT FROM. THEIR MEN ARE LIMITED, THEIR SUPPLIES ARE LIMITED, AND THEY HAVE NEARLY AS MANY DEAD AS WE DO. THEY CAN'T REPLACE THOSE MEN SO EASILY.
THEY NEEDED MY SURRENDER MUCH MORE THAN I NEEDED TO *GIVE* IT.
I BOUGHT YOU TIME.

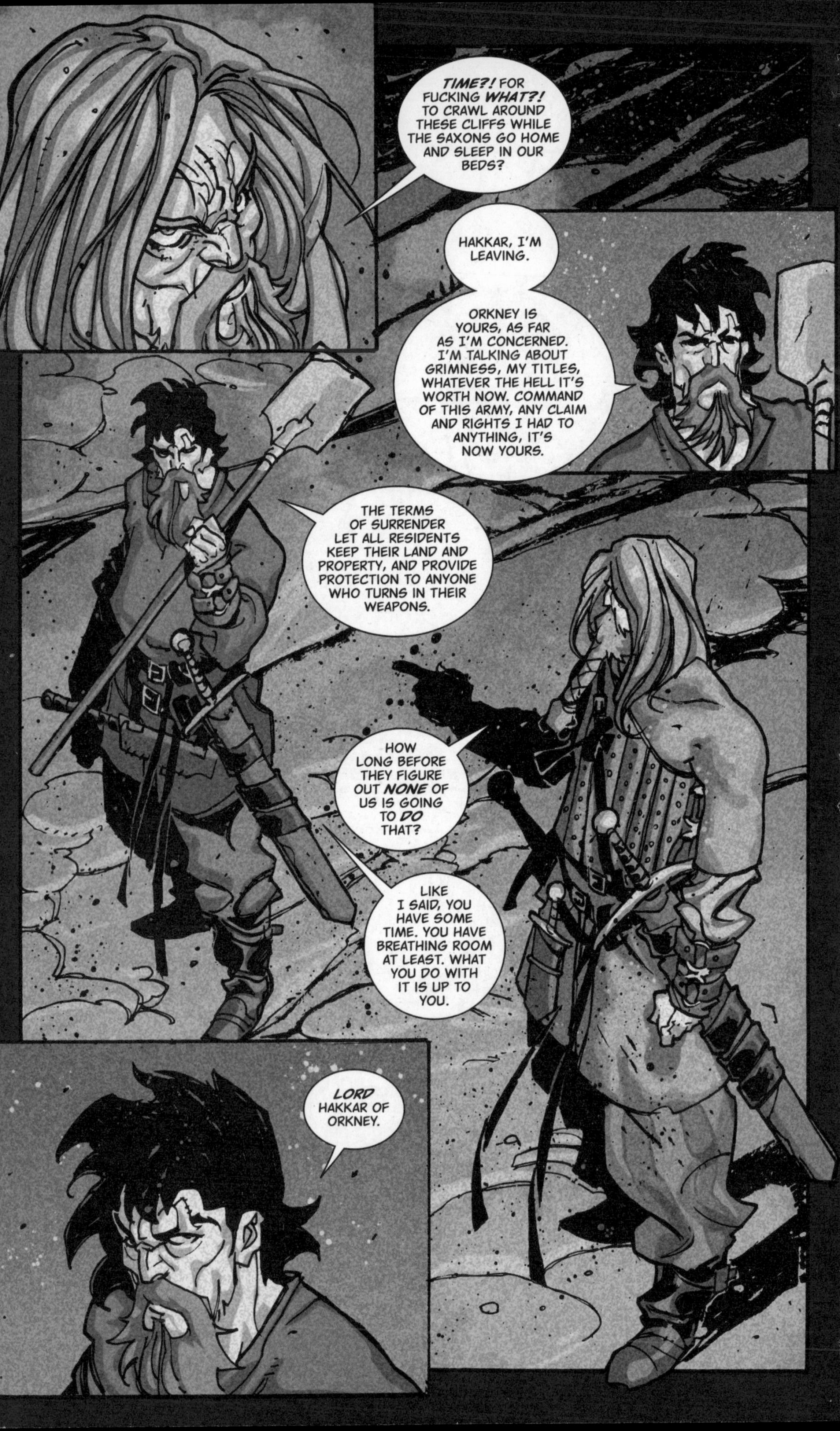
TIME?! FOR FUCKING WHAT?! TO CRAWL AROUND THESE CLIFFS WHILE THE SAXONS GO HOME AND SLEEP IN OUR BEDS?
HAKKAR, I'M LEAVING.
ORKNEY IS YOURS, AS FAR AS I'M CONCERNED. I'M TALKING ABOUT GRIMNESS, MY TITLES, WHATEVER THE HELL IT'S WORTH NOW. COMMAND OF THIS ARMY, ANY CLAIM AND RIGHTS I HAD TO ANYTHING, IT'S NOW YOURS.
THE TERMS OF SURRENDER LET ALL RESIDENTS KEEP THEIR LAND AND PROPERTY, AND PROVIDE PROTECTION TO ANYONE WHO TURNS IN THEIR WEAPONS.
HOW LONG BEFORE THEY FIGURE OUT NONE OF US IS GOING TO DO THAT?
LIKE I SAID, YOU HAVE SOME TIME. YOU HAVE BREATHING ROOM AT LEAST. WHAT YOU DO WITH IT IS UP TO YOU.
LORD HAKKAR OF ORKNEY.

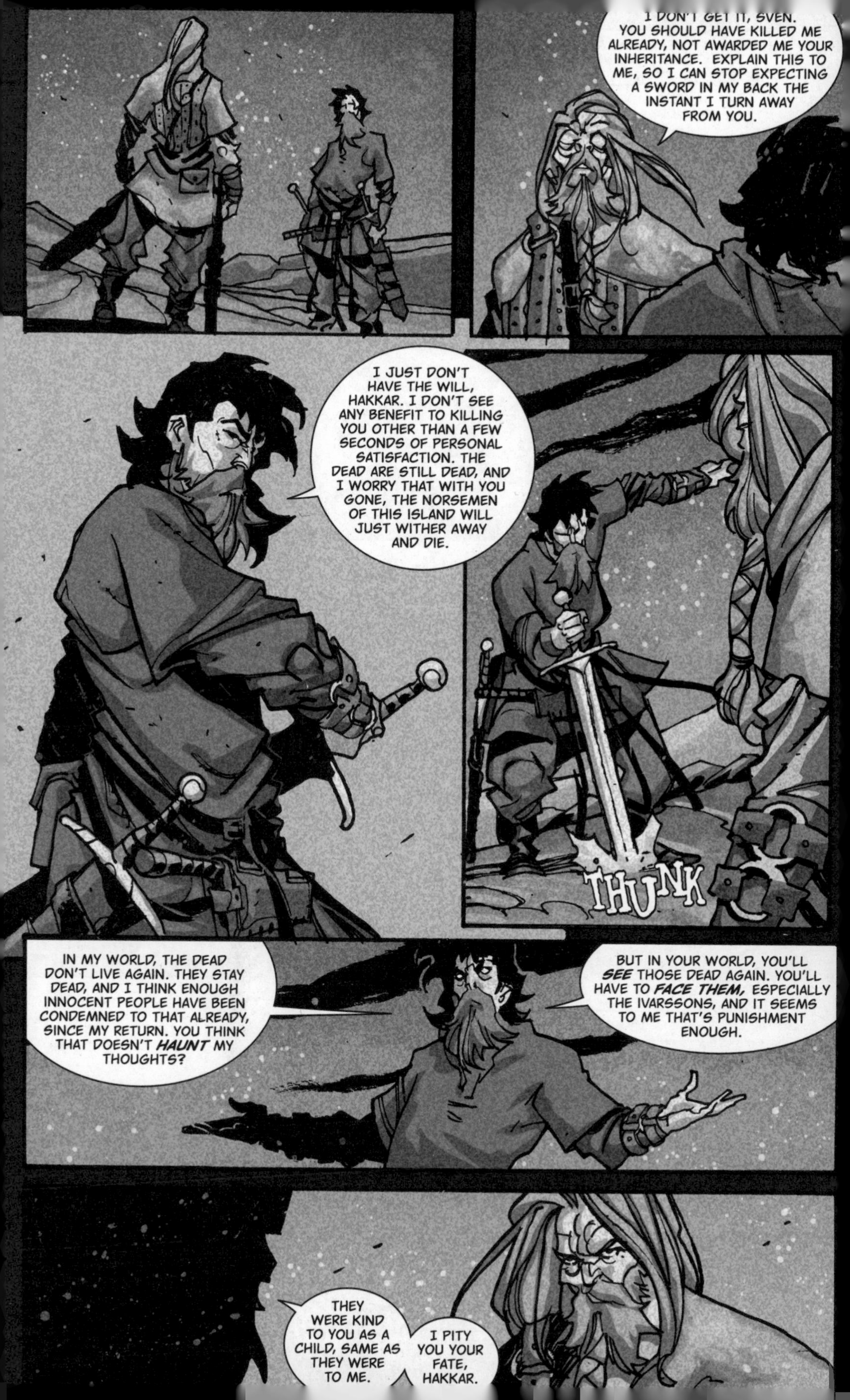

I DON'T GET IT, SVEN. YOU SHOULD HAVE KILLED ME ALREADY, NOT AWARDED ME YOUR INHERITANCE. EXPLAIN THIS TO ME, SO I CAN STOP EXPECTING A SWORD IN MY BACK THE INSTANT I TURN AWAY FROM YOU.
I JUST DON'T HAVE THE WILL, HAKKAR. I DON'T SEE ANY BENEFIT TO KILLING YOU OTHER THAN A FEW SECONDS OF PERSONAL SATISFACTION. THE DEAD ARE STILL DEAD, AND I WORRY THAT WITH YOU GONE, THE NORSEMEN OF THIS ISLAND WILL JUST WITHER AWAY AND DIE.
THUNK
IN MY WORLD, THE DEAD DON'T LIVE AGAIN. THEY STAY DEAD, AND I THINK ENOUGH INNOCENT PEOPLE HAVE BEEN CONDEMNED TO THAT ALREADY, SINCE MY RETURN. YOU THINK THAT DOESN'T *HAUNT* MY THOUGHTS?
BUT IN YOUR WORLD, YOU'LL *SEE* THOSE DEAD AGAIN. YOU'LL HAVE TO *FACE THEM,* ESPECIALLY THE IVARSSONS, AND IT SEEMS TO ME THAT'S PUNISHMENT ENOUGH.
THEY WERE KIND TO YOU AS A CHILD, SAME AS THEY WERE TO ME.
I PITY YOU YOUR FATE, HAKKAR.

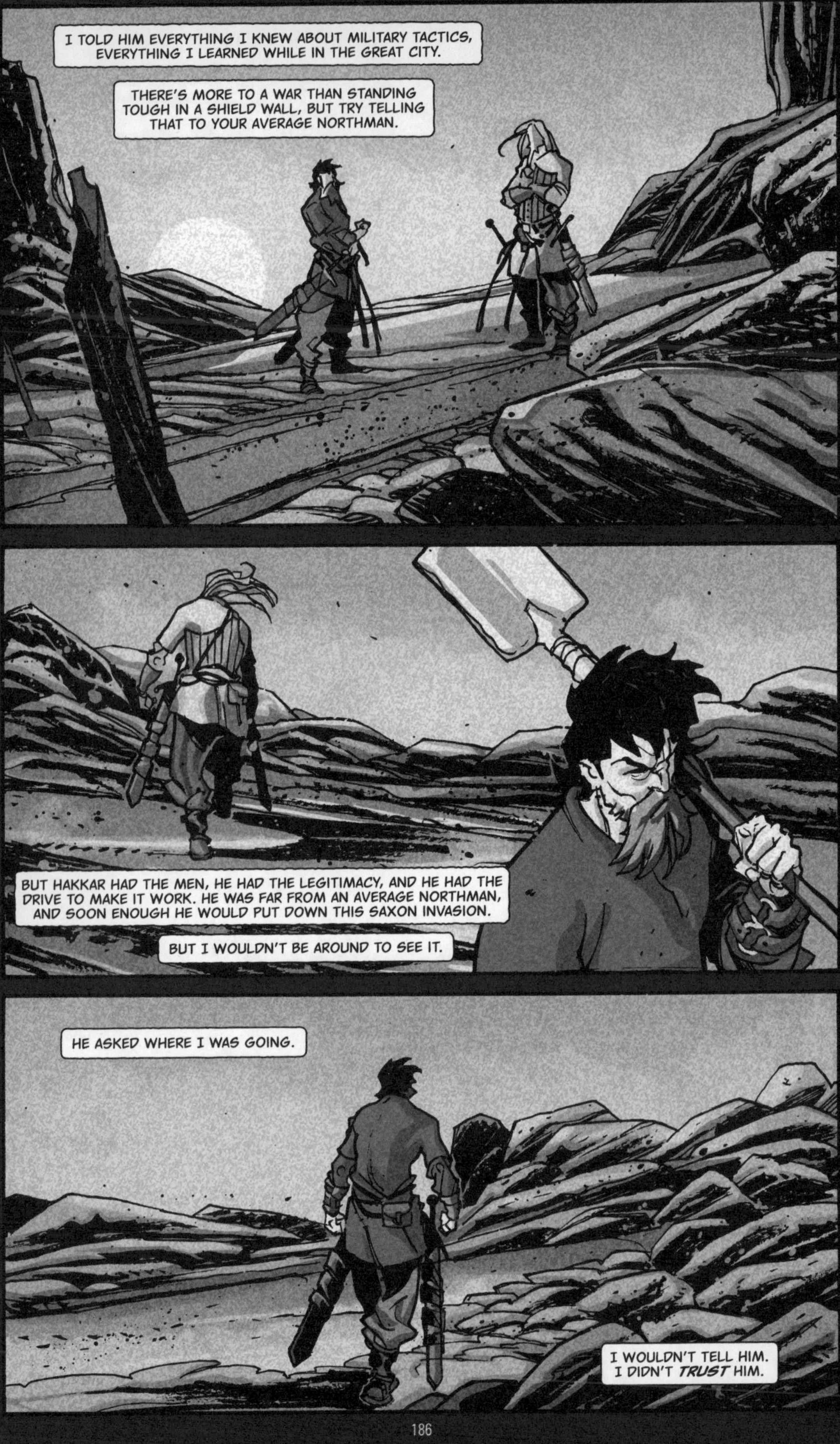
I TOLD HIM EVERYTHING I KNEW ABOUT MILITARY TACTICS, EVERYTHING I LEARNED WHILE IN THE GREAT CITY.
THERE'S MORE TO A WAR THAN STANDING TOUGH IN A SHIELD WALL, BUT TRY TELLING THAT TO YOUR AVERAGE NORTHMAN.
BUT HAKKAR HAD THE MEN, HE HAD THE LEGITIMACY, AND HE HAD THE DRIVE TO MAKE IT WORK. HE WAS FAR FROM AN AVERAGE NORTHMAN, AND SOON ENOUGH HE WOULD PUT DOWN THIS SAXON INVASION.
BUT I WOULDN'T BE AROUND TO SEE IT.
HE ASKED WHERE I WAS GOING.
I WOULDN'T TELL HIM. I DIDN'T *TRUST* HIM.

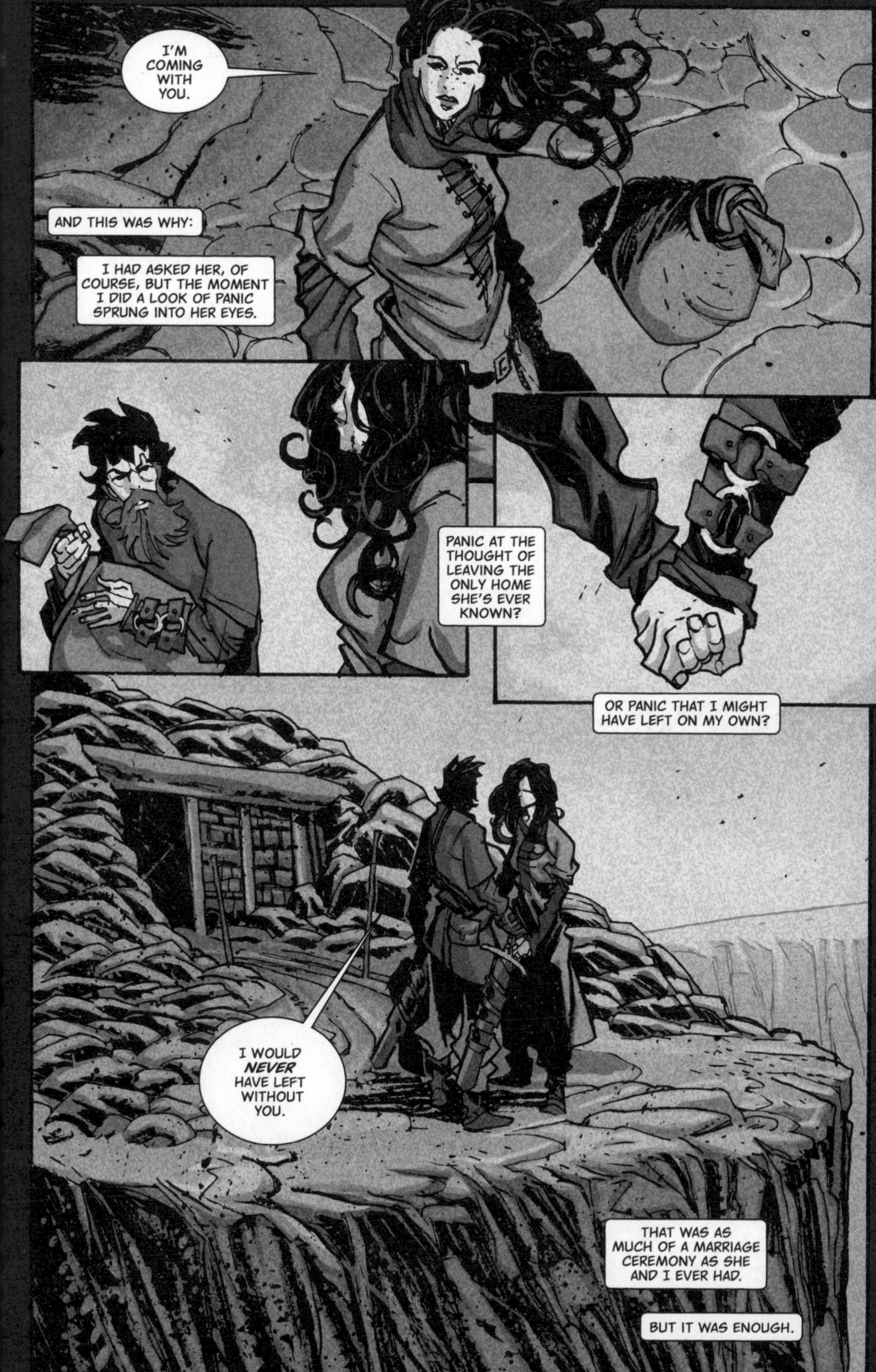
I'M COMING WITH YOU.
AND THIS WAS WHY:
I HAD ASKED HER, OF COURSE, BUT THE MOMENT I DID A LOOK OF PANIC SPRUNG INTO HER EYES.
PANIC AT THE THOUGHT OF LEAVING THE ONLY HOME SHE'S EVER KNOWN?
OR PANIC THAT I MIGHT HAVE LEFT ON MY OWN?
I WOULD *NEVER* HAVE LEFT WITHOUT YOU.
THAT WAS AS MUCH OF A MARRIAGE CEREMONY AS SHE AND I EVER HAD.
BUT IT WAS ENOUGH.

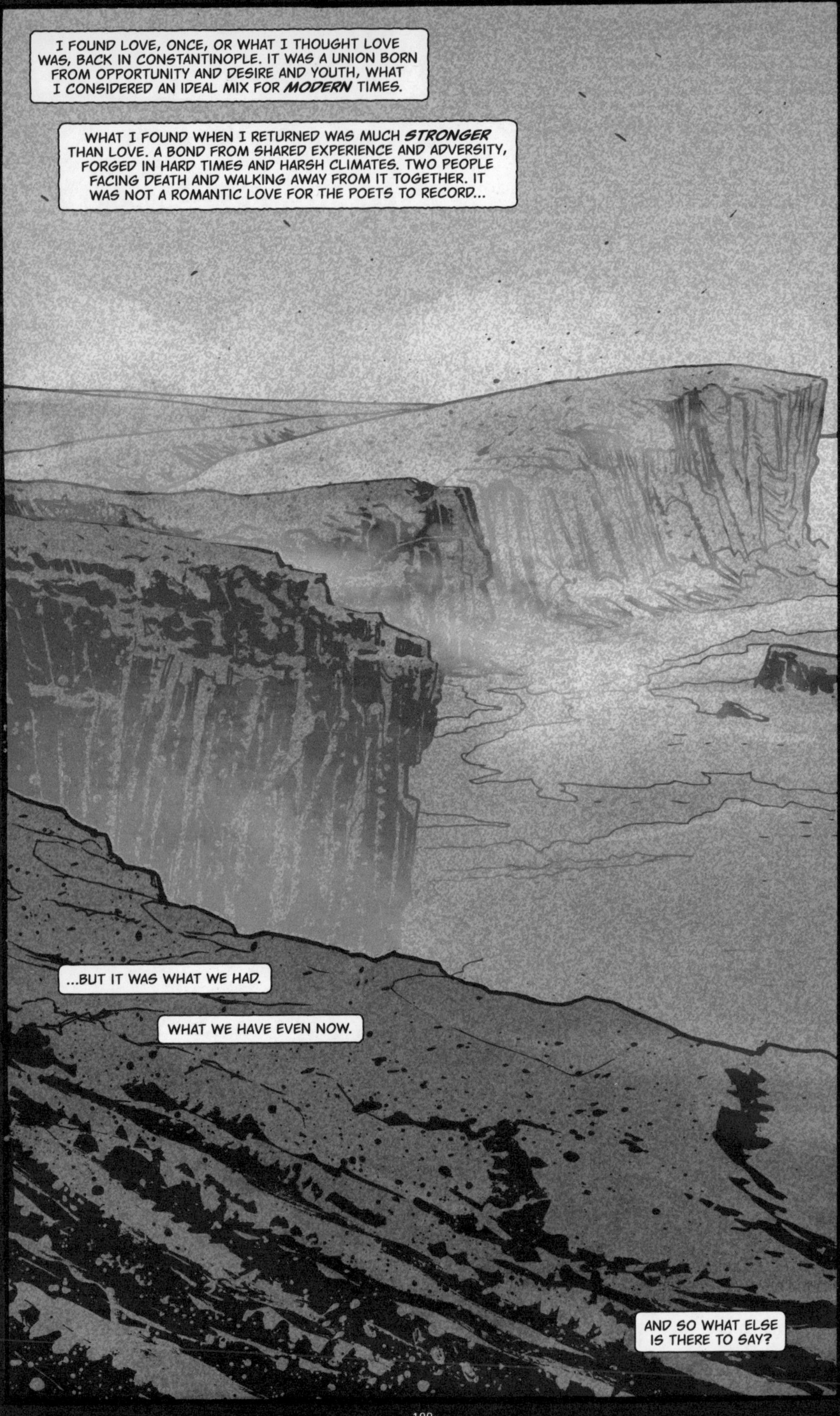
I FOUND LOVE, ONCE, OR WHAT I THOUGHT LOVE WAS, BACK IN CONSTANTINOPLE. IT WAS A UNION BORN FROM OPPORTUNITY AND DESIRE AND YOUTH, WHAT I CONSIDERED AN IDEAL MIX FOR *MODERN* TIMES.
WHAT I FOUND WHEN I RETURNED WAS MUCH *STRONGER* THAN LOVE. A BOND FROM SHARED EXPERIENCE AND ADVERSITY, FORGED IN HARD TIMES AND HARSH CLIMATES. TWO PEOPLE FACING DEATH AND WALKING AWAY FROM IT TOGETHER. IT WAS NOT A ROMANTIC LOVE FOR THE POETS TO RECORD...
...BUT IT WAS WHAT WE HAD.
WHAT WE HAVE EVEN NOW.
AND SO WHAT ELSE IS THERE TO SAY?

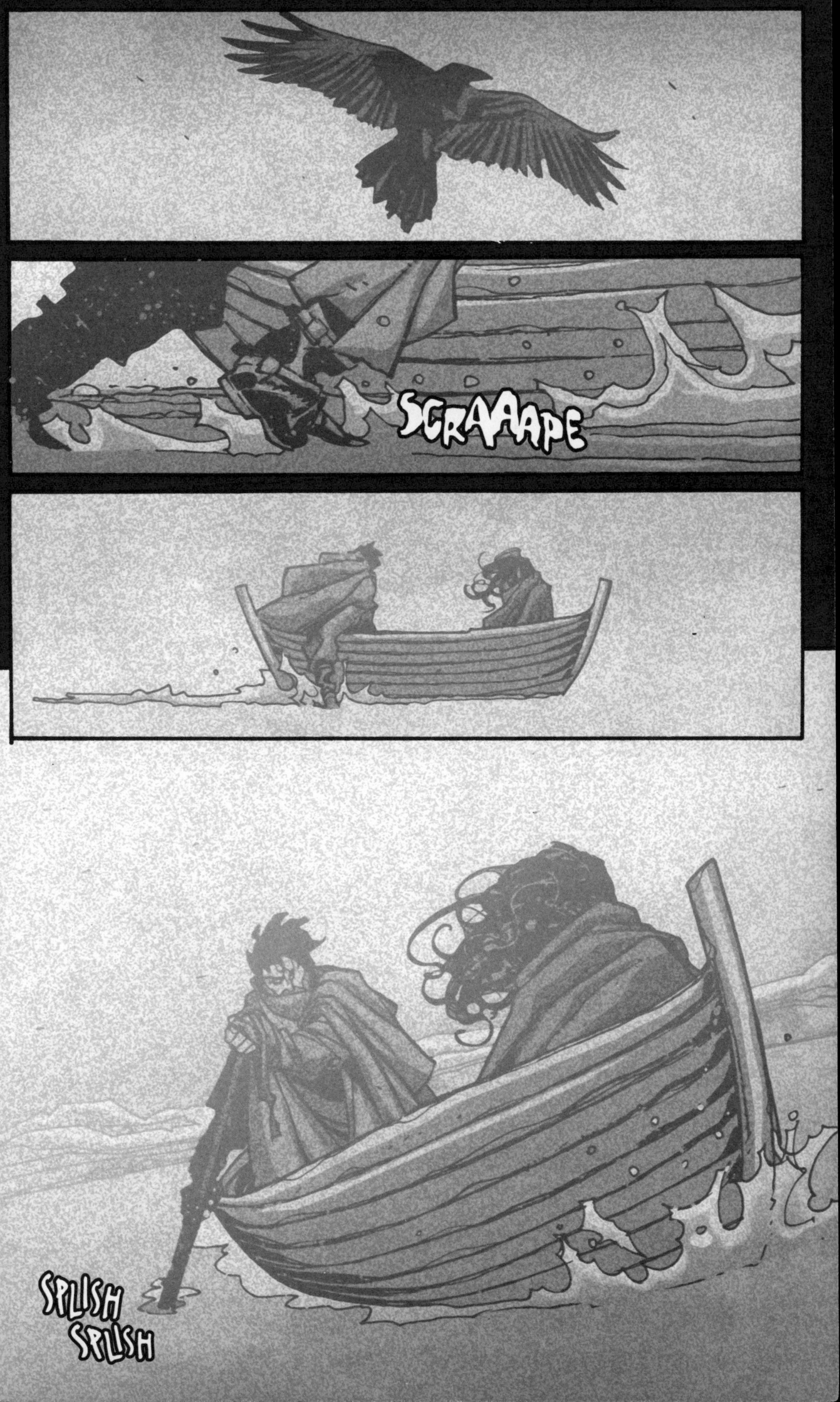
SCRAAAPE
SPLISH
SPLISH

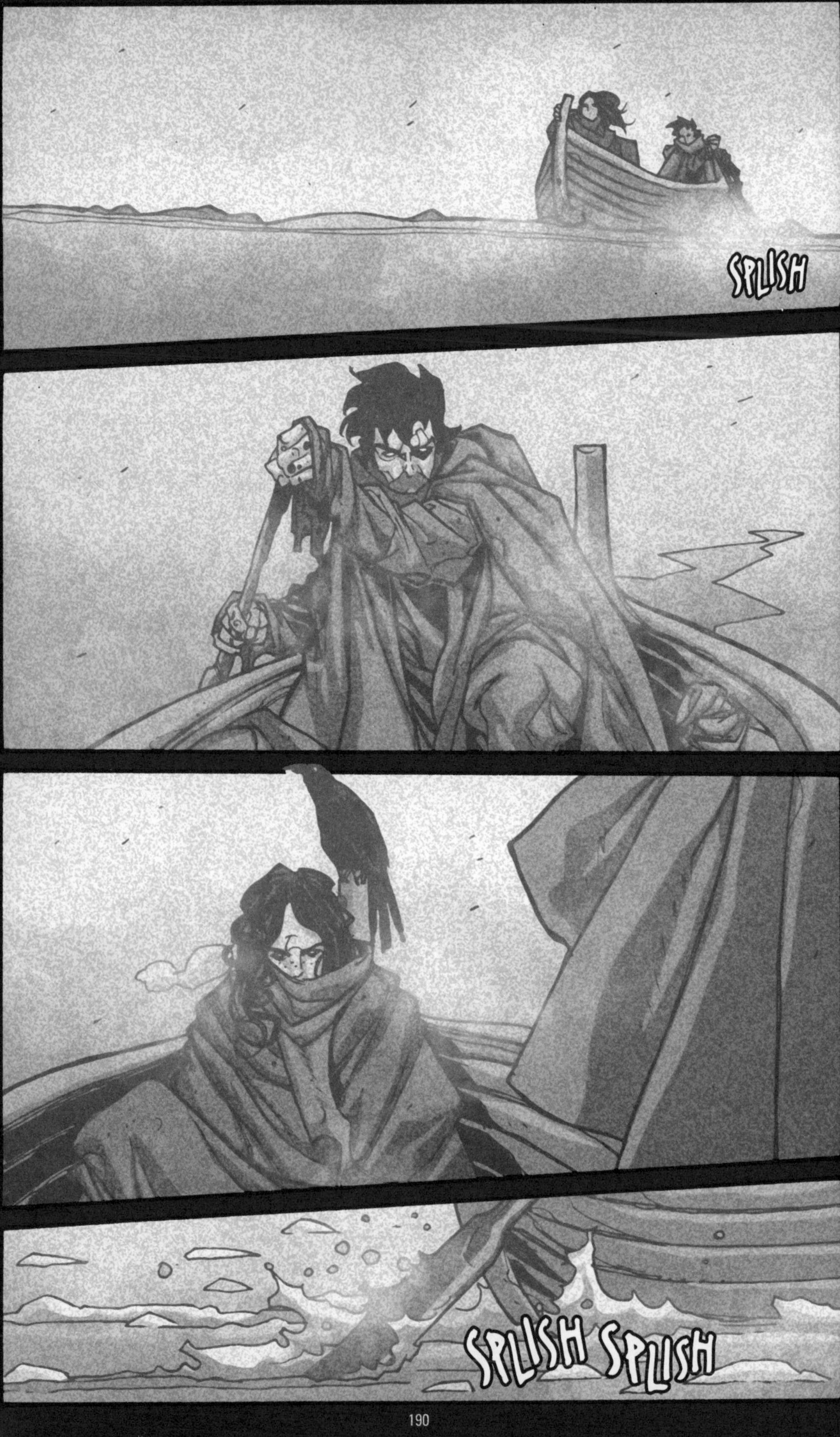
SPLISH
SPLISH SPLISH

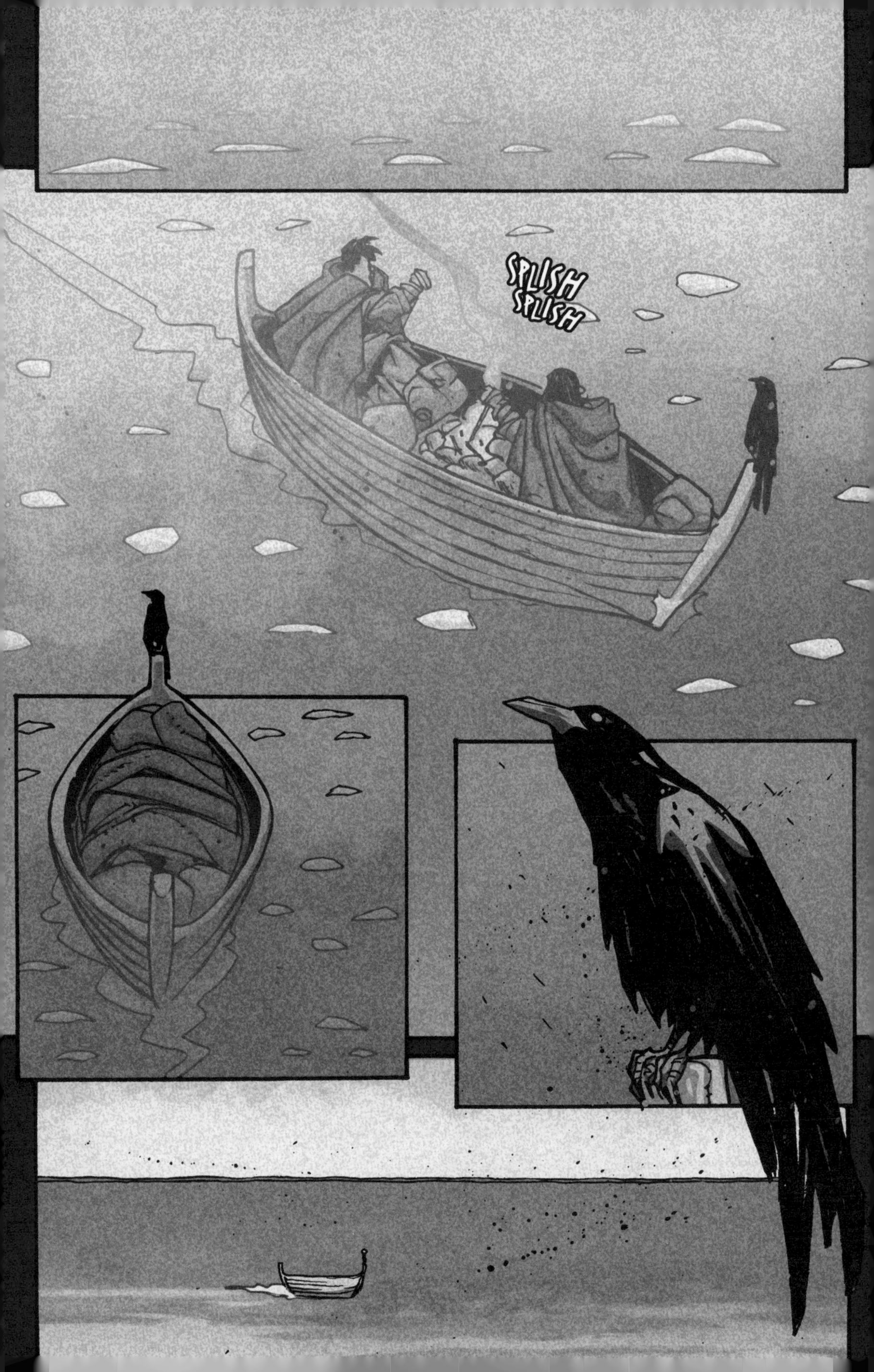
SPLISH
SPLISH

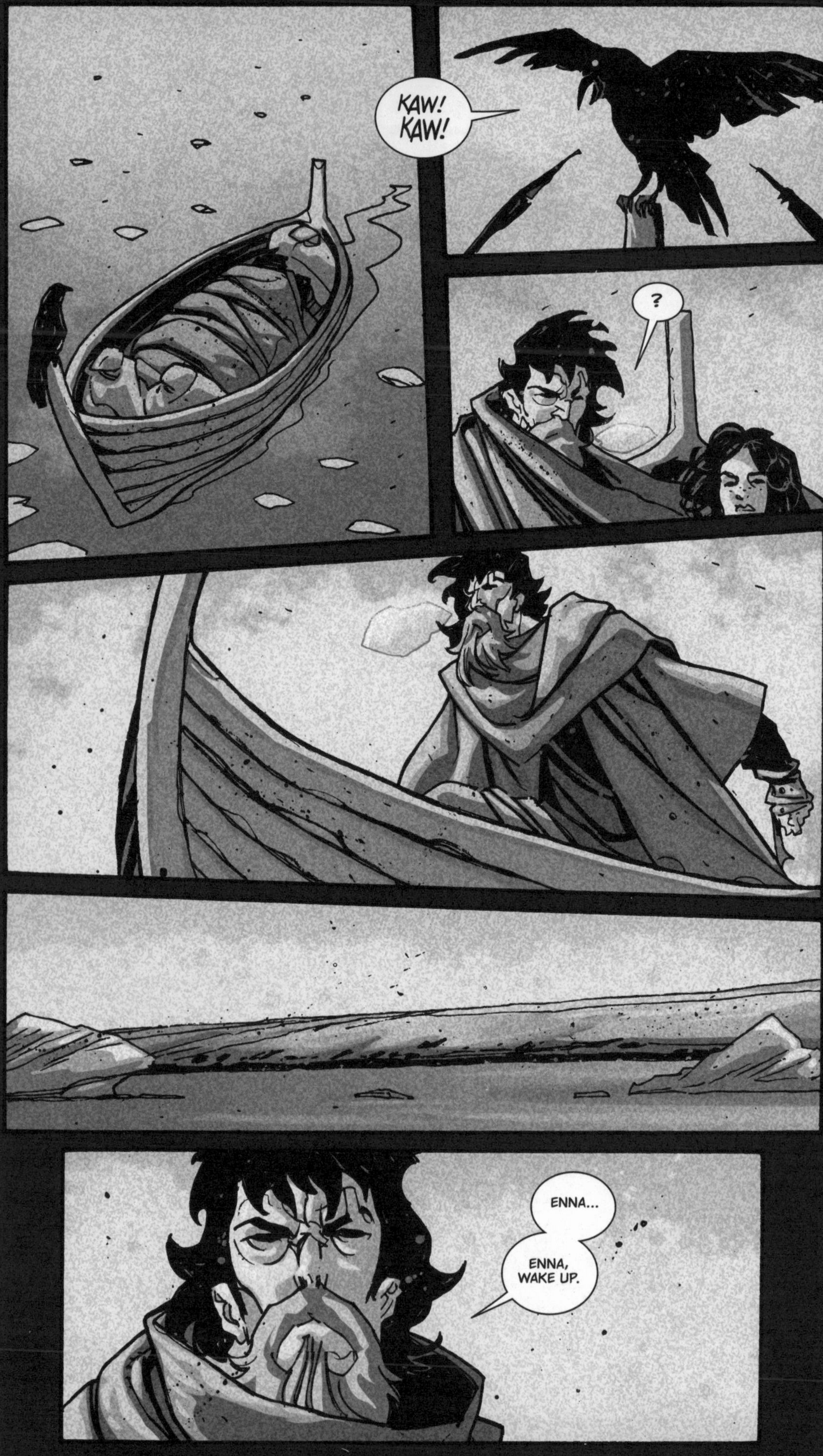
KAW! KAW!
?
ENNA...
ENNA, WAKE UP.

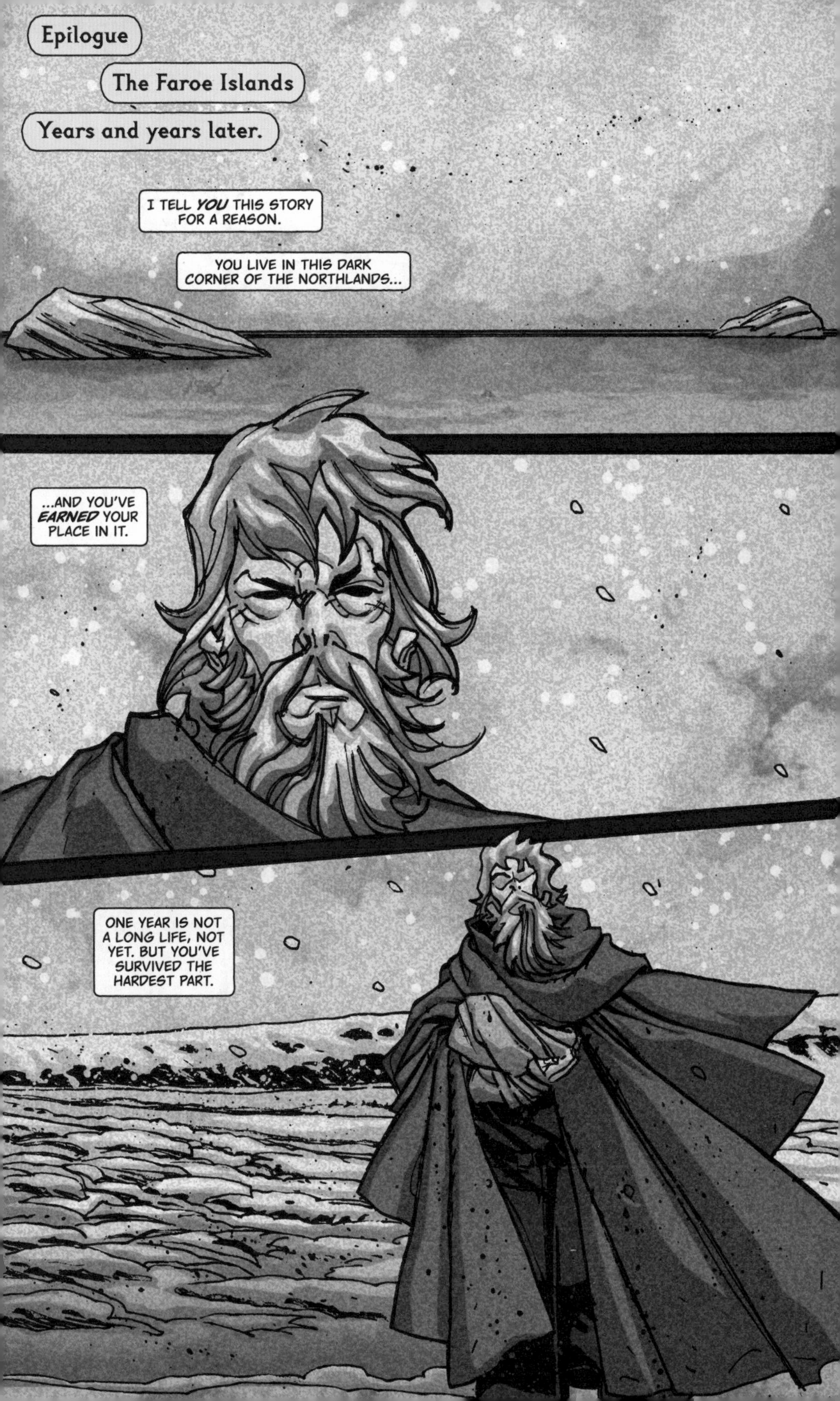
Epilogue
The Faroe Islands
Years and years later.
I TELL YOU THIS STORY FOR A REASON.
YOU LIVE IN THIS DARK CORNER OF THE NORTHLANDS...
...AND YOU'VE EARNED YOUR PLACE IN IT.
ONE YEAR IS NOT A LONG LIFE, NOT YET. BUT YOU'VE SURVIVED THE HARDEST PART.

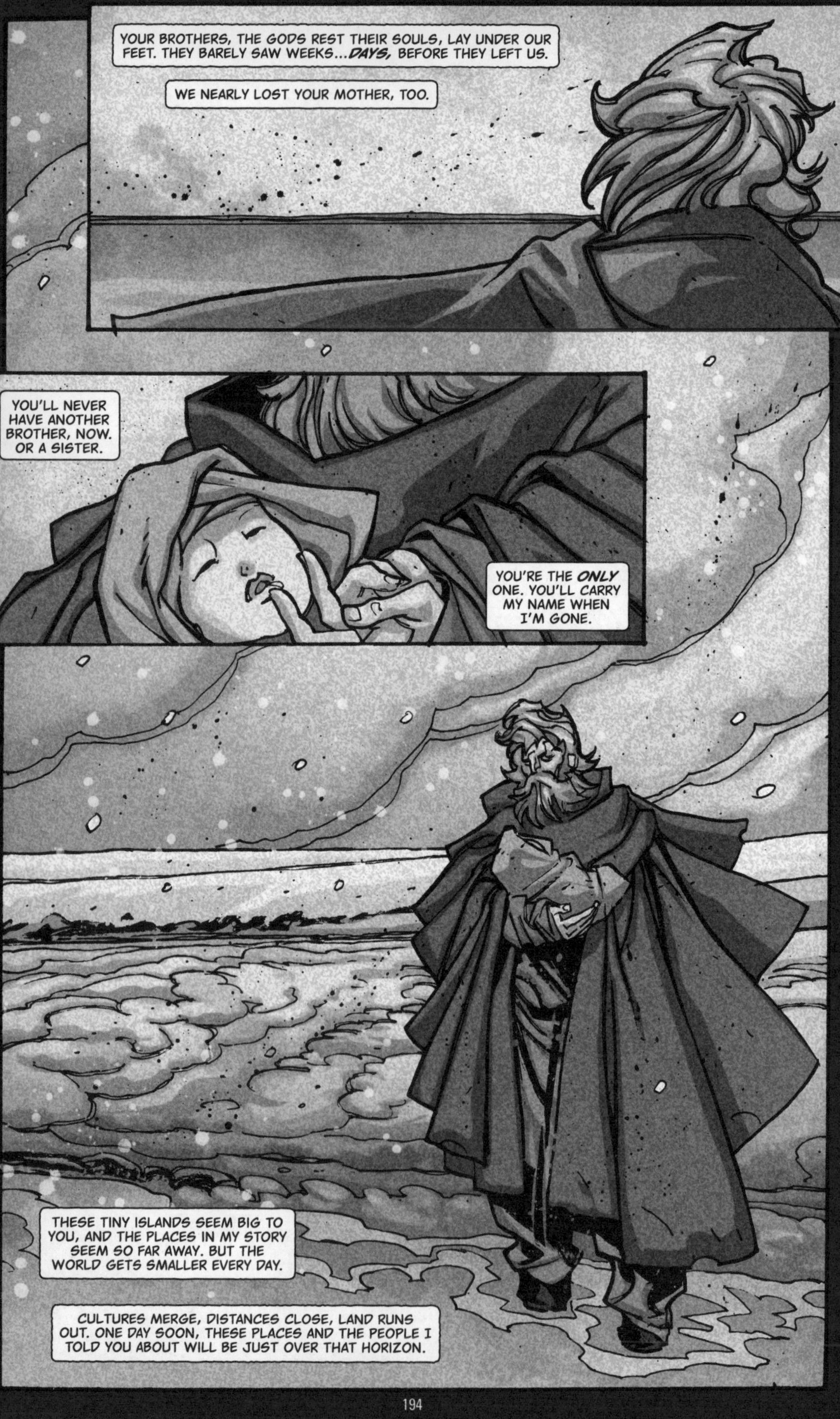
YOUR BROTHERS, THE GODS REST THEIR SOULS, LAY UNDER OUR FEET. THEY BARELY SAW WEEKS...*DAYS,* BEFORE THEY LEFT US.
WE NEARLY LOST YOUR MOTHER, TOO.
YOU'LL NEVER HAVE ANOTHER BROTHER, NOW. OR A SISTER.
YOU'RE THE *ONLY* ONE. YOU'LL CARRY MY NAME WHEN I'M GONE.
THESE TINY ISLANDS SEEM BIG TO YOU, AND THE PLACES IN MY STORY SEEM SO FAR AWAY. BUT THE WORLD GETS SMALLER EVERY DAY.
CULTURES MERGE, DISTANCES CLOSE, LAND RUNS OUT. ONE DAY SOON, THESE PLACES AND THE PEOPLE I TOLD YOU ABOUT WILL BE JUST OVER THAT HORIZON.

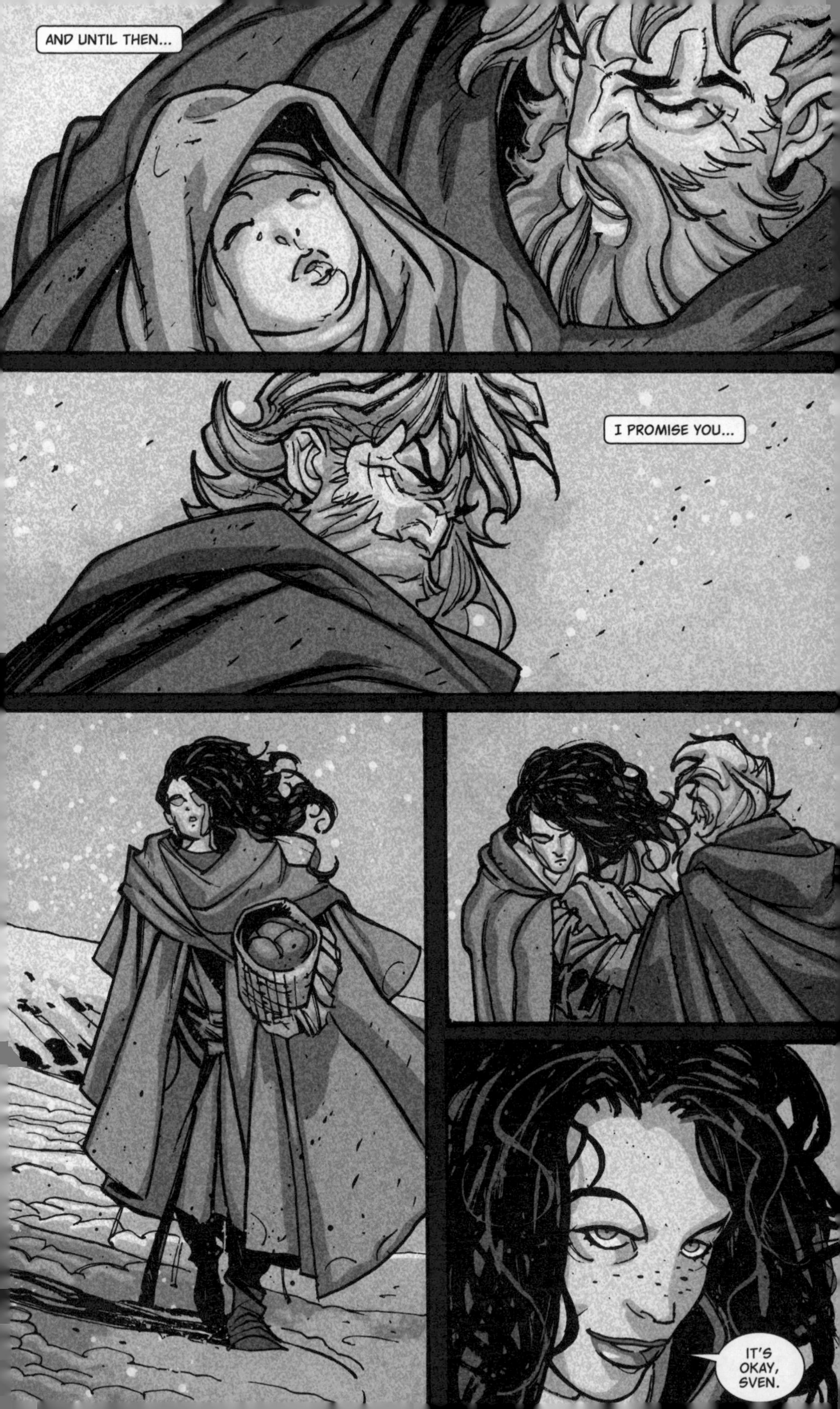
AND UNTIL THEN...
I PROMISE YOU...
IT'S OKAY, SVEN.

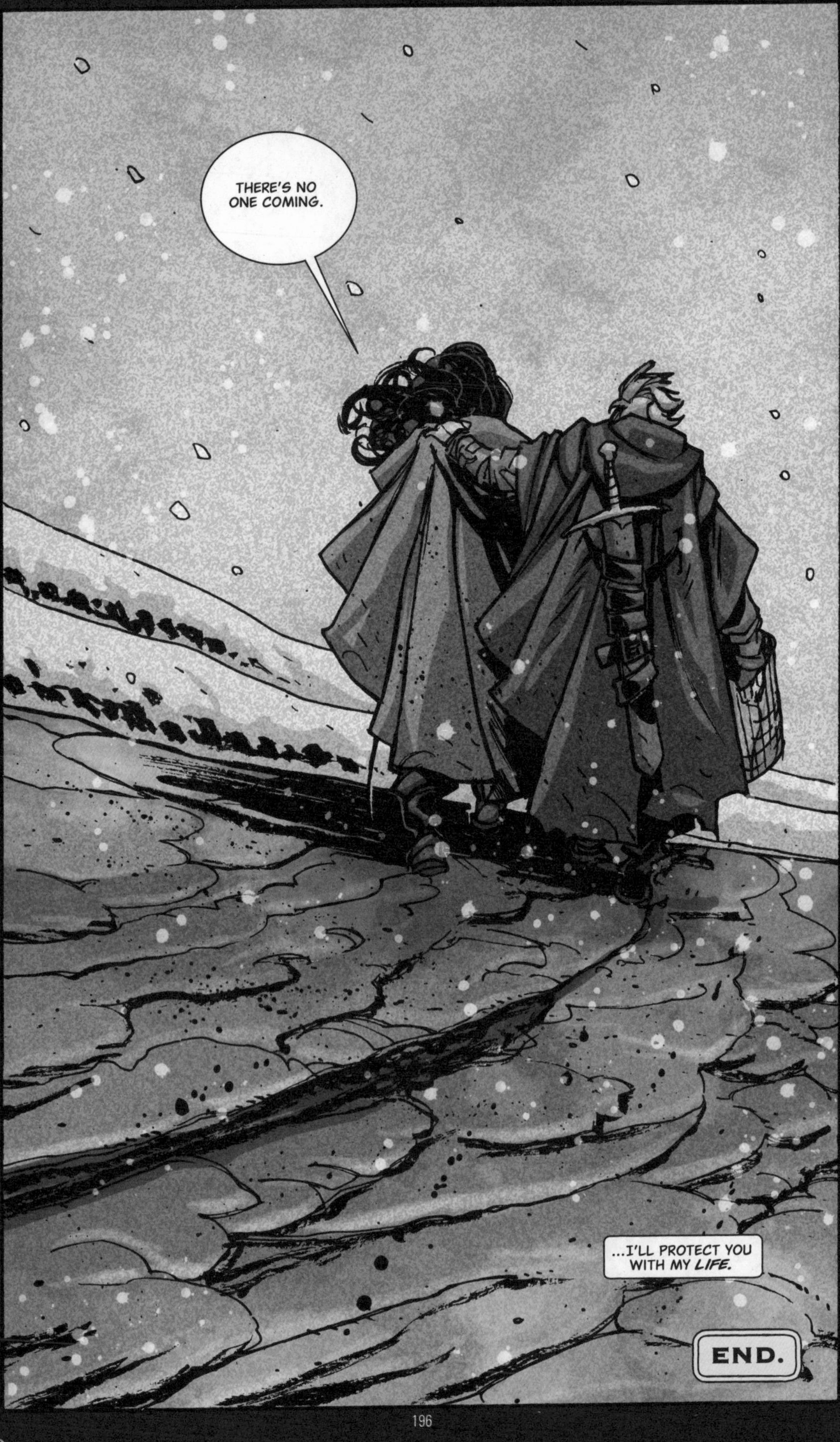
THERE'S NO ONE COMING.
...I'LL PROTECT YOU WITH MY *LIFE.*
END.

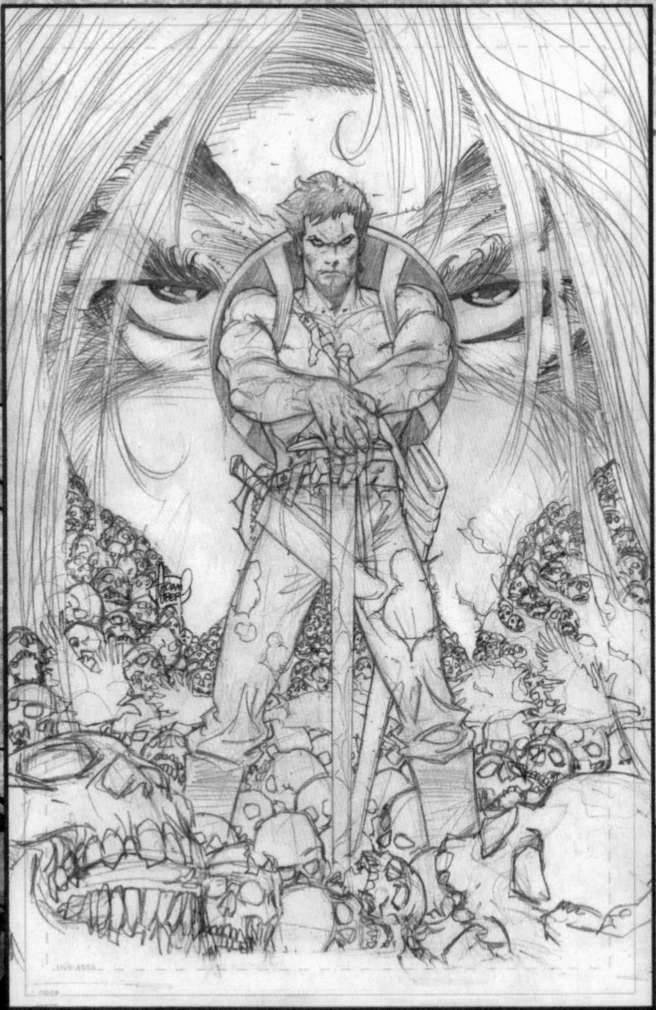

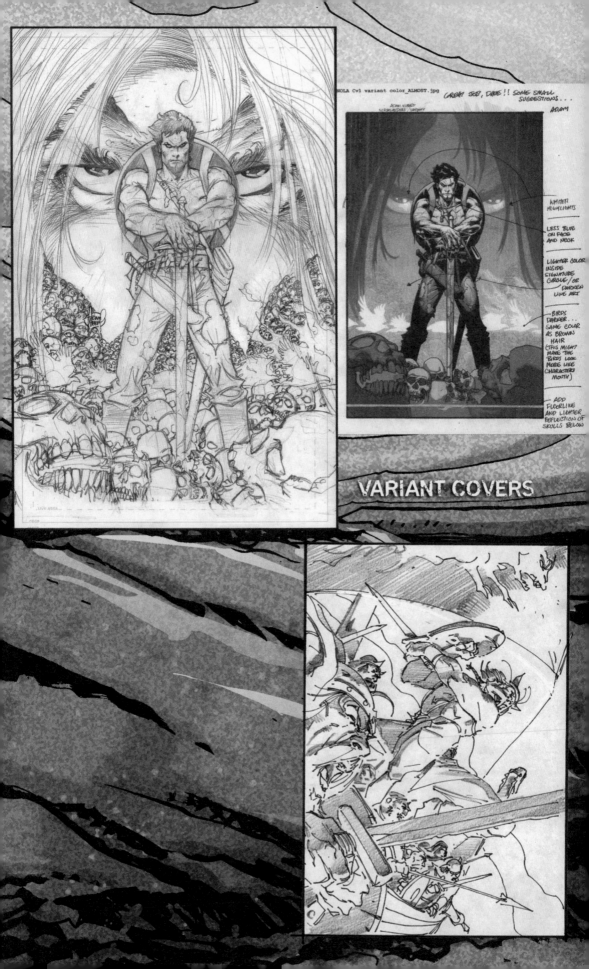

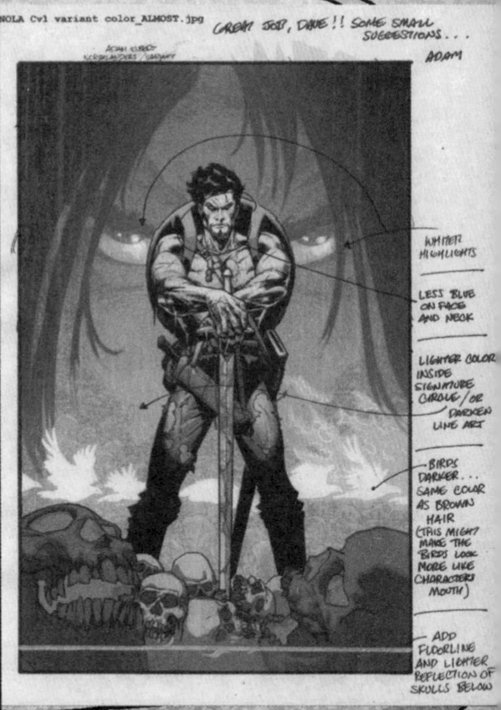
NOLA Cv1 variant color_ALMOST.jpg
GREAT JOB, DAVE!! SOME SMALL SUGGESTIONS...
ADAM
WHITER HIGHLIGHTS
LESS BLUE ON FACE AND NECK
LIGHTER COLOR INSIDE SIGNATURE CIRCLE/OR DARKEN LINE ART
BIRDS DARKER... SAME COLOR AS BROWN HAIR (THIS MIGHT MAKE THE BIRDS LOOK MORE LIKE CHARACTER'S MOUTH)
ADD FLOORLINE AND LIGHTER REFLECTION OF SKULLS BELOW

VARIANT COVERS

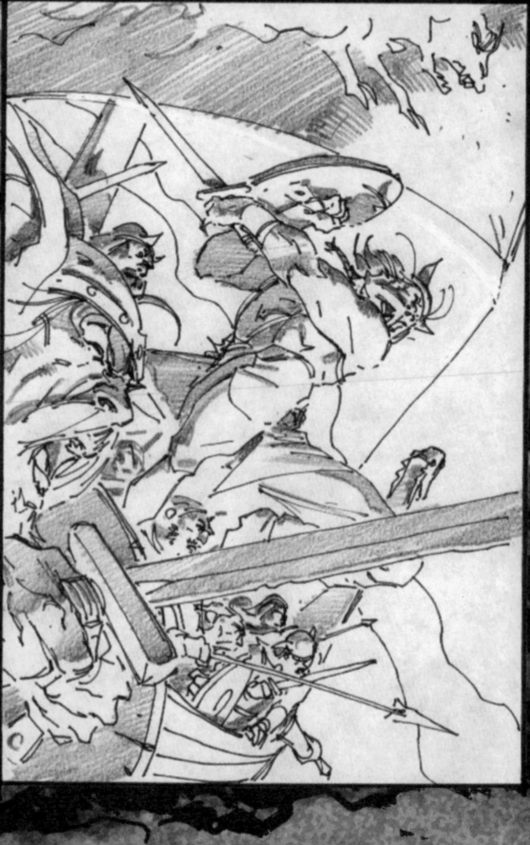

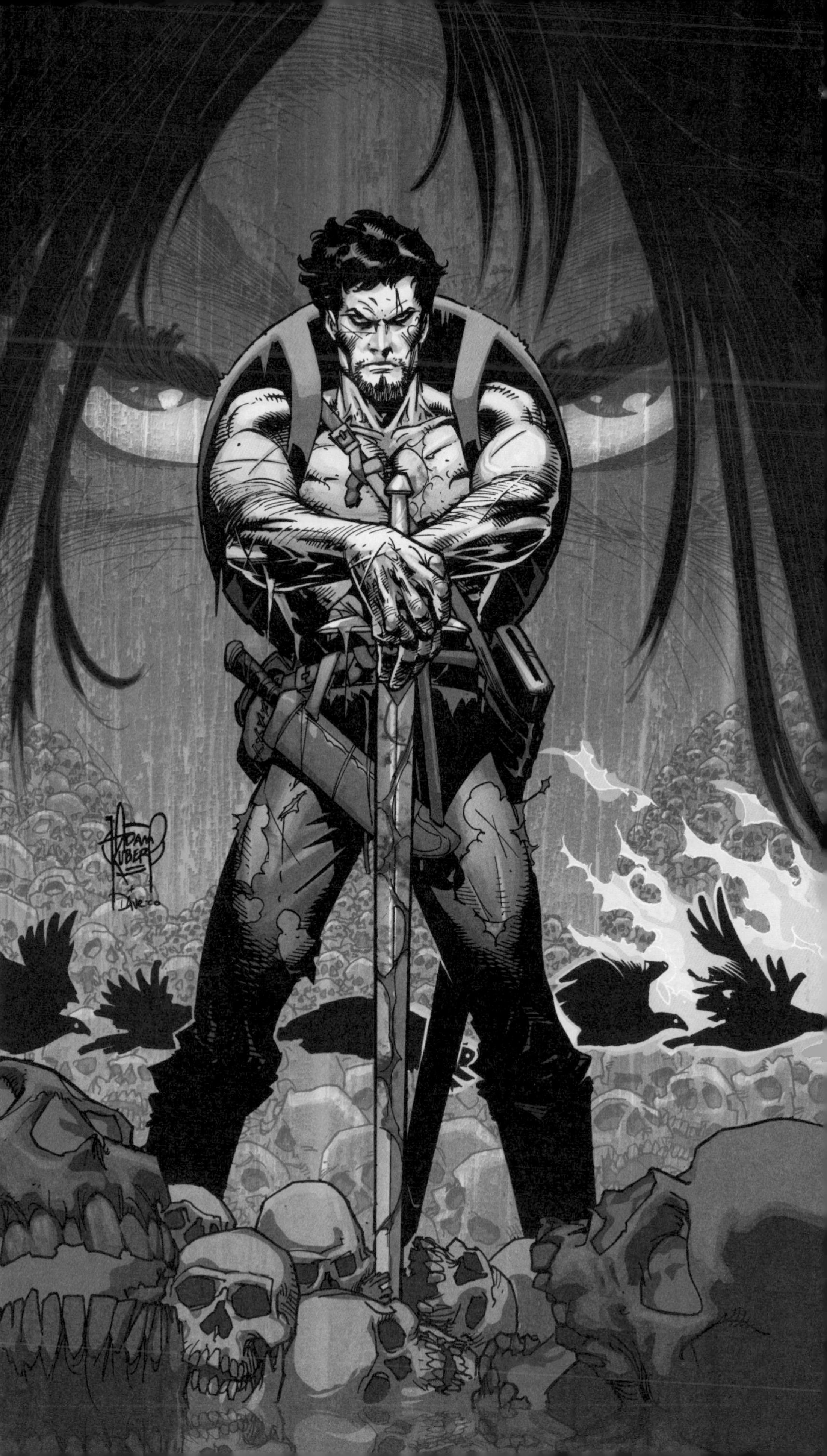

NORTHLANDERS 1 Variant cover by Adam Kubert

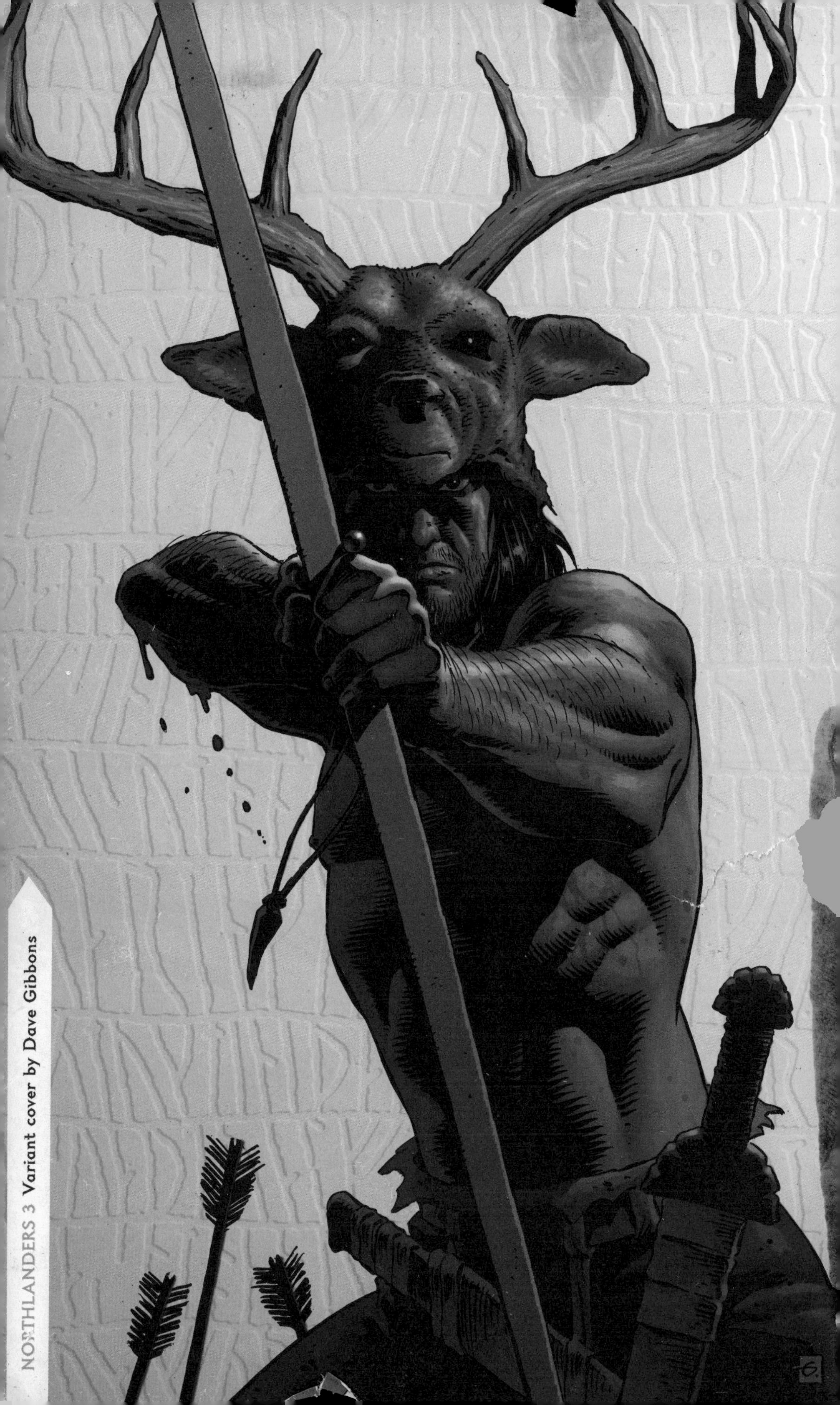

NORTHLANDERS 3 Variant cover by Dave Gibbons

NORTHLANDERS 2 Variant cover by Andy Kubert

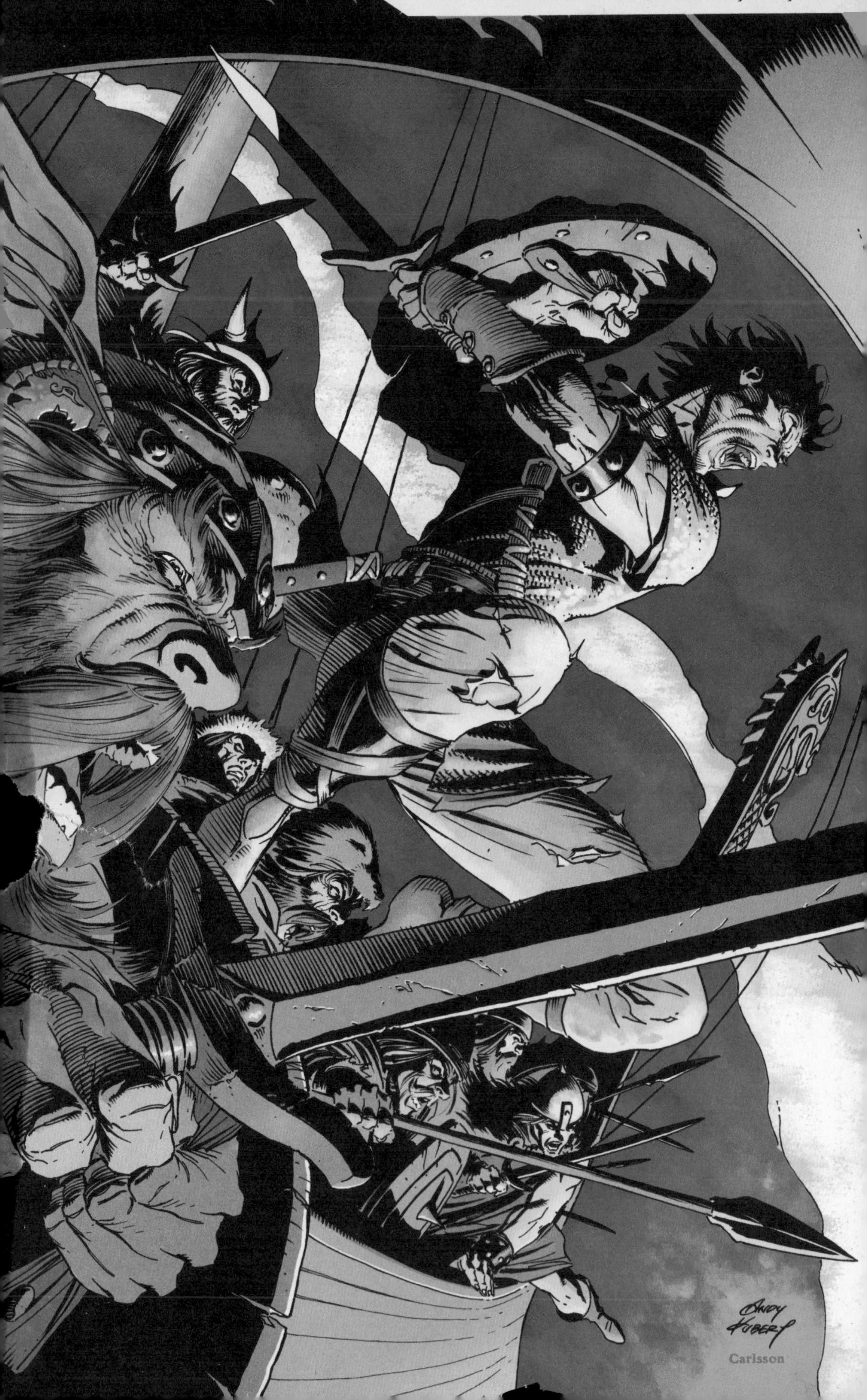

ANDY KUBERT
Carlsson